RUTGERS UNIVERSITY PRESS   NEW BRUNSWICK, NEW JERSEY

BACKTALK

WOMEN WRITERS SPEAK OUT

INTERVIEWS BY DONNA PERRY

Portions of the Pat Barker interview appeared in "Going Home Again: An Interview with Pat Barker," *The Literary Review,* 34. 2 (Winter 1991), 235–244.

The Jamaica Kincaid interview first appeared, in a slightly different form, in *Reading Black, Reading Feminist: A Critical Anthology,* ed. Henry Louis Gates, Jr. (New American Library, 1990), 492–509.

Library of Congress Cataloging-in-Publication Data

Backtalk: women writers speak out / interviews by
   Donna Perry.
       p.   cm.
    ISBN 0-8135-1991-8
    1. Women authors, American—20th century—Interviews. 2. Women and literature—United States—History—20th century. 3. Women and literature—History—20th century. 4. Women authors—20th century—Interviews. 5. Authorship—Sex differences. I. Perry, Donna Marie, 1946–
PS151.H65   1993
810.9′9287—dc20
                                                          92-41201
                                                              CIP

British Cataloging-in-Publication information available

For Neill and in memory of my parents,
Elizabeth Meagher Perry and John Perry,
who always listened

CONTENTS

Books of interviews with women writers have proliferated since the early 1980s, but most focus on white women who come from and write about the middle class. These collections tend to stress aesthetic rather than political or social concerns, limiting themselves to questions about individual texts, the creative process, and literary influences. Interviewers rarely ask writers to talk about such topics as the politics of publishing or sexism in book reviewing. And they usually ignore or downplay volatile issues—racism, classism, sexism, heterosexism, for example—even when these are central to understanding the writers' works.

There have been exceptions. Collections that have dealt exclusively with people of color, such as Claudia Tate's important early work, *Black Women Writers at Work* (Continuum, 1983), or Laura Coltelli's *Winged Words: American Indian Writers Speak* (University of Nebraska Press, 1992), in which she interviews women and men, blend aesthetic and political concerns throughout. Collections pairing writers from similar backgrounds in a discussion about literature, for instance, *Writing Lives: Conversations between Women Writers* (Virago, 1988), edited by Mary Chamberlain, also manage to put the individual writers' works in a larger political and social context.

Inspired by these good examples, I decided to interview a diverse group of successful women writers about their lives, their work, their politics, and the ways these interrelate. My criteria for choosing writers to interview were straightforward. I wanted to talk with women of different racial, ethnic, class, and religious backgrounds, sexual orientations, and countries of origin. I looked for authors who were committed to writing about people, especially women, who had traditionally been marginalized, stereotyped, or ignored in literature. I sought women who had themselves felt silenced but who had published at least three or four books. I decided to include authors of nonfiction as well as poetry and fiction, since memoirs, autobiographies, biographies, essays, and anthologies also break silences. I interviewed writers who were passionate about their work.

Because I am not fluent in another language, I limited the interviews to women writing in English. I made an exception in the case of Puerto Rican novelist and poet Rosario Ferré, who writes in Spanish and has translated many of her works into English, because I knew she would contribute a powerful perspective to the book. Another strong viewpoint comes from Chicana writer Gloria Anzaldúa, who usually publishes in English, sometimes with a generous sprinkling of Spanish or her native Tex-Mex dialect throughout.

With a small travel allowance, I interviewed writers living in the United States, England, and Ireland, although three were born and raised in the Caribbean. I spoke with the writers in restaurants, pubs, hotel rooms, and lounges, or in their own homes. My companion Neill Rosenfeld accompanied me on six of the interviews; the rest I did alone. With the exception of my first meeting with Pat Barker in 1988, I conducted and audiotaped the interviews between 1990 and 1992. Although I spoke with most of the women once for two to four hours, the Pat Barker and Valerie Miner interviews each blend two conversations I had with them.

The writers were so interesting that editing the interviews was the hardest part of the process. Basically, I reorganized material and cut each interview to a manageable length; however, I neither censored nor fundamentally changed what the writers said. If I felt explanations were needed, I put them in brackets. The few writers who asked to see the edited text clarified words or suggested changes; none of them substantially altered the interview. Graciously, Rosario Ferré and Gloria Anzaldúa corrected my errors in transcribing their Spanish.

ACKNOWLEDGMENTS

The support and encouragement of many people made this book possible. I want to thank:

My friends and colleagues in the English department at William Paterson College for giving me a community to write for, practical advice, and a title.

My students for sharing their thoughts about these writers.

Those teachers who helped me find my voice, especially Carolyn Heilbrun.

Old friends who always thought I could do it.

Leslie Mitchner, my editor, for understanding and advice.

Debra Bernardi for her meticulous copy editing.

Marilyn Campbell, managing editor, for seeing the book through production.

Sheila Yablon, transcriber, for finding voices trapped behind clanking dishes and screeching macaws.

The excellent reference librarians at Columbia University's Butler Library, the New York Public Library, and the Sara Byrd Askew Library at William Paterson College for helping me find the answers.

The New Jersey Department of Higher Education for a New Jersey Governor's Fellowship in the Humanities, which allowed me to conduct some of the interviews, and William Paterson College for awarding me released time from teaching to complete the manuscript.

I'm also grateful to Sharon Dennihy-Bailey, Joseph Bailey, and the children—Jenny, Joey, Catherine, Sean, and Teddy—for telling me their stories and listening to mine.

Thanks to my family, especially my aunts Mary Rogers and Rita Sakalinski, for their strength and caring.

My debt to these writers, for their cooperation, their good humor, and their hospitality, is immeasureable. This is their book.

I wish that my parents, Elizabeth Meagher Perry and John Perry, and my aunt Helen Meagher, could celebrate with me. I miss their dignity and grace.

Finally, I don't think I could have completed this book without the love and care of my companion, Neill S. Rosenfeld. He read and edited the manuscript at every stage, stayed sane when I went crazy, and always asked the right questions.

BACKTALK: Answering back. An impudent response; insolence, rudeness, impertinence, cheek, sass

---

To me, personally, the silencing from outside came from my family and my culture, where you were supposed to be seen but not heard. This was especially true for the girl children. You were not supposed to talk back to your elders.

—*Gloria Anzaldúa*

You will hear many different accents in these pages. The writers interviewed come from Antigua, Britain, Ireland, Jamaica, Puerto Rico, and the United States. There is a wide age range, too: from Joan Riley, who was thirty-two at the time of the interview, to sixty-six-year-old Mary Beckett. Class backgrounds differ, with most of the writers coming from working-class families, although a few were raised in the middle class and one was born in poverty. They come from different racial and ethnic backgrounds; they are gay and straight.

They write in a variety of genres—fiction and nonfiction, poetry and memoirs—and they edit anthologies of other writers' works. Some stretch or break the boundaries between traditional genres to shape forms that fit their new words; others write in more traditional ways but sound new themes.

Yet there are striking similarities among the fifteen women. Most identify themselves as feminists or political writers, and many are or have been activists. All have strong opinions about women's rights and human rights that give their work a depth and power often lacking in contemporary literature. Through their writing, they have refused to be silenced or ignored or categorized. When told to keep quiet, they have talked back.

Sometimes the threat of silencing comes from the sexism in their own families and communities, which honors men's words and rewards women for keeping their mouths shut. Gloria Anzaldúa and Rosario Ferré talk about the cult of *machismo* in Chicano and Puerto Rican cultures, respectively, and their own struggle to be heard. Maxine Hong Kingston tells of double messages from her Chinese mother—you should grow up to be a warrior, but you will be only a wife and mother. As her father and others in their Chinese American community said, "Better raise geese than girls."

As children of working-class families, writers like Pat Barker, Vivian Gornick, and Valerie Miner grew up believing that their career choices were limited to working for the telephone company or becoming a secretary or teacher. The primary goal for women was marriage and children, and writing wasn't something their people did, anyway. If you were lesbian, the situation was even worse. By coming out, like Gloria Anzaldúa, you were ostracized. Better to stay safely in hiding, like Joanna Russ and others.

For writers like Paula Gunn Allen and Leslie Marmon Silko, Native American heritage empowered them, as women, to speak. Growing up in a matriarchal culture, they weren't limited by gender. Silko says she learned to shoot and defend herself as well as any boy. And both Silko and Allen grew up surrounded by tribal storytellers and medicine women. It was the racism of the dominant culture that conspired to keep them, and all native peoples, quiet.

To Caribbean-born Jamaica Kincaid and Joan Riley, that dominant culture was equally powerful. Kincaid talks about becoming more outspoken in her criticism of racism and oppression, both in the United States and in her native Antigua. Of her nonfiction exposé of political corruption on the island, *A Small Place* (Farrar, Straus, and Giroux, 1988), she says, "I realized in writing that book that the first step to claiming yourself is anger." Like Riley, Kincaid indicts the native rulers as well as the colonizers, however. No one escapes her level gaze.

While many of the women backtalkers have drawn fire for their words, only Joan Riley has been read out in church. After manuscript copies of *A Kindness to the Children* (The Women's Press, 1992) were circulated in Jamaica, Riley, who now lives in London, was named as a sinner by the fundamentalist church. In that novel about Jamaica's working poor, she indicts church pastors for sexually abusing their young female charges, a practice she claims is widespread.

Like Kincaid and Riley, Irish writers Mary Beckett and Éilís Ní Dhuibhne (pronounced Ay-lish Ne Guivena) grew up surrounded by strong women. Beckett came from an undeclared war zone—Northern Ireland in the 1950s—where, as a Roman Catholic, she was a member of a persecuted minority. Her family lived in a middle-class, mostly Protestant neighborhood, so Beckett wasn't subject to personal attack, but she saw religious intolerance toward working-class Catholics firsthand as a Belfast schoolteacher. Living in Dublin twenty years later, she became angry that no one was telling the truth about the situation for Catholics in the North. So Beckett began writing stories and eventually a novel about the working-class mothers of her former pupils and their resistance to terrorism on both sides of the conflict.

Ní Dhuibhne, a generation younger than Beckett, angered by sexism, national policies that destroy the environment, and classism, explores these themes in short stories and a futuristic novel about Ireland. Trained as a folklorist, Ní Dhuibhne draws on Irish folktales and legends, particularly those featuring magical women and the power of female sexuality and rage, to write about the present.

Because they didn't see themselves or the members of their family or community in the literature they read growing up—another form of silencing—many of the writers have decided to tell these stories themselves. As a result, many worry about accessibility. As Barbara Kingsolver explains about her first novel, "I realized I did it because I wanted to write a book that my family or my neighbors or the guy that runs Rex and Paul's Service Station in Carlisle [Kentucky], where I grew up, could read." And most talk about feeling a strong sense of responsibility to their communities to get their stories right.

Their work is powerful and diverse. Some of the writers preserve communal voices. As an academic, Paula Gunn Allen has studied the role of women in Native American culture, religion, and literature, and edited anthologies of Native American women writers. In her poetry and her first, experimental novel, she draws on images and rhythms from her Laguna Pueblo and Sioux background to tell contemporary stories. Leslie Marmon Silko's stories and poems, many collected in *Storyteller* (Little, Brown, 1981), retell tales she heard from relatives and others on the Laguna Pueblo. Like Silko, Joan Riley captures the spirit and voices of ordinary people from her native Jamaica, and Gloria Naylor writes about the varied experiences that characterize African American life.

Other writers have assembled disparate voices in ground-breaking anthologies and nonfiction books. In two important collections, *This Bridge Called My Back* (Persephone Press, 1981; reprinted by Kitchen Table, 1983), coedited with Cherríe Moraga, and *Making Face, Making Soul/Haciendo Caras* (Aunt Lute Books, 1990), Gloria Anzaldúa brings radical women of color into prominence. Vivian Gornick's *Woman in Sexist Society* (Basic Books, 1971), coedited with Barbara K. Moran, has become a feminist classic, with contributions by important early theorists such as Nancy Chodorow, Shulamith Firestone, and Kate Millett. Valerie Miner's coauthored collections of essays and short stories in Canada and England are similarly important early works featuring women writers and feminist concerns. And, in her brilliantly argued account of the historical silencing of women, *How to Suppress Women's Writing* (University of Texas Press, 1983), Joanna Russ builds upon the work of Tillie Olsen, Adrienne Rich, and others.

Sometimes these women write family stories, preserving the voices of parents, especially mothers, and their own younger selves. In the memoirs *The Woman Warrior* (Random House, 1976) and *Fierce Attachments* (Farrar, Straus, and Giroux, 1987), Maxine Hong Kingston and Vivian Gornick, respectively, explore their relationships with strong-willed mothers, re-creating their mothers' lives and the stories of an entire generation of immigrant women in the process. Kingston's sequel, *China Men* (Knopf, 1980), presents her father's story and that of her male relatives.

Although she was writing fiction, Jamaica Kincaid claims that everything she tells in *Annie John* (Farrar, Straus, and Giroux, 1985) really happened when she was growing up in Antigua, particularly Annie's love-hate relationship with her mother, modeled on Kincaid's own. Using her family's history as former landowners, Rosario Ferré traces three generations of social change in Puerto Rico in *Sweet Diamond Dust* (Ballantine, 1988) and is currently writing a fictionalized memoir based on her mother's life.

Those who write fiction tell stories of women and men who have been underrepresented or stereotyped in so-called "serious literature," that is, fiction written by white, middle-to-upper-class, usually Protestant, heterosexual men. Their stories and novels feature factory workers, farmers, cleaning women, janitors, au pairs, bakers, waitresses, students, battered wives, happily married women, women alone, lesbian and gay couples, sisters, aunts, daughters, mothers, grandmothers, prostitutes, members of the military, veterans, dykes, and activists. Their characters lead complex lives: Old and young, straight and lesbian, of various races, ethnic groups, and religions, they are never sentimentalized.

Their middle- and upper-middle-class characters are also multidimensional. Female characters become explorers and adventurers, female avengers and amateur detectives, telepaths, shamans, rebellious wives and daughters. Exposing or replacing the marriage plot, that nineteenth-century literary staple, the writers create characters who strive to live in harmony with the earth or the ancestors or their own liberated selves. Reworking detective and science fiction genres, writers like Valerie Miner and Joanna Russ transform them.

Many of the writers create memorable male characters. As Pat Barker explains, "I never thought for a second that feminism is only about women." But when they write about men, the writers examine the meaning of masculinity in new ways: Silko imagines a World War II veteran who returns to life and health through a medicine man's healing ceremony; Barker examines the effect of World War I on shell-shock victims and the doctor who treats them; and Maxine Hong Kingston's young Chinese American Beat playwright begins to mature when he embraces pacifism.

Those who trained as journalists examine the plight of previously unexamined groups in their nonfiction. Vivian Gornick interviews women in science to determine how they are treated in that male-dominated discipline and talks with former members of the American Communist party about the impact that movement has had on their lives. Barbara Kingsolver chronicles the strength of the women involved in the 1983 strike against the Phelps Dodge Copper Corporation in Arizona.

In the personal voice of poetry, writers tell stories of their own experiences and those of the silenced ones—ancestors, parents, the oppressed. They celebrate the courage of political prisoners, the strength of legendary women, the work of other women writers. Poets Allen and Silko, in particular, write rhapsodically about their feeling of oneness with the land.

Other common threads that emerged in the interviews surprised me. I was amazed by how often the writers talk about the responsibility they feel, whether to the members of their various communities, to the characters they create, or to those they interview or write about. It's almost as though, having known personally what silencing feels like, they have learned the sacredness and power of speech.

At the same time, the writers all reserve the right to examine whatever subject moves them and to tell the truth, even when it may offend some members of their respective communities. "I never apologize," says Gloria Naylor, even if something she has written may create problems for those African American readers who want her to create more sympathetic characters. Pat Barker, Leslie Marmon Silko, and Maxine Hong Kingston talk about creating male protagonists, even though feminists have gotten angry with them. Valerie Miner and Gloria Anzaldúa discuss their conflicting feelings about pressure from the lesbian community to create positive lesbian characters as role models.

Yet most don't see themselves as isolated artists. Some talk about serving as filters or intermediaries or translators of communal stories, seeing their roles as akin to that of the tribal storyteller. Many describe writing as collaboration, either between the writer and other writers or between writer and reader in a kind of "imaginative collectivity," as Valerie Miner puts it. Ferré and Kingsolver explain how they have gone to other writers for inspiration or for help when they got stuck in the writing; Riley and Anzaldúa discuss their closeness to their readers; Gornick asserts that unless she feels some positive connection to a subject, she can't write about it. All mention the pivotal role played by special readers—husbands, lovers, friends, or sensitive editors.

They all cite anger as a positive, motivating force in their writing, whether it's the low-heat simmering of Mary Beckett over British stupidity in dealing with the Irish Republican Army or Joanna Russ's boiling rage at the pervasiveness of sexism. For Leslie Marmon Silko, anger led her to leave poetry and tribal subjects, at least for the present, to write *Almanac of the Dead* (Simon and Schuster, 1991), an indictment of the United States for five hundred years of racist extermination of native peoples.

They speak with refreshing candor about their own writing, some talking about changes they would make in earlier works if they could write them over again. Pat Barker says she would be "more careful" writing about violence against women now, and Maxine Hong Kingston wishes she had made Fa Mu Lan, the warrior woman, more like the figure of legend, who turns back into a beautiful woman. Barbara Kingsolver is even writing a sequel, in part to correct the fact that in her first novel, *The Bean Trees* (Harper and Row, 1988), she didn't take into account the tribe's claim on a Native American baby adopted by a white woman.

Although widely published, the writers talk openly about the difficulties they and others have faced trying to get into and stay in print. They discuss related issues: the politics and economics of publishing; racism and sexism and heterosexism in the industry; mainstream versus alternative presses; sexist reviewers and writers who undermine their work and that of other women; and the frustration of not finding their work in bookstores.

They talk about genres and literary definitions, about their attempts to write across conventions in new ways. Some, like Valerie Miner, place themselves in literary traditions, while Joan Riley and others chafe at the fit, claiming that no one writes about their subjects as they do. The writers wonder about conflicts between seeking accessibility and experimenting, wanting to stretch their readers and themselves.

Discussing the effect of their families on their work and the central role of women in their lives, many cite strong mothers and/or grandmothers, women authors, teachers, and friends who have inspired them, and women's writing groups that had helped them hone their craft. Some talk about their spouses, lovers, and/or children; others speak of the advantage for the writer of living alone. For all of them, writing is central to their lives.

I found the writers disarmingly frank about themselves and their work. No one refused to answer a question or sought to redirect what I was asking into a safer or more comfortable track. Although some writers, like Allen, Barker, and Silko, had just come off promotional book tours when we spoke, they didn't respond to questions with rehearsed answers. Others wedged the interview into busy schedules, but gave me their complete attention, even when the meeting ran longer than anticipated or they were tired. Joanna Russ, disabled with chronic fatigue syndrome, spoke with me from her bed.

The interviews were a delight and a revelation. I found that I respected these women whose books I admired. I enjoyed their humor and their intelligence, their seriousness about their writing and lack of pretension about themselves. I even enjoyed preparing for the interviews—the hours of reading and organizing questions. Most of all, I welcomed the chance to talk with them about their work. As one of my students said, I got to live her fantasy: I could ask these writers what they meant.

I met Paula Gunn Allen, poet, literary critic, and novelist, in Mama Bear, a feminist bookstore in Oakland, California, in June 1990. Allen, the author of twelve books and dozens of articles, was then teaching in the Native American studies department at the University of California, Berkeley, but has since joined the English department at the University of California, Los Angeles. She had just returned from a national book tour, promoting Spider Woman's Granddaughters (Beacon, 1989), a collection of tales by contemporary Native American women.

Over coffee, Allen and I spoke about many things: her diverse family background, her writing, the influences on her work, contemporary literature and criticism, the past and future of Native American literature, politics, the women's movement, and the oppression of people of color throughout the world. Our conversation was interrupted several times as women came over to our table to talk with her, but Allen never lost her train of thought or repeated herself, perhaps a result of the concentration she perfected during her recent road trip. She struck me as a determined woman used to juggling conflicting demands on her time.

The author of Skin and Bones (West End Press, 1988) and six other books of poetry, Allen writes powerfully about personal and public events, searching for interconnections. She identifies deeply with her Laguna Pueblo and Sioux ancestry, using Native American history and myth to unearth contemporary meanings in the stories of women like Sacagawea

Photo: Copyright © Tama Rothschild

and Pocahontas. Events in her own life—a grandmother's death, teaching poetry in a Santa Fe high school the week John Lennon was shot—are transformed into events of universal significance.

Her novel, The Woman Who Owned the Shadows *(Spinsters Ink, 1984), traces the nervous breakdown of Ephanie Atencio, a half-breed who eventually recovers through discovering her connection to the spirit women of her people. A lyrical, deeply moving novel about a woman's painful journey to self-discovery, it established Allen as one of the most important voices in Native American literature today.*

Allen is also respected as a literary critic. She has written a collection of essays on Native American culture, religion, and literature that establishes the centrality of women in the tribal universe, The Sacred Hoop: Recovering the Feminine in American Indian Traditions *(Beacon, 1986). In a collection published after the interview,* Grandmothers of the Light: A Medicine Woman's Source Book *(Beacon, 1991), Allen assembles twenty-one goddess stories to give an overview of the spirituality of Native American women.*

The mother of three grown children, Paula Gunn Allen has come far from her days as a "frightened little housewife in a beehive hairdo" who enrolled in poet Robert Creeley's creative writing class. Hers is a powerful, angry, memorable voice.

Q: Would you begin by talking a bit about your personal history?

A: My background was very diverse. My father is Lebanese and my mother is Laguna and Scottish. She was raised a Presbyterian and a heathen and my father was raised as a Maronite Roman Catholic. He grew up speaking Arabic and Spanish, and when she was tiny she spoke Laguna. But since her mother married a German immigrant and they moved to Cubero [New Mexico], a Spanish-speaking town, when Mother was quite small, she forgot Laguna and learned Spanish and English.

I was raised in the Sandstone Mesa in the northern part of New Mexico which is on a Spanish land grant—hardly anyone in the rest of the world even knows what a Spanish land grant is. Next to us was the Laguna reservation, which is also a Spanish land grant as well as being a federal reservation, and the Acoma reservation and Cíbola National Forest. Now this is not a typical Western upbringing, not that there are many people in Western cultures who have had a typical Western up-bringing, whatever that is. My point is that we have this official world that official humans live in, and then there is this world that most of us live in that is very different. Each of us has a peculiar history and a unique story. I have discovered this from speaking to many different kinds of people. You end up wondering where they get "typical" from.

Q: What's the impact of this diverse background on your work?

A: I have a lot of voices in my work. For instance, I'm a poet and a short-story writer and an essayist and a scholar because I have so many different personae in me and not just one. I don't think anyone is just one thing, but I really can't be because my father is very different from my mother, who is very different from my grandmother, who is very different from my grandfather. I grew up with all these things around me, so I feel like all those voices have to be there. Also, I was raised on Indian music, Arabic music, Roman Catholic music, Mexican music—so those cadences are all there inside me. My mother loved to listen to Mozart and the opera and played classical music on the piano. My father played the accordion and the piano by ear. Despite this classical home influence, I would prefer country-and-western music and the first dance I learned was the Charleston. The sounds of the Latin Mass stay with me, particularly the *Mass of the Angels,* which I sang when I was in the church choir. These are all important influences because they are bred into the rhythms of your work.

The rhythms of my novel [*The Woman Who Owned the Shadows*] are largely Indian rhythms, but a lot of my poetry sounds like Mozart or Tchaikovsky or some classical composer. My sister, who is a classical musician, can sit there and score them musically. Yet I want that clearness and clarity and richness that is there in Indian music to be in my work as well. I also think there is a lot of Lebanese in the poetry. I had an uncle who used to chant in Arabic. It was like the Jewish call to prayer—high ceremonial chanting that they would do on special occasions. I don't think I ever heard anything as beautiful as that, and I think that there are passages in my novel that sound more like Arab writers in translation than they sound like Native Americans.

Q: Your mother told you never to forget that you are an Indian. How did that warning affect you?

A: She was afraid I would be engulfed—she was afraid she would be engulfed. Her grandmother, who was the one who told her that, was really afraid that my mother would lose her sense of self. She did, actually. She lost her language and her place in Laguna society. But my mother remembered the warning and told me and all her children. Her mother—my grandmother—seemed to be busy trying to forget that she was an Indian. How you lose your Indianism and in Cubero become an Anglo-Saxon lady is beyond me, but Grandma tried.

Q: When you first went to graduate school you were told you couldn't study Native American literature because there wasn't any. I have the sense that you set out to prove academia wrong. Is that true?

A: I did, and I did it. Now there is Native American literature. I didn't do it alone, you understand. MLA [the Modern Language Association] helped a lot. But now we have a community of scholars worldwide and we study Native American literature both in its traditional and its contemporary aspects. It's a real discipline. Now we have meetings at MLA and we don't get members coming in and saying, "I know an Indian and he said so and so." Instead, we get literary questions of real substance. All of that has happened between 1970 and 1990.

Q: How did the change happen? Some of it was a result of your writing, but what else?

A: [Native American writer N. Scott] Momaday. His writing set off this explosion because it was the 1960s and civil rights issues were on the front burner. Liberals on the West Coast were publishing native people just as those on the East Coast were publishing black people. There was this flurry of colorful publishing. Then, in 1970, the MLA was doing a series of symposia on what they called "the discrete literatures"—Asian American, African American, Mexican American or Chicano, Puerto Rican, and Native American. The only two seminars MLA offered were African American and Native American literatures, as they were the only ones that got funding from the National Endowment for the Humanities. This has had a negative, long-term effect. You can see after all these years that the complexity of Chicano and Puerto Rican and Asian American studies is not that of the other two because of this early failure of support. NEH should be faulted for this because they did a serious disservice to American literature. We members of these groups are not merely colored; we are Americans. Although it is not the official America, our worlds and our experiences are American, and no full comprehension of the American experience is possible while the lives and works of large segments of American society go unexplored and unremarked.

Q: Now you are teaching Native American literature. What are your students like? Are many of them Native Americans?

A: I have great students. Most of them are white. When I taught Third World courses they were one form or another of colored—Asian American, Chicana, African American, Native American. In the Native American studies courses they are mostly white. We have a lot of students who sign Native American to their request for admission form, but we never see them. Also, somehow I got the reputation of not liking men, which is not true. I taught the women's [studies] class and a brave young man took the course and he said he couldn't understand the criticism of me. He liked the class and thought I was a good teacher.

Q: What has teaching at Berkeley been like for you?

A: In Native American studies it was pretty good. But the situation for us vis-à-vis other ethnic studies faculty—Asian Americans and Chicanos—was bad. I made a rule that I wanted to teach and get paid and be left alone. When I became a full professor they couldn't really mess with me, but the politics were silly. Someone was threatening me by saying that I wouldn't get my next promotion unless I did so and so, but they couldn't stop my promotion. I publish too much. It is difficult for women in ethnic studies. As a poet and a literary scholar, I was in isolation. Members of the English department look down their noses at us [people in ethnic studies]. Our own committee organizes a literature studies program for our graduate ethnic studies majors in which the students have to do all this course work in sociology and English. Meanwhile, [in ethnic studies] they have [prominent women of color like] Elaine Kim and Paula Gunn Allen and Barbara Christian and Norma Alarcón and others [whom students could be taking]. There is something wrong with this. I have nothing to do with it because they don't ask me to be on these committees.

I don't think I recognized how I was being treated until I started negotiating with UCLA.

Q: You've always been outspoken, Paula. How did you decide to go public about being lesbian?

A: Somebody called me not long after I came out and said they were putting together a reading for MLA. They had heard that I was a poet and Native American and lesbian. I hadn't been out three weeks! When I asked how they knew, they said they forgot where they had heard it.

So I said yes. This reading was for the Gay and Lesbian Caucus. I read with Monique Wittig and Joan Larkin and Judy Grahn and someone else. The audience was wonderful. I had always been told I was too academic or too much a street poet, but this audience was really responsive to what I was doing. By the time I came out I had no sense of hesitation about being public. I just didn't want my dad to find out. I've never made a big case of it. I didn't walk onto the campus and make a big fuss about it, but I didn't keep it secret either. I haven't had any trouble.

Then Elly Bulkin asked me to write an essay about lesbians that appeared in *Conditions* in a special issue on Native American writers. It's reprinted in *The Sacred Hoop* as "*Hwame, Koshkalaka,* and the Rest:

Lesbians in American Indian Cultures." She asked me to do it at the Gay Pride March, but it took me months to write. I kept thinking, Okay, now this will give them another reason to kill Indians: There are queers among Native Americans. I felt it was okay for me to come out, but not out the whole race.

Q: Has this bothered you—the fact that when you sit on a panel or publish something, people assume that you are speaking for all Native Americans?

A: An audience does generalize and tend to make assumptions about an entire race based on what one person says. I finally decided to publish the piece on lesbianism because I felt that we need to have many communities aware of our presence.

Q: In 1989, you wrote: "I have carried on an approach-avoidance relationship with my work; only this year have I resigned myself to what should have been an obvious fact all along: I am a writer and I love to write" [*The Women's Review of Books,* July 1989]. Do you still have some of this love-hate relationship with writing?

A: Oh, yes. Here I am sitting here when a book proposal needs to get in to the office, a book that was due two months ago is five or six hours from being finished, a book review needs to be put in the mail, and all these requests for articles need to be responded to. Actually, I just discovered what I am supposed to do: I am supposed to be a celebrity. I just got back from being on tour to talk about *Spider Woman's Granddaughters* and I loved it.

Q: What is your next book, *Grandmothers of the Light,* about?

A: Beacon is doing it. I rewrote twenty-one narratives from around Native America that are about the goddesses, spirit women, the supernaturals, and shamans. I have recounted existing stories as well as stories about things that happened to me or someone I know. So I didn't exactly make them up—[this is] in the best oral tradition. I have also added a lot of apparatus and headnotes and so on [that provide background information], so that people get some sense of [the importance of] spirituality for Native American women.

Q: Tell me about your new novel, *Raven's Road.* When will it be published?

A: I'm still working on it. It's a lesbian Indian novel, so that may affect the book's selling power. But that's okay; I want to write the book. "Deep Purple," the story that appeared in *Spider Woman's Granddaughters,* is from the book.

Q: Is it at all autobiographical?

A: This book has nothing to do with me. It's an occult espionage novel based on the adventures of five women. Three are lesbians—Allie Hawker, Eddie Raven, and Leela Sixkiller. Another is Grace, a woman who is not a lesbian and who is very traditional; and the last is Leela's mother, Maggie, who is a patriarchal woman but she's also Indian.

Then there are a group of political lesbians in the compound and an old lady in her seventies named Captain Bea who was in the army and is also a computer expert. She's heading up the feminists' antipornography campaign. She had a bevy of girls she brought out in the forties who were called Bea's Honeys. She told them all to get out of the army because there was going to be a purge, and so they did. There's a black woman named Beauregarde Baptiste who is a Yoruba American woman, a priestess, as well as a bartender and a bulldagger.

The novel takes place in the present. It's about Sun Woman who has come back and about the healing aspects of the bomb. Nobody is going to want to hear some of this! It's about God who comes home and is really pissed, but She is beautiful and She enlightens us all, like instant vapor. It's horrible, but there it is.

There's a galactic community of people whom we call spirits, but who are actually just people who have transmitters like the crystal skull. Allie and Raven and Leela are being trained to be agents for Galactic Central, just as Pocahontas and Sacagawea were agents. And they worked for Galactic Central. It's a funny story.

Q: It sounds like science fiction.

A: It's very like science fiction, except it's not fiction. It's the truth, but we'll call it fiction, in the best sense of the word.

Q: The novel sounds outspoken, particularly about lesbianism. What expectations do you have for it?

A: Assuming it finds a publisher, some will like it and some will laugh. And the ones who are lesbians will be appreciative. I expect more trouble from white liberals about its nuclear stance, and I think many Indian people would rather not touch the subject of homosexuality. I don't have a reservation to get thrown off, so I can take that risk.

Q: I found "Deep Purple" a very angry story that exposes hypocrisy and racism in the women's movement and among lesbians. Did you intend that anger to show?

A: I'm glad you said that. There has been some insightful response to it from feminist reviewers, who seem to be respectful of Leela's situation.

Q: I see it as a story about the tensions that emerge when people oppressed in one way, through sexism, can't understand the realities of other oppressions, like race and class.

A: Exactly. Those are the issues that the story is raising, and I don't have any answers and neither does poor little Leela, who's only twenty-something. The story is part of a novel about the Indian community in the Southwest and the lesbian community in the Southwest. There are all kinds of intersections between them, and the communities are very similar. They both suffer from dysfunctional dynamics that are very much alive. I want to talk about that and alcoholism and drug abuse, both of which are part of that dysfunction. So is power tripping. The white middle-class ladies in the story are power tripping all over Third World women.

By the way, there is nothing in that story that did not happen. I put three things together: One happened in the Bay area, one in Albuquerque, and one was nationwide.

Q: One scene that particularly upset me happens when Kay, the white feminist, can't understand Leela's position. This happens when Leela suggests that the group shouldn't boycott a bar that's run by an African American woman. Kay says, "Let's not think of it that way," suggesting that the woman's race shouldn't be taken into consideration.

A: They [white feminists] really do things like that. One woman once told me that women with sons are going to be the destruction of the women's movement. Now she knew that I have two sons, but because I am an Indian I don't count. And when I said, "I don't intend to destroy the women's movement," she said, "Let's not think of it that way."

Q: I bet you get angry when this kind of thing happens.

A: I do. I get terribly upset. I resign from the movement about once a month. But I learned over the years that my job is to challenge—which is the writer's job. In my case, the job is largely to challenge the women's community. It isn't right for one group of upwardly mobile, privileged women to make decisions about what we all are doing and who we all are. They don't get to do that. And they will do it if somebody doesn't stand up—lots of somebodies—and keep saying, "Hey, wait a minute." There are a lot of women doing this, but I am one of the few Native American women who stands up and does it—who can get it into print. Native women talk about it among themselves, of course.

Q: Is the situation in the women's community better now than it has been in the past?

A: There are so many ways in which it is dreadful, but at least the misunderstandings are at a more interesting level. And maybe all that has happened will lead to more progress—which is a word I actually hate because it leads to dead Indians. But certainly the community is very busy confronting itself, as America is busy confronting itself. I find the women's community more alive than many other communities.

Q: *The Woman Who Owned the Shadows,* your first novel, challenged many readers in its style and subject matter. It's not a linear book; at times it is hard to follow. What were you trying to do?

A: It is hard to talk about the book, in a way, because it isn't linear. A number of people have said that if they could get past the first thirty pages they were okay. The writing style is tough, and the story is painful. People who have had similar kinds of experiences have told me that they couldn't read it because of the pain it articulates. On the one hand, I don't want to write books that voyeurize other people. That's a real problem for native people since Indians are the subject of voyeurism all the time. People go out to the reservation and just walk into people's houses without knocking. They think they are at the zoo. So the trick for me was to make Indian people real, not oddities, not curiosities. I think I succeeded.

Q: In a recent trip to Monument Valley I overheard a tourist say to her husband, "Do you think the Indians appreciate the beauty of this land?" I couldn't believe it.

A: That's exactly why they took it—they said we didn't appreciate it. I wrote this novel in such a way that you have to join it. You have to recognize your pain, and the only way people who are not Indian are going to understand it is to connect with their own pain, with their own victimization in some way. I wanted it to be a human book. I wanted to transcend the particular and write a universal book—to put it in Harvard's terms [she laughs].

Q: Would you talk a bit about the Ephanie-Elena relationship in *The Woman Who Owned the Shadows*?

A: They're lovers, but they're children. At that point in her life Ephanie lost herself, so she turns into a nice, heterosexual, nonnative, mainstream sort of person. It is only when she goes back and recognizes all that pain and that she is Indian and that she has told all these lies to herself that she discovers who she is. She has to go back and retell her stories and then she can reclaim herself.

By then she doesn't love Elena because that would be too accessible. I wanted to write a literary book and it had to be obscure. My next book is going to be much more accessible—even obvious.

Q: What do we make of the novel's ending—where Ephanie joins the spirit dance?

A: I don't quite feel comfortable with the ending, but there didn't seem to be any other way out of the book. I understand how it ends that way. I had to do something, and I really believe that as the native people move on they go on to the next stage, a place where they can be smarter. That's how the race should be. I couldn't just stop: "Page 289, I quit." The oral tradition stories are never resolved. The storyteller resolves them in English but in the oral tradition they aren't resolved. Change is important, events are important, and in the literature of the people they go on and on. Too bad novels don't work that way!

Q: In the book time is cyclical. Is that how you see it?

A: In a way. Time, space, life itself (as we know it). Everything is always in flux. The new Americans are new, but they are going to have to take into their hands the charge that the Indians have long since accepted. Read *Indian Givers* by Jack Weatherford [Crown, 1988]. He talks about what Indians contributed to the world. I talk about their contribution to feminism—the tradition of strong, autonomous, self-defining women comes from Indians. They sure didn't get it in sixteenth-century Europe. The idea that people participate in the government—the whole idea of democracy—didn't come from the Greeks. They had a republic, not a democracy. That dream came to transplanted Anglo-Europeans from the Algonquin and Iroquois people who directly told our founding fathers— Ben Franklin, for example—that that was how they ought to do it. They should form a confederation against England. It took a long time for whites to do it, but they did it. In addition, 50 percent of all the pharmaceuticals and two-thirds of the foodstuffs in this country were Native American and they were used in the same way by native peoples. Indians are like the leaven in the bread.

The newcomers have only been here for five hundred years at most, and as they learn the ways of this land they become more and more Indian—they take off their clothes, they think child abuse is wrong, they form democracies and work cooperatively. This is proof that primitive is sophisticated. In the book Ephanie has to help Teresa to understand the spirits, the seeming naïf must guide and lead the seeming sophisticate— you see?

Q: Ephanie's attempted suicide represents her low point in the book. Did you feel that you had to push her that far before she could see the truth?

A: Yes. My own experience at the time was that one must be against the wall before she can take charge of her life. The book is sort of a distillation of everything I knew about everything before I was thirty. I began it when I was thirty, and it took me a long time to finish it.

Q: You thank Gertrude Stein in your acknowledgments to *The Woman Who Owned the Shadows.* How was her work influential?

A: I discovered Gertrude Stein in high school. My mother bought me everything she could find by her—I had a big Penguin edition of her works. I couldn't have found the rhythms I found in *The Woman Who Owned the Shadows,* which I borrowed from legend, unless I had Stein's rhythms inside me. She fractured the language, which then enabled me to do that in my way. James Joyce fractured the language in a lyric way, and, without Joyce, Scott Momaday wouldn't have gotten published.

Q: Who were some other literary influences?

A: Poems. The Black Mountain poets in particular. Bob Creeley, who was my first teacher, was one of the most important influences. He took me into his writing class. There I was this frightened little housewife from Grants, New Mexico, bedecked in a beehive hairdo.

I read Jane Austen and my very favorite was Charlotte Brontë. Louisa May Alcott was important to me: I still imagine myself writing in the attic with my candle and my curly hair and my sister at the door with, "Does genius burn?" [the question often asked of Jo in *Little Women*]. I loved *Jo's Boys,* my favorite of the books. I didn't care for *Wuthering Heights.* Emily was so hysterical she drove me nuts, and I didn't like Heathcliff. *Jane Eyre* I read five times. Rochester was another matter and the madwoman in the attic was too much—I lived with her. I felt like an orphan because I went to boarding school and I spent most of my time there looking out of the windows like Jane did.

Groddeck, a German writer. Freud influenced me. I read Marx, Freud, William James, et al., when I was a housewife. I have a poem called "Moon Shot 1969" that has echoes of Keats's "Ode to a Nightingale" in it, although I only recognized that years later when I overheard some people doing a dramatic reading of the Keats poem. I was nuts for the Romantics and Chesterton and Dorothy Parker and Robert Benchley.

Q: What contemporary writers do you read?

A: Toni Morrison, particularly *Song of Solomon* [Knopf, 1977]. I'm trying to locate Arab and Indian women writers now. I liked Salman

Rushdie's *The Satanic Verses* [Viking, 1989]. It's very funny. A brilliant book. I read another book—*The Great Indian Novel* [by Shashi Tharoor (Viking, 1989)]. I found it in England and liked it a lot. It's based on the *Mahabharata*, but it's modern. It's about Gandhi and Nehru. Neil Gunn, a Scottish writer, is wonderful. Any new Indian novels that come out, of course. I read mostly Third World people, as you can see.

There's a gay writer named Robert Glück who is terrific. I think he's one of the best writers around. He's got one book called *Jack the Modernist* [Gay Presses of New York, 1985]. He's in Italy writing another novel right now. He directs the poetry center at San Francisco State.

Q: Writers talk about the role of editors or readers of their work. Do you share what you write as you are writing?

A: I am not one of those people who shares my writing. When I was thirteen, my mother found my diary. Boy, did I get in a lot of trouble! To this day I have trouble sharing what I am working on. For a while I got together with some other writers—Sandy Boucher, Valerie Miner, Judy Grahn, and I used to get together and read one another's manuscripts. That sort of fell apart.

I have a good friend at UCLA and I show him things, but I like to get them pretty well done before I do. What I really like to do is take them out and read them at a reading. I can tell more about what's happening from that than from anything. Not from people's responses, but from what listening to your own work does. I can hear where I need to make changes.

I am getting better about using editors, but mostly I work alone. "In my craft and sullen art" is one of my favorite sayings.

Q: Some people I have interviewed talk about feeling a sense of responsibility to their group when they write. Valerie Miner says she doesn't want to betray her working-class family, for example. Do you feel this way?

A: Maybe that's why I have this approach-avoidance relationship that I mentioned. It's terrible. If I say the wrong thing, I don't know what forces I'm setting in motion. I believe that language is powerful and thought is powerful. Writing sets things in motion. There is a Theosophical principle that energy follows thought, and as I am writing I'm thinking, "They won't understand that." I'm always second-guessing white readers. Then I'm also wondering, "Will the Indian people see what I am saying as accurate?" That's my touchstone; when they do, I know my work is worthwhile. I can see that what I am "setting in motion" in the white world is present in the thought of the Indian people.

Q: I wonder if you would feel so much pressure if there were more Native Americans getting published?

A: I don't know. I never thought of it that way. I feel a terrible burden. People always make generalizations: "I knew a Catholic and he said . . ." or "I knew an Indian and he said. . . ."

But most of the Indian people are so good to me, so I know that I'm okay. If I'm distorting their stories, then I'm in trouble. I do want the world to know how wonderful the Indian way is. Maybe that's wrong, but it's what I want to do.

I don't want to sugarcoat things; I don't want the people to see a lie about themselves. I want them to see the truth as I understand it, and that's all you can do. It's dreadful to go through the world and never see yourself anywhere. We live in a world where we expect to see images of ourselves in the media, and there are very few for Indian people, especially Indian women. I tell you, they come to me in tears, and they are in college and they are in graduate school and they say that they are going to do it, too, because I have. I always say that *The Woman Who Owned the Shadows* is about a half-breed woman, but full bloods, traditional ones say, "No it isn't; it's about me." A young man who is Sioux-Lakota said they respect me and teach the book at the community college. That matters a lot.

Q: What about the publishing situation for Native Americans now? Louise Erdrich has made it, but is it easier for Native Americans in general to get published today than it has been in the past?

A: It is getting better and better. Louise Erdrich hit it big and that helped. This book [*Spider Woman's Granddaughters*] is selling very well. It got good reviews—the *New York Times,* the *Los Angeles Times,* the *Philadelphia Inquirer.* It was a notable book of the year for the *New York Times* for 1989. Ballantine bought it, and Beacon ran out of copies. The writers who appear in it are doing well. Vickie Sears now has a book out [*Simple Songs* (Firebrand Books, 1990)], and she was barely published. Elizabeth Cook-Lynn's collection of short stories is coming out with Little, Brown [*The Power of Horses and Other Stories* (1990)], which is exciting because her work is very traditional. I didn't think that a white audience would get it.

Q: What do you mean by saying that her work is traditional?

A: They are books that need a lot of glossing to understand the dynamics, the relationships, the plot. She had a book called *Then Badger Said This* that was published by a small but respectable press [Ye Galleon Press, 1983]. It has some excellent vignettes, very beautiful. But she might as well have translated them from her language. To my sense they are pure Indian. But because she is stubborn, she does what she wants to do. I hope the book gets the attention it deserves. If that book makes it in a respectable sense, it will open up a readership.

Reading Erdrich is different because she is easy to read, except for *The Beet Queen* [Henry Holt, 1986], which is her best book. It comes directly out of her core.

Q: I'm interested in that core, in the ways in which the literatures of different racial and ethnic groups are similar and different. How is the work of Native Americans different from that of African American writers, for example?

A: Native American writing is less political, less Marxist, less polarized. It is much more spirit-based and land-based. The land plays a central part and the spirituality has a deep connection with the land.

Now, Toni Cade Bambara does most of these things in *The Salt Eaters* [Random House, 1980], but she is more urban in her focus, and more definitely politicized. Momaday, even though some of his settings are urban, writes from "the res." I can't think of any Indian who has written an urban novel, at least, not yet.

Q: Nature plays a central role in your work, doesn't it?

A: I think that's what I'm best at writing about. The most important influence in my work has been the land. It is so big to me, so huge, so compelling. It makes up all my dreams.

Q: The group as a source of strength for the individual seems central to the literature of both African American and Native American writers. Does Native American literature resist the dominant notion of the autonomous individual finding herself or himself?

A: I can't think of an oral story that has to do with finding yourself. I can think of a lot that have to do with finding spirits, finding power, finding knowledge, but I have never heard of one that has to do with finding yourself. Nor have I ever heard of one where they find their place to be that's different from where they were raised—not ever. It is always about transformation. Magic is always at work. Momaday, in *The Ancient Child* [Doubleday, 1989], and Gunn Allen, in *The Woman Who Owned the Shadows,* both deal with this. At the end of my book, Ephanie is transformed into a spirit.

Q: This represents a break from the Oedipus story, one of the central myths of Western literature. The idea there was that one had to destroy the parent to find the self.

A: But, in my mind, the Oedipus story says that such killing is the worst thing that you can do. Of course you need to become an individual—how can you not? The real issue is: How can you maintain community? You must. As I understand the Indian world, you have to do both. You become self-responsible—you are responsible for what you do—and you are part of the community. That community is not just those around you; your responsibility extends to the whole group.

Q: Given this sense of responsibility, what do literary critics who are reading Native American texts need to be doing now?

A: They need to be developing critical dimensions that allow us to assess all American literatures. We can't read American literature until we get out of the Harvard-of-the-mind insularity in which we intellectuals live. Maybe we should quit having departments of English, since their brand of English is a foreign language to most of us. I discovered that I don't speak English when I went to England and couldn't understand anyone. I learned that I speak English as a second language, and that British, Scottish, Welsh, and Irish cultures are ethnic cultures, just as Pueblo, Lakota, or Cherokee cultures are.

Q: How do you respond to reviewers who dismiss work by women as small, or who want writers of color to deal with more [so-called] universal themes? It seems to me that they want everyone to write white.

A: Yes, and to write white in terms that only Harvard minds understand. Ed Abbey, a western writer who has written three novels, is not big either. *The Monkey Wrench Gang* [Lippincott, 1975] is one I particularly like. He has also been writing environmental-ecological essays since the 1950s. He just died. One of the funniest writers I've ever read. He's not going to be canonized until we change our definition of what constitutes great literary works.

   All of Melville's works about race never get in the canon either. And Whitman is kind of tangential because he's a faggot and they're stuck with him because they are overwhelmed with the power of his work. There is something very wrong with a criticism that denies the particularity of experience.

Q: In a recent *Michigan Quarterly Review* article [vol. 28 (winter 1989)], Toni Morrison talks about the importance of reading American literature from different perspectives. She talks, specifically, about how she, as an African American, reads the references to the whiteness of the whale in *Moby Dick,* for example. In *The Sacred Hoop,* you interpret a Keres Indian tale in three ways, depending on the perspective of the reader. How important are these new readings for our understanding of literature?

A: They are central. Native American critics need to be critiquing American literature from a Native American perspective. Not politically, but asking what those metaphors mean in our framework. And, of course, politics will have something to do with it. The experience of reading *Moby Dick* is going to be different for me than for someone from New England, for example, or than it was for Melville. These are the exciting critical questions and the questions that we should be asking and arguing about, instead of deconstruction. Perhaps deconstruction could be turned to great use, but as it is now it seems so insipidly silly.

Faculty attitudes have to change. Starting this fall [1990] I'll be at UCLA. I'm doing a faculty seminar on integrating Third World women's literature into the curriculum. This is the fifth year they are doing this, with support from the Ford Foundation. I will be teaching with a fellow named Eric Sondheim, who is in African American literature. This training of faculty is what has to happen.

Q: These faculty workshops are often difficult because traditional English departments think that transforming the curriculum simply means replacing a James Joyce story with one by Alice Walker.

A: That's why we have to change the critical underpinnings. James Joyce and Alice Walker have more in common than they have as difference. If you understand the history of Ireland and you understand the history of black people in the United States, you realize that you are talking about analogous situations.

Q: What do you say to people who say that the readings you are proposing are too political?

A: I tell them that I have been working on a theory of the politics of aesthetics. I give them Edward Said. Don't tell me that any aesthetics do not have a political dimension. Your aesthetics lead to dead Indians, I say. Don't tell me that you're not political. You can say that—you're the conqueror. I can be really special, too, when I own the world. I can afford to be pure. It's like Ursula Le Guin, who said in her review of *Spider Woman's Granddaughters* that she didn't know if the idea of war could be redeemed [*New York Times Book Review,* 14 May 1989]. If I were her, I would say that, too.

Q: You've said, here and elsewhere, that native peoples around the world are in danger. Would you expand on that?

A: What do you think they are doing in Guatemala right now? The whole issue is to kill the Mayas. Twenty-four thousand live in the Highlands. They are moving. They are coming up here like crazy because they are under assault. The United States is trying to help the Guatemalan government buy the Toledo district in southern Belize, which is Mayan country. The theory is that this is because the Guatemalans need a seacoast. Bullshit. The reason they want it is to control the majority of the Maya population. Those people will be killed. They will be infected with diseases. And people will say, "Oh, isn't it sad." But the net result will be dead Indians because the war isn't over; it moved south.

[In proportion to the population] there are more Indian men on death row than any other group in thirty-three states. Now, why is that? Today, Indian women and men have been forcibly sterilized—25 percent of the women; 10 percent of the men—without their consent. Fetal alcohol syndrome, Michael Dorris says, will be 100 percent at Pine Ridge and on White Mountain Apache Reservation by the turn of the century. That means no one over the mental age of six to run tribal affairs.

Do you see what I mean? It is focused. It is concerted. It has never stopped, and it is not going to stop while there is a single Indian alive. Roxy Gordon, an Indian poet in Texas, has statistics on this. There is a group called something like the Custer Brigade—they advertise in *Rifle* magazine—who kill Indians. All over the country you can humiliate or torture an Indian and no one cares. A friend tells me that even in the Tenderloin [in San Francisco], Indians are at the bottom of the pole and everyone spits on them. At every single level in this society, Indians are painted as drunk, derelict, no good, as people who "can't appreciate this land." Therefore, it is common to believe, they should die. It's not said this way, but it is assumed.

Phil McGee at San Francisco State, who is a black psychologist and ethics studies dean who also teaches in the African American studies department, says that he believes the foundation of racism in this country is Indian-hating and every American and immigrant to America learns it right away, even within the first few weeks of their lives. They learn that Indians are dead or should be dead because they are bloodthirsty savages who kill innocent people and who are mean to women. Of course, they aren't mean to women—they are much less mean to women than most other groups.

In Argentina, they moved all abandoned people—the Mapuche, etc.— onto rocky, barren reservations where there is no way to make a living. Of course, you don't hear about this. Who is going to tell you? We hear all about South Africa, but we don't hear a damn thing about Argentina, except that Maggie Thatcher launches a war there and we are supposed to sympathize with the Argentinians. Not that I sympathize in any way with her, but the Argentinians are not clean. They speak Spanish, a

European language. Most Argentinians immigrated there from Europe. It is not a colored nation. The fights in Canada are terrible, too.

You see, if native peoples are alive we can keep saying, "Look what you did." Once America can get real about its history and talk about it and come to terms with it, we can begin to deal with the past in a legitimate way. Native peoples do not want the Europeans dead, but it would be nice if those colonizing people could admit what they did. Maybe that will happen with the number of writers, nonnative and native, who are writing now. Maybe by the turn of the century we can have a real dialogue about the past—not just, "You're guilty," or "How awful," but a real dialogue about what happened and what is still happening. We need to make it stop.

Before I interviewed Chicana poet and fiction writer Gloria Anzaldúa at the Conference on College Composition and Communication in Cincinnati in March 1992, I felt I knew her through her writing, particularly the now-classic anthology she coedited with Cherríe Moraga, This Bridge Called My Back: Writings by Radical Women of Color *(Persephone Press, 1981; reprinted by Kitchen Table, 1983). Her own essay in that book, "Speaking in Tongues: A Letter to Third World Women Writers," evokes strong reactions from my students; she warns that women of color must unlearn "the esoteric bullshit and pseudo-intellectualizing that school brainwashed into [their] writing" and criticizes white feminists for "tokenizing" women of color.*

Anzaldúa wants her readers, both women of color and white women, to get upset. Writing matters to her. It has been her means of survival, a way to maintain her sanity. And her message isn't an easy one to take, particularly for those white feminists who are uncomfortable acknowledging their privileges of race and class.

Yet Anzaldúa sees herself as a mediator, a facilitator. A graduate student at the University of California at Santa Cruz, she travels throughout the United States attending conferences, giving lectures, and reading her poetry and fiction to diverse audiences. Using her own experiences as text, she establishes an immediate rapport with workshop participants, often pausing to ask, "Does this make sense to you?" and responding candidly to questions and comments.

I saw Anzaldúa in action at a workshop on the creative process. "How's that for drama?" she asked us, having covered a portable blackboard with drawings. "I lecture with pictures," she explained, going on to trace the significance of these personal hieroglyphics. After she read us one of her poems in Spanish: "I know that was frustrating for many of you, but I wanted you to see what it feels like to be locked out of the language because you don't know it. I was punished for speaking Spanish in school."

Anzaldúa grew up near the Rio Grande in south Texas, close to the Mexican border. Since her parents were ranchers and sharecroppers, Anzaldúa, her sister and brothers joined them in the fields, and, for a time, the family raised chickens. School introduced her to English and to racism; sexism she encountered closer to home, in the Chicano community's gender stereotyping. As a dyke (her term), Anzaldúa found her family and community's expectations particularly galling: Loving women and resisting pressure to marry and have children, she found herself an outsider among her own people. As she explains, she began to feel more at home in the (predominantly white) lesbian feminist community, although racial and class differences eventually made this an uneasy alliance, too.

Just as she resists being pigeonholed into any one category, Anzaldúa's writing transcends boundaries of language and genre. In Borderlands/La Frontera: The New Mestiza *(Spinsters/Aunt Lute, 1987), she blends prose and poetry, cultural history and personal remembrance in an exploration of what it means to occupy the place between two cultures. Individual poems and essays flow from English to Spanish, with a scattering of Tex-Mex, suggesting that language, too, is fluid in this meeting place. In another edited collection,* Making Face, Making Soul/Haciendo Caras *(Aunt Lute Books, 1990), Anzaldúa assembles seventy pieces from new and established women writers of color in a book designed to let them talk to and with one another in a variety of forms—from formal essays to poems, notes, and stories.*

There's no difference between the Gloria Anzaldúa of her essays and the woman I met in Cincinnati. In person, she's thoughtful and candid, her speech (like her writing) interspersed with Spanish, her convictions strong. In the interview, which she sandwiched between conference commitments, Anzaldúa talked about her published works and two forthcoming ones: Lloronas/Women Who Write: Autohistorias, Teorías, and the Productions of Writings, Knowledge, and Identities *(1995), which she described as "sort of a sequel to Borderlands," and* La Prieta *(1994), a collection of stories, many of which are based on her own life (both to be published by Aunt Lute). When I left her hotel room, Anzaldúa was ordering her dinner from room service. She still had to look over her notes and drawings for the next day's workshop on multiculturalism.*

Q: Let's start with the idea of Borderlands [a term Anzaldúa capitalizes], from which you took the title of your latest book. How has this idea affected you and your writing?

A: Having been raised in the border [area] of south Texas near the Rio Grande—the river that separates Texas from Mexico—I was very conscious of how people cut off sections of land and say, "This is mine and this is yours and this is for corn or squash or cotton." I became conscious also of how the borders shifted—how, when the river changed its bed, a Mexican family who lived near the edge of the river would one day find themselves on the U.S. side of it, or vice versa.

I got to thinking very early on what this crack, this borderline means. When you're right in the middle, your identity and your language partake of both sides. I consider Chicanas and Chicanos, my people, as in-betweens. We mediate between the Mexican side and the American side, speaking both languages. Chicano Spanish, especially Tex-Mex, is made up of both. I extended the physical Borderlands to the psychological metaphor. Border people are in an in-between state, able to have two or three points of view because we've been on all these other spaces, worlds, and cultures.

Q: So the Borderland is the place where different viewpoints come together.

A: Yes. It is a place or a state of awareness where we could all listen and talk to each other, where divisions may be breached, perhaps even healed. There are little Borderlands everywhere. And multiple perspectives seemed a key to understanding one another and then living and working together. If we can make this empathetic leap to the other side and listen, we could come to a deeper understanding of each other's positions. I don't think we can "resolve" our differences right away, but a lot of work can be done in the dialogues.

Q: Is it difficult to straddle two cultures?

A: Yes, but I see that if we could get an understanding of this crack, this Borderland, our situation would be less chaotic and painful and we could understand both sides better. It would give us a makeshift map or tracking device.

Q: So you've turned the chaos in your situation as a border person into something positive?

A: Yes. In *Borderlands/La Frontera* I talk about a constantly shifting, very fluid space, where you can also keep a toehold. People kept saying, "Marginal people, minorities are pushed to the margins," which were seen as poverty-stricken areas deprived of culture, almost like prisons. So I thought, What if I take this space that I have been pushed to as a lesbian, as a Mexican, as a woman, as a short person, whatever, and make this my territory? Make it a place where I can function and work and be creative? What if I start pushing to enlarge that crack so that other people can also be in it?

I want to take the attention away from the center and place it on the periphery and the margins. Once that displacement happens, there is no center. One of the fears that a lot of academics have with multicultural education and with people like myself is that they will be replaced. But they are wrong. I'm not interested in *replacing* them but in *displacing* them—from the center. I'm exploring these ideas in a book that I'm working on now, *Lloronas/ Women Who Write: Autohistorias, Teorías, and the Productions of Writings, Knowledge, and Identities.*

Q: This is an essay collection?

A: It's sort of a two-volume sequel to *Borderlands,* with autobiography, aesthetics, and theory all together. It is about identity, about what it means to be a *mestiza* [half-breed], a Chicana, an academic, someone who is interested in psychoanalysis. I rely on little pictures to kind of tie it together; they are my hieroglyphics.

In a third book, *La Prieta* [an upcoming story collection/novel], I'm doing the same thing: I have some stories about Prieta finding herself in this abyss, in between different spaces. So the theoretical and the fictional pieces are dealing with more or less the same ideas. I use the stories to dramatize the theory.

Q: In *Borderlands* you make your reader stretch more than you did in earlier works because you don't always translate the Spanish into English.

A: *Sí.* Sometimes translations will appear at the ends of the poems. In other places in the prose section I didn't translate all of the Spanish poems into English.

Q: Why did you write this way?

A: Mostly because it's the kind of Borderland dialect that I grew up with, talking both Spanish and English. But I also wanted the readers to start thinking about the myth of a monocultural U.S. There are people of other cultures that speak Italian, the different Jewish languages, Native American dialects, black English, plus all the Asian languages. By speaking and writing both languages, I wanted to force that awareness that this country is not what those in power say it is. It's a *mestiza* nation.

Q: Do you write in English or Spanish or both?

A: I have a fiction project that I just started that is entirely in Spanish. Most stories are predominantly English with some Spanish, unless it's a kind of a regional piece about south Texas, and then a lot of Spanish comes in. It depends on the mood and the character how much Spanish is used. In *La Prieta* I have a story called "Las Movidas of a Baby Butch Dyke," about a young butch dyke who decides that she wants to become a femme because femmes don't have to initiate intimacy. In that story, every line has Spanish colloquialisms because I had that particular setting and age group in mind.

Q: When you were growing up, you spoke Spanish?

A: Yes.

Q: You learned English in school?

A: None of us "Mexican" kids knew English. We were supposed to pick up a little bit of English in Beginners I and II. So when we got to first grade, we were supposed to have an understanding of English. Of course, there's no way that a little *chicanito* with a year of English could understand and have a mastery of the language like the white guy who spent six or seven years practicing it.

Since my birthday is on the twenty-sixth of September, I didn't enter the first Beginners until I was almost seven. So I must have been about nine before I could speak and write in English. I like English; it's a good language, just like Spanish is and Nahuatl [a group of languages spoken in central Mexico and El Salvador]. I love English literature and English writers. What I'm opposed to is shoving this English-only thing at us.

Q: Do you think in Spanish or in English?

A: Right now I am thinking in English. When I visit my mother I think in Spanish. And when I'm talking with my sister, I think in Tex-Mex [she laughs].

Q: Rosario Ferré told me that there were some things that she couldn't translate from Spanish to English, and she said that she hated most translations of her work. What's your experience?

A: I usually like the translations, but it's hard for the translators to hit the same register of vernacular and formal language that I do. I liked Maria Margaret Navar's translations. Then Ana Castillo translated *Prieta* and the "Dear Women of Color" letter, which don't correspond to what I was trying to do. I usually do my own translations. I translated some poems in *Borderlands,* such as "Sea of Cabbages" and "In the Name of All the Mothers Who Have Lost Children."

I couldn't translate "Cagado abismo"—the more spiritual stuff is harder for me to translate. I couldn't translate "mujer cacto" nor "sobre piedras con lagartijos," the one about the Mexican hiding under the brush in the desert so that the border patrol can't find him.

Q: In *Borderlands* you're also forcing the reader to rethink genre. You blend the personal with the academic, poetry with prose.

A: I was trying to accommodate all of my selves. Sometimes one theory will blossom in a poem, or a story, or creative nonfiction, or a letter.

Q: You have this formal section with footnotes at the beginning.

A: And some of the stories I'm working on will have footnotes or endnotes because they're supposed to read like essays. I got tired of being taught in these cubbyhole disciplines, taught that you couldn't jump over the fence into another genre.

Q: Is writing poetry different from writing fiction?

A: In *Borderlands,* I wanted some of the prose sections to read like poetry. I was trying to make the point that in writing prose, one can use elements of poetry, and vice versa. Good writing uses every technique and tool available in order to make its effect. I put snippets of verse in letters, journal entries, and theoretical pieces to prove my point. But it's also difficult to read because I often have to shift registers and languages in almost every passage.

Q: I liked the switching of voices from personal to academic to poetic; but I had a problem because I never studied Spanish in school.

A: *Sí.* You have the monolingual dominant culture to blame, not me. Some of the younger white readers and readers of color act like this difficulty is all my fault; and they curse me for making it hard on them. My intent was not to exclude certain groups of readers but to *not* make my work so easily assimilable, so easily tokenized.

Q: Many of the poems in *Borderlands* express your rage over racism and sexism. Would you talk about "el sonavabitche," the poem about the migrant workers being cheated of their pay by the owner who turns them in?

A: About 1973 or '74, after I got my master's, I applied to be one of two selected public school teachers in the state of Texas to travel with the migrant families. I chose to go to Indiana, where I was the liaison between the school officials and the migrant workers. The other day I met some people from that area in Indiana and they actually knew the grower [she laughs]. They recognized him from reading this poem.

Q: That's great, since you say in the poem that if he doesn't give you the people's money, you'll tell on him.

A: That's right.

Q: Is "Corner of 50th St. and Fifth Ave.," a poem about New York policemen beating up a Puerto Rican man, based on a true incident, too?

A: Yes, when I used to live in Brooklyn I would walk around 50th and Fifth Avenue to get the groceries. This incident happened one day. I witnessed all sorts of social injustices in the streets every day.

Q: Tell me about "Holy Relics," the poem about Teresa of Avila, where you talk about how her body is being dug up by these so-called worshipers. You connect her with all women.

A: It belongs to an unpublished manuscript called "Tres lenguas del fuego" ("Three Tongues of Fire"). I was trying to deal with women figures from medieval Renaissance Spain and colonial Mexican women.

I found out that Santa Teresa was sent to the convent by her father because they caught her kissing a woman cousin. I had been reading Judy Grahn's poem "I Have Come to Claim Marilyn Monroe's Body," and at the same time I was reading about what happened to Teresa's body: how they dug her up, how people had taken different pieces of her, and how her body did not really belong to her but to the Church. I started making the connection with what happens to women's bodies now.

By the way, my grandmother's name is Davila, which was originally d'Avila; somewhere or other, some of my ancestors originated from Avila.

Q: Did all of that really happen to Saint Teresa? Was her body moved all those times?

A: Every single thing that I've put in there I researched and it is true—the names, the places. The only thing I didn't mention which I wanted to put in there was that you could go into one of these stores by the church and buy a piece of her. It's on display, in a reliquary. I haven't done the research for some years now so I don't know if she's sold out [she laughs].

Q: These women in "Tres lenguas del fuego" are historical figures?

A: Most are. I have Juana la Loca, who was supposed to have been the queen of Spain but was kept off the throne by first her father, then her brother, then her husband. I had a poem about a Jewish woman in dialogue with Philip II [a Spanish king who oversaw the Inquisition, which persecuted alleged heretics, including Jews]. One poem is about a woman alchemist, another about a woman who went on the Crusades. Others are about a woman pirate who dressed as a man and a woman abducted by the Moors in Spain who falls in love with her abductor.

Q: Was the Jewish woman–Philip II poem true?

A: Philip was true and the Jewish woman was a made-up composite. I had a poem called "Slow Growing Fire," about two nuns. The older one gives away the younger one who is burned at the stake as a witch because the older one can't tolerate the sexual feelings between them. I have "Basque bruja," a Basque witch's poem—Anzaldúa is a Basque word. I have Basque blood. I have a Gypsy poem. Another poem was about Sor Juana Inés de la Cruz, who was the first feminist on this continent, a Mexican nun and an intellectual who wrote poems and treatises about the oppression of women and the rights of women.

I spent years doing tons of research on all of these persecuted groups. I see these women as models: They were writers, readers, intellectuals, and activists.

Q: You've used the idea of women's bodies being taken over elsewhere. In "Canción de cascabel" ["Song of the Rattlesnake"], which you gave me in manuscript, the medical profession appropriates a woman's body, and she finds out that she nearly died only when, at the end, she reads her own medical report.

A: That woman was me. I was hospitalized for infected fibroid tumors in 1980. The surgeon didn't tell me that I had actually died for a moment on the operating table. I felt I had hallucinated my death because of all the drugs they had given me. In writing about this I had to improvise a little bit about the place where I was dead, where the soul went because I didn't know how much I had imagined and how much I actually experienced, or whether there is a difference between the two realities. When I write my stories I often don't know if I am imagining them now or whether I went through that experience in another state of mind.

Q: But it almost doesn't matter whether it happened or not, does it? As long as the spirit is true.

A: Yes. Originally, "Canción de cascabel" was a three-part story. The first part, "He Couldn't Find the Hole," was about the three months of illness they spent trying to find out what was wrong with me. They dilated my cervix. They gave me half-a-dozen different antibiotics. In the third story, "The Second Day Home from the Hospital," I keep crossing the border between life and death. I would look out the window of my apartment in Noe Valley and hear and see, very clearly, people who were on Twenty-fourth Street, two-and-a-half blocks away. I could see them as clearly as though they were right outside my window.

Q: What happened to those stories?

A: As I was limited to a certain number of pages I cut the first and third parts of "cascabel."

Q: Since so many of the *Prieta* stories are based on your own experiences, did you worry about the reactions of your family and friends?

A: Yes and no. Yes, they are very opposed to my writing about them. But I continue to write about us and our culture. One of my chief problems is that I don't want to "incriminate" people who are going to see themselves in my stories. So I dwell a lot on Prieta's emotional life, rather than fleshing out some of the other people. In the stories involving sexual or romantic relationships, I made composites of people rather than represent actual persons because I didn't want to hurt them.

In the story "Her First Fuck," the guy's going to know I'm writing about him. I don't mind his feelings being hurt. But I don't want to hurt the feelings of some of the other women for whom I care a lot. These people are alive and I respect their privacy.

Q: Silencing is central in your own work and in your edited collections, *This Bridge Called My Back* and *Making Face, Making Soul/Haciendo Caras.* How have you felt silenced?

A: You're right that these are central themes in my work. For me, personally, the silencing from the outside came from my family and my culture, where you were supposed to be seen but not heard. This was especially true for the girl children. You were not supposed to talk back to your elders. You were not supposed to have an opinion that deviated from the tribe's. Because my culture is very family and extended-family oriented, the individual is not that central. It's the family. I had to fight that when I was growing up. Because of the Anglo-American influence, Chicanos have become more individualistic nowadays, but, when I was growing up, being different from the crowd wasn't allowed. I was also sensitive to the fact that males could talk at any time but not girls.

Q: Were your brothers treated differently?

A: I think that males are privileged in most cultures, although, in some, it's more subtle. My brothers could say bad words and I couldn't. They could go out at night, but I wasn't allowed. A lot of la Llorona stories in the Chicano/Mexicano culture are used to control the children, to keep them from venturing out, especially the girls.

Q: These were the stories of that female spirit who would follow you and harm you.

A: Yes, of the ghost of la Llorona. Her folktales are about several kinds of silencings—silencing that has to do with gender, being silenced by the dominant class, race, or culture. One of the silencings that has been important for me to write about is the censorship against the writing and speaking of the artist. For a Chicana of *campesino* origins, and for most women of any class, race, or culture, there is always that censorship.

"Carta a colón-nialism," an essay I wrote, is about all these sorts of silencings. It's a chapter in *Lloronas,* a book I'm writing on the production of writing and knowledge and the construction of identities. It's a book about different kinds of storytellings.

Q: Native American poet Joy Harjo has said that a major assumption in Native American literature is that myth is alive and very much a part of the culture. Leslie Marmon Silko and Paula Gunn Allen said this, too— that myth was missing from white culture. Do you think there's a difference between your sense of myth and that of the mainstream culture?

A: Yes. I realized when I was trying to conceptualize the dissertation book that I needed a central figure, and the one that spoke to me is la Llorona, because she has to do with utterance. She also has to do with insurrection against the patriarchy, with sexuality, with women's roles and conditioning, with women's bodies, with motherhood. Also, in the bad and the good kind of dichotomy that gets placed on women, she's on the bad side.

I remember the stories I was told. The first story happened five hundred years ago, before Cortés came and slaughtered the Aztecs. It's a myth, a legend, a folktale that has existed among every generation. When I was in Vermont, I heard Chicana people telling me Llorona stories. When the Vietnam veterans came back, they had seen la Llorona in Vietnam. I heard stories of la Llorona when I was in the Midwest. I read an article about Chicanas in juvenile centers who had encountered la Llorona.

So, with all these Llorona-encounter stories, I started thinking about how people use myth as a way of dealing with lots of things. The story represents what that ethnic group wants to transmit from century to century. And the stories and myths stay alive because they resonate in our daily experience.

Q: They speak to something universal.

A: Yes. So here's a woman whose lover leaves her. Well, women are being abandoned all the time. Violence against women is also prevalent today and that's there, in the myth. And the idea of fighting back, speaking out.

Q: And you have a central figure, like Silko's Yellow Woman.

A: Yes, I use Coatlicue and Tlazolteotl. And this may be the Indian part of the Mexican—you know I'm three-quarters Indian. But I think that myth is very much alive in my culture. People tell stories of la Llorona, all kinds of stories, all kinds of folktales. It's not an element that I play up in my writing, but it's there. And in several of the chapters of the Lloronas book I talk about myth and folktale and what are called *casos,* or cases, where the story is told in order to teach a lesson; it has a moral. A lot of that teaching of what it is to be a Mexican girl and how you should be a Mexican macho is told through myth.

Q: In *Borderlands,* you say, "Nudge a Mexican and she or he will break out with a story," and you say that your father and your grandmother told stories.

A: And my mother. But my mother not so much, I think, because some of the stories are probably not that pleasant and she didn't want to be reminded of poverty and other painful things. Stories brought back memories that were not too happy for her. The Llorona stories were the ones my mother told. She would say, "If you don't do this, Llorona will come and get you."

Q: Did people in your family tell stories about their own lives?

A: Some of the stories had to do with animals. My father told about black ghost dogs, *espantos,* and Mamágrande Ramona told rabid coyote stories and stories of Pancho Villa coming across the border and raiding the pueblos. My grandmother Locha told the family histories, stories of when she was a little girl. The stories were both cultural and personal.

Q: Your essays suggest that class is especially important.

A: Words and literature were a luxury that only middle- and upper-class people could afford. When you work twelve to fifteen hours a day, you're so tired you don't have time to do anything but flop in front of the television. Because of this, what I was doing—writing—felt to my family like play. My mother felt studying was a nonessential activity; I had to fight for the space and the time even to do my homework. At the same time, my mother was very proud that I was going to school.

The silencing that I have been writing about in *Lloronas,* especially in that chapter I mentioned before, "Carta a colón-nialism: Surpassing the tongue, mujeres que tienen mano." This will explain what I mean [she draws a left hand with eyes and a mouth from which comes a tongue whose tip is the writing end of a fountain pen]:

Los ojos, the eyes, are seeing and understanding, *conocimiento,* getting

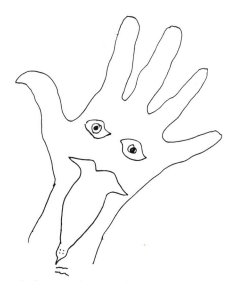

Con los ojos y la lengua-pluma en la mano izquierda
(With eyes and tongue-pen in the left hand)
Drawing by Gloria Anzaldúa

to know things. *La lengua,* the tongue, has to do with speaking, with, writing and communication. But it's not enough to understand, and it's not enough to write and communicate. You have to do something about it, which is activism, being engaged, and that's *la mano izquierda,* the left hand.

I don't know who to credit for this hand idea. I did find *con la lengua en la mano* in the work of Margo Glantz, the Mexican Jewish writer whom I read from today at the workshop [from the introduction to *Haciendo Caras*]. But I had originated *El Mundo Zurdo,* the "left-handed world," in *This Bridge* in my essay "La Prieta" in 1978–79. And now, a decade later, I've added the tongue-pen and the eyes.

I wanted to acknowledge that Glantz had this concept as well; that we're all working with similar ideas, and that they don't belong to any one person—they're part of the collective consciousness.

Q: I know that you've been an activist for many causes, Gloria. Do you consider your writing as activism, too?

A: Yes, I do. A lot of the networking that I do and acting as a resource is teaching women skills, pushing them to have a sense of self-confidence so they'll say, "Yes, I feel good enough about me and who I am and my writing so that I can send it out." I spend many, many hours a day editing, counseling, being a resource, and getting them published in my anthologies, other anthologies, and various magazines and quarterlies. When I talk about writing, I bring in the obstacles and problems that women of color and lesbians of all colors have, the issues of appropriation and those that have to do with racism. By tying issues of race and class to writing and how women writers and artists are treated, I feel like I'm addressing the same issues that other activists are.

Q: There's a myth that many women of color are getting published today when only some are.

A: In order to appease the masses and stop the insurrection of the oppressed segments of the population, the mainstream will take one or two of us in and make us represent all the others. They'll say, "Well, look here, we've published Amy Tan or Toni Morrison." Even with my own work, nonmainstream, there's been a kind of appropriation and tokenizing, especially of *This Bridge* and *Borderlands/La Frontera.* Some academics have somehow taken the sting out of whatever is dangerous or unsettling or too confrontative and focused on what is nonthreatening to them. They've found a way of diluting the radical aspects and whitewashing the books. The ideas in *Borderlands* that often get paid attention to in classrooms, such as the concepts of the Borderlands and of the *mestisaje,* are ideas easily accessible to whites because they speak to their experiences as well. The angrier passages or ideas in *Borderlands* get less critical attention. This kind of selective critical interpretation is a form of racism.

There are a lot of progressive, culturally sensitive white feminists who have been very helpful to women of color. They stretch emotionally and try to understand our experiences. But then there's this large percentage of people with blank spots who don't try at all.

Q: How do you deal with this kind of colonialism, this taking over of your work?

A: It is colonialism. There are several ways I deal with the frustrations. In a kind of solitary way, through meditation and talking to myself in affirming ways. In a collective way, through writing and sharing my writing and talking—with other writers, graduate students, in Santa Cruz or other communities and colleges throughout the U.S. and Mexico. Giving interviews is also a way to share this pain. As a kind of border/bridge person, I've always mediated and translated and negotiated. I have a great deal of patience. I would make a good diplomat—I can look at people who think they're different from or superior to me, and I can find something in them to empathize with. I find myself having real conversations with people, instead of making small talk, just because I open up.

But, there's always a risk—I have been put down with little jabs, barbs, and slurs by people who are insecure. But most of the time when I open up to another person and expose my vulnerabilities, he or she becomes a little vulnerable too, and then we can really talk.

Q: You've written that you sometimes get tired of being a bridge for others ["Bridge, Drawbridge, Sandbar, or Island, Lesbians-of-Color Hacienda Alianzas," in *Bridges of Power: Women's Multicultural Alliances*, ed. Lisa Albrecht and Rose M. Brewer (New Society Press, 1990)]. Do you still feel this way?

A: Yes and no. Being a bridge is my way of life, but once in a while I have to be drawbridge in order to recuperate my energy and to get any serious, extended writing projects completed. Being a bridge is not for everybody. Women of color, especially, need to be aware that this mode of living often depletes and burns them out. I respect various forms of occasional, temporary, and long-term separatisms, though I myself advocate connection.

Q: Today at your workshop on the process of writing, you talked about language, describing yourself as a "dyke." I know you think "lesbian" is a white, middle-class word.

A: I also used the word "queer," originally a working-class term, now appropriated by gay academics. I think this is part of my strategy for jerking people out of their tracks, out of habitual ways of thinking, speaking, and acting. When everybody says "lesbian," a word connected with Sappho and the island of Lesbos, that automatically means that your forefathers and foremothers are European, that George Washington is the father of our country and Columbus discovered America—all false assumptions.

The word "lesbian" was sufficient when I first came out: Being a lesbian meant that I had a community, albeit a *gringa* community. When I was growing up it was okay that they were *gringos* and we were Mexicans. But those terms don't work anymore. The term "white people" doesn't work anymore because of the different ethnicities and classes: Working-class people do not have the same power and privilege that the dominant people do and it's not fair lumping them with their privileged brothers.

I feel the same thing about the term "the other." It becomes locked into an us-against-them, subject-object, binary trap. I'm using the word *nos/otras*. *Otras* means other and *nos* means us, we. We don't have to keep using the oppositional language of the fathers. We were taught to write and think like these theorists. It's complicitous for somebody who is an "other" to be using "their" terms and "their" styles all the time. It's like fighting them with their own language. Audre Lorde said it very succinctly: "You cannot use the master's tools to dismantle the master's house."

Q: In *This Bridge Called My Back* you bring together the voices of so many women. How did it get written?

A: When I was in graduate school at the University of Texas at Austin, I was one of two Chicanas in the comparative lit program, but I didn't see the other woman, Maria Margaret Navar, who later translated some of my Spanish poems into English. When I went to talk to my advisor about research and dissertation topics—feminist studies and Chicano literature—I was told that those were not legitimate areas. I felt that I was not being heard. I tried to explain how Mexicans had lived in Texas for a long time and how we had a literary tradition, just like anybody else; but it didn't matter. The silencing and exclusion of Chicanos and our culture made me aware of other kinds of censorship—of women and working-class people. I quit the doctoral program and moved to San Francisco.

Even before starting the Ph.D. program, I had felt this kind of censorship and silencing when I was teaching high school at PSJA, Pharr-San Juan-Alamo Independent School District, around 1971–72. The required texts in American literature had nothing written by Chicanas or Chicanos, so I would do these little supplementals—Chicano stories and poems. The principal caught me and said that I should stick with the assigned book or I'd lose my job. It didn't matter that Chicanos are also American.

Q: What were your students' backgrounds?

A: The students were 90 percent Chicanos and about 10 percent white. I kept bringing in Chicano texts, but I told my kids not to tell because my job was on the line. So they didn't.

Q: What happened when you came to California?

A: I started participating in an organization called the Feminist Writers' Guild. I served on the steering committee for about two years. I also got involved with the Women Writers' Union, which was a little more radical.

Q: Who were some of the writers in that group?

A: In the Feminist Writers' Guild: Susan Griffin, Cherríe Moraga, Kim Chernin, Elizabeth Lynn, the science fiction writer. I think Valerie Miner was part of it, too. These are the ones that have published and have made it. The Women Writers' Union had Nellie Wong, Merle Woo, Karen Brodine, and others.

Q: Was this in Berkeley?

A: This was in San Francisco, Oakland, and Berkeley. During our discussions some women would ask, "What do you feel is the Chicana perspective . . . blah, blah, blah?" and I would start to talk and some of the white women would interrupt me, or, if they didn't interrupt me, when I was done talking they would interpret what they thought I had said. They tried to impose their ideas of who I was and what I had experienced on me. That made me really angry.

Q: So this sparked *This Bridge*?

A: It added fuel to the spark. Around this time Merlin Stone was in town doing a workshop on women and goddess images at a retreat north of the city. I knew that she was very political and more sensitive to women of color than most white feminists were, so I decided to go. She had offered two scholarships: one for a woman of color and one for a working-class white. I applied and got a scholarship.

We each were given a little room. We all ate together: vegetarian food prepared by the two white middle-class lesbians running the place. It was very nice. On the second day, they found out that I was there on scholarship, so they moved me out of my little room and into the bunk area. When I sat down to eat, they watched to see how much I was eating. I felt so bad.

Q: That's terrible.

A: The other dozen or so participants were friendly, but there was a distance between us. It was 1978, and white women were not aware of the differences among us—or they did not want to be aware. They assumed that since we were all women, we were all oppressed equally and we were all in this together.

One night I couldn't sleep, so I went down to the kitchen for some tea. Merlin Stone was there, smoking away. She said, "What's up?" And I said, "I'm really upset because they're treating me really different. Not only that, but the women in the workshop don't recognize or acknowledge the differences between me and them." She said she'd noticed that, and we ended up talking all night.

I had been wanting to compile and edit a collection of women-of-color voices. She encouraged me to do so and her enthusiasm was the inspiration that initiated *This Bridge*. I am eternally grateful to her. I went home very exhilarated and wrote up a soliciting letter from the notes I had jotted down that night. Then I got a friend who had access to a Xerox machine to make copies. I didn't even have money for postage; I just handed the letters out!

When I asked women of color to contribute to *Bridge,* many said, "I can't write, I don't know enough, I feel really inadequate." Then I would tell them, "Oh, but your words are important, your experiences are legitimate. I'll help you with it." When I met with several of the contributors who considered themselves non-writers, they showed me their drafts. Then I'd say, "What about exploring this thread?" or "Can you elaborate on that?" A couple of weeks later, we would meet again and we'd do another round.

Q: Sounds like you were really helping these women see themselves as writers.

A: There was a lot of evoking and midwifing going on; I like drawing the writing out of people.

Six or nine months later, I realized that it was an overwhelming task for me. So I asked Cherríe Moraga, who is really a hard worker and a good editor, to be coeditor. And so we started it.

The impulse behind the anthology was to expose the racism in the women's movement and to share information among women of color about each other's cultures. This was in 1978, 1979, 1980. Women of color were outraged but did not have a vehicle for their voices. I wanted *Bridge* to be that vehicle and also, ultimately, to be a bridge to the white community.

Q: How is the new collection, *Haciendo Caras,* different?

A: *Haciendo Caras* is more of a bridge to other racial and ethnic groups and does not address white people or try to educate them as much as *Bridge* does.

Q: So was your editing job different in the two cases?

A: No, except that I edited *Haciendo Caras* by myself. It was ten years later and the times had changed slightly—women of color had grown up reading *This Bridge Called My Back,* as well as [The] *Third Woman* [ed. Dexter Fisher (Houghton Mifflin, 1980)] and *Home Girls* [ed. Barbara Smith (Kitchen Table, 1983)], and [*But*] *Some of Us Are Brave* [ed. Gloria T. Hull, Patricia Bell Scott, and Barbara Smith (The Feminist Press, 1982)]. They had writing models and established subject matters from which to write. Therefore, a lot of their essays were a collective, ongoing dialogue which these books initiated. The contributors to *Haciendo Caras* were tired of putting their energy into educating white people. We wanted to deal with our own issues, to educate ourselves.

For *Haciendo Caras,* I put the word out, did a lot of research, compiled important previously published work and encouraged unpublished writers to write pieces especially for the anthology. The organizing meta-phor for the book was "making face." The task was to weave seventy-three different voices into this central metaphor. Trying to create a single entity out of all these voices was a challenge. There are gaps in this many-faceted face: A Jewish-Native American woman who is differently abled didn't finish her essay, and five people who were writing good stuff didn't turn it in. I had to cut some good pieces because the issues they dealt with were covered elsewhere and because it's a very big book. *Haciendo Caras* is 446 pages, twice the size of *This Bridge*.

Q: What's your own writing process like? Do you get input from readers as you go along?

A: I read a lot of rough stuff to audiences and I have a writing group, a support group. To me writing is very collaborative. I feel that all these people who are my readers are cowriting the stories.

Q: What about revisions? How many versions would you do of a story?

A: I think "She Ate Horses" [a *La Prieta* story about a woman's fear of her own sexuality] has gone through thirty, but I don't know if you would call these all drafts or just continuations. The story starts out a page long and I keep elaborating. Then, when everything is there, the real editing starts. And I may do three or four or five revisions. "She Ate Horses" has gone through a lot just because it was really hard to write. I wanted the metaphors to be there but not too obvious, and I didn't want to intellectualize a lot. On the other hand, "Canción de cascabel," the operation story, did not go through that many drafts. So it's not so much revising as rereading and seeing different things that could go in there. To me, rereading is revising.

Q: Why did you decide to go with Aunt Lute publishers?

A: My association with Aunt Lute began with *Borderlands*. I was in Minnesota for the Great Midwestern Book Show, on a panel with several writers discussing whether the writer should be an engaged writer. A couple of black male writers on the panel attacked Alice Walker and other black women writers, accusing them of emasculating black men in their writings. Then they turned on me, and the facilitator, who was inexperienced, didn't intervene. From the audience, Barbara Smith, writer and cofounder of Kitchen Table Press, spoke up on behalf of Alice Walker and all the other people. She was great.

Also in the audience was Joan Pinkvoss, a printer in Iowa City. She came up to me afterward and said, "I would like to publish your stuff. I'm moving to California and merging with Spinsters." [The new company was Spinsters/Aunt Lute.] I told her I had a couple of projects in progress; one was *Borderlands* and the other was *La Prieta.*

So here was a white feminist operating a small press who wanted to promote my work. Thus far Chicano presses had refused to publish me, mainly, I think, because I was a lesbian. The people who have supported me have been feminists—Jews, white lesbians, and feminists-of-color. I liked Joan and sensed that she was excited about my work and would push it. Since I do my own PR stuff anyway, I decided to go with Aunt Lute. Then, after *Borderlands* came out, I got deluged with offers from other publishers, university and mainstream. But I stuck with Aunt Lute because Joan was there for me and because she listened to my ideas for book design, cover, marketing strategies, and even future goals and visions of the press.

Q: *Haciendo Caras* must be one of their biggest sellers.

A: *Borderlands* and *Haciendo Caras* provide about 75 percent of their income. They're also publishing *La Prieta.* By sticking with Joan, I know that I'm missing out on big advances and mainstream readership that has the money and gives out the awards grants. But I figure later on those readers will catch on [she laughs].

Q: So you're loyal to these people who have published your earlier books?

A: Yes. I think that if I did go to a mainstream publisher now it would be okay because I did *Bridge* first with Persephone, then with Kitchen Table; I did *Borderlands* with Spinsters/Aunt Lute, then *Haciendo Caras* with Aunt Lute.

But I also look at people like Rita Mae Brown and some of the writers who were supported by small presses that have switched over to mainstream presses. That's all right—that's their choice. But the fact is that I'm sensitive to the publishing history of dykes and women of color. It was women who put my work in print and I'm not going to turn my back on them. Ideally, I would like to do both: publish with a small press and enlarge my audience by publishing with a mainstream press.

Q: Both Valerie Miner and Paula Gunn Allen talked about the difficulty of getting published by mainstream presses when they choose to write about lesbians. Do you think that would be a problem for you?

A: Before *Borderlands* came out, they would probably not have published me because they can't categorize my style, genres, and the English-Spanish language mixture that I use. But now, I think they'll want to publish me because they see my books are selling. But I'm more concerned about having the right publisher—that the editor like my work, that the book get produced quickly, that it be distributed and not sit in some warehouse, that it not be remaindered. And I'm not sure that mainstream presses would be the right ones.

Q: Are there other reasons to stay with smaller houses?

A: One of the reasons that I think it's important that feminists, lesbians, and women of color publish with small presses is that it keeps the presses alive. They're constantly on the edge of bankruptcy. Another reason is that we also have more control over our product. I am able to tell Joan Pinkvoss, "This is the kind of cover I want. Could we have this kind of break in the print, this kind of design?" Besides having more say in production, we're also allowed more input into what markets to push.

Q: I guess if you went to a big house they might not feature it.

A: I don't know how Random House is doing with Sandra Cisneros. She's the first Chicana to make it to the mainstream.

Q: Besides the autobiographical stories, you've written science fiction and mystery stories. Would you talk about those?

A: I have one story, "Pulgada," which means "inch," about a Chicana dyke private eye. "Sleepwalkers," the story that I gave you, is a sci-fi spy story that is still very rough in a manuscript tentatively entitled *Fic-19*. I have a western romance written entirely in Spanish that takes place around 1890 and a dyke story with horses [she laughs] and a horror and a couple of fantasy stories in *La Prieta.*

Q: When will they come out?

A: *La Prieta* will be out in spring 1994. Several stories from *La Prieta* have been published: "Lifeline," "People Shouldn't Die in June in South Texas," about my father's death, and "El Paisano Is a Bird of Good Omen." *Fic-19* will be ready for publication in ten or fifteen years. There are seven other books that I've got in the works and that are ahead of it.

Q: How is your detective story different from others?

A: I have been thinking about the different kinds of detectives. There's Sherlock Holmes, who was using deductive observation; there are the male hard-boiled detectives, like Philip Marlowe. Then you have male writers who are more sensitive to women's themes, like Robin Cook. In *Coma* [Little, Brown, 1977] the woman is the heroine; the woman takes risks; the woman saves herself. Then you get to the women writers: Agatha Christie and P. D. James and all those that have women detectives but do not call themselves feminists. Then there are the feminist detective fiction writers, like Linda Barnes, who present strong women, but there is always a connection with a man.

Q: That's like Sue Grafton and Sara Paretsky?

A: Yes. Then you get to the dyke writers. And they make the most radical departure from the hard-boiled detective, in that the misogyny is not there; they contest the violence, the use of weapons and the use of people as objects. And the dyke writers deal with political issues, like sexual abuse or battering, often from the point of view of the victim. They have an understanding of women's issues.

Q: These are not just issues to be dealt with; this is life.

A: Yes. And so they question the cool distance that hard-boiled detectives always had from the people they were investigating for. Dyke writers' detectives get really involved with the people who hire them.

Q: Who are some writers that you like?

A: One of the classics that I like is M. F. Beal's *Angel Dance* [Crossing Press, 1990], about a Cuban dyke detective. I like Karen Saum's first mystery, *Murder Is Relative* [Naiad Press, 1990]. One of my favorite woman sleuths is Kay Scarpetta, a medical examiner in mysteries by Patricia D. Cornwell—*Postmortem* [Scribners, 1990] and *Body of Evidence* [Scribners, 1991]. The dyke detective writers need to get their stuff together, to get more skill. It's a young subgenre.

I like some male writers, too. Dick Francis is entertaining. I like Jonathan Kellerman, a child psychologist who does books in which children are the victims—they have been molested or they have been shot or intimidated. In *Silent Partner* [Bantam, 1989], *When the Bough Breaks* [Atheneum, 1985], and *Time Bomb* [Bantam, 1990], he has some insights into children-parent relationships.

Q: So you like to read popular fiction?

A: Yes, especially horror, also science fiction, espionage, romance—all the popular genre stuff.

Q: Do you like horror movies, too?

A: Yes. One of the chapters that may end up in this particular book, *Lloronas/Women Who Write,* deals with how I see similarities between the everyday lives and writings of women of color and the aesthetics and themetics of the horror genre. Did you see the movie *Alien?* I identified with both the alien and its victims. I also think that reading escapist trash, or whatever you want to call this type of literature, has helped me deal with the oppression of women and violence in my own life. It's helped my writing, teaching me how to keep the reader's attention and interest. You have to have vitality in terms of sensory, concrete images and a plot that moves along.

Q: Were there any novels that you remember from your childhood?

A: *Jane Eyre.*

Q: So many writers I've spoken with have mentioned that book.

A: For me, I think that it was because there was hardly anything on the shelves that centered on girls coming of age. I was always reading books about boys, horses, dogs, and wolves—books like *Call of the Wild.* Recently I found a copy of *Jane Eyre* in Spanish and I bought it, but it's not the same.

Q: A lot has been written about Bertha as the woman of color, locked away in the attic. When did you recognize that aspect of *Jane Eyre?*

A: It wasn't until I got to college and I started reading more critically. I remember really early on reading some of Proust and never realizing he was homosexual, for example. Once I did recognize Bertha as being a woman of color, then I could say, "Oh well, they put her in the place of the Mexican villain." She was the madwoman. She was excessive in her sexuality. She was excessive in her emotions. She was dangerous, violent. The scene where Jane looks across the bedroom and sees Bertha in the mirror is when I first thought, "This is the other side of the image of Jane Eyre."

Q: It's interesting that Bertha never talks.

A: No, she shrieks, but she never talks. I read "The Yellow Wallpaper" [by Charlotte Perkins Gilman] and found another example of a woman who was locked away by her husband because she was different from other women—too strong, too assertive, and a writer. The captivity drives her mad, too.

Q: You have a story about a prospective bride who escapes, too. Is "El Paisano Is a Bird of Good Omen" based on a real incident?

A: No. The terrain and the character Andrea, the grandmother, the mesquite—all the stuff is real. The groom is a composite of two people. The story is mostly true but not necessarily happening to me, but to my grandmother or to other people. And then I set it back in time. I wanted the time to be ambiguous. People can think of World War II or Korea or the Vietnam War. But it focuses on Andrea sitting down and thinking about her past and her culture.

Q: You have a lot of pictures of imprisonment; I think of "Ghost Trap," for example—the wife who is haunted by her dead husband until she destroys him. You write about people who are contained until they can free themselves. Whether it's the person saying, "I'm not going to be abused anymore," or whether it's that wonderful wife getting her skillet and threatening her husband—

A: I wanted her to use a woman's tools. I think I wanted to present new models in that story. There's always the woman in the novel who suicides, goes crazy, has the man come and rescue her. I want new models; I want new stories.

Q: We certainly need new stories.

A: Yet I put in the temptation to suicide in stories like "She Ate Horses," so that I can present some of the history of women having been victims and not getting out of it. Ultimately, she gets out of the victim role in that story.

Q: That question of control is central in "She Ate Horses." It has something to do with sexuality, too: to access your own sexuality and your own power, and then be able to control it yourself.

A: I feel that a lot when something is really clicking in the writing. I feel that's a sexual energy.

Q: One of your new poems, "Old Loyalties" [in *Third Woman*], struck me because sometimes I've felt displaced in my own friendships with women.

A: That was a painful poem to write. Originally, I had dedicated it to the friend who I had this friendship with. But then I thought, I can't use a poem as a weapon of revenge. When she reads it, she'll know. The situation had happened several times: When you're friends with somebody who becomes coupled, you're left out. Or the other person feels jealous, or the friend thinks that he or she is being disloyal by having such a tight relationship with you. The theory is that there's a scarcity to human emotion; but I think the more affection and love and friendship you have, the more you have to give to other people. That's why I wrote that poem.

Q: So you don't see this sort of exclusivity as necessarily just a heterosexual thing? You see it as a problem among lesbian and gay couples, too?

A: Yes. Because the lesbian community is under siege, we always try to present to the heterosexual community the idealized version, but I do not think that's a good way to do it, even though I can understand where it's coming from.

Q: Valerie Miner talked about the kinds of self-censorship she finds in her work when she starts thinking she should present only positive images of lesbians or working-class people.

A: Yes. In that poem and also in the poem "Night Voice" I do that. There's this whole controversy now over media images of lesbians and gays and bisexuals. It's brought out in movies like *Basic Instinct* and *Silence of the Lambs* where they are presented as killers. It comes up in the novels of P. D. James, where she has these criminals who are lesbians or gay men. And I hate that. But, at the same time, I want the dirty laundry to be out there, whether it's on the Mexican culture or the lesbian culture or the bisexual. And I'm not sure how you do that.

I think Hollywood has to be a little bit more fair, but I do not believe in idealizing any way of life. It's dangerous when the lesbian community puts out all these idealized coming-out stories. Then the young potential dyke of color comes out and she finds out that the lesbian community is not what she was told it was. She's confused.

Q: You mention resenting pressure to write only about lesbian characters or to write only about certain situations.

A: Or to write only about Chicano themes or to write only about feminist issues. Yes. These are issues I explored in "To(o) Queer the Writer" [in *InVersions: Writings by Dykes, Queers and Lesbians*, ed. Betsy Warland (Press Gang Publishers, 1991)].

Q: Can you resist that pressure?

A: At the beginning I felt very much the pressure to write from a [so-called] "lesbian" perspective or from a "Chicana" perspective, but now I just feel the pressure to write, to put out my work. Because I have the privilege of having my books out, I can now say I feel secure enough about my identity and my writing that I'm going to continue to push against these walls, as I have been doing for the past ten years. What does the reader good is what hasn't been written about in this particular style or this particular way. If I re-cover the same ground, I want to do it from a different angle, using a different kind of language.

British novelist Pat Barker and her husband, David, a university professor of zoology, drove over one day during their vacation to meet me at my hotel in Exeter, England. It was July 1991, and Barker, relaxed and tanned, had just finished the British launch for Regeneration *(Viking [London], 1991, and Dutton [New York], 1992). She was between books, a rare situation for someone with five novels in nine years.*

Barker's first four novels draw directly on her own experience of growing up in the industrial northwest in a working-class family of women. Whether they are factory workers, as in her first novel, Union Street *(Virago [London], 1982, and Putnam [New York], 1983), prostitutes threatened by a serial killer, as in* Blow Your House Down *(Virago [London], 1984, and Putnam [New York], 1984), or an elderly pensioner about to be evicted, as in* The Century's Daughter *(Virago [London] and Putnam [New York], 1986), Barker's women have fashioned for themselves complex coping mechanisms for survival. Without middle-class privilege, with minimal help from men, they turn to one another—to mothers, coworkers, neighbors, and friends—for support and help. Occasionally someone rebels—a prostitute goes after the man she thinks killed her lover, a mother lets her daughter's illegitimate baby die after a botched abortion—but usually the women accept their lot as inevitable and struggle on.*

For her next two novels Barker creates male characters as victimized as

Photo: Copyright © William Abrahams/Dutton

her women. In The Man Who Wasn't There *(Virago [London], 1989, and Ballantine [New York], 1990) she imagines what her own life might have been like if she had been born male. Her lonely protagonist, a twelve-year-old fatherless boy raised in the aftermath of World War II, prefers an imaginary world based on heroic war movies to the grim everyday world where his mother waitresses and his schoolmates taunt him for being different. In* Regeneration, *her latest novel, Barker examines the treatment of shell-shock victims at Edinburgh's Craiglockhart Hospital during World War I. Writing about the real-life relationship between Dr. William Rivers and his patients, particularly the poet Siegfried Sassoon, she shows how the humane and sensitive Rivers comes to love the men entrusted to his care at the same time he begins questioning the rightness of the war. Barker introduces the class issue in two ways: by creating Prior, an antagonistic second lieutenant from a working-class family who becomes the doctor's questioner, and by demonstrating the horrible treatment enlisted men who were shell-shock victims received in London at the hands of Dr. Lewis Yealland, another historical figure.*

I had interviewed Barker in 1988 and looked forward to seeing her again. I wanted to get her reaction to Stanley and Iris, *the Jane Fonda–Robert De Niro movie based on* Union Street; *to find out where she got the idea for* Regeneration, *which had received rave reviews in Britain (and would go on to do the same in the United States); and to expand upon some of the questions I had asked earlier. As before, she was warm and totally unpretentious, this time joined by David, who provided additional information and humor. The following blends material from both interviews.*

Q: You have been praised for your realistic portrayals of poor and working-class people. Do you consider your books "political," in the sense that you are offering a critique of society?

A: It makes people in this country [England] nervous to call books "political." There is a definition of literature which excludes making political points of any kind. In my [early] books, the characters themselves are not political. People want to read a message of hope for the people in Britain in my books but it isn't there in political terms. When Liza [a former activist in *The Century's Daughter*] has to go out scratching for coal, she has to fall out of political activity.

Q: If the British are nervous about political books, why did you take the plunge with *Regeneration*?

A: I think *The Man Who Wasn't There* was perhaps an intermediate book. I just write what I want to and don't think about the way people will react until after I write the book. Also, I think you can get away with saying more if you put it either in a fantasy world [like *The Man Who Wasn't There*] or in the past [like *Regeneration*] because people are prepared to consider things then. If you attack a subject which is very contemporary and very controversial, the danger is that people either meet your work knowing what they think about the subject beforehand or avoid reading your work because they think your views are different from theirs.

Q: Maxine Hong Kingston told me that she wants to change the world when she writes fiction. Do you have any aspirations like that?

A: I admire her work very much, but nope, I don't. If you wanted to change the world by writing a novel you would first of all have to secure the fact that politicians would read other novelists besides Jeffrey Archer [she laughs]. In this country, at least, they don't. I suspect your lot is the same. Maggie [Thatcher] used to read and reread Frederick Forsyth.

A: Before *Regeneration,* which seems thoroughly researched, did you do research for your novels?

A: No, I wrote about what I saw happening in depressed regions. We are becoming a much more deeply divided society. Even in the north where nobody works and young people are bored and drinking too much and creating disturbances, there is still tremendous wealth living beside poverty. There are people spending enormous amounts of money at Metrocenter, the largest shopping center in Europe, yet in Newcastle you see people queuing for day-old bread.

About research, I have never, ever gone out to try and meet someone who would be useful. I use women I know. I don't need to know an awful lot. I haven't been in a chicken factory, for example, but I have done bloody awful, monotonous jobs. In *Union Street* I wrote about something I had not done: working on an assembly line in a cake factory, where the women working the line can use the machine against one another by speeding the pace up.

Q: What is the relationship between your own life and these works?

A: It's probably different for the different books. I think the starting point is inevitably always something in your own life, just as the source of every single character you create has to be yourself. But quite often you are going off on a tangent—taking a fact in your own life and saying, "What if? . . . " and from that point you are going away from your own life at right angles, although the bedrock of the book was your own experience. For example, in *The Man Who Wasn't There* it's simply the sex of the child. What if you had been born into an all-female family as a boy rather than as a girl? Would you not have been debilitated by the same facets of your life which for a girl were sources of strength? Or perhaps you wouldn't be. Perhaps they would still be sources of strength. If a boy were raised by these women, to what extent could he take strength from them and to what extent would it be a threat?

Sometimes I've used a particular episode which actually occurred—like, for example, the hemorrhage in *The Century's Daughter* and *Union Street*. That's something that actually happened to me: I have had to pull clots of blood out of someone's throat. But, in each case, by giving it to a different person and making the relationship between the person watching and the person dying a different relationship, I've changed the significance of the episode. Basically, I'm not interested in writing autobiography in any way, shape, or form, although I think at the end of the day when you look at the books on the shelf they are—for every writer, not just for me—the spiritual autobiography. And probably far more honest in their devious way than an actual autobiography would ever be, if you ever felt moved to write one.

Q: Is that painful birth certificate scene in *The Man Who Wasn't There* autobiographical?

A: That is very autobiographical. You could have a small birth certificate at a time when everyone had a large one. It meant either that you were adopted or illegitimate.

Q: Like Colin, were you the product of a wartime romance?

A: I never knew my father. He was in the RAF [Royal Air Force] where the death rate was very high.

Q: Besides Colin, whose life has parallels with your own, are any of your other characters like you?

A: Kath's [in *The Century's Daughter*] is the closest to my own experience, but even that is changed, mainly by leaving out a lot of things that happened. I was brought up by my grandmother and I had a whole string of great-aunts who used to get together and quarrel about things that happened when they were growing up in Victorian England.

Q: Were they storytellers?

A: They weren't telling stories so much as arguing about a past that was very much alive to them. They were always coming to blows about something that happened before the first world war, like was their father drunk or not the time he came home from the pub on a particular night and Mother said—no she didn't—this kind of thing. That was interesting for me growing up.

For *Regeneration* I had stories from my grandmother's second husband—who was my grandfather as far as I was concerned—about the first world war. He only told them towards the end of his life because they were so horrific that he didn't want to tell them before then.

Q: Can you give me an example of that kind of story?

A: I was thinking of the time that he was bayoneted. He had a bayonet wound in his side which I used to stick my finger into when I was a charming little girl [she laughs]. With his consent, of course. It was quite a horrific scar. He had been bayoneted and he was an officer's servant. And just as he was bayoneted, the officer got his revolver out and shot the German between the eyebrows, which meant that he didn't have the chance to twist the bayonet and pull it out, which is the bit that really does all the damage. So he survived, but he had to lie on the battlefield and he got flies all around and maggots in the wound. He lay on the floor of the hospital for hours and hours before he was treated.

Q: How did the wound form a hole?

A: Because he was a very thin young man and he became a very fat old man, the scar tissue didn't seem to grow out with him. The tragic thing was that when he was dying—I think it was of stomach cancer—the doctors, who were not very much into telling people the truth in those days, told him it was his bayonet wound that was killing him and he believed them. So he thought, "Well, it's getting me in the end."

Q: Since you write often about mothers and daughters, I am curious about your own mother. How has she reacted to your success as a writer?

A: She doesn't read. She reads the Bible but hasn't read my books. She has seen me in the newspaper now [as a result of the publicity surrounding the movie *Stanley and Iris*]. She read a piece in which I was asked whether Jane Fonda should get silicone injections in her boobs [she laughs]. My mother reads that kind of paper. I don't think she knows I'm successful. I think she's happy because I'm married to a successful man.

My mother has never really worked out who I am. She thinks I'm her sister. For her to have had an illegitimate child in the 1940s was a terrible thing to have happened. I was hidden in a cupboard when people came to call. She explained me away as her kid sister or niece so often that she ultimately forgot who I was. So sometimes I'm her daughter but sometimes I'm not. She's even less able to accept the relationship now because she's a Jehovah's Witness and goes door to door preaching. My mother would have liked to have given me up for adoption but my grandmother found it inconceivable that any part of your family should be given away. If you were down to your last crust of bread you would not do it.

My grandmother was very strong. As an example of that, when my mother was a child she had erysipelas and one of the great traumas was going bald. When a teacher made my mother take her cap off, my grandmother chased the teacher.

Q: When did you first start thinking of yourself as a writer?

A: I wrote my first novel when I was eleven. It was then I decided I would be a writer. My grandmother said, "There's no money in it." She said, "Work in the factory over the road and write in your spare time." While I was teaching, I found writing fiction and writing critical essays so different that I put fiction apart. I feel as though fiction writing is the art of middle age because you have to have an accumulation of people to do it well. There are two novels, which I used to think were quite good, that will stay in the back of my drawer. They nearly came out and it's good they didn't.

Q: I know you majored in history at the London School of Economics and taught for a while. How did you get back to fiction writing?

A: I specialized in diplomatic history. Maybe that's a connection with my writing. Then I taught history and government in the college of further education until I started a family. I've never gone back to teaching on a permanent basis. I was first published when I took a creative writing course with Angela Carter and she sent the manuscript of *Union Street* off to Virago and they took it.

Q: Did she recognize that you were good right away?

A: I think she did, yes. She is very good at recognizing people with very dissimilar talents from her own. I think it is basically because she is a born teacher as well as a born writer [Angela Carter died in 1992]. And what I gave her to read, in fact, was the scene with the two old ladies in *Union Street*—the old lady who is going and picking up condoms with the sugar tongs. She is actually a character from life, of course. I knew an old lady who used to do that. Anyway, I read this and Angela said, "You know, you really ought to do some more things along these lines." The actual thing I read was really rough—it was not a good piece in any way at all. But the character, she could see, was alive and the setting was alive.

It's a marvelous course—I don't know if you [in the United States] have anything like it. It's not teaching—it's not a creative writing course. It's a matter of apprenticeship. You simply go and sit in this farmhouse in the Yorkshire moors and you work in the presence of two published writers who then comment on what you do—if you want them to. They will set you things to do if you want them to, but if you've got work in progress you just bring your work and work on it. And you do the cooking and the cleaning and the bed making yourself—you're not waited on in any way. And it's just a very good, a very intense atmosphere.

Q: Is this like Yaddo, the writers' colony, without room service?

A: Sort of, except this is for beginners, whereas Yaddo is for established writers.

Q: What got you to the point where you went to the farmhouse and took this course?

A: Not being published, basically. I had written several books that were not getting anywhere. One of them, I think, was good enough to have gotten somewhere if I'd persevered with it. But, in fact, I wrote *Union Street* and you can't really have two books circulating at the same time because it looks terribly desperate. So I took the other one off and circulated *Union Street* instead.

Q: I find a similarity between your working-class characters and themes and those in fiction by African American women writers. Do you?

A: Gloria Naylor wrote to me when *Union Street* came out. As we corresponded we became frightened because I realized she was going to write about a group of prostitutes, just as I was. I wanted her to do it, of course—and good luck to her—but it would have been hard to market two books about prostitutes. [Naylor has since dealt with this topic in *Bailey's Cafe.*]

A while ago I went to a group which studied black women writers. Only women turned up. The attitude was that we were going to study black women without studying black men. I argued that you can't do that. Then they [the women in the group] were equating the experiences of middle-class white women with working-class black women. Obviously, there are a hell of a lot of differences. A white South African woman said, "We share a common oppression as women," and spoke about having the same experiences as those of a black woman who lived on her land. Of course she hadn't.

Q: You portray a lot of violence in these women's lives—besides rape and sexual assaults, wife batterings, and illegal abortions, older women are targets for thieves.

A: I think my own attitudes about portraying violence have changed. I think I would be a lot more careful about who I portrayed as the victim of violence now because I can see that, first of all, it isn't true that women are the main victims of violence. The main victims of violence are young men, just as young men are the main perpetrators of violence. And I think portraying violence can have a terrible effect. There are old ladies in English villages where a crime wave was fifteen years ago when somebody stole a bike—that is the level of crime in those areas—and these ladies are not going out because they watch a program on British television called *Crimewatch*, which deals with real violent crime and reconstructs it. And they are sitting there shivering and they are in no danger whatsoever. I think the portrayal of violence is a very dangerous thing.

Q: The elderly character Liza is beaten and robbed at the end of *The Century's Daughter*. What were you saying here?

A: Their vandalism of her box [containing mementos of her life] is the last straw. There was a spate of granny-bashing going on in the northeast when the thugs had too much lager and welfare payments. The feeling I meant to convey is that in isolated pockets of total depression people turn on each other.

There are minor acts of violence all the time. At a launch dinner in Denmark [for *Blow Your House Down*] I met someone who worked three months as a prostitute to do research. She said she recognized Danish prostitutes in my book. Also at the launch, a man who was introduced to me as an opera singer told me he had been a male prostitute. He said he cried when he read the book because they were like the women he worked with. And many were dead. He said his ration was fifteen men a night. There's a woman in my region who does it for empty beer bottles.

Of course, class is a factor, too. Nobody paid any attention to the Ripper killings until a middle-class girl was killed. [Barker was alluding to the murder of thirteen women and the maiming of seven by Peter Sutcliffe, the "Yorkshire Ripper." The case served as a model for *Blow Your House Down*.]

So, I think the lives these women lead are in fact very violent lives, but it is easy to present women as foreordained victims. I don't think my women are victims in that sense because I think they are coping with it rather than succumbing to it. Even so, I would think more carefully now.

Q: Your mentioning the killer reminds me of a criticism occasionally leveled against women writers—that their portraits of men are too negative. How do you respond to this?

A: You can't have a socially conscious pimp or a nice torturer to soothe reviewers. Sometimes reviewers miss the point completely. In *Blow Your House Down*, you expect it to be about the killer but it isn't. A feminist writer said after reading it she didn't understand Peter Sutcliffe. But the point is that he isn't in it. The book isn't about him at all. No one says Dickens's women are too negative.

Q: The bonding of women is a theme running throughout your work. How do you see that working itself out in your characters' lives?

A: I'm surprisingly ambivalent about women's friendships in these cases. If you look at what women in *Blow Your House Down* are doing for one another, there is support, but it is support for the status quo. When I was writing, I was thinking that they shared the kind of humor men had in the trenches, fighting a war that should not have been fought. Women who are tremendously supportive of a woman who is being battered, giving support on how to deal with it, are not helping her get out of it. There's a stoicism without any idea of what the alternatives are. These friendships were serving exactly the same purpose as men's friendships in World War I.

Q: I notice that you have moved from writing about women in your first two books, to writing about an elderly woman and a male social worker in your third, to writing about a boy in your fourth and men in your fifth. Did you feel some pressure to create a male protagonist?

A: No, because I always knew I could. It's not a pressure. Fay Weldon says men are a different species. I don't feel that. I feel I could do either. I hope I will find a woman I want to write about. Some people may criticize me for deserting the cause, but I never thought for a second that feminism is only about women.

At the moment, I find more interesting what society does to men because I think I've gone as far along the road exploring what society does to women as I can. In a sense, you can't deal with one gender in isolation from the other. I'm more interested in looking at the pressures on men, which in wartime are specific and worse than those on women are, but not, I think, essentially different.

Q: Where did the idea for *Regeneration* come from?

A: Oh, several channels. I first read [Dr. William] Rivers's book, *Conflict and Dream*, when I was in my early twenties; I had read [poets] Wilfred Owen and Siegfried Sassoon in my teens. I had always wanted to write about Rivers and shell shock and about the first world war, too. That first thing I ever wrote was a terribly bad poem about the first world war when I was eleven. So the urge to write about it was there, but I wanted to wait until I could find a sufficiently original way of doing it because, obviously, it's one of the most overdone topics that has ever been. And it's been done brilliantly by people who were actually there.

Q: How did you find that angle?

A: Basically, by resolving not to write about the trenches themselves, but to put it on the home front. And to write about the treatment of shell shock, which has been done—Rebecca West did it—but I don't think it's one of her best books [*The Return of the Soldier*, 1918].

I would say that basically *Union Street* and *Regeneration* are both books about trauma and recovery. Everybody says, "But those are upper-class men instead of working-class women," but I think the feeling for the people involved is similar. I would say that Burns [in *Regeneration*], for example, is a similar character to Maggie in *Blow Your House Down*, the woman who is knocked on the head and has to sort out what she feels about it and behaves in a rather similar way to Burns, in fact. So I think the theme of trauma and recovery comes from my own background.

Q: Have people recognized the feminist perspective in *Regeneration*?

A: A lot of rather simple-minded people think that if you stop writing about women you have given up being a feminist. I must say that here in Britain men have tended to see this feminist perspective [in the novel] rather more than women.

I think the analysis of men's dependency and their lack of autonomy in that war, a study of why they suffered from hysterical symptoms rather than paranoia is a feminist analysis. But it's not any kind of feminist tract. And above all I'm not saying, as one woman suggested, that being a housewife in suburbia equals being a man in the front line. Anyone who believes that is so sunk in self-pity that there is no hope for them at all.

Q: How much is your portrait of Rivers like the real-life man?

A: He's as like as I could make him, which is a very enigmatic, a very mysterious sort of man. He's not easy to research. I think he is very like the real-life person.

Q: What about the historical basis for the other characters? We know about Owen and Sassoon, but what about the others?

A: They are all basically based on Rivers's case histories, with [the character] Prior very slightly based on Rivers. I needed Prior to bring out certain facets of Rivers's character that I couldn't bring out through Sassoon or any of the others. I needed someone basically to be fairly antagonistic to Rivers. Burns, the man who got his head stuck in a corpse and had all those terrible experiences, is very closely based on an actual case history. The young man who is treated by [Dr. Lewis] Yealland with electrodes is also entirely drawn from an actual case. The patient is hardly an individuated personality, but his problems and his method of treatment are entirely what happened.

Q: Was Yealland really this awful, treating enlisted men with shock therapy?

A: Yes, he was incredible. This very wooden dialogue is what he represents himself as having said. And he is clearly proud of having said it. [See his *Hysterical Disorders of Warfare*, 1918.]

Q: Rivers, treating officers, is compassionate; Yealland, treating enlisted men, is cruel. Which approach was more typical?

A: Neither Yealland nor Rivers was really typical, but the balance, at least for the [enlisted] men, was tilted more towards Yealland than Rivers. It was certainly tough treatment. As you say, officers and men were treated differently.

Q: What was the treatment for women suffering mental breakdowns at the time?

A: I think the treatment for female hysterics could be rough, but I don't think it was ever as rough as that. It could be quite hostile, but then I think psychiatrists tend to be hostile towards hysterics even today. I think hysterics are totally infuriating people, and they are manipulative.

Q: Well, it's about power and control, isn't it?

A: Yes, and it's about somebody who is evading responsibilities, and it's very hard for some people to go on being sympathetic. I think what made the treatment of the male hysteric during wartime so hostile was precisely that it was thought of as a female way of responding to stress, so the feeling was that he wasn't just shirking or being cowardly: He was also being effeminate. And this made them [the psychiatrists] very, very anxious. In the things Yealland says, he shows this: "You must behave like the hero I expect you to be." There is no shilly-shallying about it. You have to get back into line, and you will be prodded back by electrodes if you don't do it.

Q: Rivers has a theory that the men who were most like women were the ones in the observation balloons, who floated passively over the battlefields doing reconnaissance.

A: Yes, and in the observer's seat in the plane.

Q: That seems to be a remarkable insight into the reality of women's lives at the time.

A: He was asking the question, "Why is hysteria so common in women in peacetime and so relatively uncommon in men?" The first answer he gave was that, in fact, women in peacetime have actually far more reason to be frightened than men. He was thinking about sexual assault, but he was also in that time thinking about the dangers of childbirth—that women just had reasons for being scared that men didn't have. They were helpless—just floating along till whatever might happen did, feeling that they couldn't control it.

But then he also got to the idea of women's lives being more passive and more circumscribed [than men's] and the paradox that when you sent men to the front thinking they were going off to do this great big, masculine, hairy-chested thing—no, they were actually going to sit in a hole and do as they were told and wait to be killed. It's total passivity. Far worse passivity than the majority of women would ever experience. And yet if you crack down under this total feminine passivity, you're told you're unmanly [she laughs]. So there's no way they can win.

Q: Prior introduces the class issue—he's a fish out of water because he comes from the working class and he is an officer.

A: There was a category of men in the first world war who were like that. Because the demand for officers was so great, the social qualifications for being an officer were relaxed. These people were known as not just temporary officers, but "temporary gentlemen" was the phrase at the time. And they were held with great scorn, though with less scorn in the front line than behind the scenes.

Q: Rivers says at one point that he thinks that enlisted men don't have as complex a mental life as officers.

A: Yes, he did think that.

Q: So Rivers is a snob?

A: Yes.

Q: Is he less of a snob at the end?

A: Well, he is slightly less a product of his time by the end, but I think the class culture permeated everything in that time and nobody could hope to be free of it. You could tell whether somebody was a lady or gentleman simply by looking at them. It was as obvious then as race is obvious today. And it is true that the men presented different symptoms on the whole. It was the [enlisted] men who presented the mutism and paralysis and deafness, and the officers didn't present that. So, in a sense, it wasn't just that they were being treated differently; it is that they were responding to the intolerable situation in different ways. And this, too, has its modern parallels, where unskilled, unemployed people don't go to the doctor saying, "I'm thoroughly depressed because society doesn't seem to have any use for me." They go and say, "My back aches," or "I've got headaches," or "I can't sleep." Anything. It's acted out rather than verbalized.

And if you are into psychotherapy, of course, the patient who can verbalize in the way that is required by the treatment is a patient you can relate to. The patient who is just lying there saying, "I cannot walk," is that much more difficult to deal with.

Q: So it is significant that early on Prior isn't talking?

A: Yes, that's the point that Rivers makes and then Prior turns it on him and says, "Well, if mutism is because you daren't say what you have to say, perhaps a lifelong stammer like yours is because there is something you daren't say that you want to say." Prior makes the book, I think. It would be too bland without Prior.

Q: Silencing is central in the book, as it was in your earlier ones. I'm stuck by Rivers's dream where he imagines that he is putting the bit on the patient, just as slaves were given the bit at an earlier time.

A: Yes, and the book actually ends, in a sense, with the silencing of Rivers. He comes to write the final word for now on Sassoon, and he says there is nothing more he wanted to say that he could say. So, in the end, Rivers is silenced, too.

Q: What other silencing is there in the book?

A: Oh, a tremendous amount. There's the mutism of Prior and Callan. When Prior is goading Rivers about his lifelong stammer being a result of his having been silenced, that is meant to be taken seriously, not just to be one of Prior's gibes. And the people, I think, who are not silenced, exactly, but not listened to very much, are the women in the factory. Somebody pointed out to me that what I had done was to establish two groups who find these men totally, outrageously laughable—one are the women in the factory and the other are the people [Solomon Islanders] on board the *Southern Cross*, who turn the tables on Rivers and laugh at the life of an Edwardian don and think that it is the most amazing, bizarre thing that ever was, too hilarious for anything.

Q: As a psychiatrist at that time, Rivers is supposed to "cure" people who are homosexual. Why doesn't he do that with Sassoon?

A: [A pause.] I think, you see, that Rivers is homosexual, too. I think that he is in love with Sassoon. One of the things that can't be said, in fact, is the depth of the feeling he obviously has for Sassoon. Whether he even says it to himself I don't know. There is one time when Sassoon is talking about Owen's feelings for him and these amazing letters that Owen wrote to him. Sassoon thinks that Owen was in love with him and he hopes that he was kind enough, and Rivers simply says, "It happens." That is Rivers with everything hanging out.

Q: Many of your male characters are uncomfortable with their emotions.

A: I think there's a lot of great pain in men growing up without fathers, you see. I'm very much aware of that. I think that's what Robert Bly [author of *Iron John* (Addison-Wesley, 1990)] is tapping, that need for some type of validation from the older man. And he's become a tremendous guru on the basis of it. There's a great irony, too, that he is quite perceptive in analyzing that what has gone is the father-son relationship, but the solution is for the father to go off for a weekend and leave Mum with the boy yet again while he does his drumming and his initiation ceremony [she laughs].

Q: Twelve-year-old Colin, the protagonist of *The Man Who Wasn't There,* spends a good part of his life imagining what his father was like.

A: There was an absence of strong men after the [second world] war because they had been blown up. Women tended to bring up children on their own. On the whole, Colin came out more optimistic than I thought, and I think Viv is a good mother for him because she isn't too devoted to her own chick.

Q: In the climactic scene, Colin faces this man, who is really a figment of his overactive imagination. But the man is more than that.

A: Yes, in that encounter Colin is also facing and destroying a future self. The temptation with Colin is to be a traitor, which is why he is fascinated with the traitor in his fantasy. He is getting an education which distances him from his [working-class] family. At the time, the grammar schools saw themselves as taking kids from poorer cultures and giving them a culture. The idea that they *had* a culture wasn't recognized. We don't know who his father is, just as I never found out. I still don't know. And you live with it. It's harder for a boy to live with than a girl.

Q: Lorimer [a weak, often ridiculed character in the novel] seems to be Colin's alter ego. He's what might have happened to Colin if he weren't strong.

A: Yes. Colin's thing is that he is able to fit in superficially because he is tall and clever and can play games. He survives but he knows there is a Lorimer who is there. The potential to dissociate yourself from Lorimer is also there.

Q: The scene with Mr. Boyce, his mother's boyfriend, is wonderful—the way Colin gets rid of his rival by leading him to believe that his mother is planning marriage.

A: He's a nasty little boy, but so clever. Colin is dealing with his own sexual ambivalence, which he inevitably has because he has no one to model his behavior on, except his mother. In the course of the novel he gets a sense of how little courage has to do with stereotypes being fed to people by the media. The fifties war films here in England portrayed a false image of the people who lived through the war. You had officers with clipped accents who did not get killed and men with cockney accents who often did. And Germans, who always got killed.

Q: Speaking of movies, what was your response to *Stanley and Iris,* the Hollywood movie made from *Union Street*? I missed the realism and the social criticism of the book.

A: I think it abandoned the attempt long, long before it actually got into the cinema. Who knows why they do it? They buy a book for certain qualities and then when they are trying to write the screenplay they get terrified of those qualities—they screen them all out—and produce something totally innocuous and you wonder why. There are certain things that you can't say, you see—the girl has to have the baby. She can't have an abortion. And they have to have a love story, and it has to end happily, and even then they are still nervous. It doesn't just end happily—she has to have a five-bedroom house with two bathrooms. He has to have his name on the office door. And the ultimate irony for me is that what he's doing—robotics engineering—is going to make all of those women in the factory redundant because you're going to have a machine that does the whole cake easily.

Q: So we still need a movie of *Union Street.*

A: Well, you can't have one because the rights have gone. You could do a movie of *Union Street* which wouldn't take any of that material at all because very little of that material comes from the novel anyway. People imagine that you have more control than you have. In fact, once you've sold the option, your control's gone.

David: About 2 percent of the movie comes from the book.

Q: I understand you became a bit of a celebrity when the movie came out over here.

A: I got a lot of publicity. Very stupid sorts of things.

Q: Like the tabloids asking you about Jane Fonda's silicone. I wonder where these people are coming from?

A: I don't know where they were coming from but I know where they were—they were sitting outside my house. One of them was. All these reporters were walking around knocking on doors looking for the address of the character Jane Fonda played, Iris King. They had no idea of the difference between fact and fiction. So they wanted to look up Iris King and ask her how she felt about being played by Jane Fonda. Great idea: photograph of Iris King, photograph of Jane Fonda.

Q: You have an impressive record—five successful novels in nine years. How have you done it?

A: It doesn't feel like a lot. I always feel like I'm lazy. I write every day. I'm not making a tremendous amount of money at it, but it mounts up with translation rights from Scandinavian countries.

Q: What's your process of writing?

A: There's a long period before the start of writing of bringing the characters to life and knowing them. When they start talking to each other, you start writing. Then I just grind away at the computer every morning, basically, producing all this drivel until, occasionally, I think, Well, that has a spark in it. I'd better press on [she laughs]. It's a depressing business, actually. I try to write every weekday once I've started the book, because otherwise nothing would happen at all. I have, in fact, abandoned books. Oddly enough, the books that get abandoned, in a superficial sense, probably look better than the ones I go on with, because they're neat, and they're coherent and have all the grisly virtues, and they're completely dead. And sooner or later, I'm between page 60 and 85 and I think, Oh God, this is dead. It's gone [she laughs].

Q: What makes you decide what to continue with and what to drop?

A: It's a certain liveliness about the characters, a certain feeling that I'm interested in. In the end, of course, it's a business that's done in solitude. And the person who matters then is yourself—if you're interested, you go on. If you're not, it's fatal. But it's very mysterious: You can write a marvelous synopsis which everybody says is fascinating and you try to write it and it's dead from the word go. And yet something else, a vaguer, a much less impressive sounding idea, once you try to start working with it comes to life. I suppose because it's because you're tackling something deep down in yourself, whether you know what that something is or not.

It always amazes me when some writers say they take ideas for books from newspapers—it seems to me so risky, because that may be keying into something very deep in your past, but it's much more likely that it just caught your attention in a fairly surface kind of way, and I wouldn't want to commit myself to any idea that hasn't been around for a long time. *Regeneration* is an example of an idea which was around long before *Union Street*—a long, long time.

Q: When we spoke right after *The Man Who Wasn't There,* you were working on a book about a man obsessed with a sense of his own guilt. Why did you scrap that idea for *Regeneration*? Did it lack that liveliness?

A: I decided that I couldn't stop the book I was trying to write from turning into a psychological thriller. A lot of the impact of that book would have been derived from staying inside this one character and never quite knowing whether his perceptions of the world were accurate or distorted. In addition to being a double and all the other things, he was going to be an unreliable narrator, and I decided I didn't want that kind of claustrophobia. I'm not sure I ever want it again. A lot of very good books that are being written at the moment are single-viewpoint fragmented narratives in disturbed minds, and that's okay, but you can only take so much of that. I found it actually quite a challenge in *Regeneration* to write from several points of view, with quite a few people fundamentally disagreeing with each other and yet very often respecting each other. I think that's the way I want to go. I want to be able to breathe in the work.

Q: As you are writing, does David read your work?

A: He read *Regeneration* as we went along. That was simply because the actual story of Rivers was historical, and he knew the story. He hasn't read previous works during the writing, but he is my first reader at the end. And my most important reader.

David: This book was totally different from the other four because this time we did a lot of research together. I'd grab the car and find a place on a map and all that sort of thing, so I'm involved. I can't just be a chauffeur, so I have to be told.

Q: With your other books, did you have somebody reading it as you went along or just when it was all done?

A: I showed it when it was all done. I don't like anybody reading in this way, though my editor at Viking saw a very late draft of *Regeneration* and made comments which were helpful.

Q: Do you read reviews?

A: Oh yes, I read them [she laughs]. I know people who say they don't, and I know other people who wait until they've got them all and then they sit down with a very large bottle of wine and drink their way through them. I'm afraid I read them as they come out, which is not the way to do it actually, because everybody gets bad ones sometimes. To do a public appearance or an interview on a day you've had a bad one is actually a very difficult thing to do. On the other hand, to do it blind, knowing that everybody else has read it, might be even worse. I think I prefer to know the worst. The thing is, I don't know if it's because I'm a depressive personality, I find that bad reviews are much more depressing than the good ones are elating. The tendencies are almost always down [she laughs].

Q: What would you read in a review that would get you angry?

A: It hasn't happened to me very often, but when you know that somebody has been given the job to do a hatchet job on—a set-up thing. You're always aware of that. But it doesn't happen to you until comparatively late in your career. You would never get that kind of review with a first novel. For example, in *The* [*Times* (London)] *Literary Review*, this woman said, "The word 'bum' appears twelve times in this book." And I thought, Well, hell's bells, babe, I hope they were paying you well to count because I'm blowed if I would spend my time doing that [she laughs].

Q: I understand you've recently gone back as one of the teachers at that writing workshop where you got helped by Angela Carter. What was that like?

A: It's very, very hard work, of course, because it's all about establishing the writer's voice. There was one lad who had been sent to boarding school when he was five because his parents were missionaries. He hadn't grown up to be a Christian—he had been sent away and been thoroughly miserable at that age for something he didn't even believe in. So we said, "Aren't you slightly cheesed off about this?" "No, no," he kept saying. So we kept pressing him, trying to get that true voice out. Finally, he said, "What did upset me was when I knew a boy and I had made friends and I felt safe and then the boy left the school." That was the moment that upset him. And he wrote a lovely story in the end about his feelings when one of his friends just didn't show up at the beginning of the next term and suddenly the place was dangerous again. So he got there.

Q: Did you like teaching?

A: Yes. I like that kind of teaching. You have to be very, very delicate, though. It's like being Rivers because you are dealing with terribly explosive materials.

Actually, the majority of the people who come on those courses are not looking to become professional writers necessarily. You get people who are sorting out their alcoholism or their bereavement or their drug addiction or their habit of flashing [she laughs]. There was one course Angela Carter was teaching where she had a flasher, but he chose to flash at the heroin addict. So when this happened all the addict would do was blink, so it was totally wasted effort this man was putting in [more laughter].

Q: What are you working on now?

A: Nothing right now. I'm taking a rest and hope to start when the launch is properly over. I hope that the American launch doesn't interfere too much.

I met Mary Beckett on a chilly, rainy July afternoon in 1991 at her home in Templeogue, on the outskirts of Dublin. A fire blazed in the front parlor as we sat over tea and homemade buns discussing a writing career that began when she was twenty-three and teaching at a school in her native Belfast. She won a BBC radio story contest and more stories followed, most of them inspired by the painful lives of her students and their mothers. These are meticulously crafted stories of ordinary women's struggles and disappointments, painted against the background of Northern Ireland's political violence.

In 1956, Beckett married and moved to Dublin with her husband, Peter Gaffey. After the death of her first child at birth, she had four children in five years; another son was born seven years later. For twenty years she lived a traditional middle-class life as homemaker and mother, occasionally thinking about writing but lacking the time to do so.

Consciously or unconsciously, Beckett must have been storing up material for fiction. In the 1970s, frustrated over the southern attitude toward "the troubles" in the North, she began writing stories that put a human face on the headlines. A Belfast Woman (Poolbeg [Dublin], 1980, and William Morrow [New York], 1989), a collection of eleven stories set in and around Belfast, depicts women trapped by inarticulateness and rage— against domineering husbands, unplanned-for pregnancies, bone-wearying factory work. Beckett gives us individual acts of courage: A mother goes

*after the teacher who has beaten her child; a wife pushes her drunken hus-
band in front of the fire. She sets their personal tragedies within the
context of a country destroying itself from within, with Catholic and Protestant forces making violence a way of life.*

    *Beckett, a Catholic, condemns the violence on both sides. The narrator
of her novel* Give Them Stones *(Bloomsbury [London] and Morrow [New
York], 1987) is a woman spurred into action when the Provos (provisional
wing of the Irish Republican Army) shoot a boy in both legs outside her
home-bakery shop. When she refuses, on principle, to continue paying
protection money to the IRA, the Provos burn down her house.*

    Beckett sets her next collection of stories, A Literary Woman *(Blooms-
bury, 1990), in and around Dublin, and moves the focus to the middle
class. The struggles are more personal, but still powerful: A woman breaks
her engagement to a man who has kept her waiting too long; another, em-
bittered by her loveless life, sends anonymous letters that explode like
terrorist bombs destroying her neighbors' serene lives; a mother copes with
the accidental drowning of her child.*

    *In articles in the Irish press, Mary Beckett is usually presented as a con-
tented housewife who happens to write stories, as though they were made
as effortlessly as the delicious buns she serves. Downplayed is the econom-
ical style and ear for dialogue that make you remember why the Irish are
known as storytellers. By giving voice to the nonliterary women of Ireland, she has honored their lives.*

Q: You gave up writing for twenty years while you were raising a family
here in Dublin. Did you quit because of the children?

A: It was partly that I was busy with five small children. I didn't feel the
same necessity to express myself that I had felt before. But, apart from
that, I had always written about Belfast or the country right near Belfast.
So I came here to Dublin and I thought, The language is different, the
intonations are different. I won't get it right. I was afraid of that, and I
was afraid that maybe I didn't know the people. Actually, I discovered
there's no difference, although Dublin people are gentler, more relaxed.

Q: What do you mean the language was different?

A: The people talk Dublin here; I talk Belfast. It means some different
words, but mostly different inflections and intonations. Years ago I sold
stories to BBC radio, so I have to hear the whole thing when I write. In
this new collection that I did [*A Literary Woman*] I was very keen that
the dialogue had to be exactly right. I didn't want Dublin women talking
like Belfast women.

Q: So you stopped writing because you were away from Belfast?

A: Also it was 1956 when I came here and the little magazines that I wrote for—like *The Bell* [from Dublin] and *Irish Writing* [from Cork]— were collapsing, one after the other. There was no place to send short stories. English and American magazines weren't ever very interested in me. I only wrote to *The New Yorker,* never for *The New Yorker.* They kept writing back saying, "Yes, we're very interested, but try it again," you know [she laughs]. So it wasn't purely the family; it was also that the opportunities weren't there.

The stories in that first book, *A Belfast Woman,* were written mostly in the late forties and fifties when I was teaching in Belfast.

Q: When did you get the urge to write again?

A: It wasn't until the troubles [in Northern Ireland] started that I began wanting to write about that. Also, when the children were a bit more grown up and I had more time, I began not being happy and I used to wonder why. My husband said, "I know what's wrong with you. You should be writing." He was very disappointed that I stopped writing. In fact, he may have married me because I was a writer [she laughs].

Q: Why do you say that?

A: We met on the Aran Islands—on Inishmore—where I went on holiday. Very windswept and wild and all the rest of it. When we got to know one another slightly and he wanted to know what I did, I said that I was a writer, and I knew he hadn't heard of me at all. When he got back to Dublin, he got the mail and there was one of my stories in a current *Irish Writing.* Then he started writing to me in Belfast and our whole courtship was letter writing. If I hadn't been able to write a decent letter, he mightn't have married me at all.

Q: Did you enjoy teaching?

A: I taught for eleven years, from when I was nineteen, in a school in Ardoyne in a very poor area. I didn't like teaching, although I was very fond of the children. I didn't think I was any good at it.

Q: Why not?

A: The classes were enormous, and I always felt that if you weren't sort of controlling every mind in the class all of the time that they would slip away from you. So it was a strain. I was good at teaching English. I taught them all to read and write and all that kind of thing, but I wasn't clear-cut enough in maths.

Q: Did you teach small children?

A: Yes, some of them were from four years of age. I taught all year at all ages from four to fourteen. The ones I really loved were the twelve- and thirteen-year-olds. The eleven-plus [qualifying exam] had come in, which meant that at eleven years of age the good ones were weeded out. But there was no place for the others to go, and the person who taught them the year before me had a nervous breakdown [she laughs]. I taught eleven- to fourteen-year-old girls for two years and loved it because they weren't expected to be good at algebra and things like that. We read *The Mill on the Floss;* we read Jane Austen; we read poetry; we learned Shakespeare's plays. It was marvelous.

Q: How many students in a class?

A: That class was only about forty. In the infant room at one stage I had one hundred twelve in a classroom built for forty-eight.

Q: Why was it so crowded? Was there just a baby boom?

A: No, there were always boom times for children in Ireland. An English school inspector—they didn't make Irish men school inspectors in Belfast—came over and looked at my class once. And this Mr. Tulip looked at my class and said, "They breed like rabbits around here, don't they?" I thought that was none of his business.

But we didn't have enough money to build on [classrooms] in those days because the Catholic school didn't get much of a [government] grant. They just took all the children in. Also, this old school had big high ceilings, and for some reason or other they counted the amount of room per child in cubic measurement.

Q: So you just stacked them up?

A: That was the general idea. My confidence wasn't helped when another Englishman called Mr. Grey came in to examine me and postponed my diploma for six months because he said I wasn't good enough at teaching. I had to go home and tell my father, who was a principal-teacher, and that put him in the depths.

I got my diploma in the next six months. My mother wrote to me years later when I was married down here [in Dublin] that she had two pieces of news for me: One was Mr. Grey had died, and the other was that our dog Teddy had died [she laughs]. So I said I had equal regrets. Teddy was not a nice dog.

Q: Is much of you in these early stories?

A: Probably, yes. Certainly the events that are in it. When my children read them, they laugh, because they can recognize so many bits. But the sum total would not be the same. When I was young, I was lonely, the way most people are lonely. You feel that you should have someone you can tell all sorts of things. Then you learn, later on, that you'd be a right fool if you told everything to anybody. For instance, the loneliness of the wife in the first story ["The Excursion"] was my loneliness when I was twenty-three and I didn't seem to have anybody. I had friends, and we went to the pictures together; we went dancing; we went out. But I didn't feel that I had anybody that I could unburden myself to. So I put that feeling into the marriage that wasn't working. I think that you put a little bit of a thing into a story and then it's exaggerated.

But a lot of them [the stories] would be just from observation. The people who came up to the school—the mothers and families and children themselves—told me their life stories.

Q: So you stored them up and they came out in your own stories?

A: You do. This is one of the things I missed dreadfully when I left Belfast. It wasn't only a matter of leaving Belfast, but leaving all that huge gravel hill of stories that was with those children and their mothers.

Q: You said in an interview that one of the reasons you started writing was that you never saw Catholics in books.

A: That's right. I never did until I read the short-story writer Michael McLaverty. He's old now, practically dying [McLaverty died in 1992 at age eighty-eight]. He was a Belfast teacher who published in places like *The New Yorker* and *The Atlantic*. I'd say that would have been the first Catholic I ever read about in any book, except that you'd see Catholic characters in novels by the Brontës, with people looking down their noses at them.

Q: So many of those British novelists wrote like that.

A: Yes, and the American writers I would have read in my childhood, like Louisa May Alcott, weren't Catholic. You never met very much that was recognizable in that way in a book. And in the children's books at school it was the same: They never would have met Catholic characters either. It needed a certain amount of courage for me, as a Catholic, to write.

Q: So a Catholic writer wasn't readily accepted in the 1950s?

A: I'll give you an example. That first story in *A Belfast Woman* ["The Excursion"] was sent for a BBC short-story competition, and it won. I was very careful not to have a Catholic or anything suggesting it in that story because I thought, I'm not going to shoot myself in the foot. And one of the people in the BBC said afterwards that one of the judges was a playwright who would have been absolutely incapable of giving the prize to a Catholic.

My name, Beckett, is a Protestant name, so I could sail through under false pretenses. Because people in the North go by your name, I would have to make it very clear, when I was in company that didn't know me, that I was a Catholic for fear they would say something that would embarrass them.

Q: Is there still this prejudice against Catholics?

A: Oh Lord, yes. Against Catholic writers, no. That's gone. In fact, I think they probably would have an advantage in Northern Ireland.

Q: Religion is there in your books, but it's not a big deal. You don't have any priests in them, for example.

A: No, I have none of that because I don't think the priests and the nuns and so on are the essential part. They're the servants. For instance, in this house I think we had a priest here three times in the thirty-five years. The priest is up there on the altar and gives Mass and hears confessions, and, as far as I'm concerned, that's it. Sometimes they say something that gives you a little bit of enlightenment, but it's rare.

Q: If you look at writers you read as a young person, who influenced you?

A: I'm sure Michael McLaverty did, as a short-story writer. And Frank O'Connor and Seán O'Faoláin. Not that I would have ever written the same kind of thing, but they showed me what short stories were like. But once I started to write, I wouldn't have wanted to think I was writing the same as anybody else.

Q: You wanted a different voice.

A: I would have hoped for that. It's always a delight to me when I'm told that I have.

Q: Would you explain just how you got back into print after twenty years?

A: I had completely cut myself off from any writing people. Nobody around here knew that I had ever written anything. Then Sean McMahon, with Poolbeg Press, who had read the stories at Queens [University, Belfast] when he was young, phoned me. Of course, it's always easy to find anyone in Ireland. So he gave my number to David Marcus of the *Irish Press* who rang me up and said, "Start writing again."

As I said, I had been a bit restless and thinking about the North, and so I wrote "A Belfast Woman," and David published it on the literary page. Then he said, "Gather up your stories and Poolbeg will publish them." So I thought that was marvelous. In those days that was really all I wanted. I thought Poolbeg was very good about it: They made me feel that I was a success. And the papers were, mostly, very kind.

Q: Do you read reviews?

A: Oh yes. I'm always happy enough to get reviews. The things I don't like getting are people writing about this woman who had five children and stopped writing for twenty years and bakes bread and has a kitchen and suchlike, as if it was a wonder I could string a few words together. That's the kind of thing that really annoys me, but that's what the publicity people want from you.

Q: I read one article about you in which the writer seemed amazed that a housewife could have written these books, as though your brain is supposed to die when you have children.

A: Exactly. Although, to a certain extent it does [she laughs]. I get very worried nowadays because words escape me. I know it's in there someplace, but there's something wrong with the computer. That started when I was forty-three and expecting my last baby. I got a wee bit of that into the last story in *A Belfast Woman* ["Failing Years"] where the woman gets the words wrong. She says "rashers" instead of "wafers" or something like that—because that was happening to me. There's always a connection in the word—either sound or the way they look or something, as in this case, but there's just that little bit wrong, that bug in the computer.

Q: I see a lot of anger in your stories: the scene in "The Excursion," where the wife pushes her husband into the fire and almost kills him; the tension between the wife and mother-in-law in "Saints and Scholars."

A: Why not?

Q: So this image of you as this contented homemaker . . .

A: But you can only stay contented if you accept that sometimes you'll be angry. There were a lot of very nice women around here for the past thirty-five years that I've been in this house. Then, ten years or more ago, all the nice women, who never complained about their children, who never complained about their husbands, developed breast cancer and they died. The nasty ones are left.

Q: So how does women's rage come out? In talking with other women?

A: Yes, in venting it. I remember telling Gerald, my middle son, about attacking Peter, who's my husband, about something. I said to Gerald, "What he did was sit smaller and smaller in the chair." And Gerald said, "Well, when you come on heavy like that, there's no place you can be" [she laughs].

Q: Your novel, *Give Them Stones*, is an indictment of the violence in Northern Ireland as seen through the eyes of this ordinary woman. What led you to write it?

A: It took about four years to write, from the early to mid-1980s. I wrote it because I was meeting people down here [in Dublin] who would say, "Why are the people not content in the North? Why is there this trouble? They have free health, they have free education, nothing is wrong with their housing. We have unemployment down here— what's wrong with them?" They didn't seem to understand at all. Now I wouldn't have minded English people or Americans not understanding, but I was very upset that they didn't understand.

So I wrote *Give Them Stones* to explain to people down here what it was like for a Catholic woman on the back street in Belfast. It is entirely one-sided; I knew that. I didn't take in cross points of view at all. So I wrote it in the first person, which I thought made it fair, and I thought I would leave it to Jennifer Johnson and these other people to do the same thing for the other side [Dublin-born Johnson lives in Belfast and writes fiction about the Anglo-Irish].

I got the impetus because [British literary agent] Christine Green read *A Belfast Woman* and rang me up and said I was to write a novel. I said that I couldn't, but she insisted. "Listen, it's the same as asking a four-minute-mile man to run a marathon," I said; but she said, "Take another Belfast woman and write about her." So I thought, "Well, sure, maybe I can." So I wrote it and she sent it to Bloomsbury who took it right away.

Q: Martha Murtagh, your protagonist, is so clear-sighted about her life. She doesn't sentimentalize anything.

A: Oh no. Belfast people don't.

Q: She left school at fourteen, she goes out to work while her sister is educated, and there isn't any resentment of her sister.

A: Because she loves her sister. And because she felt she had chosen this life. She hadn't actually; she hadn't any choice. But then there were so many, many people, men and women, clever, intelligent people, all over Ireland, not only in the North, who never got any chance at all. That was part of it.

Q: Did you pick the names Martha and Mary on purpose, to echo the Bible?

A: Martha I always had terrible sympathy with, in the Bible. Nowadays it's not so bad because they don't read that bit [about her being the housekeeper] so much, but they do nearly always at funeral masses read the other bit in John's gospel where Martha comes out to meet Christ after Lazarus is dead. Mary's still sitting in the house. She was a bit lazy, I always thought. I called her Martha also because she was going to do the bread baking. And I called her sister Mary Brigid because I had a little girl in school called Mary Brigid who had the same little face I thought would do for the sister. It was Christine Green who said to me about Martha, Mary, and Lazarus—that [the brother] Danny was Lazarus. That had never struck me at all [she laughs].

Q: You have all these critics finding things in your books.

A: Yes, you don't know how clever you are. And then all the other things you do put in people don't notice at all.

Q: Why did you take your title from Nathaniel West's *Miss Lonelyhearts* [1933]? [The title comes from the quote: "When they ask for bread don't give them crackers as does the Church, and don't, like the State, tell them to eat cake. Explain that man cannot live by bread alone and give them stones."]

A: That was a joke. We couldn't think of a name, and Christine Green looked in a book of quotations and found just the one [she laughs]. She said I didn't have to get it into the book, but I said, "I know exactly where I'd like to put it."

I went and got *Miss Lonelyhearts,* and I was so delighted when I read it. I thought that terrible cynicism and bitterness fit in so beautifully with those out-of-work men sitting in Belfast—that they'd realize they're not the only people in the world who are in this pitiable state.

Q: It seems to me that's a book about one woman's radicalization, about one woman's coming to political consciousness.

A: But she was reared that way; the same way that I was reared. She was reared with an absolute awareness of politics, as I was. My father was not pushing politics, but it was a very strong aspect of his life. I used to ponder, when I was about four or five years of age, why the unionists [those Northern Irish, almost all Protestant, who wanted to maintain union with Great Britain] were called unionist, whereas we wanted a united Ireland. Why weren't we "unionists"? I hadn't even started school when I remember asking my mother that and she explained it to me. We were brought up that way—not with the bitterness that they keep on telling you that children were brought up with. There never was any of that. My father was principal in the school for poor children, and we couldn't live in those streets—this sounds dreadfully snobbish—but anyway we had to live up the upper end of the parish. And we had no Catholic neighbors.

Q: So you grew up with Protestants?

A: We did, and they were excellent neighbors. We all got on the best at all, you know?

Q: I don't sense in your book that you're blaming the Protestants. You're blaming this military establishment.

A: Yes, and the Orangemen [Protestant extremists belonging to the Orange Society]. On the news today this Catholic village of Pomeroy asked that the Orangemen would not walk through there today [12 July, the anniversary of the defeat of James II by William of Orange at the Battle of the Boyne; this is the occasion for parades by Northern Ireland's Orangemen]. And the high court asked the RUC [Royal Ulster Constabulary, the police force in Northern Ireland] to consider rerouting them. Well, the RUC appealed to the Supreme Court and they sat for five hours. Now, how judges can sit for five hours saying will they or won't they go through the village is beyond me. And they decided late last night they're to go through: The Orange procession, 100,000 Orangemen, are to walk through a Catholic village. But the Orangemen, themselves, at the place said, "No, we'll reroute it a bit." So the establishment is much worse than the people on the ground.

Q: You really underscore the economic reality of Martha's life when you say that she wanted to marry her future husband when she saw his gas cooker.

A: That was a joke, but some people do that in earnest. So it's only half a joke.

Q: I think part of the reason the marriage works, later on, is that she has her own money earned through her baking.

A: Absolutely.

Q: In "Excursion," the father says, "Money's power, me girl, money's power!"

A: My father used to say that, but he never had any money [she laughs]. That is absolutely true. The only purgatory in my life, other than when my children failed exams, was the fact that for the first twenty-five years of my married life I was entirely dependent on my husband. And although ordinary, decent husbands don't ever refuse to give you something, the fact of having to ask was terrible. You get the housekeeping money and that's fine, but to have to ask because your thirteen-year-old wants a new dress really is dreadful. That's the only thing in feminism I feel really strongly about. I don't know how it can be avoided, except that nowadays the women all go out to work. Of course, there's all kinds of trouble with that, too. But I think that money is grand. The pittance that I get [from writing] still gives me that bit of independence.

Q: I like the fact that she gets the money from the aunts, too. It's a nice touch, like handing down this freedom.

A: Yes. That never struck me when I was doing that.

Q: What about this catering to men that I see in some of your characters?

A: Oh, that's right. I used to see men favored all the time. When I was at school at the poor end of the parish, sometimes the children would have to do a message in the butcher's [go to the butcher's with an order], and it would be a pound of sausages and a quarter pound of steak. And the steak would be for the father, even though he wasn't working, you know? But the sausages were for the children.

Q: Does that anger you or do you just accept it?

A: That would anger me, and certainly I never would have experienced that. In our household at home, in my mother's view, the children would have come first. No difference between the boys and the girls. I had two brothers, myself and my young sister; she was six years younger. But it would be one set the table, the other cleared it, one washed the dishes, the other dried. After I left home, my brother who was still at home brought my mother her breakfast in bed every morning.

Q: I like the fact that Martha makes the connection between what she sees happening around her—the shooting, the kneecapping—and the tyranny of Miss Cooney in the school when she was a girl. Suddenly there's this integrated political consciousness.

A: I didn't see it as clearly as that. But when I was at that school that's written about, there was a tremendous amount of walloping and it made me sick. I never was touched. My father was the principal teacher downstairs in the boys' school, so nobody ever slapped me. But there were children who were really murdered, and it made me cross just to think back about it. So Martha was me getting it out of my system. And that gave you an abhorrence of any physical cruelty. It doesn't matter what it is. Because of that horror, I really did feel as a child that my hair was standing on end.

When my children went to school, they weren't touched, but there was one dreadful schoolteacher who slapped some poor, unfortunate child who couldn't learn quickly enough or who blotted his copy. I remember my middle son, Gerald, coming home and not eating his lunch because he was so upset. So for me, and for them, any physical cruelty is just out.

Q: When Martha tells the Provos that she won't pay protection money anymore because they shot the young boy, she knows she's put herself in limbo. She's brave to take that stand.

A: Yes, she is. You see, there are a lot of people in the North who would like to protest, but they can't. She couldn't have protested it if her children were still around. Because she's only a fictional character and she can get away with it, she's speaking for the people who want to protest and who can't.

Q: But when she does that, could she have envisioned that her house would get burned down?

A: She thought she was going to get shot, because people have been shot for refusing to pay the protection.

Q: She says to her husband, "You know, they won't hurt you."

A: Yes. You hear on the radio that a man in a car traveling down such-and-such street was shot. And here, we wouldn't know what happened. When I'd ask at home what that was about, they would say he didn't pay his protection money. All the small businesses had to pay up. I don't know if it's as bad now, but certainly a few years ago if they lived in Catholic streets they had to pay up to the IRA. If they lived in Protestant streets they had to pay up to their fellows [the Protestant paramilitary group].

Q: Did you have to do research for the novel?

A: I only had to do two kinds of research. I had to find home bakeries to find out how they worked. There were very few of them left because they'd all turned into chains. They all baked the stuff in the big places. But I went up there and found a couple, and they were very nice and good to me. Mind you, having seen the back of them you wouldn't be too keen eating the stuff, even though it might have tasted all right [she laughs]. And the other thing was I had to go through newspapers to make sure I had the years right for things that happened.

Q: For a lot of the novel's years you weren't living in Belfast, yet you capture pretty well what it must have been like.

A: Maybe I don't, you see. That's what I'm afraid of—that people who have lived through it might say, "Sure, she hasn't a clue."

Q: How have they responded? What does your sister say?

A: She didn't say much. She was afraid I was pro-IRA. I don't know how she got that notion, but in the book she thought I was far too easy on the IRA. I'd never ever excuse the IRA, but I can understand them. That's what I wanted to convey—that they're not psychotic. They know exactly what they're doing. They're not mindless. To them terror is necessary, you see. They felt somebody ought to be killed to make sure that others handed up their money.

Q: So what's life like for most Catholics in Belfast today?

A: It depends on where you are. Where my sister lives, and where I lived, it's quiet. She teaches in west Belfast and she lives in north Belfast, which meant that during troubled times she would have to go right across through bad streets and so on, where she'd come across burning cars and all of that. When the hunger strikes were on, there were, all the time, protests—burning buses and cars, barricades across the road, cars being seized. Of course, those children going to school had to go through all of that, too. My brother taught in Saint Marcus College and said men teachers used to have to go out into the road to make sure that the teenage boys were in and were not holding up the lorries.

But the people in the ghetto areas have a dreadful time of it. When the children—the young fellows—go out, they're stopped; they're searched by the soldiers; they're shouted at; their houses are searched. And unemployment is terrible. If they can't get employment for all those young men, there's going to be an IRA there, no matter what they fix in talks. What other way have they of asserting themselves?

Q: They have to feel like men, that they have some sort of power.

A: Yes. When I was growing up, during the war, there was full employment, but other than that, there was never employment for Catholic men. And the priests would always be preaching all the time that you have to put up with it. You know, offer it up. You get your reward in the next world. It's only when all of that stopped and the young men who got free education went to university that they said, "What the blazes is this?" And they thought they'd fix it by marches, but it got out of hand. It was bound to.

Q: Are most Catholics in Belfast pro-IRA?

A: No. In the ghetto areas a certain number would say, "We need them to protect us." But most of them would not want the violence and would condemn the violence. At the same time, they would say, "Well, they're neighbors' sons. You can't do anything nasty about them." And the hunger strikes were such a terrible, stupid thing of Margaret Thatcher's, so stupid that she kept them on until eleven of them died. They could have been given all those things they asked for—they now have them. And there's nothing wrong with having those things: to have their own clothes, to run the place [the prison] themselves.

Q: It sounds like the IRA can draw on people's righteous anger.

A: You remember the three IRA people who were killed in Gibraltar? Two fellows and a girl. They were brought home to be buried, and at the funeral, a loyalist hid in the graveyard and shot and killed two or three mourners. And at the funeral of one of them, an army car appeared on the scene with two or three army men in it. They came right into the funeral procession. What did the men do? They stopped the car; they took the soldiers out; they killed them.

Everybody in that whole district who had any slight connection with that—if they had a speck of blood on their clothes, if they let the people into their houses—they have all been up and tried, you see? The whole district has been persecuted for that, which builds up support for the IRA. The English establishment are so stupid! They want compromise, but they won't compromise themselves.

Q: How do you see this working itself out?

A: I don't. I don't see it at all. When these [peace] talks began, down here they were so optimistic and they said, "Everybody is in such a mood to compromise and be generous." I thought, "My God, they're mad." In [the story] "A Belfast Woman," when I wrote that she thought she had cancer and she hadn't cancer, the cancer was meant to be the hatred between the Catholics and the Protestants. And it wasn't really there, as I thought at that time. But now I wouldn't be so sure. So many dreadful things have happened that I think there's a lot of hatred.

Q: The title, *A Literary Woman*, seems intended to be ironic. In the story of that name the literary woman is an angry woman sending false letters to people.

A: It's a joke.

Q: So you're sort of exposing the pretentiousness of that kind of title?

A: It's partly that. It's partly me. First, I was a Belfast woman. Then I was a literary woman. Secondly, the literary women in Dublin that I meet, generally, I think, have got things all wrong. One of them said to me at one lunch that husbands are so much baggage. I think these women are just building up misery. I don't find my husband baggage.

So the literary woman in that story got everything wrong. She wrote a letter to every house, and it was wrong, and it hurt. That was part of the joke, but it was entirely private, and nobody got it at all [she laughs].

Q: She's such a quirky, angry character. Was that fun to write?

A: No, it was very hard to write because she was so horrible. I had to have the whole life [condensed] into a short story, and where do you start, and how do you get at it? To write it in the third person, from the writer's point of view, it's as if you're condemning her. So, again, you have to resort to the first person: She can judge herself. But then you have to be careful not to make her too literary—you have to bring her down a bit. You see, she is a woman who would have been intelligent, who would have been capable of great things, if she'd had a chance.

Q: You give her such a lonely childhood.

A: The theme of the whole book is family. Not the family as in America, where they all love each other so much [she laughs]. I have an American friend whose daughter got married to someone they didn't like and they had family counseling. They brought the whole family—who are all grown up in their twenties and thirties—together for counseling. That strikes horror. My family separated from the door, you know?

Q: You're not interested in all that coming together?

A: [She laughs.] No, not at all. We come together for meals once a week or so. When my husband wants to know how I feel, he says, "Are you warm enough?"

Q: The story "Sudden Infant Death" was very painful. Where did that come from?

A: That wasn't written until the book was nearly finished. During the years when I wasn't writing, I never kept any commonplace book or journal or anything, as you do when you are writing and immediately put it in words when you see something. But I remembered hearing about these people who had gone on holiday and their child was lost. Then he was found drowned. And I remember thinking that was such a dreadful, awful thing to have happened that I wanted to write about it but didn't feel I could. Then I was going out in the car the following Sunday with the children in the backseat—we used to take them out every Sunday afternoon—and the sky was a summer gray—and I remember thinking,

"Haven't I described that?" So I thought again of writing. I felt I had to write that story.

Q: The mother says at the end, wondering how she'll save her marriage, "Maybe when the children, whatever number there were, grew up she would not care anymore and he [her husband] would have to take life as it happened. But now, dependent, she would cater to his wishes." The story ends ambiguously.

A: I do that on purpose. "You take it from there" kind of thing. This is why people don't like short stories—because you have to work along with them. In London, when I read "Cypress Trees," which I found more painful to write than "Sudden Infant Death," some of the people coming out said to me, "What happened to this boy afterwards?" And I said, "It's as plain as a pike staff!" But they wanted it written down, they wanted it word-for-word, which is why they read [Irish writer] Maeve Binchy.

Q: In "A Ghost Story" you're pretty critical of that yuppie couple who are so obsessed with material things.

A: That was one story I didn't have any very strong feelings about. I just was looking at them. A lot of my neighbors' children are getting married, and so I had heard of this young couple who were just married, just home after their honeymoon, both working, came to the shopping center to buy the food for the evening. The young man, who was driving the car, said, "Don't be too long now," and she said, "You're coming in, too." And he said, "I am not." So she sat back and said, "Well, I'm not going either." And they sat there till the place shut and they didn't have any dinner [she laughs].

When I heard that I said, "This is it. We have trained them to decide for themselves what they're doing, not to give in, stand up for their rights, and now they're doing this to each other." That was really what I had in mind in that story, but also this whole business that so many of them have dropped their religion. I can't think that wouldn't cause a bit of a problem internally—not to the fellow in the story. He didn't have any trouble with that; he was so full of himself. But I would have thought that it would affect her: pretending at home to be a good devout Catholic and still, to please him, she wasn't. That that would have set up trouble in her that she wasn't admitting to.

Q: The story "Under Control" is written as a letter from one sister to another. It's interesting to do that in a book about lying letters. What sparked that?

A: I don't know. I'm very fond of my sister, and she does an awful lot for me. I don't think she knows I appreciate her because we're not great at saying things to each other or hugging each other. I don't do that with my children either, once they get to a certain stage. Something wrong with me, but nothing I can do about it. So I wanted to present in it an appreciation of one sister for another.

Q: That woman is such a controlling mother.

A: I was sympathetic with the mother in that, but I met a young Irish woman who teaches in university in Italy, and she had read that story and wanted to put it on the course for her students. But she hated that mother, she detested her. She thought that the mother was too much keeping them under control. But I felt, in a way, she had to.

Q: She feels that she's doing the right thing by raising her daughter's illegitimate daughter as her own. Is that still common—that unmarried girls give their babies away or have the birth hidden?

A: No, that doesn't happen. Girls have babies now—there's no stigma, but it still is a burden.

Q: For the women in your books marriage is a necessity. If they don't get married they are out there in limbo.

A: Well, that's my feeling, unfortunately, about life for women. I know that's altogether out of date, but I had that feeling when I was young and I still have it.

Q: Is it just getting married or is it also having children?

A: [She ponders.] I don't know. When I got married I didn't care whether I had children or not. I was really very upset when I found out I was pregnant the first time, and all of the other times afterwards, too. It never gave me any great thrill. All this ecstasy that people have when their babies are born skipped me.

Q: Your women don't seem to have a lot of that, either.

A: Not at all, because I know nothing about it. I read about it in books, that's as near to it as ever I got. My devotion to my children is much the same as a tiger to its young: absolute commitment to it. I was in such a state when I was pregnant. I was happy with the four. And then I was pregnant again [with the youngest] and I did not rejoice one little bit. Whereas before I would feel affection for the baby in the womb before it was born, I had none for him. Then, when he was born and I got him home, I had such pleasure with him because I had time for him.

Q: In "Heaven" you have this older woman who says she doesn't want the burden of caring for her grandchildren. I wish she didn't give in and agree to do it.

A: She had to because she had to have someone stop her hating her husband who was underfoot. So they were it. That was all. A woman told me the actual bit about the grandchildren and being left. She was very upset because her daughter-in-law was leaving the grandchildren with her. She was so cross, saying, "It should not be put on me," and I sympathized with her so much. The woman in "Heaven" also didn't want the grandchildren because she was afraid of becoming a perfectionist with them.

Q: I kept thinking, as I was reading about these women, how their lives could have been different if they didn't have to have all these children, if they had used contraception. Is that dilemma anything that you would ever write about?

A: Yes, their lives would be different. I don't know whether I would write about it or not, because I'm not sure of it myself. You see, I myself cannot see anything wrong with contraception, but I would never have used it. I would have been afraid that when I did, I'd say to God, "Well, I thought it was all right," and He would say, "But the Church told you it wasn't all right."

Q: What would you say to your daughters?

A: I wouldn't say anything. The only one of my children who's married is a son, and my sister said to me, "Any sign as yet?" And I said, That doesn't even occur to me. It's entirely up to themselves to decide when to begin having children.

Q: It's a different world, isn't it?

A: It is a different world, and it's much better.

Q: Can women get contraceptives in Ireland now?

A: It depends, but they mostly would be on [some form of contraceptive].

Q: Wasn't there some debate about that?

A: That was about the condoms. They made such a fuss about them. I go to Mass every morning, and I was saying to this woman who is similar to myself, "I wish to God they'd get their condoms quietly and stop shoving them down our throats!" I was raised in Belfast, where such things would have been available, but you never did see them. I don't see why they couldn't be similarly available here, without offending anybody.

Q: How has your family responded to your work? Do they think you're a literary woman?

A: I don't think so. They're good about it. They kind of get annoyed with me when I'm not writing, tell me that I should be writing when I'm not. My eldest son was a bit dubious to start off with because he was afraid that maybe I wasn't good enough, but he would never say anything. And the other sons wouldn't say anything, except to hope it was going well. When *A Belfast Woman* came out, the two girls would go around the bookshops and turn it around on the shelf so that the front cover was facing out. They wanted people to see it.

Q: This was published in the states by William Morrow, wasn't it?

A: William Morrow brought it out in hardback, but I notice that your copy is from here. Anybody from America who has mentioned that book to me has read the Irish edition. They haven't seen the William Morrow edition at all.

Q: Has that been a problem?

A: Well, it shows they didn't give it any publicity at all. And they refused to take *A Literary Woman* because they said the book of short stories hadn't sold. They weren't going to publish another book of short stories unless I wrote a novel in between. I haven't done so.

Q: I've heard that before—that publishers don't push the books.

A: This really gets me down because you are such a perfectionist when you're writing the blessed story, and then you give it to them, and they don't bother their heads about getting it out. It's not just the American publisher; Bloomsbury's the same. Books wouldn't be on the shelves, and you'd say to the people in charge, "Why aren't the books out?" And they would say, "It's up to the bookshops to ask for it." But it's not. *Give Them Stones* is not kept on the shelves, and it's out of print now. Being out of print for England is fine, but it shouldn't be out of print for Ireland. They should keep it here, and it would sell, the same as *A Belfast Woman* has sold for eleven years.

Q: Do you know Éilís Ní Dhuibhne's work?

A: I don't know her work. I know herself. She's a lovely girl.

Q: In the interview I did with her, Éilís said she felt that Irish women, for a long time, didn't get the same attention as men, and that even now the Irish literary establishment didn't consider women in the same way.

A: To a certain extent I would go along with that. *Give Them Stones,* got a lot of attention in the Irish papers because it's political. I wrote *A*

Literary Woman, but it's about families, so they sent these people to interview me in my house, but they don't give it any kind of a literary review. If you're a woman writing about something, presumably, outside the home and outside women's concerns, you'll get the attention. But if it's just about a woman's world, the papers just aren't going to bother.

Q: It's interesting, because *Give Them Stones* is about a woman's world, too.

A: It is.

Q: Have you gotten any kind of insight from being a mother that helps in your writing?

A: I'd hope so. It's the only consolation I have. When the troubles started in Belfast, I thought, Why am I not up in Belfast? Look at the number of stories I'd have known about if I were up there. But then I consoled myself: But you're down here, and you have these people and you know more of this side of life than if you had stayed up in Belfast.

Q: Do you think you'll write another novel? I hope you do.

A: At the moment, I'm not writing anything. But I had a kind of an idea that I would write Mary Brigid's story—where Martha would have been really Republican, Mary Brigid would have stepped away from it. She would have said she didn't care about it, that she would bring up her children where I was brought up. I've started writing, but I'm stuck at the moment.

I worry a lot about the children. I know I shouldn't, but I do. And I get tired. I know quite well that if I started to write I'd stop being tired. I get ideas, but what I need is a lovely plot. . . .

In 1974, Puerto Rican artist Francisco Rodón displayed a portrait of writer Rosario Ferré, surrounded by flames and wearing newsprint. Entitled Andromeda, *the painting invokes the mythological daughter sacrificed for her mother's follies and, with her father's complicity, put on a rocky ledge to be devoured by a serpent. Andromeda was rescued by Perseus, but no one rescued Ferré when the furor arose which led to the painting.*

The daughter of a former governor of Puerto Rico and a graduate student in Spanish and Latin American literature at the University of Puerto Rico, Ferré had broken a cultural taboo. In 1972, in the seventh issue of Zona de carga y descarga *("Loading and Unloading Zone"), a literary magazine she founded and edited at the university, she published "When Women Love Men," a short story she had written to shock. In sexually explicit language, the story explores the thoughts and person- alities of an upper-class widow and a prostitute who meet after the death of the man they shared. So outraged were some Puerto Ricans that they burned the magazine (thus the flames in Rodón's painting). They labeled Ferré a traitor to her class and her gender.*

Ferré laughs as she remembers the scandal, but copies of that issue are collector's items today. For Rosario Ferré has emerged from the ashes to become one of Latin America's most powerful writers. Still controversial, her works critique Puerto Rican society with detachment and precision: a

Photo: Courtesy of Rosario Ferré

cultural sexism that makes middle- and upper-class wives and daughters into dolls; the moral bankruptcy of a corrupt aristocracy; class conflicts that erupt into random violence; the desperation of women and men who are marginalized by poverty and racism.

To date, only two of Ferré's books have been translated into English. Her widely acclaimed Papeles de Pandora *("Pandora's Papers" [Joaquin Mortiz, Mexico, 1976]), a collection of short stories and poems in which she revived the Greek myth of Pandora, was published, minus the poems, as* The Youngest Doll *(University of Nebraska Press, 1991). A novel and three short stories,* Sweet Diamond Dust *(Ballantine, 1988), appeared originally as* Maldito amor *("Damned Love" [Joaquin Mortiz, 1986]). Much of Ferré's work has remained untranslated, mainly because translation is very time-consuming, whether she translates the works herself or works closely with the translator. As she says, she would rather write.*

Her untranslated works include a book of children's stories, El medio pollito *("The Half-Chick" [Ediciones Huracán, Puerto Rico, 1976]); a collection of feminist essays,* Sitio a Eros *("Eros Besieged" [Joaquin Mortiz, 1980]);* Los cuentos de Juan Bobo *("The Stories of Juan Bobo" [Ediciones Huracán, 1981]);* Fábulas de la garza desangrada *("Fables of the Bled Heron" [Joaquin Mortiz, 1984]);* El acomador Felisberto Hernández y la literatura fantástica *("'The Usher': Felisberto Hernández and Fantastic Literature" [Fonda de Cultura Económica, Mexico, 1987]); a collection of literary essays,* El árbol y sus sombras *("The Tree and Its Shadows" [Fonda de Cultura Económica, 1989]); and a book of fables,* Sonatinas *(Ediciones Huracán, 1989). A book of poems and short stories,* Las dos Venecias *("The Two Venices") is forthcoming, and Ferré is working on a memoir.*

The interview took place in June 1991, in Washington, D.C., where Ferré lives with her husband, architect Agustín Costa. In our time together over iced tea in a hotel restaurant, she discussed her background and writing, as well as other topics: the advantages and difficulties of the author who has left the homeland she writes about; the role of anger and magic in her work and in that of other Latin American writers; the significance of race, class, and gender for the woman writer from Puerto Rico; the art of translating fiction; the relationship of autobiography and fiction; and Puerto Rican culture and politics. In person, as in her fiction and essays, Ferré is unsentimentally honest about her country's past. You sense that Rodón was correct in depicting this rewriter of myths as a mythic figure, although not Andromeda. Opening the lid on deeply buried secrets, she's more like Pandora.

Q: When you were growing up in Puerto Rico, did you want to become a writer?

A: I wanted to be a dancer at first. I didn't just want to have a career, in the sense of a business career. That wasn't interesting enough. In Ponce, where I was born, my father had a little newspaper, *El Dia,* which my brother later developed into the island's most important newspaper. I might have liked to be a newspaper person, but my father wouldn't let me work there. When I was a college student—I graduated from Manhattanville College [in Westchester County, New York] in 1960—I did a couple of features for the summer issues. I would write when I went home. I wrote little cameo articles; I really liked it.

Q: Why couldn't you work at the paper?

A: They wouldn't let me even consider a career as a journalist. Women weren't supposed to work at that time, so I got married and had three children. After ten years I got a divorce and then went to the University of Puerto Rico to do my master's degree in Spanish and Latin American literature.

Q: Many of your stories use dolls as symbols of women's restricted lives. Were you sort of a doll in your marriage?

A: Yes, I was. Definitely. But in Puerto Rico most of the women of my generation were in the same situation [Ferré was born in 1942]. I was no exception. Women who wanted to change that or go against that stereotype would be considered odd or slightly crazy. The only reason they couldn't say the same about me was because I made it in the world of literature. At the university I started a literary magazine called *Zona de carga y descarga*, with some of the other students. We started publishing unknown writers and it was unusually successful, so we went on for two years. I would publish something for every number and that's how I started writing. Those first two years gave me about half the material for the first book, *Papeles de Pandora,* which came out in 1976. Then I got into writing; I came to the United States and got my doctorate at the University of Maryland, and they couldn't say I was crazy. I was just doing my thing. Things were changing at that time; feminist issues were becoming more and more important. I was lucky. I probably took the last train that went out for my generation of women. I always look at myself like that [she laughs].

Q: Besides dolls, you write a lot about women's friendships. "The Gift" celebrates the relationship between two girls from different classes who love one another despite attempts to break them up. In "When Women

Love Men," a friendship is established between the white woman who is the widow and the black woman who is the mistress of the rich landowner. And in "Pico Rico Mandorico," there is the love between sisters. Did you grow up among women?

A: My mother had eight sisters and they were always very close, so our house was always filled with aunts. It was a very feminine environment. Women used to communicate a lot between themselves; and I had a lot of girl cousins. It was definitely a matriarchy.

Q: Did the relationships cross classes?

A: It did, in a sense. In Puerto Rico people adopt a lot of children. That's why we haven't had any problem with homeless children until just recently. If someone died and there was no one to take care of the sons or the daughters, the aunts and uncles would adopt them. So that happened in my family, too, and my grandmother adopted a couple of children. And we could establish friendships, but we knew they weren't our flesh and blood; we weren't really related.

Q: Would the family support them if they wanted to go to college, for example?

A: No. When they grew up, they would probably get married and the family would help them to establish themselves. They wouldn't be poor; the family would give them a hand. But they wouldn't go to college, not at that time. But my grandmother didn't go to college either. My mother went to college and it was something extraordinary because my father's sisters didn't go to college. They were more on the lower social scale. If you had the money to send the girls to school, this was a maximum luxury.

Q: You're very critical of the Puerto Rican landed aristocracy in your works. Was that hard for you to write?

A: I think that the sugarcane aristocracy did a lot of bad things. *Sweet Diamond Dust* is more or less the picture of what happened in Puerto Rico in the first half of the twentieth century. But they were also, in a paternalistic way, very much aware of the people who were working with them. It was a lot more human than what happened later, when the big corporations were there and exploitation became totally dehumanized.

Q: You mean the aristocrats were more humane exploiters?

A: Yes. They lived nearby to the workers, on the fields themselves; they knew the names of the persons who were cutting the cane. When a worker cut his arm or something, the owner rushed him to the hospital and tried to save him, or maybe he adopted his child or gave the worker some other type of help. When it really got bad in Puerto Rico was in the 1930s, when these big, absentee-owned corporations were dominating the scene. They weren't just Americans; some of them were Puerto Ricans. Sugar processing ceased to be under small ownership and became incorporated into mega-enterprises.

Q: Was yours an aristocratic family?

A: My mother's was; my father's was not. She was from a very good family. In a way it was all a myth, though, because my grandmother was from Corsica. Her parents were lower middle class. Once she married my grandfather, then that fact was sort of hidden—nobody would talk about it. My great-grandfather, her father, was probably a smuggler, as well as a merchant. In Puerto Rico there are lots of Corsicans.

Q: How has your family responded to your critique of aristocracy?

A: Well, they are not that aristocratic anymore [she laughs]. That's the way it used to be. They've lost a lot of money; agriculture on the island has gone down the drain. The grandchildren of all these people are lawyers or architects or engineers. They are all professionals. I do have a couple of very old aunts and uncles who are still alive, and they were upset that some of the places described in the novel were the same as in real life. I used the family house to create the right ambience, and they recognized it. But I didn't use their names, and, of course, the anecdote is totally imagined.

Q: So *Zona de carga y descarga* got you started? Tell me more about that magazine.

A: It came out bimonthly, and the students did all the work. We did the art, the layout—we even sold it. We took it to the bookstores; we had this whole network of people involved. Distribution was two thousand copies and it sold for fifty cents. That's when I started to write, because we needed to fill the blank pages. My first story, which was "The Youngest Doll," came out in the first issue, and in every number I would publish something. My cousin Olga Nolla, who is also a writer, very well known in Puerto Rico, would also publish, as well as other young Puerto Rican writers. Of course, we never paid anybody anything; it was done from scratch. We didn't have any advertisements at all.

Q: Why did you all feel that impulse to make a magazine?

A: We were filling a vacuum. There was one magazine, called *Sin nombre,* which was published by Nilita Vientós Gastón, who was the "great lady of letters" in Puerto Rico. But she only published writers who were already famous, who had written books. Nobody would publish the new writers; they thought we were too radical. In Puerto Rico the sixties arrived four years late—in a colony everything gets there a little late. So from 1968 to 1972 we were right in the middle of all that. Drugs, marijuana, rebellion. Everybody wore long hair.

I remember one day we were sitting in the campus in front of the tower at the university, on this big lawn. All the people from the magazine were there, talking and reading poems. Maybe we were smoking some pot, I don't remember exactly, but all of a sudden I saw this huge truck going down this arched road quite far away. It was pulling an advertisement for Coca-Cola, a billboard, and from the window of the truck this man with a telephoto lens starts taking photographs of us. Of course, the police probably thought we were revolutionaries. Actually, the magazine did have some political overtones, but they were more anarchist than anything else.

Q: Carlos Fuentes says, "To be a witness of Latin America in action or in language is now, and will be more and more, a revolutionary act." Does that apply to the Puerto Rican writer too?

A: I think he's probably talking about the fact that as a writer you have to be there when the massacres take place, like in Tlatelolco [in Mexico] for example. Mexico is a very violent country. We have a lot of violence, too, in Puerto Rico, but not as much. I think he is right, and I admire him a lot. He has done a lot to bring the Latin American situation to the American consciousness.

Q: Is there a lot of repression in Puerto Rico?

A: There is less now than there was seven or eight years ago. Now it's become better, but I do think that everyone who has anything to do with independence—the artists or writers—is on some kind of a list.

Q: You probably were on a government list when you were a graduate student publishing this radical magazine. Who were some of the others involved?

A: My cousin Olga Nolla, whom I mentioned. Yvonne Ochard, who is also a poet and a novelist. Manuel Ramos Otero, a poet and a short-story writer who just died of AIDS. Also, from the more academic establishment, there were some very fine people, like Mercedes Lopez Baralt and Luce Lopez Baralt, two professors of the Spanish department. They both published articles with us.

Q: Was anything ever censored by the government?

A: No. Censorship doesn't exist in Puerto Rico, as it does in Argentina, for example. It would have been really a scandal if they had tried to do that.

Q: So this graduate school publication enabled you to find your voice?

A: Yes. When I started to write I realized that I could do something that not everybody could do. I was surprised. I didn't expect people would listen. I remember the first thing anybody ever told me about "The Youngest Doll." A professor from the university said, "I liked your story very much, but it was too short" [she laughs]. I got the idea that maybe he might like for me to write more.

Q: It was just long enough for you to tell the story.

A: That's right. That's what I should have answered.

Q: Who influenced your work?

A: When I was fourteen I used to read literature in English. I read textbooks and the newspapers in Spanish, but when I really started to get into literature was when I started reading *Jane Eyre* and *Wuthering Heights.*

Q: Many of the writers I've interviewed have mentioned those books.

A: When I started reading *Wuthering Heights,* it just put my hair on end. I couldn't put it down. I read it two or three times, one right after the other. Another book that was very important for me was *A Thousand and One Nights.* I used to read that when I was around ten or younger.

Q: You sound like Scheherazade in "The Poisoned Story," for example. The story itself is poisonous.

A: In *A Thousand and One Nights* there is a story about a king who is reading a poisoned book, which the wizard has sent him. I think probably Umberto Eco read it, too. *The Name of the Rose* [Harcourt Brace Jovanovich, 1983] has a similar theme. The idea he has is similar: a book that poisons the reader.

Q: Did you grow up hearing a lot of tales?

A: Yes. I had a nanny who liked to tell stories and read to me. She would make up many of the stories. I have a book which I dedicated to her, called *El medio pollito.* They are stories she used to tell me, and then I sort of rewrote them in a literary way.

Q: Did you also have family stories?

A: My father made one story up: "The Wise She-Frog." I rewrote it a bit and put it in the book. But that's the only one you might call a family story.

Q: Let's talk about the process of writing a novel. Was that different from writing your short stories?

A: It took me longer; it took me about six years. *Sweet Diamond Dust* is four short novels which are related to each other. All the characters belong to the same family. The first part takes place from the 1890s to the 1930s; the second part is in the 1950s; the third is in the 1970s; and the last part in the year 2000. The first short novel, especially, was very intricate because there are four characters, and they each tell the same story from a totally different point of view. Each version cancels the one that came before. It was like trying to write a literary version of [Akira Kurosawa's film] *Rashomon;* I was fascinated by the idea. I was trying to bring out the fact that in an island, Puerto Rico, the atmosphere is always so claustrophobic. Everybody is criticizing everybody else, saying bad things about them and making up all kinds of calumnies and false stories. You never know what the truth is, because everybody's lying; everybody manipulates the truth to a certain extent.

Q: So can we ever find out what really happened in the past?

A: Truth is always relative because our perception of it is always subjective, but there is a core to truth. I won't say that I agree with the structuralists or the poststructuralists who believe that history doesn't exist and is just something a historian makes up. I think history does exist, but you have to analyze the points of view from which it is being seen. You need to see it from many different points of view to really understand it.

Q: In *Sweet Diamond Dust* you touch on the race issue. Would you talk about racism in Puerto Rico and its significance in your work?

A: Puerto Rico is very much built upon that conflict, the same as the southern states in the United States. You see it here [in Washington, D.C.]; it's all over. I think probably we [in Puerto Rico] have been able to deal with it better; that's a plus for us. We have been able to become an integrated society, but not completely.

Q: In your work you also seem to suggest that blackness is a source of power.

A: Yes, I think it's like that in all the Caribbean. The black race has been very vital in the contribution of their traditions to Puerto Rican culture. In the face of oppression the black people's traditions often have to do with the joy of life. They are the ones who play the best music. They make up the best music. The food that comes from the black culture is fabulous. These traditions are more present in the coastal towns, where the slaves were brought. Inside the country, up in the mountains where the white population stayed, people are always sad. There, they played sad songs—beautiful songs, something like those of the Indians in Peru, but totally different from what went on by the coast.

Q: Racial differences show up in several of your stories. In "When Women Love Men," for example, two women named Isabel—white wife and black mistress—get together after the death of the man they shared. The black woman ends up getting the house and also bringing the white woman to life.

A: There is a metamorphosis in the end, when they merge. The story has to do with the idea of miscegenation, the merging of the races, in Puerto Rico.

Q: There's an association with sexuality, too—much more of an acceptance of sexuality on the part of this prostitute than of the repressed wife. Were you working with the virgin-and-whore idea in the two women?

A: Yes. This is very typical of Puerto Rican culture and of all Latin men. Women are either the Madonna or the whore. It's very difficult for them to have an idea of a woman who is neither, or perhaps both.

Q: In "When Women Love Men" you write, "Every lady hides a prostitute under her skin. . . . A prostitute, on the other hand, will go to similar extremes to hide the lady under her skin." What were you getting at here?

A: [She laughs.] Well, I was trying to show how every woman who is sexually repressed would like to break those taboos and simply be sexually free. If you read Freud or a little psychoanalysis, you know that society has to control that or there would be total anarchy. But everybody has the same desires. The important thing was that when this story came out no Puerto Rican woman had ever written about sex. My story is just a little story, and it's not Henry Miller's *Tropic of Cancer,* but I think I was trying to go in that direction.

Q: You have some very graphic descriptions and language here.

A: I was trying to shock everyone, out of a repression of centuries.

Q: Did you get a reaction?

A: Yes, very much. People were very mad. That story came out in the seventh number of *Zona de carga y descarga* along with a story of a friend of mine, Manuel Ramos Otero, which is about the same prostitute. His story hasn't been translated into English. His story was just as shocking as mine, but of course because he was a homosexual and a man, he was looking at the thing from another point of view. The magazine's format was very large. We published it in two or three colors. It was beautiful. We published those two stories side by side, in parallel columns. The text was white on a black background: totally black, the pages all black.

Some people would buy the magazine and burn it, because they thought it had to do with witchcraft. I realized how much it had shocked people because the issue didn't sell. All the other numbers had gone like hotcakes, but that number was considered to be banned. So we had to go to the bookstores and pick them all up.

Q: What year was this?

A: 1972. I still have about two hundred in my garage in Puerto Rico [we both laugh].

Q: In 1974 the Puerto Rican artist Francisco Rodón displayed a portrait of you in which you look like a nun in a habit made of newsprint. Was that image reflecting the controversy?

A: Yes. Rodón is one of the best-known painters in Puerto Rico. I look like Joan of Arc in a pyre, which has something to do with the scandal at the time. The newspapers are like flames that are eating me up.

Q: Do you like that image for you?

A: I didn't much like it [at the time]. I didn't buy the painting. Of course, it's a wonderful painting. Later I regretted not having bought it, but at the time I didn't really have the money. And he could sell it to anyone he wanted. After a while, I felt the painting was not just about slander. I'm just burning up because it's about literature, and language is that powerful. I'm burning up in a pyre of printed pages. Well, that's a great idea [she laughs]. I sort of liked it. I hadn't written *Sweet Diamond Dust* at that time, but in a way he was making a prophecy. I like it now.

Q: What about the role of religion in your work, particularly your presentation of nuns?

A: I was taught by nuns when I was a girl, and we used to have a lot of fun with them. I remember I had a nun who used to have a whole closet full of lipsticks and makeup. I was about twelve at the time, and she would teach us how to put makeup on.

Q: You seem critical of nuns because they are so interested in money. I'm thinking of "Sleeping Beauty" or "The Gift."

A: They were, very much so; but only because they were very poor. They had to survive somehow. They weren't getting any help from the government, that's for sure. The school was for rich girls, but the landed aristocracy was going through a great crisis, and there wasn't enough money to help them out.

Q: What about the role of sexuality in your writing in general? How does it figure in your thoughts?

A: Well, I think of the discovery of sex as a liberation for women, which is why I like that picture *Thelma and Louise.* When you search yourself and realize that you can have your own life, that you don't have to live dependent emotionally on a person because you get sexual satisfaction from being with them, then you can be on your own. But it breaks something; there's a dangerous point of no return, which was shown in the movie *Thelma and Louise,* and it's important to keep that in mind. I think probably the pill has been the greatest invention of the twentieth century.

Q: Certainly one of them. Moving to a story that deals with repression and anger, let's talk about "The Youngest Doll." This is your best-known story—about an aunt who makes dolls and her niece who leaves her husband the hideous doll that she has become. In your essay "The Writer's Kitchen," you say that it was based on a story your aunt told you about a distant cousin of hers—a woman, victimized by her husband, who made honey-filled dolls for the girls in your aunt's family. But you fleshed out the story.

A: "The Youngest Doll" is a story about writing. The old aunt who makes the doll is like the witch; she is the weaver of spells, which is what a writer does. And each doll is like a story or a potential story. Actually, in the memoirs I am writing now, I'm writing the story of all those dolls. I just wish I could make it in a novel, because I still haven't been able to write a long novel. This book is already two hundred pages, but it's a memoir, not a novel.

Q: Why do you need to do a long novel?

A: It's a challenge. A story is like building a chapel; a novel is a cathedral: That's the difference.

Q: It's like the Renaissance poets wanting to write the epic.

A: That's true. And they always wrote sonnets. "The Youngest Doll" was a very important story. It was the story that showed me how to write. It was my first breakthrough.

Q: Did you revise that a lot?

A: No. Some things I revise a lot: for "The Poisoned Tale" I must have made fifteen versions. But I didn't have to change "The Youngest Doll" at all.

Q: Another story inspired by a previous story was "Pico Rico Mandorico," the story of two sisters who escape the power of a devil figure. Wasn't that influenced by Christina Rossetti's "Goblin Market"?

A: Yes, in fact my story is a prose rendition of the poem. I said so in the introduction to *Sonatinas,* the book in Spanish.

Q: Joanna Russ was also inspired by this Rossetti poem. How did you transform the story to make it your own?

A: I liked it so much I said, "I want to do my own version of this." I've done a lot of things like that. In fact, I taught a course in creative writing at the University of Maryland for a semester—I did it on my own, "unofficially," because the students didn't get any credit. We met once a week for the duration of the semester. I would tell them to pick a fable, a short story by Scheherazade, for example, read it, close the book, and then rewrite it in their own terms.

Q: What happens when you do that, when you retell a story?

A: You put yourself in the situation of the original writer and simply tell yourself: If I were she, how would I have reacted to this situation? What would I have done? And then tell what happens.

Q: You change the Rossetti story considerably. Most significantly, the girls castrate the man. These sisters are much more empowered. It's more obviously feminist than Rossetti's, which has a more covert message. You also give it a political dimension.

A: Writing is a lot like sewing: You bring pieces together and make a quilt. What brought me to Rossetti's story was a dirge, a little ditty called "Pico Rico Mandorico/Quién te dio tamaño pico?" ["Pico Rico, far and wide/leaves a mark where others hide"]. In this nursery rhyme there is a man dressed in black who comes to the house of a little girl. It's always on Sundays—that's very important. He has a very long nose and he spills everything on the table, so they have to cut off his nose. The man is really a devil, and he wants to steal the little girl and take her away with him. The Christina Rossetti story reminded me of the nursery rhyme, and I made a quilt of both.

Q: Did you like teaching writing?

A: Very much. I taught at Rutgers University and the Johns Hopkins University last semester. It was only part-time because I travel to Puerto Rico so often.

Q: What about your situation as someone who lives in the United States and writes about Puerto Rico? How does the distance affect what you write and how you write?

A: Well, you always feel that you're betraying someone. Puerto Ricans are a little bit like cats: they always want to be on the other side of the door [she laughs]. There are one and a half million Puerto Ricans who commute to the island every year, so I suspect guilt feelings abound. But then on the island, you have so many relations whom you are expected to visit often and take care of, because you are there. There is no way you can get away from it. But if you are here, then you can see them and leave.

I also found out distance gives me a lot of perspective. It's easier to write about a place when you're not living there. It's like being there in a different way; you have to re-create everything from memory.

Q: So you have a sort of psychic distance by not living in Puerto Rico?

A: Yes.

Q: And anonymity?

A: Yes, that's very important. In Puerto Rico people are more interested in the life of the writers than in the works. In the United States it's different. If you like Maxine Hong Kingston or Toni Morrison, it's because you like their books, not because they may lead interesting or uninteresting lives. In Puerto Rico there is no way you can get away from close scrutiny. It's impossible to write a novel there because people always think it is autobiographical. It happens to all the writers, not just to me. Some of them don't mind it and others do. It depends on the way you function.

Q: So here you are living in Washington and writing about your home country. Is the picture you have in your imagination more real than if you were actually there and looking at it?

A: Sometimes it worries me that my picture may not be the right one, that time has left me behind. I fear this because every time I go there, even though I read the papers all the time and I know what is going on, it's like going back seven years ago, to what the island was like when I left. You never see things the way they really are, but how you remember them. This worries me because I don't want to start writing about a Puerto Rico that doesn't exist anymore. But I think maybe this has to do with age. As you get older, you start to write about a certain time and a certain place, and the world that you're writing about gets smaller.

Q: This idea of multiple perspectives is central in your writing. I think of "Sleeping Beauty," where you put together letters, newspaper articles, photo album captions, etc. What made you choose that form in which to write the story of this woman who becomes mad?

A: At that time I was reading a lot of Manuel Puig's novels and I read one which I loved, *Boquitas pintadas* [Sudamericana, 1969], "Heart Break Tango" in translation. This is a short novel and is all made up of letters. So I read this and I said to myself, "Oh, I can do a version of this [she laughs].

I applied to myself the same lesson I gave to my students in my writing class. I took different stories from the ballets I knew, because I had danced parts in them as a student: *Giselle, Coppélia, Sleeping Beauty.* I combined this idea with Manuel Puig's idea of writing a novel out of letters, and the story came out.

Q: One of your most obviously political stories is "Captain Candelario's Heroic Last Stand." Is this a cautionary tale or a predictive tale?

A: I think it is probably both. Since it is supposed to happen in the year 2000, it is predictive. And it is a cautionary tale in the sense that I think it points out the dangers in our political situation, which are not solved. We are a divided country, and when this happens, there is a possibility that war may break out. Voting on whether to become a state or not is split down the middle: Half of the country wants to be a state and half wants to be independent, sort of like Cyprus. But the half that wants to be independent doesn't want to be totally independent: It still wants to be a part of the United States.

Q: What do you think will happen?

A: I think it's going to stay the way it is for a while.

Q: Candelario's problem seems to be an excess of idealism, in a way. He needs to see things and people for what and who they are.

A: I think that also has to do with Puerto Rico: The Puerto Rican ethos, or character, is precisely defined by its undefinition. We are always trying to define ourselves and never get there; but it is part of our definition that we keep looking. It's like Diogenes, who was always looking for truth with his lamp; and although he never found what he was looking for, the important thing was that he kept on looking.

Q: Is that situation inevitable, given Puerto Rico's history?

A: Unless we become strong enough economically and psychologically to be able to make a break, I think we will stay as we are. Unless the United States decides for us, which is another possibility. They could say, "Just make up your minds; we can't wait any longer." You are dealing with injustice in two different directions, because we have become used to a certain standard of living. For about a hundred years we have been a part of the United States; this is like being in paradise compared to how people live in most of Latin America. Therefore, not belonging to the United States, if things are brought to that point, is also going to be an injustice.

Q: What about the role of music in "Captain Candelario's Heroic Last Stand"? You talk about salsa as a political force. Is there really a relationship between music and politics in Puerto Rico?

A: I was in Europe recently, and I noticed how dominant the United States still is in terms of popular culture. Everyone wants to hear rock music, and American pop culture is all over the place. This happens in Puerto Rico, too, but the salsa is different because it has political connotations. It comes from the lumpen, the unemployed, people on the streets peddling drugs, who are really the worst; all of the salsa composers have been in jail for drugs. There is the idea that there is something lawless, there is something socially threatening coming out from these people's music.

They don't play salsa in the elegant nightclubs. They play mainly avant-garde rock.

Q: Ruben Blades is the closest to a crossover there is, isn't he?

A: Yes, he would probably be played in elegant nightclubs.

Q: So which are you? Are you also someone who listens to classical music, like Captain Candelario, or are you a *salsera*?

A: [She laughs.] I listen to both. I like salsa, but I have to be in a special mood. If I listen to it here [in the United States], I get too sad.

Q: How is your work seen in Puerto Rico today?

A: It's still controversial, I think. The truth is that our men writers get a lot more attention than our women writers. There are some very good female writers, like Magali Garcia Ramis, who has a beautiful novel, *Felices dias, Tio Sergio* [Editorial Antillana (Puerto Rico), 1986], translated as "Happy Days, Uncle Sergio." Her novel is as good as Luis Rafael Sánchez's *La guaracha del Macho Comacho* [Ediciones de la Flor (Buenos Aires), 1976], published in the United States as *Macho Comacho's Beat* [Pantheon, 1981], but it hasn't been admired as much.

Q: Why do you think that is?

A: There's still a fraternity of men. They admire themselves, and they admire each other's works. I think they are a little bit scared of women, too.

Q: Scared of women's power?

A: Yes. And their rage.

Q: I see that rage in your works, particularly in the stories where women are continually struggling to be heard, to be understood by those around them, other women and men. In "The Writer's Kitchen," your essay on your own creative processes, you said: "I write to build myself, word by word, to banish my terror of silence. I write as a speaking human mask." Would you talk about the "terror of silence" that you wanted to banish?

A: I am dealing with that issue of silence now, in a memoir which has to do with both my father's and my mother's family. My father's family was very male-oriented. Only the men were the important ones. When the family would be sitting at table, only the men would talk. There were four brothers and two sisters, my grandfather, and all the brothers' wives. My mother was one of them. My grandfather was a Mason; he believed that there had to be a fraternity amongst men, like Mozart says in *The Magic Flute*. He would say, jokingly, "Women talk when chicken go peepee," which means they never speak because chickens never go peepee [she laughs]. Women weren't supposed to have an opinion. If they did, they were never taken seriously. They were treated like children.

I have the idea that people who are very repressed tend to be inner-oriented; they talk to themselves more than other people. People who have difficulties making themselves heard have usually been brought up in stifling environments. Maybe that's why I felt as I did—because I was very timid. Maybe that's why my writing is so violent, in a way.

Q: What about the other part of that quote, when you talk about being a human mask? That phrase sort of mystifies me.

A: Right now I'm reading Mark Twain's *Autobiography*, which I like very much. There is a part where he talks about his love for Oliver Wendell Holmes's writing. Twain tells of how he was accused of plagiarism because once he took a quotation from Holmes and used it as his own. He says that plagiarism does not exist in literature, and I agree. Literature is made of many pieces, of a reinterpretation of similar themes, of a recycling of materials. Only the mask exists, and the writer wears it to interpret the manifold possibilities of humanity that exist around him. He learns to be a writer when he can take someone else's mask and make it a part of himself and talk from that mask.

Q: Is this why your stories are layered? You move from one character's mind to another's effortlessly.

A: I learned how to do that from Latin American writers like José Donoso, a Chilean writer I like very much.

Q: What about Virginia Woolf?

A: Well, I would like to have written *Orlando* [she laughs]. But I'm very far from that!

Q: In "The Writer's Kitchen," you talk about leaving Woolf and Simone de Beauvoir behind.

A: I believe they belong to another generation; they are in another stage. Women now have more of a sense of control, a little bit more. Not a lot, but a little bit more than they used to have at the time of Virginia Woolf. Women's lives were even more restricted then.

Q: You also say, "In a way, all writing is a translation, a struggle to interpret the meaning of life, and in a sense the translator can be said to be a shaman, a person dedicated to deciphering conflicting human texts, searching for the final unity of the meaning in speech." Could you talk a little bit about this idea of the writer as shaman?

A: If the writer is trying to interpret the meaning of life, all of what he writes is autobiographical. Think of Mark Twain, for example. You can tell from Twain's autobiography that Tom Sawyer and Huckleberry Finn are versions, or imagined stages, of Twain himself. He was writing about his own life, about how it was or could have been. And he's still trying to reinterpret his life or to translate it when he is writing his autobiography, only he is not doing it with a mask anymore, rather as a testimony. When you write fiction, you are wearing a mask, you are dealing with magic. The novelist is like the shaman; he reinterprets the life of the tribe in terms of his fictitious characters, in order to bring out the devils. And that's what literature does.

Q: So you're trying to interpret the tribe?

A: Correct, yes.

Q: So, in a way, all of your stories are about you?

A: Yes, and they are not about me. About everyone else. Let me read you this from the Twain book, where he talks about Oliver Wendell Holmes's response to the accusation of plagiarism. This is what I want to say [from *The Autobiography of Mark Twain,* the response of Holmes to a letter from Twain apologizing for his unconscious plagiarism of Holmes's ideas]:

Dr. Holmes laughed the kindest and healingest laugh over the whole matter and at considerable length and in happy phrase assured me that there was no crime in unconscious plagiarism; that I committed it every day, that he committed it every day, that every man alive on the earth who writes or speaks commits it every day and not merely once or twice but every time he opens his mouth; that all our phrasings are spiritualized shadows cast multitudinously from our readings; that no happy phrase of ours is ever quite original with us; there is nothing of our own in it except some change born of our temperament, character, environment, teachings, and associations; that this slight change differentiates it from another man's manner of saying it, stamps it with our own special style and makes it our own for the time being.

Q: If the role of the writer is to be a shaman, what is the role of the critic? What should critics be doing?

A: I had two reviews for *The Youngest Doll:* one in the *New York Times* [a positive one] and another one in the *Chicago Tribune* [a negative one]. The man who wrote the *Tribune* review thought the book was depressing because it was about women who had psychological problems. He criticized the stories for not having a logical construction; he said that they escaped into surrealistic poetic endings. And I wondered if he wrote that because he was trained in a literary convention which answers to books written by men.

What I think criticism should do is teach literature from different points of view. Stories may or may not have an ending; may or may not have a logical construction. This doesn't mean that they are bad. I believe women are more flexible in their criticism, and I'd like men to look at our books with the same openness that we look at theirs. That would be a great addition.

Q: What about the fact that you work in Spanish and English? You've said: "Only a writer who has experienced the historical fabric, the inventory of felt moral and cultural existence embedded in a given language can be said to be a bilingual writer." Do you write first in Spanish?

A: Yes, I never write in English. I translate my own work.

Q: Could you write in English or would it be too different?

A: It has to do with the way things come to mind; it has to do with dreams. I dream in Spanish and like to play with words. Many ideas for the things I write come from words themselves. If I am writing in English, I can't play this way. I'm not working with the language in an unconscious way.

Q: Your stories are very dream-like; they remind me of Kafka. You've written that the imagination and fantasy have freer reign in Puerto Rico than in the United States. Why is that?

A: I think, in part, because of the influence of black culture that I mentioned before. The world of magic is very real in Puerto Rico.

Religion there is very mixed with superstition and white magic, such as *Santería*. I don't think that's present in the United States, except maybe if you go further south [than Washington, D.C.]. I think some of the black writers in this country have been dealing with this.

Q: So if you said to someone in your family that you saw a ghost, no one would be surprised?

A: No. They would probably say, "Oh, I did too, a few weeks ago," or, "I dreamt such and such a thing, and then it happened." And they would start bringing all these stories out. It used to be more like that in the past, when people would get together and start talking about the supernatural things that happened to them. And always death was an important part of it—the premonition of death. I'm using part of that in my new book of memoirs. People have premonitions that they are going to die.

Q: How do you translate your writing? Do you have to reinvent things in another language?

A: I take four or five dictionaries and I pore over them. Once the meaning is there, it is easy to play with the sound. Sometimes for the sake of sound I change the meaning, but these are just nuances. The main thread of the story remains the same as it was originally written in Spanish.

Q: You mean you change details when you move from one language to another?

A: Yes, I change details.

Q: Are these changes just translations or are some of them a result of your seeing things differently? Some of the translations are done years after the original works.

A: Yes, it has to do with that. It has to do with changes of the mind perhaps, also with changes in feeling. Language has a lot to do with feeling, and you can't talk about certain things the same way, when you talk in a different language. Also, you're writing for a different audience. The traditions in literature are different. Here, a story has to have a beginning, a knot, and an end. Otherwise they think it's just a lot of hot air. Fleeting impressions are not important; they're not interesting. Everyone gets bored. In Spanish, we have a tradition of open-ended, poetic stories. It's a very popular genre. Bequer, Lorca, Dario all wrote in this way. There are lots of writers who never wrote stories that had the knot-and-ending style. And they are considered great writers; they give a lot of pleasure.

But here it is just not done. Edgar Allan Poe, whom I admire enormously, set a model for the American short story which is very tough to break. He is the one who established that the traditional short story has to be like this. When I translated the stories of "Pandora's Papers" [in *The Youngest Doll*], I tried to give more importance to action and to structure; not in all the stories, but in some. In Spanish, you can be more poetic and imprecise; things can be put more generally. It is more difficult to generalize in English; you have to be more precise.

Q: Has the fact that you have translated your work into English affected your writing in Spanish?

A: I don't know, maybe. I think I am a lot more precise now than I was before: In everything I am writing now, action is always very present. I guess it also has to do with the way your mind matures as a writer. I still think that you can write very well in the other tradition, but I get bored myself. That must mean that I am getting Americanized [she laughs].

Q: How do you choose your translators?

A: Diana Velez, a good friend of mine, is very good. She did a basic version of the translation of *The Youngest Doll,* which saved me some time, but then I took it and reworked it. When I worked with her I told her that I would only do so if I could do what I pleased with her version of the translation—that she couldn't have the final word. That was the only way I'd let her do it. I had that experience once with another translator, who started telling me, "Oh, you can't change this or that because it's in the original." I said, "It's your translation, but it's my story!"

Q: Only two collections of your work have been translated to date and some poems. Do you have plans to translate the rest of your work?

A: I wish I could. It's just that in translating you have to sacrifice the time that you would be using to write something new in Spanish. It's self-defeating, in a way. But then, when I see the translations they do, I get so upset that I say, "No, I don't want anything else translated. I want to do it myself." So I haven't tried to have anything else translated, especially the poetry.

Q: Are you still writing poetry?

A: Yes, I have a book of poems and short stories which is coming out in Mexico. It's called "The Two Venices" [*Las dos Venecias*], but it isn't going to be translated for a while.

Q: Let's talk about that memoir you mentioned. What is it about?

A: It's called *Eccentric Neighborhoods*. I got the idea one day when I went to visit my mother's tomb in the Cemetery of Old San Juan. This cemetery is next to the walls of the Old City, next to a very violent slum, where only drug addicts and criminals live, and also next to the sea. Why was she buried there, in such a strange place, that did not have anything to do with her? And I got to thinking of all the places she had lived in which had led her to lie there; and the idea of writing her life talking about them came to me. I wanted to combine threads so it was not just the story of her life, but also the story of those neighborhoods she had lived in—the type of thing Naguib Mahfouz does in his books about Cairo's neighborhoods, like *Miramar* [Heinemann (London), 1978]. It's a fictional memoir—I have done some research into what was happening at the time, but I've made up a lot of things, because the people I'm writing about are all dead. So I have been making up their lives, in a way.

Q: In writing a memoir, are you doing anything different from what you do in writing fiction?

A: No, it's pretty traditional. Mahfouz has helped me a lot for this particular book. He has this style that goes very quickly through generations, giving little cameo portraits of people and sort of bringing it all together in a very exciting way.

Q: Would you say something about "magical realism," the term so often used to describe the work of certain Latin American writers? Is it a useful term and does it describe your work?

A: All writers are unhappy with reality and so they want to build a world where things are open to change. They have created a different space where they would like to be. All writing is, in that sense, a meeting of reality but also an escaping of it.

In Latin American countries, magic is an everyday event; we hear people talk about how they were healed by the Virgin of the Well of Sabuna Grande, for example, a small town on the southern coast where the Virgin appears every Saturday. I believe being an underdeveloped nation has to do with this; people still have faith; they believe in "wonders." This is what is called magical realism, as opposed to the concept of the fantastic, which is an inner phenomenon. The fantastic, as Poe understood it, deals with the subconscious, with the nearness of madness. Our vision is altered, much like what the Surrealists believed, and we see things in a different way. But that doesn't mean they *exist* this way in the outside world. In magical realism miracles do happen, and our literature takes part in them.

According to journalist Vivian Gornick, there's no place like New York City. Sitting in her comfortable sixteenth-floor Greenwich Village apartment on an unusually balmy January afternoon in 1992, she explained the pivotal role the city has played in her life.

Gornick grew up in a working-class, Jewish, socialist family in the Bronx, a subway ride away from Manhattan. Like others from similar class and ethnic backgrounds, she was educated at City College of the City University of New York in the 1950s. After marriage and divorce, she came back to become a writer in New York, publishing in the Village Voice, where for a time she was a reporter, and free-lancing for publications such as the New York Times and Ms. Most important, she discovered feminism in New York in the late 1960s, an event which changed and shaped her life.

With "The Next Great Moment in History Is Theirs," an essay about the founders of the contemporary women's movement that appeared in the Village Voice in 1969, Gornick traced the movement's roots and examined its principles, but she also examined the meaning of her own life in feminist terms. This personal journalistic style must have fit because it became her trademark in essays she wrote throughout the seventies on topics including women and success and love-work conflicts. These essays, many of which are collected in Essays in Feminism (Harper and Row, 1978), demonstrate Gornick's broad frame of reference and willingness to take

Photo: Copyright © Thomas Victor

chances. She said what she thought, even if it put her at odds with the feminist establishment, as when she defended the rights of lesbians within the movement, an issue much debated at that time.

Gornick also edited and wrote books on a variety of themes, all somehow related to gender, class, or ethnic identity. With coeditor Barbara K. Moran, she collected twenty-nine essays from a who's who of the movement in the ground-breaking anthology Woman in Sexist Society: Studies in Power and Powerlessness *(Basic Books, 1971). Her own books took her across the United States and abroad to interview those whose lives embodied seeming contradictions. When a book editor suggested she go to the Middle East, she went to Egypt, a former lover's homeland, to try to understand the Egyptian character. For* In Search of Ali Mahmoud: An American Woman in Egypt *(Dutton, 1973), the book that resulted, she assembled the impressions and experiences that led her to find surprising temperamental parallels between Egyptian men and American women.*

Trying to understand more about her parents and those like them for whom Communism was the defining experience of their lives, Gornick researched and wrote The Romance of American Communism *(Basic Books, 1977). Traveling around the United States for a year interviewing former party members, she made their stories the raw material of the book. Her next book,* Women in Science: Portraits from a World in Transition *(Simon and Schuster, 1983), found her interviewing another outsider group— women scientists—and unearthing the same kind of passionate involvement her parents had felt with the party.*

Gornick turned from journalism to autobiography in Fierce Attachments: A Memoir *(Farrar, Straus, and Giroux, 1987), an examination of her complex relationship with her mother. An intimate, often painful story of two strong women locked in a kind of struggle-to-the-death, the memoir is amazingly honest: There's no tearful reconciliation scene, no catharsis. Mother and daughter never fully understand one another; the best they can achieve are temporary truces as they take walks around Manhattan talking about the past.*

In this interview Gornick talks about her mother and those walks, and about the twin passions of her life: writing and feminism. Blunt and outspoken, she's as controversial in person as in print. Why not? As she explains, "Seeing myself as an outsider has helped me call the shots as I see them." No wonder she loves New York, the subject of her next book. It's as bold and passionate as she is.

Q: How did you become a writer?

A: I wanted to write since I was a child, but I didn't do it. Part of my feminist education was to understand why I couldn't write. I think it was the woman in me rather than the Jewish girl or the working-class girl or the socialist daughter or any of those things that kept me from writing. I was always divided; I was always afraid of writing. I had a big mouth. Everything I said in *Fierce Attachments*. I was unable to resolve many conflicts which are psychologically difficult to identify. I just couldn't find my way, like many writers couldn't, for many different reasons.

But the important thing is it [writing] wouldn't let go of me, and I was finally forced to do it. That's how you know you're a writer.

Q: So it took you a long time to become a writer?

A: I came to it late. I really didn't start writing until I was thirty and I do believe it was that conflicted female in me that just did not allow it to surface and make its way into the world.

Q: How would all of this have been different if you were your brother?

A: If I were my brother I think that I would have been writing without conflict and steadily since the teenage years.

Q: You would have known this as an undergraduate at City College?

A: I think so. There were girls who did, of course, but I think that I suffered from these tremendous conflicts that I could not identify early. My mother had said to me, "You're a smart girl, make something of yourself, but always remember love is the most important thing in a woman's life." And that went into me like a knife, and it divided me against myself for life. I think that's as good a simple explanation for the development of my psyche, my life, as anything else. I think whatever my brother's psychological struggles, they never divided him from his work. And, as far as work is concerned, I was divided against myself from childhood on, and he absolutely cohered around it. It saved him from himself, and it did not save me. If it wasn't for feminism, I don't think I ever would have understood that.

Of course there were always women who were so powerfully strong-willed, so undivided that they could prevail, and they became the lady eccentrics of every previous generation.

Q: Those older scientists you write about in *Women in Science?*

A: Exactly, my scientists.

Q: And the teachers that we all had.

A: Yes, of course. The spinsters.

Q: I think a lot of us didn't want to become those women.

A: I think so, too.

Q: So how did you finally start writing?

A: This is exactly how I started: It was the late sixties when I was about twenty-eight years old. LeRoi Jones was about to name himself Amiri Baraka, and the black militant movement was about to declare itself. And, in contradistinction to the shared white-black civil rights movement, they were about to say, "Okay, you motherfuckers, get out." And they did say it one night here [in New York] at the Village Vanguard at a Monday night speak-out. They had these regularly at the time. And at one of them LeRoi Jones, [musician] Archie Shepp, Larry Rubin, who was white and a painter, and I forget the fourth—three black guys and one white—got up to talk about art and politics and essentially lashed out at the audience, saying, "You white ofay, blood is going to run in the streets of the theater of revolution and guess who's sitting in those seats?"

Well, the whole place went up in flames. It was filled with white middle-class liberals who were all big in civil rights and they were in great distress. It was a time when the three boys in Mississippi were killed [civil rights workers James E. Chaney, Andrew Goodman, Michael H. Schwerner], so I was terrified like everybody else. But I thought he was wrong. He kept saying, "When we get there we're going to do it different than you guys." And I thought, "You can't get there without becoming us." So I thought he was making a crucial mistake in class and race. He did not understand, and I wanted him to understand, but I was afraid of him.

I went home and I sat down to explain to Mr. Jones why he was wrong. It seemed natural to me to first recapitulate the entire evening and then to write an impassioned interpretation of the event. So I had stumbled on a style which became my style and which was known as personal journalism. Of course everyone who was writing or trying to write was infected with this style in those days.

Q: Did it get published?

A: I sent it over the transom to the *Village Voice,* and they published it. The editor, Dan Wolf, called me up and said, "Who the hell are you?" And I said, "I don't know, nobody. You tell me." Anyway, he asked me then to write for them, and I couldn't do it. So I got out one piece a year for the next five years. Which is still not so different from my style [she laughs].

Q: Why couldn't you do it? Here was this editor wanting to publish your work.

A: Right, and I was still fighting my own demons. I couldn't discipline myself to the task. Meanwhile, I was doing other things—I got married a second time; I was trying to teach; I was trying to be in love; I was trying aimlessly to put together a life but drifting in some deep way. So I left New York, left teaching, and went away to New Mexico with my husband, thinking that marriage would cure me. But I was moving close to the climax of this unformed life. And the marriage was doomed. These were years that I would describe as a huge piece of inchoate life, in which a young woman who was terrifically split was dovetailing with a time which luckily was going to resolve her.

Q: You found feminism?

A: If it had not been for feminism I do not know how my life would have taken shape, although I think I would have struggled toward writing anyway. At any rate, in New Mexico my husband was working as a psychologist, and I was going to write. And I vegetated, and I didn't do anything. A year passed, another year, and then we separated, and then I went to California.

Q: Is this when you went to Berkeley?

A: Yes, that was when everything sort of exploded at once, and I realized that I wanted to write more than anything. I didn't know how to make myself do it, so I decided to come back to New York and try to get a job in journalism. I had been trying to write the great American novel with no success. Reality was at a premium. I was going to get a job as a writer.

Q: What happened in New York?

A: I'd been sending the *Voice* one piece every year when I was gone, so I went to to Dan Wolf, the same editor, and I said, "Give me a job." And he said, "You're a neurotic Jewish girl who can only produce one piece a year. How can I give you a job?" And I said, "Not now. Anything you ask me to do I will do." So he said, "Free-lance for a while, and we'll see how it works out." So here I was, a Jewish working-class girl who had to have a job. And I had to make this decision whether or not I was going to take this chance on a writer's life or ditch the whole thing and go look for a job and write at night. And I decided to take that chance.

Q: How did you support yourself?

A: Luckily, before I got married I had lived in a tenement apartment on First Avenue where the rent was something like sixty-seven dollars a month, and for some damn reason I did that thing that New Yorkers always laugh about: I kept the apartment. So, when I came back to New York, I still had that apartment, and that allowed me to work for nothing for years. When I finally got a job at the *Village Voice,* I was bringing home $117 a week. But, twenty-five years ago, you didn't really didn't need that much. I was thirty years old then. I think I made six or eight thousand dollars a year. You could live marginally in a way that I think is very difficult now.

Q: What was your first assignment?

A: Jack Kerouac's funeral in 1969. That was a funny story. I didn't know what to do. When I got to Lowell, Massachusetts, and found my way to the funeral parlor, there was this big, burly guy there that I spotted right away as a cops-and-robbers reporter. Turns out, he was from the *Boston Globe.* After I walked up and introduced myself and told him that I had never done this before, he said to me, "Kid, you know the writers?" I said, "I do." He said, "You show me the writers, I'll show you how to do this." So it was hilarious: We were partners at this funeral. I pointed all the writers out to him, and he told me how to get to the cemetery. So I did it, and I came back. And, again, I found my way into my style. I reread all of Jack Kerouac, then I sat down and wrote a long piece in which I first placed Kerouac in American literature and then described the funeral. After I did two more like that, he [Wolf] gave me a job.

Q: Shortly after this you wrote "The Next Great Moment in History Is Theirs," about the feminist movement in New York at the time. How did that come about?

A: At the time I got this job, American feminism burst on the scene. Of course it had been building. But the *Voice* sent me down to Bleecker Street, saying "Why don't you go do a story on these liberationist chicks?" They, of course, thought I would do this tongue-in-cheek, clever *Village Voice* put-down. And in one week I met Betty Friedan, Ti-Grace Atkinson, Susan Brownmiller, Nanette Rainone, Myrna Lamb, Shulamith Firestone, Anne Koedt, Ann Snitow, Alix Shulman, and Phyllis Chesler. And in forty seconds I was a feminist. I just heard three sentences, and I got the whole thing, and I got it whole. And then I wrote that piece that did become important. It was that first piece in my life that laid the whole thing out.

Q: Let's talk about *Fierce Attachments,* your memoir. You were thirteen when your father died. How did that affect you?

A: His death so completely unhinged and destabilized my mother that I experienced his absence more through the trauma of her inability to remain a stable human being. It was a common trauma for us. We became women without men.

Also, my father's death turned us into pariahs. The Jewish working class we lived among was crude in a thousand ways. They were urban peasants. There were so many people in our tenement who became frightened of us because we had the stigma of death upon us . . . we'd be avoided. It was a superstition that they could catch death. This wasn't uniformly true, but there was enough of it so that I felt one of those first senses of stigma.

Q: Your book describes a great deal of tension when you went away to college. Was that because you were living the life your mother wished she had lived?

A: I think it's always that, isn't it? But I think it was more. There are essentially two responses of mothers to their daughters who are going to go out in the world. One is very passive and superficially loving: "Darling, I didn't do it; you go do it." They don't really mean it. The others are openly belligerent like my mother: "I didn't get out, and I'll be fucked if you're going to get out." And the way it comes out is: "This is wrong; this is right. These girls are good girls; these are whores."

Q: But your attachment to her was so intense.

A: We identified fiercely with each other, she and I. That's the source of the tension. There are girls and their mothers who don't really have much to do with each other emotionally. My mother and I were locked into a life-and-death struggle for the good of our mutual souls. It got bitter when she saw that I was going to live a life really at variance from hers, but the antagonism preceded that.

Q: What were the sources of the anger between you?

A: I think my mother was hungry for the world, didn't know it, and the ignorance thereof was treacherous. I, in turn, was volatile, explosive, and enraged from the time I can remember, because I wanted something from her I didn't get. I think if I'd been the good girl of her dreams and become a schoolteacher, married the boy next door, and moved in next door, she still would have been raging at me all her life. I was her and she was me; therefore, I wasn't owed civil rights.

That kind of intimacy is the first example of what is most hateful to me in intimate relations. I hate the incivility between husbands and wives, between lovers, between parents and children. Feminism is responsible for making me think harder and longer about that than anything else.

Q: What do you mean by incivility?

A: It's an incredible presumption of right, of the imposition of will on another human being. People feel that in intimacy they have the right to impose their will on another. Kate Chopin is a writer who has really understood this presumption in marriage. It's not that she's a feminist; it's just that, as a woman, she has quicker access to this penetrating piece of truth. It can be a man doing it to a woman or a woman doing it to a man, but it's at the heart of so much of marriage.

Q: Is that inevitable in marriage?

A: No, I don't think it's inevitable with self-consciousness. A lot of people do it a lot better now. But the old idea "that two shall be as one" was awful. The isolation of sexism by feminists led them to that piece of understanding—that what we're talking about here is the imposition of will; usually it is a woman's will that is being subordinated to a man's.

Q: *Fierce Attachments* has these wonderfully strong women who were your mother's friends. You say, "They never spoke as though they knew who they were or they understood the bargain they had struck with life. But they often acted as if they knew." What is this "bargain"?

A: They acted as if they knew that marriage had enslaved them. They knew, with every natural sense of muffled instinct and emotions, that they were not free inside their lives. That they did not have freedom of will, freedom of consciousness. Now, of course, no working-class people are free, women or men. And these were immigrants. But at the bottom of the bottom were women. The men, who were not free in any sphere of their lives, nevertheless could act like little dictators in their homes.

So the women knew that they had contracted to be servants, that they had contracted in a power brokerage—these are contemporary terms, but they work. That famous passion and volatility on the part of working-class women, especially, is due to that acting out of what they couldn't articulate. Every time a group of women sat around the kitchen table talking about "him," they were acting as if they knew who they were, without saying it. They would speak of their husbands as if they were strangers and antagonists. That's what I meant when I said, "They didn't know, but they knew."

Q: And the source of power of your mother's friend Nettie was her sexuality?

A: Yes, but it was a false view of power. She didn't have any power at all. She had the illusion, as any woman does who gives her body. Any woman who contracts through sex to gain a place in the world knows the bitter truth that it doesn't work.

Q: As I read your book, I felt so sorry for these women who were so trapped by the choices they had made.

A: Listen, it was 1940, but it might as well have been 1880.

Q: How did you decide to organize *Fierce Attachments* around these walks you took with your mother?

A: That was the luckiest accident of my life. I started to tell the story chronologically in the past about me, Mama, and Nettie. And I don't know how much I wrote—not much—and I saw that I had a lot of unfinished business with my mother and that this would not tell the whole story. I wasn't even sure I knew what the story was. I just knew that that was not it.

Then I fell into a kind of depression, and I didn't write for quite a while. And one day, something had happened with my mother and I wanted to describe it. So I found myself going back far enough in my mind, to the mythical, nonexistent reader who wouldn't understand unless I explained, "Look, my mother and I always walk and this happened on a walk." And I described what happened. I also had to explain that my mother and I are at our best when she's telling stories from the past, that her story never varied, but my questions always varied. It happened just like that. I suddenly realized that I had stumbled on exactly what this book was really all about—which was that I was going to keep asking the question until I got the right answer.

Q: So your mother gives you a little more information each time?

A: Yes, if I ask for it.

Q: Why does she tell stories?

A: It makes her feel good. She has a natural storyteller's enjoyment of making sense of things. She enjoys the function in narrative of telling a story in order to understand what happened or to make it up so that it has shape.

Q: Did you grow up with people telling stories in your house?

A: They were all great talkers. But no, she wasn't a self-conscious storyteller. They all had the ability to know that a story has to arrive at a point. They would set out and detail for us a circumstance and people in the circumstance in order to make a point.

Q: Would the adults tell stories to teach you children something?

A: When we were kids, children were not central. Children were being educated only peripherally in our homes. I was not important to my mother's household. My mother never set out deliberately to civilize me, socialize me, never.

Q: Do you think it was unique to your particular situation?

A: It wasn't just my case, no. These people were harried, working-class immigrants. It was the times.

Q: The role of work is interesting in the book, too. Your mother was obviously getting such pleasure out of being an activist, being involved. And then your father said, "Don't work," and she quit.

A: That's it.

Q: Did she ever say after that, "I wish I hadn't"?

A: Always. She always knew. She couldn't imagine that far. She only knew that she had a hunger for involvement and that she felt very bad that she had to quit. But the idea that she had to was immutable. Papa wanted it, and what made Papa happy made her happy in her view. It was also inconceivable for her to defy the wishes of her husband. That is what is hard to understand for people who don't understand what feminism has done. Feminism made conceivable the inconceivable.

Q: The women writers who I've talked to from working-class backgrounds, people like Valerie Miner and Pat Barker, talk about feeling a sense of responsibility to their people. Valerie talked about wanting to "get it right" and not have working-class people seen as stereotypes. Did you have any of that kind of feeling at all?

A: I feel that in relation to women, not class. I did as a kid, but I don't anymore. That's not really my politics. Valerie Miner has a view of class as the most powerful piece of identity; I don't. I'm sure I would have twenty years ago. But the Jewish immigrant working class has been done to death. My experience is psychological in its cast; it's no longer social.

Q: How come?

A: I remember reading [Philip Roth's] *Portnoy's Complaint* when it was published [Random House, 1969] and thinking, You fucker, you don't know those women. You're making cartoons out of them. I know those women. I know all that passion and energy and articulateness trapped inside these cartoon-like figures. And I realized that was my subject.

Q: Jewish women?

A: The reality of those lives. I felt it was important to get the idiom right—the way they were, which carried within that, implicitly, class. They're Jewish, they're working class, but that's not my subject. That was Kate Simon's subject in *Bronx Primitive* [Viking, 1982]. She was twenty years older than me, and it was proper that her sense of life in that same piece of world was so overpoweringly social in its construct. She did a piece of social history very elegantly. The language is very elegant, but she's talking about the crude power of being those immigrant people. Maybe if you're Spanish you can do class, but it's too late in the game for an evocation of working-class life as such.

Q: Did your mother like this book?

A: My mother—she's eighty-nine—is so involved in the celebrity of this book she thinks she wrote it. She walks around signing it. When she's feeling good she says to me, "You enlarged my life." When she's feeling bad she says, "You held me up to criticism." The book is the book, the woman is still the woman [she laughs].

Q: New York is so visual in the book, and the conversations are so lively. Have you ever thought about basing a screenplay on it?

A: A friend of mine who was a theater director came to me about a year ago and said, "Why don't we try and write a screenplay and make a small, good, New York movie out of this book?" Well, for a year I've been trying to do it with no success at all because I don't know how to write a screenplay. The idea that those walks are the story is not true. What I discovered in extracting it from its narrative context is that that narrative voice is a character. And it's out of the character of that narration that everything takes its life and its meaning. The women, the conversations between the daughter and the mother, everything. I have to find an equivalent for the screen, and I don't know how to do it.

Q: *Woman in Sexist Society,* which you coedited with Barbara K. Moran, has become a feminist classic. What was it like writing it?

A: It was like we were archaeologists in the Pleistocene age. Everything was original discovery. Everything was as if it had never been thought before, even though we immediately went back and traced our history and realized that modern feminism was two hundred years old and began with Mary Wollstonecraft and *A Vindication of the Rights of Woman* [1792]. There was this explosion—Wollstonecraft comes out of the Enlightenment; she writes this great book; there are others like her. It puts the idea on the map in modern terms, and then it dies away. Fifty years later you've got abolition and the American feminists. Fifty years after that you've got ERA, suffrage, and then fifty years later you've got us again. And each time we come up out of the cave all over again, as if it never happened before. We were the reincarnation of the New Woman. The Platonic model. We come out blind and deaf and dumb and saying all these primitive things. *Woman in Sexist Society* was written out of the energy and amazement of original discovery.

Q: That must have been an incredible time to be in New York and writing. *Sisterhood Is Powerful* [ed. Robin Morgan, Random House] came out in 1970, too.

A: And Shulamith Firestone had just written *The Dialectic of Sex* [Morrow, 1970]. It was all happening at once. It gave people of my generation an identity that is strong, excited, exuberant. It will last me a lifetime; I will always be that woman who will take strong refuge in this feminist identity.

Q: So what's different now?

A: What you have now, twenty years later, is the long, hard, grueling work of making that really part of the changed fabric of social life. That insight is something like the insight in analysis. How many times do you have the same insight in analysis? And you have it because the job of that insight is to change the compulsions of behavior. That happens over a long, grueling, hard time.

Q: What would a second edition of *Woman in Sexist Society* look like?

A: I was actually asked to do this, but I wasn't interested. Now what you have is an immense proliferation of testament from every quarter—sociologists and economists and historians—and journalism by the mile constantly telling you what everything means. It's an incredible industry, where there was nothing before. So what you would have would be this charting of slow internal change.

If I were putting together *Woman in Sexist Society* today, I would have a piece on what it's really like to be married today. What actually happens in a contemporary marriage? Who does what? What are the new ideas? To what degree is a woman's life as real as that of a man's life in a marriage? And I guess from every discipline we would have a new piece of testament. And what you would end up with is a volume with more thoughtfulness and a thousand times more uncertainty than we had. We were certain. And you would have a picture, not of assertion, but of people struggling in a live way with issues that have been made palpable by that volume and everything that it represents. What we put into the world is the idea that what happens between men and women is a serious matter. And how one negotiates that territory bristles with questions now.

Q: I admire the piece you published in 1971 about lesbians in the women's movement ["Lesbians and Women's Liberation: In Any Terms She Shall Choose," reprinted in *Essays in Feminism*]. You criticized those who objected to an open acceptance of lesbianism in the feminist movement because they were nervous about the movement's image.

A: I was afraid to write that piece. I think if I had not been a child of the Communists I wouldn't have written it.

Q: Why did you write it?

A: It was one of those many moments, and I wrote every single time it happened, in which I felt that we were doing ourselves in. I feared that independence of mind would be forfeited to a political expediency, and fear of the mob that would make us sacrifice each other. That's really what the piece is all about. It's not about lesbians, as such. It's about the fact that we were very quickly becoming politically correct and incorrect, saying, "This is a feminist, this is not. And, essentially, we're all hetero-sexual women here, and this [movement] is only about equal pay for equal rights. And is this going to play in Peoria? And, if not, we're not getting behind it." And I knew that that was wrong. So it wasn't at all that I was particularly interested in protecting the rights of lesbians within the movement, and certainly I never thought of lesbians taking over anything.

Q: What were you afraid of?

A: I wasn't afraid of being called "unnatural" and/or a "man hater," which, of course, we were called. This was immediately not a thing to be taken seriously. I was afraid of Betty Friedan when I wrote that piece. I was afraid of being censured by my own comrades. I was afraid of losing the affection of my comrades.

Q: In *The Romance of American Communism* you make a connection between the role of feminism in your life and Communism in the lives of all these people whom you interviewed. What surprises did you get interviewing these one hundred former Communists in 1974?

A: One thing that came as a terrific shock was how subjugated women who had been Communists were. Another thing was that I discovered that they were not extraordinarily intelligent—I used to think they were—but that they had these great, strong feelings. This was the whole population of my childhood. I discovered that the Communists were people who had an immense amount of emotional energy to live life in a serious way.

Q: So that connected with feminism?

A: I felt that way, of course, as a feminist. I realized that I was a person, too, who had the ardor for political passion.

Q: I was surprised when you said in the book, "Almost none of the ex-Communists were now political activists of any kind."

A: Right. Because they couldn't make themselves liberals. Having conceived of the world in such ardent, radical terms, they were not capable of converting that political excitement and meaning into liberal causes. It was through radical politics that they felt themselves extraordinarily expressive. They couldn't come down from that particular high. I associate to that because for me feminism is a tremendous high. I wasn't political for years before it, and I doubt very much if Latin America could become my cause if I had to lose feminism. Or ecology, or cerebral palsy, or some good cause.

Q: So you think that for these people Communism was a kind of self-actualization?

A: Absolutely. . . . It was a piece of politics in which they felt themselves living at a level of intense expressiveness. And that, it was my contention, was what they craved. I felt the same thing with the scientists; I feel the same thing with myself. It's why we are attached to what we're attached to—because we feel ourselves alive in it, and anything else is really platitudinous.

Q: *Women in Science* must have been interesting to write.

A: It was interesting to research. I loved meeting those scientists and living with them for a year. When it came to writing it I felt like I had said all of this already, and I really didn't have that much of a contribution to make. It really felt like freshman feminism all over again. But it was reissued recently, and I reread it, and I thought a lot of what I saw was true and is still true. I'm glad I wrote it.

Q: This book appeared ten years ago. In regard to the issue of whether women do science differently from men, you wrote: "One day there may develop a practice of law and medicine, some of whose traits may be traced to the influence of vast numbers of women, but today isn't the day."

A: Right. No, today isn't either. This book was republished because ten years later there is so little change. The contention of backlash, which I don't follow in a specific and pointed and concrete way, is everywhere. There has not been a steady progress toward the eradication of discrimination. So that's true in science, too. The book was republished because now we know there's discrimination. I was interviewed over the telephone by people from all over the country who hadn't known the book the first time around. Now they did know about it, and now they said it was new news.

I just got this book, *A World without Women: The Christian Clerical Culture of Western Science* [by David F. Noble, (Knopf, 1992)]. It's the story of the same piece of history: the systematic exclusion of women from Western science. Why are they publishing it now? It's certainly because there has hardly been significant progress. There's been immense change among *us* [feminists]. We have put into the world a piece of consciousness and that consciousness will last us our lifetime. We [feminists] are a vast, motley, unshapely group who are temperamentally joined at every age by this piece of consciousness that now exists. But we're ricocheting and reeling around in a world that will change very slowly. Institutional change is the last thing to go.

Q: It surprised me that most of the women did not become politicized as a result of the blatant sexism they encountered. Why do you think they didn't?

A: Most of the women in science did not call themselves feminists and had no conscious affiliation with feminism because it's one of the most conservative, male-identified of all of the enterprises. Yet, at the same time, there wasn't a woman I interviewed in 1980 of any age, from twenty to eighty, who did not acknowledge the changes that the women's movement had wrought in her own profession. They knew that we had raised the issues of power politics within the profession, issues that never would have been raised by the profession itself. But you don't get ahead by being a maverick in science. You get ahead by identifying with the aggressor, as they say. That was true in 1980, and I'm sure it's still true, although I think there are probably many more feminist women in science today.

Q: Among many women I know, political consciousness came when something made them recognize political realities, like not getting tenure or an appointment that was due them. You write about how politics diverts women away from being primary researchers into being research associates, for example.

A: I think that's still true, but it's nowhere near what it was. There's one woman who said to me, "I'd rather be a professor at East Jesus Tech than a research associate at Harvard." And until that happens in great numbers, there will be no brilliant women in science.

Q: Yet, as you point out, they all love science so.

A: They're artists and revolutionaries, and that was a great surprise. I wrote that, too. I thought I would find a lot of victims, but I found women who made me see what women had done: that they had hung on by their fingernails for one hundred years just to do science. Even though they were victimized, they didn't act victimized. It was beautiful to see that passion.

Q: How common is this impressionistic journalism that you do? Would you call this a woman's approach to journalism?

A: No, it's an old-style journalism. Probably more women do practice it; I don't know. Maybe it's more congenial to women.

Q: It's an approach that's less interested in objectivity and empirically verifiable truth, and more interested in impressions and people's stories.

A: It's a very chancy thing to do, and you can do it either better or worse. I think that I did it very well in the book on Egypt and I did it much less well in the book on science.

Q: Why do you call it "chancy"?

A: Because you are always accused of not having enough facts, of not having done enough research, and of not being definitive in any way. And that's an absolutely legitimate charge. I have seen myself practice this with more and less skill and discipline in different pieces of work.

Q: Why do you think the approach succeeded in *In Search of Ali Mahmoud*?

A: I was much more invested in the entire enterprise because I was a character in it. I was much more invested in getting to the bottom of things, trying to figure out what was happening better, and trying to be more inclusive in my descriptions. I took a wider canvas, a deeper bite. It was one of the books that taught me the direction that I had to go in, which *Fierce Attachments* is the logical conclusion of. Now I understand that when I write I'm really writing memoir or nonfiction of a certain kind, in which I seek to tell a story out of my own experience that will be as whole as a novel is. *In Search of Ali Mahmoud* was confused. It was half nonfiction writing of this kind and half journalism. *Women in Science* was all journalism, and it wasn't a thing that I felt I could really do well. I wasn't invested in it anymore.

Q: As I was reading *In Search of Ali Mahmoud*, I was struck by the fact that the affair you have when you are in Egypt becomes part of the fabric of the book. That's when the focus for me became your personal story instead of a reporter's assignment. Did you know that you were strad-dling two sorts of styles when you were writing the book?

A: No, I didn't. It's one of the reasons the book is so overwrought. I reread that book recently for the first time since I had written it, and I was shocked at all the purple prose. I saw how out of control I was. No, I didn't know what I was doing. I certainly wouldn't write it like that today, but I was deeply disturbed, and I just let all the disturbance hang out all over the page, as if that were real writing. One of the failings of that book—which is a subject of mine now—was the absence of control and proper distance. I learned these things by the time I wrote *Fierce Attachments*.

But I think the book has wonderful things in it, and I still stand by it. It's got really some of the best descriptions of contemporary Egypt written by anybody [she laughs]. There are people who go to Egypt who use that book as the only guide that they have.

Q: Do you still share the conclusion you reached that Egyptian men are so much like American women?

A: The one thing feminism really made you see is the political and social meaning of this deep psychological and emotional disenfranchisement and the way women in this country have struggled up from under this immense unconsciousness. In a country like Egypt, the women are utterly out of the picture. So the men are the ones making that struggle for consciousness out of a humiliated and wounded state of social non-being. They feel and act like immigrants in their own country. When I saw this I thought, My God, these guys are so nervous and high strung. They're just like us [women]. It was a remarkable moment, that recognition.

Q: It seems that they're in this state also of perpetual adolescence.

A: Adolescent is exactly the word, just as we were.

Q: They're overwhelmed with emotions which American men are trained to suppress.

A: Right, exactly.

Q: If you were writing that book now, how would it be different?

A: It's hard to say. I went to Israel in 1977, six years after I'd been in Egypt, and I thought that I was going to write a book about Israel without the politics, the same kind of book. But I saw that I didn't have any real sympathy anymore. I came back with one hundred pages of notes, and every single story I had was negative. And I knew enough as a writer already to know I was not going to write out of that spirit. Without an affectionate heart never write, never. I learned that pretty fast.

Q: So the difference wasn't just that Israel was a different kind of country?

A: No. I'll give you a better example of this difficulty [of lacking sympathy for a subject]. I've been teaching in different universities, one semester a year, for seven years. And I came to feel this was a piece of experience that was collecting in me that I could write about. I dislike university life very much, and I felt I suffered at its hands in ways that were very illuminating. I felt like little murders of the soul were being committed all the time and that I had become part of it. So [because I am such an outsider there] being in a university is like being a traveler to another country. I feel there's something there I have to write about because there's something important to discuss about the human condition, but I have not yet found a way because it's all negative.

Q: Why do you dislike academia so much?

A: It's been stultifying. Why? Because when I go away to teach in these university towns, the whole world becomes the department. And the life of the department, I finally came to understand, was like the life of the family [she laughs].

Q: We're back to *Fierce Attachments* again.

A: That was a better family. More interesting, anyway. What I feel in the university is a whole lot of people are locked up together for life in a very static situation. Two things: stasis and homogeneity. Everybody's like everybody else; and the terrible stasis of it makes people get involved with each other in very deleterious ways. I reached a point where I used to brood about not being invited to dinner by people I didn't like [she laughs].

This startled me into seeing what it is about New York City that I love so much. Essentially, it's the fluid nature of exchange. It's the extraordinary openness. The other side of which is marginality, obscurity, uncertainty, conflict, and danger.

Q: Is it the universities or small towns that depress you?

A: It's institutional life, small town life. It was like a kibbutz in Israel. It's that small, tight society. The thing that is different at the university, that is painful, is it's all in the name of highmindedness. There are lots and lots of intelligent, marvelous people at the university doing interesting and incomparable work, like everywhere else, but for the most part the life is not characterized by devotion to the life of the mind. I found that most academics have the souls of insurance agents.

Q: Yet you've said that your years at City College changed your life because you were exposed to the life of mind. . . .

A: Well, I was a kid and it was an urban university. It was a working-class school absolutely teeming with excitement—I guess, in a way, City

College was at one remove from the Zionism of immigrant excitement. But my experience is only one experience. In the Ivy League you could have a different experience.

Q: How are the places you talk about different?

A: I teach in writing programs that are mostly housed in large, state universities where the life is very prototypic; it's not special. At City College we were the last generation of what was called the proletarian Harvard. We were kids who were on fire with the discovery of our own lives. It isn't that it doesn't happen anymore; it's just that the idea of pursuing the life of the mind is, at the present moment, a tired one in American education. What you're involved in now is an immense socialization project in which intellectual excellence is really at a very great low, both as a value and as a practice. More important, there's no shared value. I don't have to tell you what grim business teaching is.

And these writing programs are a total scam. They are good for us [instructors] because they give us patronage. It's just like the courts of the sixteenth century. They give writers a living, but I am in there teaching a mass of people of absolutely mediocre mind and spirit, sensibility, talent, everything. Most of them are there to kill time, no matter what they say and no matter what they think.

Q: I take it you don't like teaching.

A: I hate teaching because they [the students] don't give me anything. When I sit and I struggle with writing it can be a bitch, and it is difficult and it is depressing, but at the end of it I have something. I have more of myself. When I began to teach, people said to me, "You'll be a natural; you're such a great talker." But I got in there and I found myself paralyzed by anxiety brought on by all these recalcitrant people whose attention I had to win. It was a nightmare. I would say repeatedly, "Well, we just read this, what do you think of that?" And then they would tell me, and they would destroy my mind. They'd give me an answer, and I was lost.

Then, somewhere in the third year I think, I was in Colorado at Boulder, I literally stopped on a dime, in the middle of a sentence. I suddenly realized, I'm not going to have a conversation anymore; I'm going to tell them. And I just turned myself in that instant into a teacher who delivered herself of her wisdom and her experience. I made myself into a old-fashioned teacher who gets up there and lectures. I work very hard in the classroom, very hard. I talk nonstop for two hours, giving everything that I can. And then I walk out, and I'm wiped out, and I recover.

Q: Isn't it hard to teach and write at the same time?

A: It's hard to write while I'm teaching, but, you know, I'm really free the minute I walk out of that room. I just have to recover from the exhaustion. I teach on a Tuesday–Thursday schedule, so I have four full days in which to forget about teaching and write and three days in which I'm in the grip of the teaching.

Q: So teaching is a way for you to make money?

A: For me now, yes. I worked as a journalist for many years, and then it became intolerable. After *Women in Science,* actually, I thought, "I do not want to be a stranger in other people's lives anymore as a writer. If I have to be a stranger, let it be as a teacher." That's when I began to write *Fierce Attachments.* It was difficult to earn a living as a journalist and try to write in another way, consulting inner experience. I wanted to make literature. It's not impossible: Many great writers have done it. But I had this other way out and I chose it. So yes, for a writer it's either journalism or teaching. I'm grateful for the writing programs being there and giving me a living, but it doesn't make me appreciate the condition.

Q: What is your writing process?

A: I get up every single morning at 8:00. I struggle out of bed by 8:30, and by 9:00 I'm at that desk. If I didn't do that I'd be dead. I'm always at it all morning. Now, many of those mornings I may be overwhelmed, as I often am, with mist, fog, cotton wool, depression, or anxiety, and I won't get anything done. But I stay there. As long as you're there, something is happening, whether you're conscious of it or not. Sooner or later, something breaks. I have terrible, terrible trouble working. It remains a demon that I can't conquer. I still consider myself in thrall to a lot of neurotic conflict about writing. And the only thing I can say for myself is that I wanted it more than anything in the world. When I work I feel more alive than under any other circumstances. There's not an "I love you" in the world that can match it. I feel safe, excited, at peace, erotic, centered. Nothing can touch me.

Q: Do you have people reading your manuscripts as you go along?

A: That changes as the years go on. When I wrote *Fierce Attachments,* that was the first time that I had a really steady editorial relationship. I worked with a wonderful editor, Jonathan Galassi of Farrar, Straus, who I indeed hope will be my editor for years to come. I was showing him stuff as I went along.

The one thing that I have stopped doing is just giving it to the wrong reader—friends, family, all this bullshit. Even when they are friends who are literate, the right reader is often not among them. The right reader is as important as lover, editor, anything. At a certain point in the manuscript you need criticism that is also a certain kind of encouragement. But you need intelligence. You're not a fool.

Q: I was struck in reading your reviews by how independent-minded you are. Every time you write something, in the *New York Times,* for example, there are all these letters saying, "She doesn't know what she's talking about," or, "She should read this other book."

A: Seeing myself as an outsider has helped me call the shots as I see them more than wanting in. Also, when you speak as I do, you inevitably discover that there are so many people who are thinking exactly the same thing and people are being frightened for nothing. The punishments are so petty. I discovered that if I speak my mind I always have enough people to befriend that position. I may become a pariah in certain circles, but there are all the other circles. And the proof is that there's always somebody to publish it. So I don't think of myself as courageous—but I think my only strength is calling the shots as I see it.

Q: What are you working on now?

A: I'm struggling to write a book about myself and New York City that grew out of my university experience. I began to realize that it was my love of New York City that was really a subject for me. So I'm struggling to make that cohere.

Q: Is this going to look like *Fierce Attachments?*

A: In a certain sense. It's in sections; it alternates. It's about loneliness and friendship and the streets of New York. The woman who walks the streets is not the woman who narrated *Fierce Attachments.* She's closer to the woman you're interviewing today. It's this writer in her fifties who's a feminist and who lives alone and has opted for friendship rather than marriage. And she's walking the streets, tramping the streets of a great city, feeling marginal [she laughs].

Q: But, in a way, you have to feel marginal in New York.

A: Why do you say that?

Q: Because in New York there's such diversity that there's no one central identity; everyone is marginal.

A: That's a good point. Yes, I think that is the great thing about urban life, and it's been like that for a couple of hundred years. Dr. Johnson walked the streets of London in 1740 feeling the same way. And purging himself of daily depression in the same way [she laughs].

*"What a way to meet someone," Jamaica Kincaid said, as she greeted me
in her home in North Bennington, Vermont, in April 1990. Wrapped in a
terry cloth robe, her hair still wet from the shower, she was headed upstairs to dress but stopped in the living room where I was talking with her
husband, composer and Bennington College professor Allen Shawn.
"Don't sit on the children's toys, now. They've got them all over the
place."*

*Her lack of pretense made me feel comfortable right away. It's obvious
in her surroundings—there's no formal dining room and the kitchen,
covered with daughter Annie's drawings, looks like the most lived-in part
of the house. It's obvious, too, in the effect she has on people—the owners
of the Japanese restaurant where we had dinner greeted her like an old
friend. As we talked for the next few hours, I found myself recognizing
that lyrical, direct voice I had heard in her prose.*

With the appearance of her first collection of stories, At the Bottom of
the River *(Random House, 1983), Kincaid was praised by establishment
critics as an important new voice in contemporary fiction. In these experimental, impressionistic stories, she re-creates her experiences growing up
on the island of Antigua, hinting at themes she would expand in later
works: a fierce desire for independence, the struggle to escape a domineering mother, a joy in sensuality and physical beauty.* Annie John *(Farrar,
Straus, and Giroux, 1985), Kincaid's autobiographical first novel,*

continues this exploration in a straightforward episodic account of her growing up and away from her mother. Again, the critics praised: lyrical, charming, haunting, a universal story of one girl's coming-of-age.

Kincaid's next step was riskier. Her earlier works, written for and published by The New Yorker *magazine, were mostly apolitical. Criticism of colonialism occasionally surfaces in* Annie John—*young Annie compares a tyrannical grandfather to Christopher Columbus, for example—but the novel doesn't explore the significance of colonialism in Annie's life. Kincaid's political awareness becomes clearer in her controversial nonfiction work,* A Small Place *(Farrar, Straus, and Giroux, 1988), a series of essays written after a visit back to Antigua. Again drawing on firsthand experience, Kincaid exposes the racist underpinnings of British colonial rule and the effect it had on her as a child. But she goes beyond this to criticize the corruption and mismanagement of the native government (Antigua gained independence in 1981). In this book of many moods—at times lyrical, sardonic, accusatory—Kincaid demonstrates that she is not a writer to be neatly categorized. Not surprisingly,* The New Yorker *declined to publish the work.*

In Lucy *(Farrar, Straus, and Giroux, 1990), her next novel, Kincaid again transforms personal experience into powerful fiction. But this time her protagonist has left an unnamed Caribbean island for a large U.S. city to become an au pair for an upscale white couple and their four children. Lucy's love-hate relationship with her absent mother, her affection for her employer Mariah, her friendships and love affairs form the main text of the novel, but there's a different consciousness at work here. Lucy is aware of her situation in ways that the isolated Annie couldn't be, making connections between her own experience of oppression and the domestic politics and racial policies of her adopted country. The novel is never polemical—Kincaid knows the difference between fiction and nonfiction—but the consciousness is different, perhaps because this protagonist is older.*

Kincaid left her own family at an early age. Shortly after her sixteenth birthday, in 1965, she came to New York where she worked as an au pair, a receptionist, and a magazine writer. She studied photography at New York's New School for Social Research and spent over a year at Franconia College in New Hampshire. Her first published piece was an interview with Gloria Steinem that appeared in Ingenue *in 1973.*

The turning point came when she became friends with George W. S. Trow, a writer for The New Yorker, *who started writing "Talk of the Town" pieces about her. Soon she met the editor (and her future father-in-law) William Shawn, who began publishing her stories.*

Kincaid's parents named her Elaine Potter Richardson, but she took the name Jamaica Kincaid when she started writing—the first name because it evoked the West Indies, the second simply because it seemed to go well with the first. The same independent spirit that led her to change home and name characterizes everything this writer does. In her new stories, one of which she read at the 92nd Street Y in New York in 1992, she writes about a determined woman's sexuality (a theme in her work from the beginning) with power and exuberance.

During the interview Kincaid said of her writing, "When people say you're charming you are in deep trouble." As charming as she is in person, no one will call Jamaica Kincaid's current work charming anymore.

Q: Could we start by talking a bit about *Annie John,* your first novel? I know that the situation is autobiographical. How do you translate what has happened in your life into fiction?

A: A lot of what happens in *Annie John* were things that actually happened to me. But one of the things that I seem to do in writing is [that] I often take a lot of disparate events, and, I don't know how, but sometimes they make a kind of psychological sense that I couldn't have foreseen or I can't see until I'm writing. I would say that everything in *Annie John* happened—every feeling in it happened—but not necessarily in the order they appear. But it very much expresses the life I had. There isn't anything in it that is a lie, I would say. For instance, the story of the long rain and the girl's illness. Both really happened—I had whooping cough when I was about eight or nine—but in the book the girl is older, about fifteen. These feelings and some of the things that happened—like the bathing of the pictures—happened when I was about nine.

Q: Why did you choose to write fiction instead of autobiography?

A: Because autobiography is the truth and fiction is, well, fiction. In an autobiography, for instance, I could not have had the long rain coincide with the girl's illness. One of the things I found when I began to write was that writing exactly what happened had a limited amount of power for me. To say exactly what happened was less than what I knew happened. Mr. Shawn used to say I was a terrible reporter. I like the idea that when something happens it has a more powerful meaning than the moment in which it actually happens. When I started to write these autobiographical things I was told, "Oh, why don't you write a sort of autobiographical reminiscence about life?" but I wanted something more than that. I could see that if you put it in a sort of straightforward memoir that it would have a sort of bitterness that I didn't want—that wasn't the point. The point wasn't the truth and yet the point *was* the truth. And I don't know how to explain that.

Q: So you were after something more universal?

A: More universal. Yes. But at the time I did not know that, and now I make it a point not to know that.

Q: Would you ever write a story about something that hasn't happened to you?

A: I don't know how to do that, no. I read sometimes that a writer says, "Oh, I overheard a snippet of conversation and I went from there." I can't do that. If I overhear something I have to totally internalize it. I can only find the thing inside me. If it's not there, then I'm not able to figure things out. It's not that I couldn't write about something that didn't happen to me, but I would have to find the emotion somewhere inside myself.

Q: I gave the book to a young woman from Jamaica who enjoyed it, but she didn't like the ending because Annie leaves home. Have you heard that reaction before?

A: That's happened a lot among West Indian girls who have read the book. Many teachers have told me that. One teacher in Queens [New York] said that the class split over it: The West Indian girls said it didn't have a happy ending, the other students—not West Indian—disagreed. I don't know if it is, but I have noticed that black people don't like unhappy endings. Perhaps we have too many. This reality of life is perhaps hard for us to face. Another reality is that life is ambiguous; it has many meanings and many endings. Most endings in life, I have noticed, are not happy. Death, of course, is the most common one.

I wonder why it is that Africans like a one-party state. Even when they are not Communists, they insist on one party. They can't stand the idea of many opinions, where the one that is most popularly expressed is the one that will go, but that the other differences are accommodated also. It's as if we must all think alike or nothing, and we must all think happily. And this idea that it must be happy and it must be the same means that there is deception all the time. So, yes, the reality of the ending of *Annie John* is very disturbing.

Q: I see the central character in *Annie John* as an outsider in some ways. Did you think of yourself as an outsider then?

A: I didn't think of myself as an outsider because of my race because, for one thing, where I grew up I was the same race as almost everyone else. And I did not feel I was an outsider because of my sex. Many people were the same sex as me also. But still, I did feel that I was an outsider.

It is true that I noticed things that no one else seemed to notice. And I think only people who are outsiders do this. I must have felt very different from everybody. When I tell people there now how I felt then, they look at me with pity. For instance, I have a friend now who is a little bit older than I am, who grew up in the same area I did. Our families were not acquainted—her parents are practically aristocrats, my parents are peasants. But she and I have now become friends, and I can tell her all of these things that I noticed about her. But at the time I was little and observing her I wasn't observing her for any reason I knew of. I mean, some of the people I knew were, like her, from a different class—they had land and money—and most of the people I knew were like me, just from working people.

So why did I notice her? I remember an incredible number of things about her, and it was just from seeing her come and go. We weren't friends. We never spoke to each other. She has two sisters and a brother and I can even tell her what they were like. I just knew the kind of people they were then.

Q: Would you say that you grew up with a consciousness of class difference?

A: No. Not really. I noticed things that came under that heading, but I noticed other things also. I just noticed things, a lot of things. I had all this information about everybody. I can just imagine that if it had not worked out this way I would have been someone who would have caused enormous mischief, because I knew so much about everyone that I would either have spread rumors or engineered catastrophes, including the catastrophe of my own life, I'm sure.

Q: Getting back to something you said earlier about drawing from experiences in your own life, did the "Columbus in Chains" episode really happen to you—the incident in *Annie John* when you write under the picture of an enslaved Columbus the words your mother spoke about her father: "The Great Man Can No Longer Just Get Up and Go"?

A: Yes, but my mother had really said, "The great man can't shit." I had written that and it wouldn't go in *The New Yorker,* so I changed it. Then I left it that way for the book because I realized that it had a more profound meaning, and now I can't exactly remember why. But I thought about it for a long time—I had a long conversation with my editor at the time because "shit" was not a word that appeared in *The New Yorker* then—appropriately, I have now come to feel.

The two incidents [hearing her mother and writing the caption] happened separately in real life.

Q: That section seems to be the part of *Annie John* that most clearly reveals a political consciousness. Do you agree?

A: I think that's the first place I began to know how to express it. I think in the things I just wrote [in 1988 and 1989], it becomes clearer, and it becomes clearer, also, to me, how to express it. But the typical reality of someone like myself in a place like Antigua is that the political situation became so normal that we no longer noticed it. The better people were English, and that was life. I can't say that I came from a culture that felt alienated from England or Europe. We were beyond alienation.

It was amazing that I could notice the politics the way I did, because most of those who took notice did so in some sort of world context, like the man who became prime minister. But I took notice of it in a personal way, and I didn't place it within the context of political action. I almost made a style out of it.

Q: Speaking of political consciousness, why did you write *A Small Place*? That's a very political book.

A: I really wrote it as a piece for *The New Yorker*. Mr. Shawn, the former editor, loved it and bought it; then Bob Gottlieb, the present editor, hated it [since the interview Tina Brown has become editor]. He said it was very angry. Not badly written. Angry. I now consider anger a badge of honor. It had a sort of traumatic history because it was so intimate. It was written for the readers of *The New Yorker*, whom I had come to think of as friends in some peculiar way. And then it was very much loathed by the new people.

I don't know how it is for most people—other writers—but I feel that I am sort of lucky or privileged to get to do this thing called writing, in which basically all I am doing is discovering my own mind. I'm very grateful that I am able to make a living at it, but that's all it is, discovering my own mind. I mean, I didn't know that I thought those things. I didn't go around saying them to myself. But then, somehow, once I had the opportunity to think them, I just did. I went to Antigua, and I began to see things again about it, and they turned into this article. So when *The New Yorker* didn't buy it, Mr. Shawn thought that it should be presented as a book, all by itself. He was right of course, as usual.

Q: I felt when I read *A Small Place* as though it was a kind of turning point in your writing, a growth in political awareness in some way, and that your works to follow would be different. Is that so?

A: Yes. I thought it was a turning point in me. I wrote with a kind of recklessness in that book. I didn't know what I would say ahead of time. Once I wrote it I felt very radicalized by it. I would have just thought of myself as a liberal person until I wrote it, and now I feel that liberal is as right as I can go.

Q: There's a lot of anger in it.

A: Yes, that's right, and I've really come to love anger. And I liked it even more when a lot of reviews said it's so angry. The *New York Times* said that the book didn't have the "charm" of *Annie John*. Really, when people say you're charming you are in deep trouble. I realized in writing that book that the first step in claiming yourself is anger. You get mad. And you can't do anything before you get angry. And I recommend getting very angry to everyone, anyone.

As I wrote it I realized that I had all this feeling and that it was anger. I wanted it to be crude and impolite—and all the other things that civilized people are not supposed to be. I no longer wanted to be a civilized person. Really, for me, writing is like going to a psychiatrist. I just discover things about myself.

I can see that *At the Bottom of the River* was, for instance, a very unangry, decent, civilized book, and it represents sort of this successful attempt by English people to make their version of a human being or their version of a person out of me. It amazes me now that I did that then. I would never write like that again, I don't think. I might go back to it, but I'm not very interested in that sort of expression anymore. Now, for instance, I've become very interested in writing about sex, or smells. I'm interested in being not a decent person.

Q: You said earlier that if you hadn't become a writer you might have caused a lot of mischief because of what you knew. Did *A Small Place* cause mischief? Were there repercussions in Antigua?

A: Not really. I think people thought it would and they talked about it. There's a section of the book that very much describes the reaction of Antiguans to the book. It was sort of a great event, and now it's just part of what happened that someone wrote this book and said these things that we—they—all know happened. There wasn't anything in it anyone learned, except that someone would make an attempt to tell the world about them. They have always seen themselves—we see ourselves—as little, insignificant people that great things happen to: slavery, America, the British, whatever. They never really thought that any of us could just stand up and say to the world the things that we know about ourselves.

So the world looking at them has become part of their everyday life. And I think the government was a little afraid that it would hurt them at first, so they sort of banned it, but then they were reelected by an overwhelming majority.

One thing Antiguans said about *A Small Place* is, "It's true, but did she have to say it?" No one says that it's a lie; the disagreement is, did I have to say it.

Q: In the book you mention that the library was closed. Has it been reopened?

A: No. But you know, yesterday I was reading an article about a newspaperman in Zambia who writes satirical articles about his government and he said that there isn't one bookstore in Zambia. There isn't a library or anything. So there is this incredible, almost conspiratorial effort on the part of the people who rule in the black Third World to keep any institution of learning out of their country. Mobutu, apparently, simply closed the universities when the students protested against him.

Q: Do you see this as similar to what happened in China [during the Tiananmen Square demonstrations]?

A: To some extent, but the Chinese want their students to be educated—in their own way. It's quite a big difference; the Chinese don't mean to do away with education. The Africans and the West Indians don't make that fine a distinction. They just don't want any opposition. The fact is that a lot of the things that are considered essential to having a nation are not in existence in black Africa or in the West Indies. We had better health and education under colonialism.

Q: The saddest part of *A Small Place* is that after colonialism many things in Antigua seem worse than they were under the British.

A: It's absolutely true; it's not an exaggeration. In the hospital in Antigua—the children's ward—most of the children are there because they suffer from malnutrition. And Antigua has the highest standard of living in the eastern Caribbean. I have no idea, by the way, what that means, but that's what they say. You do see people with a lot of things. Everyone has a car, everyone has a television. They have cable television, and they get something like thirty channels from North America. It has all of what looks like prosperity. My mother, who lives in a tiny house, has a refrigerator and a better television set than we do. It's really quite remarkable.

Q: Could you talk about "Ovando," a short story of yours that appeared in *Conjunctions* [vol. 14 (1989)]? As an allegorical portrait of the horrors of colonialism, that work seems to continue this concern with domination.

A: I can only say that story is something that I stopped because I realized I didn't know enough to go on. As I go around the world I understand it better and better. I think in some way I am very interested in domination. I suppose we all are. I feel that, in particular, my own history is so much about dominion; in fact we were called "the dominion," and all the colonies were "the dominions." So when I started to write "Ovando" I thought I was going to write a grand work about the question of dominion.

The other insight I have into history is that it's a bit like musical chairs. When the music stops some people are standing up and some people are sitting down, but at any moment you don't know if it will be you among the stand-ups or the sit-downs. I feel as though, if I am among the people sitting down, I always will identify with the people who are standing up—that my knowledge of my history tells me that I have to always make room on the chair for the people standing up. In writing "Ovando," I was trying to understand how, for some people who found themselves sitting down, it would become important to try to remove the apparatus for the game to continue—so that they would never again be standing up.

Q: Do you see this as the situation of the colonizing countries like Europe and the United States?

A: Yes. On the other hand, we know that every relief also bears its own prison. If you remove the apparatus for the game to go on, then permanently sitting down is its own prison.

I realized that in order for me to finish "Ovando," I would have to understand more about the reality of someone like Christopher Columbus than I know now. His journals are in Seville and you can go and read them. I really need to know more about these explorers themselves. I need to be older.

All these people are very admirable when you think of what they did—these "great men." People thought the world was flat. A very poetic idea.

In some ways, these explorations to the New World were very touching. I realize that one of the things that is bound up in this horrible thing that happened (slavery—the domination) is the great curiosity in every human being. I mean making maps, building a boat—there's something really extraordinary about it, very moving, when you think of these people just going somewhere without knowing what really they would find. It's not like going to the moon at all, which has this incredible support. It had an individual element that was admirable or inspiring.

But, of course, by the time they made their discoveries, everything admirable about them becomes lost.

Q: They became the conquerors?

A: Yes.

Q: At the end of "Ovando" you say that "a true and just sentence would be imbued with love for Ovando." That suggests that you think it would take a great-hearted person to understand Ovando.

A: It's a funny thing. I grew to understand that, too.

Q: "Ovando" seems very medieval. I kept thinking of Barbara Tuchman's *A Distant Mirror* [Knopf, 1978] and the cult of the Black Death. Were you suggesting parallels with the medieval period?

A: Yes. When you read the history of what the Europeans left behind, it is a record of disease and incredible suffering, poverty.

When I hear people talking about the "Great Western Tradition," I think, wait a minute, what are they talking about here? All I see is a tradition of incredible cruelty and suffering and injustice—not to mention murder, complete erasing of whole groups of people. Everybody is always looking for a way out. And what was their way out? The New World. Start fresh. But of course you can't. There's no such thing as a fresh start.

Q: Can you talk a little about your writing process? How do you write?

A: I read about writers who have routines. They write at certain times of the day. I can't do that. I am always writing—but in my head. I just finished writing a book [*Lucy*] about a month ago. I started it when Harold was three months and then I finished it when he was a year and six months. It will be published in the fall. It will be some stories that have appeared in *The New Yorker*. I don't know how I did it. I wrote in between things. I have to figure out how things will go—what we will have for dinner, how the children's lives will be, Allen's life, my life. I sort of expect that I'll figure it out.

I think I have to have a great deal of domestic activity to write. I am essentially a person very interested in domestic life and very interested in things that we think of, either in a good way or a bad way, as women's things. I know a woman and she comes to see me in the morning and we sit at the kitchen table. We just sit and talk. That's not how I write, but in a way it is. I sit with this woman and we sort of arrange the world. We talk about Bush. We talk about the Russians. We talk about Nicaragua. We talk about the homeless. We sort of settle the day—the world. Then, about 11:00, I say, "Well, goodbye," and I go off to my office—a room at home. And I do whatever I do.

I may do absolutely nothing but read the newspaper and then for fifteen minutes I write a paragraph or maybe a sentence or a page. I can't tell how it may go. But that's how I write. I sort of think about it as part of my domestic life. In fact, I think I reduce everything to a domestic situation. I wouldn't be very interested in putting the world in the way the world is actually arranged. If I actually ran the world, I'd do it from the kitchen. It's not anything deliberate or a statement or anything, that's just how I understand things. It's arranged along informal lines. I don't like formality. I realize, for instance, that I would never live in a house with a dining room. I couldn't stand a room in which you only ate.

When I was little I had this great mind for history. And I never really understood it until I realized that the reason I liked history is because I also reduce the past to domestic activity. History was what people did. It was organized along the lines of who said what and who did what, not really unlike how the society in which I grew up was organized. The idea that things are impersonal occurrences is very alien to me. I personalize everything.

Q: That personalizing is what enabled you to make the connection between Columbus and your grandfather.

A: That's right. You see, I reduce everything to a domestic connection. It's all the great men who have been humbled. Finally.

Q: What difference have your children made in your life? You described the domestic arrangements that make writing possible—your friend who comes over to help out—but I get the sense that motherhood takes a lot of time.

A: Absolutely. I have two children: Annie, who is named after my mother and Allen's grandmother, and Harold, who is named after Allen's father's brother. Annie is five and Harold is a year and a half.

I don't mean to be one of those people who says everything happens for the best, because when you hear someone say that you are listening to a defeated person. But I have these two children, and yet I wrote one book in a year and three months. There was a long period after I had Annie that I didn't write at all. I don't know if I didn't have time to write or if I was gathering. You know there is a fallow period that one gets frightened of. You think, "Maybe I'll never write again." I never felt that way. As long as I can have some way of earning a living or doing something, I don't worry too much about it. I think, "Well, I haven't quite figured out how to say what I want to say."

That was true after I wrote *Annie John.* I wanted to say something but I didn't know what, and it turned out to be *A Small Place.* And then I planned to write a book after that, but I got pregnant and couldn't write. Then I had Harold. And then, just to earn some money, I started to write the first story of this new book. I didn't mean to write the whole book at all. And then within a year and three months I finished it.

Q: Is it harder to write now that you have children?

A: It's hard to write now, but it was hard to write before. I feel incredibly free—I feel I could have more children, I feel that I can write. I don't feel writing is cut off for me because I don't feel having experience is cut off from me. I think somehow if I didn't have the children I might feel that way. But, you see, being so interested in domestic activity, having children can only add to my feeling of domestic life. I am beginning to see their life as going out into the world, whatever it is. But I can only see that from the kitchen table.

Q: When do you let other people read your work? Does your husband read what you have written when you think it is ready?

A: He reads it daily [she laughs]. Probably I couldn't be a writer without Allen. When I'm writing, every night before he goes to sleep, he reads. It's not quite a joint project, but I really depend on him as a reader.

The way I wrote *Annie John* was that I would get up every day and I would say to him, "Well now, today I'm going to do . . . " and I would say pages and pages of how I would write. And he would say, "Oh, that sounds good," or, "Well, but what happens when this . . . ?" And I would say, "Oh, but this. . . . " Then, just as I told him, I would go into my room and write, and later I would show him what I had written.

He's not a writer, but he is very interested in writing and very interested in me, I must say. He's great fun to be married to. It's wonderful to have this great companion, in every way.

The terrible thing about traveling is that he doesn't like to travel, and so I travel alone. It is a great loss because I have all these experiences, and usually when we have these experiences we just chatter, chatter, chatter all the time. And when I'm alone there's no one to talk to. So then we just have these huge phone bills.

Q: These stories [in *Lucy*] seem harder edged than *Annie John*.

A: I think they are more frank. I think that after writing *A Small Place* and seeing the reaction to it, I realized that people couldn't stand a certain sort of frankness. But I knew that what I wanted to be, more and more as a writer, was frank about what the lives I wrote about were really like, as frank as I could express or as I could know. I didn't know if that would be possible, but that was what I wanted.

In the context of that, I'm still very conscious of art, of making something, and I'm always very interested in the right word. I want to use the word that would best express something. But yet I wanted to be very frank and to be unlikable within the story. To be even unpopular. In the last two stories I wanted to risk more.

As I go on writing, I feel less and less interested in the approval of the First World, and I never had the approval of the world I came from, so now I don't know where I am. I've exiled myself yet again. In fact, the world that comforted me and made me a writer is now the world where I don't care about their approval: *The New Yorker.* I used to care about *The New Yorker.* I used to feel I had a personal stake in it. Now it's just another thing owned by someone with a billion dollars. Like everything else in the world.

Q: Yet they are still publishing your stories, aren't they?

A: Yes. I'm shocked. They bought all of them.

Q: This couple whom you describe in your last stories—Lewis and Mariah—seem like readers of *The New Yorker,* actually: white, upper middle class, politically left of center, city dwellers. But they also seem somewhat vapid to me. Is this your idea?

A: Yes. Well, you have to read the other two to come because the couple divorce. I really was an au pair, and I was writing about my own experience. The other people are incidental; they are not anyone I actually knew. I went out of my way to make the other characters not like people I actually knew.

Q: On a recent trip to the New York Botanical Garden [in the Bronx] I found a place called Daffodil Hill, a hill covered with daffodils that reminded me of the garden where the wife takes the narrator in the story "Mariah" [from *Lucy*]. Was that the place you had in mind?

A: No. I had never been to a specific garden; I just imagined it. This story of the daffodils did not really happen. But it is amazing to me that there is such a place and so it could have happened.

Q: Were you really forced to memorize Wordsworth's "I Wandered Lonely as a Cloud," the poem where he praises the daffodils?

A: Every colonial child has to do that. It's a two-edged thing because I wouldn't have known how to write and how to think if I hadn't read those things. I wouldn't have known my idea of justice if I hadn't read *Paradise Lost,* if I hadn't been given parts of *Paradise Lost* to memorize. It was given to me because I was supposed to be Satan. The last chapter of the book I have written has a lot of things about that. The book is called *Lucy,* short for Lucifer.

Q: So in this work, as in *Annie John,* there is some of what really happened and some manipulation of what really happened.

A: Like *Annie John,* everything happened but not necessarily in this way. I want the truth. I begin to understand this thing about the mind, and I'm sure it's not just true of me. I'm always shocked to see that things are more neatly connected than we think. I really manipulate the facts, but within the manipulation there is no lie. I believe I can safely say that—that in everything I say there is the truth.

I arrange things in a way that I can understand them, but it isn't completely fiction; it is, in fact, not in my imagination. I have no imagination when it comes to that. It's as if you were given a broken plate and you rearranged it into a pitcher. The rearrangement wouldn't deny the fact that the plate and the pitcher are made of the same stuff. I use the same material, but I make it into a different thing, something new.

In these stories, the place and the girl herself aren't named. It is New York, but it could be anywhere. I didn't want to specify because I didn't want any preconceptions about the place. She doesn't even name the island she comes from.

Q: Your stories seem seamless—both these new ones and the parts of *Annie John*. How do you account for the particular shape they take?

A: I just write, and things come to a crest, and that's how it is. My mind works in this way—its sort of like a puzzle. I know where the pieces are, but I don't want to fit them for myself or for the reader. I just write.

Q: It sounds like *Lucy* has an unhappy ending, too.

A: Yes. The last two stories are very painful, even for Allen.

Q: What contemporary fiction writers do you read?

A: Do you know any of the French West Indian writers? They are amazing. There is a collection of Caribbean women's writing, *Her True-True Name,* that is amazing [ed. Pamela Mordecai and Betty Wilson, (Heinemann, 1989)]. The French writers are much more frank, much more exciting. You can see the French influence in *Wide Sargasso Sea* [by Jean Rhys (André Deutsch, London, 1966)] and *The Orchid House* [by Phyllis Shand Allfrey (Constable, London, 1953)]. *The Orchid House* is very good. I can understand if someone would think it was deeply flawed if they don't know the story, but I think it's very good.

If you don't know something intimately, you might not know if it is good. I'm supposed to write an introduction to a work by Zora Neale Hurston, but I don't know what to say. I think that I do not appreciate her as some people [do] because I have not had a certain kind of experience. The language makes assumptions about things that I just don't understand.

These French writers are also unbelievably bold about sex, and of course, sex is everything. The world starts at the crotch, essentially. And it's not that people are a slave to the crotch, but they are a bit. I once read an article about AIDS in Africa and the writer said that the reason AIDS is spreading so fast there is that Africans are sex-positive. I thought this was a wonderful phrase. For example, prostitution was not known in Africa until Europeans came. An African woman would have many lovers, but there was no money exchanged. A man would bring a gift, but it wasn't in exchange for the sex. It was to show affection. And I think there's something like that where I come from, and so almost all the most basic arrangements are made on that basis: no exchange, just a gift.

I'm just about to get to this in my own fiction, this commodification of relationships. The commodifying of things is what I wanted to discuss in "Ovando."

Q: Before we end, I want to ask you about the role *The New Yorker* has played in your development as a writer. How important was it?

A: I don't think I would have become a writer if it wasn't for *The New Yorker*—the old *New Yorker*, that is. Not the thing that still calls itself *The New Yorker*. It was writing for them—for Mr. Shawn, really—that helped me learn how to write. I'm very grateful to him for that.

Although she's lived in Tucson for years, Barbara Kingsolver still sounds like her native eastern Kentucky. It's not just her accent that gives her away; it's a certain way of talking—a down-home, no-nonsense style, metaphoric and rich with vivid detail. Close your eyes and you could be listening to Taylor Greer, the quick-tongued protagonist of The Bean Trees (Harper and Row, 1988), her first novel.

Born in 1955, the daughter of a doctor more interested in healing than making money, trained as a musician and scientist, Kingsolver grew up among Kentucky's rural poor and working class—people a lot like Taylor. From observing her neighbors and listening to her father and grandfather, Kingsolver learned early on about social responsibility and community, principles that play a central role in her life and writing.

This emphasis on connection and interdependence makes Kingsolver's fiction similar in spirit to that of fellow-Southerner Eudora Welty; they share a sympathetic attitude toward characters, as well as the journalist's sharp eye. But Kingsolver grounds her characters' stories in a broader political context than Welty does. And her definition of community extends beyond the biological family. Thus, just when she thinks she's managed to leave home, Taylor becomes saddled with an abandoned Native American child she ends up adopting. The new family she builds in Tucson includes an abandoned wife who becomes her best friend and a pair of Guatemalan refugees, for whom Taylor risks her own life. Communal claims and re-

Photo: Copyright © Susan Pearce

sponsibilities are central themes in Pigs in Heaven *(HarperCollins, 1993), a sequel, in which Kingsolver shifts the focus to the tribe's efforts to reclaim the child after she has been adopted by Taylor.*

In the collection Homeland and Other Stories *(Harper and Row, 1989), Kingsolver explores connections within families and among neighbors. A young girl connects with her Cherokee great-grandmother (in "Homeland"); a harried single mother recognizes her daughter's resiliency (in "Quality Time"); a small-town girl defends a beloved friend who is labeled a lesbian (in "Rose-Johnny").*

The question that led to Animal Dreams *(HarperCollins, 1990), Kingsolver's second novel, was, Why do people make the political choices they do? It deals with the awakening of a young woman's political consciousness when she comes home to Arizona to care for her ailing father. Aided by the example of her sister who is working for social change in Nicaragua and the love of a Native American man whose communal ideas challenge her own notions of independence, the main character finally recognizes her dependence on others.*

Before earning a living as a fiction writer, Kingsolver worked in Tucson as a journalist. For eighteen months she researched the role of women in sustaining the strike against Phelps Dodge Copper Corporation. The resulting book, Holding the Line: Women in the Great Arizona Mine Strike of 1983 *(ILR Press, 1989), filled with vivid portraits of individual women, celebrates their solidarity and bravery as they faced economic hardships and the Arizona National Guard, the same kind of courage Kingsolver writes about in her fiction.*

She claims to have written poems in the margins of her biology textbooks in college, and Kingsolver's poetic ability is obvious in Another America/Otra America *(Seal Press, 1992), her first volume of poetry. These "little stories," as she calls them, describe personal and national violations and praise individual acts of heroism in the name of justice. With Spanish translations by the Chilean writer Rebeca Cartes, the poems remind us that America is more than the United States, that this other America to the south must be embraced and not exploited.*

When I talked with Barbara Kingsolver over lunch in an Indian restaurant in New York, in January 1992, she had just returned from several months in the Canary Islands. She went there with her husband and daughter to do research for a future book and to escape for a while from the rising militarism surrounding the Persian Gulf war in the United States. Her escape was only temporary, however, and Kingsolver is back in the struggle, working as a political activist and writing fiction that she hopes will help change the world.

Q: You've been a political activist as well as a writer, Barbara. What in your background led to this activism?

A: One thing is the time in which I grew up, going to college in the early seventies when convictions were not only fashionable, they were greatly rewarded. We were out in the streets yelling about an unjust war [Vietnam], and the war stopped and the president resigned. It was magnificent reinforcement for a lasting sense that I can—and really have to—do something about the stuff that's bothering me.

But even more important is the fact that I grew up in an impoverished, rural place in eastern Kentucky that was right next to a really rich place. Borderland Appalachia butts right up against the Blue Grass, where there's enormous wealth, where there are horses with their own swimming pools. That's not an exaggeration. And in my whole county we didn't have a swimming pool. I never swam in one until I was an adult.

A: You mention that in one of your books. So living in this area made you aware of injustice?

Q: Appalachia has a history of militancy that comes from this juxtaposition of extreme poverty and extreme wealth—for example, the miners who had to work in the shadow of the huge capital of these enormous mining companies. There was a primordial sense that there are people a lot better off than we are and that's really unfair. Also, the sense of community was really strong.

Q: Were people dependent on family or the larger community?

A: Neighbors. In a rural place the connections between people are really obvious. You know where your food comes from; you might know the person who grew it if you didn't grow it yourself. You literally know the person who laid the sewer pipes. There's this human connection and you understand that your life depends on the people around you. If your barn burns down, you know the people who will come and help you build a new one. If you have a devastated crop one year, you know the individual people who will help you survive. If you live here [in New York], if you have a really bad year, some agency will help you—or won't. But you don't know the people by name.

Q: How has that experience shaped you?

A: I didn't appreciate it at the time. I just thought that it was hell to live in this place where everybody was into your business and watching who you're going out with and having so much to say about how much you've grown since last year. But once I was out of it I realized how rare it is to live in a place where people care.

Because of my background I feel like I'm always running up against this wall of what an American is supposed to be like. To be American is to be independent. We celebrate Independence Day and heroes like Charles Lindbergh who flew across the ocean all alone. We even celebrate the single mother who can manage to do everything with no help. And I feel no kinship with that cultural value. I feel that independence is stupidity [she laughs]. If you're that independent either you're really kidding yourself or there's something wrong with you.

I celebrate dependency. I love the idea that a lot of people have contributed to my life and a lot of people have been involved in making the things that I use.

In the Canary Islands, where I've been living for the past year, you go to the market and buy bananas from the person who grew them. You buy a chicken from the guy who grew it and get the chicken with its head still on and its feet, which he would cut off if I asked him to. Here [in the United States] I go to Safeway and I buy this thing wrapped in plastic that theoretically was a chicken once. And there are no human faces attached to any of this. The only human face is the checkout clerk.

Q: What's the difference in having a human face attached?

A: I feel like I belong to a crowd, like I'm a part of a tribe. We're all here making a lot of noise and in this together and looking out for each other.

Q: It seems to me in your work that the idea of community extends even beyond the human. There are strong connections in your books with the animal world, for example.

A: I'm attached to the chicken, too [she laughs]. Growing up on a farm was an important part of who I am: seeing where things come from and what goes into life and what comes out of it. And seeing that everything kills something else in order to live. In Tucson I have a little piece of ground where I grow food and we have chickens; after they stop laying eggs, we eat them.

I know a lot of very good people who are vegetarians and would never eat an animal, but that distinction seems quite artificial. There's this continuum of life, and why is it better to decide that this half I will kill and this half I won't? It's my science background, too. I got degrees in ecology and evolutionary biology at DePauw University in Indiana.

Q: Didn't you do doctoral work in science, too?

A: I got a master's at the University of Arizona some years later. Then I had a crisis in the middle of my doctoral dissertation and realized that the genetics of termites wasn't really my first concern [she laughs]. Keeping termites in a laboratory in an old wooden building is not the best idea. Those suckers were always escaping. A scientific writing job at the university came up and I told my committee, "I'm going to take this job and take a year off and think about my life." And I really liked getting paid to write.

Q: What was the attraction of biology?

A: I think biology is my religion. Understanding the processes of the natural world and how all living things are related is the way that I answer those questions that are the basis of religion. What's the purpose of my being here? What happens when we die? So when I say I feel a kinship with a chicken, I don't mean anything New Age. I just mean that we have ancestors in common.

Q: Was your family religious?

A: In a very peculiar way. My mother was some sort of fundamentalist, but my father has been uncomfortable with any sort of organized religion since he was a boy. His idea of worship is to sit in a forest and listen to the birds. And although my mother really felt differently, she was submissive to him. Sometimes she would whisk us off to church, but I also got these ideas from my father that creation is about acorns and trees, instead of some guy with a white beard saying, "Zap! There you are." I appreciate the fact that, accidentally, my parents brought me up with a good deal of broad-mindedness concerning spirituality and creation myths and world-views, because I'm really interested in learning about the different ways that cultures explain their existence in the world. I think that goes a long way in explaining our behavior.

Q: For example?

A: I think the Christian creation myth, which says the world was put here as a little garden for us to use, goes a long way in explaining how we've really devastated that garden. We feel this entitlement. We have about used up what there is to use, and yet we continue looking at nature in terms of what we can exploit—the idea that this mountain is put here for me to mine and get pumice out of so I can make stone-washed jeans. Feeling that morality has nothing to do with the way you use the resources of the world is an idea that can't persist much longer. If it does, then we won't.

Q: This idea is totally at odds with the belief of Native Americans, for example.

A: Exactly. The Pueblo creation myth is that the world was here and people were down inside of it along with other animals. One day, with the help of a badger, they figured out how to burrow up through the mud and arrived on the surface. They looked around and said, "Wow, this is terrific. If we're really good maybe they'll let us stay." It's a completely opposite way of looking at the world, and it brings a sense of morality into every single act that you perform in connection with the ground that you walk on, the trees that you sit under, the animals that you kill to eat, the corn that you grow to eat.

Q: So you consider yourself closer to a Native American worldview than this Judeo-Christian one?

A: Yes, I do. Also, something that I didn't realize till I was much older is that my Grandfather Kingsolver's mother was Cherokee. She's a big blank spot on the family tree.

Q: Do you think that's intentional?

A: Absolutely. My Cherokee great-grandmother was quite deliberately left out of the family history for reasons of racism and embarrassment about mixed blood. But her photograph captured my imagination when I was a little girl, and I always felt a longing to have known her. I felt that there was some sort of wisdom there that I needed.

Q: You grew up aware of the difference between rich and poor, yet your father was a doctor.

A: Not a very rich one. My Grandfather Kingsolver, his father, was a sort of moral voice in my life. Moral isn't the right word, but he had a way of doing things, slow and careful, deliberate and connected. He always thought a lot about the consequences of things, even so far as if you put the same size nails in this jar, then tomorrow when you look for nails, you'll be able to find them. He came from deep in the mountains, Ashland [Kentucky] I think, and never had very much money.

Q: So how did your father go to medical school?

A: He got put through medical school with a lot of jobs, and he was always driven to serve people who needed him, whether they could pay or not. When I was in grade school we lived in Africa and in the Caribbean for a while. We didn't have very much. In Africa we didn't have running water. We lived in even more difficult circumstances than in Appalachia. And then my dad and mom settled in Nicholas County, Kentucky, which is really foothills. I think some of his family had come from there. It's not mining country; it's tobacco country. But it's not wealthy at all. A lot of his patients paid in vegetables, and we grew a lot of our own food on the farm.

In school there were these class differences. There were the town kids whose parents were merchants who had the clothes of the year. And then there were the country kids who had questionable wardrobe skills [she laughs]. And I was certainly in the latter group.

Q: So you would have been a "nutter," as you say in your fiction.

A: I was a nutter, yes. We picked up walnuts and got stained hands.

Q: Did you feel a pull to go into medicine the way Codi did in *Animal Dreams?*

A: It interested me. But, more than medicine, I felt from my dad this obligation to do the right thing rather than do the thing that rewards you financially. I felt a pull to do something useful to people, which is why I didn't study writing. I really wanted to be a musician. I started playing the piano really young and I played in bands when I got older. I got to college in Indiana on a music scholarship, and I went to conservatory for a couple of years. But there was a voice in me—that maybe was partly my father and maybe was partly the working-class community that I grew up in—that really didn't have a lot of respect for the arts as a way of life. And so it didn't even dawn on me that writing novels for a living was something I could do. I never met any authors, either.

Q: Valerie Miner said the same thing about writing not being seen as a legitimate option for someone from her working-class background.

A: You could say, "I want to be a ballerina when I grow up," or, "I want to write novels when I grow up." But unless you were a five-year-old, you would get laughed at.

Q: Were you a reader when you were growing up?

A: Yes. When I was growing up our TV broke, and it took twelve years to get it fixed because my dad just hated TV and really didn't want one in the house. For that I'm enormously grateful because there were no other entertainment options in the place where I grew up except for catching butterflies in the alfalfa field behind the house or reading. And I did a lot of both of those things. Reading was my escape from the mundane.

Q: What did you read?

A: I was crazy about children's classics like *Treasure Island* and the novels of Louisa May Alcott. I wanted to be Jo [in *Little Women*]—not the writing part of her, the tomboy part of her. I don't think that contemporary juvenile fiction had really reached Nicholas County, so I went straight from things like *Little Women* to William Saroyan.

Doris Lessing I started reading when I was in high school. Somehow a copy of *Martha Quest* had gotten left in Nicholas County one time by mistake [she laughs]. Later, when I was in college, I read everything of Lessing's. She was probably the first huge literary influence on me: I loved the way she evoked Africa. But more than that, maybe on a less conscious level, I loved the fact that she was writing about something real and important—the frustration of women who had absolutely no choices in their lives but to marry these hideous men who treated them badly. I couldn't get enough of reading about real issues.

Q: What do you read now?

A: I read more women than men, partly out of principle, but more because I read what I like. I think I prefer books by women because women tend to write more about relatedness, and men tend to write more about conflict and overcoming and manipulating the environment. It's a huge generalization, and there are many male writers I like a lot, but it seems true to me.

Q: Have other writers influenced you?

A: I was very much influenced by Flannery O'Connor and Eudora Welty, the Southern writers. Faulkner, also.

Q: You sound like Welty sometimes, like the voice she uses in "Why I Live at the P.O."

A: Exactly, that story I've reread a hundred times. I go back to it as a lesson in how not to sound self-conscious, how to get the writer out of the story. Where is that voice coming from?

Q: Reviewers have said that you're a "regional" writer. Do you see that as praise or criticism?

A: It can mean that you're of interest to a region and none other, like maybe you write books about farming in the prairie and only other farmers in the prairie will be interested in your book. But Southern writers have always written books that are deeply rooted in that place and culture but say something beyond that place.

It interests me that if you write a book about Manhattan, that's considered of general interest, but if you write a book about all the states west of the Mississippi, that's regional. I think that historic geographic provinciality in the publishing industry is changing a lot. My books are more widely read in the West than the East, but I can't complain that I've suffered a huge amount of discrimination because I'm living in the West instead of New York.

Q: How did *The Bean Trees* get published?

A: For five or six years a story set in an imaginary place that was populated by these various women had sprouted in the back of my mind and was growing. I had written a few short stories about the people, but I was working first as a scientific writer and then as a journalist, so I didn't have a lot of time to write fiction. It was a hobby that I did around the margins.

When I got pregnant in '86, I immediately got insomnia and slept almost not at all for months. My doctor told me to scrub the grout on the bathroom tile so that I wouldn't be rewarding myself for being awake. "Do something you hate," the doctor said. So I did that one night, and then I said, "Screw this; I'm writing a novel."

We had this really tiny house and there was just one room that was my bedroom and study. The clicking of the typewriter kept Joe [Hoffmann, Kingsolver's husband] awake, so I moved my desk into the closet and closed the door. And I would write for four or five hours every night, just for my own entertainment. And in nine months I got this novel written. I didn't give one thought to its publication.

Q: So how did it get to a publisher?

A: I had been working with Frances [Goldin, literary agent] on placing this copper strike book [*Holding the Line: Women in the Great Arizona Mine Strike of 1983*]. I wrote her a letter, saying, "By the way, I wrote this thing I think is a novel, but I'm not sure. Before I put it away in the drawer forever, do you want to take a look?"

She called me up the morning after she had gotten it—at 6:00 A.M. or something—raving about this novel. I thought she had a wrong number. And she said, "I'm going to auction it. We're going to get this much money for it." I was completely astonished. And within a matter of weeks I went into labor and the book was auctioned. The day after my daughter was born, I was just home from the hospital, and Frances called with the offer from HarperCollins [then Harper and Row]. I had been in labor for twenty-four hours and was still in this euphoric stage. I said, "Sure, whatever, I'll sign."

It didn't really sink in until I realized about a month later that I didn't have to go back to work as a journalist because I was getting this nice fat check from Harper and I could write another book.

Q: You said in another interview: "Every character in *The Bean Trees* is a piece of me."

A: Almost all of my characters come from me. I don't base characters on people I know or family members, God forbid. I make up a shell and then fill it with my own experience. For example, if this character needs to be insecure I think about the insecure part of myself. How would I feel if I were moving to a town and didn't know anybody, and what would I say, and what would I act like? Or if the character is cocky, I try to remember my cocky moments and think about what I would say in that situation. This process must be akin to acting.

Q: For *Bean Trees* you envisioned Taylor, this working-class character who, like you, leaves one part of the country to live in another. Why did you make her working class?

A: Oddly enough, I feel that I do come from a working-class background, even though my father is educated. There was never quite enough to go around, and you had to stretch stuff and be concerned about whether the garden will do well. All of my friends were working class.

So almost all of my characters are working class because those are the people that I know about. I know their language; I know how they dress; I know what they're worried about. I don't have to do research. I don't have to call up a friend and say, "What's the brand name of your sheets?" [she laughs].

Q: So you write about them because you know them?

A: That's why they're generated; I continue to write about these people because they matter. I believe that everything you write is a stream feeding the lake. People like this are worth writing about. People whose main concerns are not the meaning of life necessarily, but, "Who's going to take care of my kid?" or, "How am I going to pay the electric bill and the rent?" or, "How can I bring some joy into this life that seems so constrained by simply trying to survive?"

Q: These are people who have, for the most part, been left out of literature.

A: Exactly. I didn't grow up with the sense that their lives were the stuff of literature. What I learned in English class is literature is what happens between three men with swords or a man and this great white whale. Those are the elevated, glorious lives which are worthy of being immortalized in literature. And I think a lot of people believe that.

Q: What do you think is the effect of this exclusion on people themselves?

A: Because people don't find themselves in books, their lives don't feel very important.

Q: Are you writing for those people?

A: Accessibility is extremely important to me. When I wrote *The Bean Trees* in the voice of Taylor, someone who barely finished high school, I very soon realized how confined that voice was because Taylor doesn't know words like "vermilion" and "astute." She's really smart, but her vocabulary would fit in one of those Berlitz books for foreigners. So it was a challenge to describe scenery that Taylor had never seen before or thoughts that Taylor maybe never thought before from that small vocabulary. Time after time I would write a scene that I thought was quite nice but it had to go straight in the trash can because Taylor couldn't have said it.

There were times when I wondered why I had set this job up to tell this story in the voice of a person who was not very educated. After the book was published I realized I did it because I wanted to write a book that my family or my neighbors or the guy that runs Rex and Paul's Service Station in Carlisle [Kentucky], where I grew up, could read. I wasn't really thinking they ever would, but that's the kind of book that I wanted to write. And I still do. I would feel very embarrassed if I were writing books that they felt were too highbrow for them.

Q: Yet your novels have been acclaimed by critics.

A: I would also like for there to be enough complexity to keep more educated and more sophisticated readers interested and challenged. So the references to Homer's *Odyssey* or the references to Walt Whitman are in there, and some people will get them. And that's nice. But for all those people who missed those references, it's still okay because they're still going to get the rest of the story.

Q: How did you know that some of Taylor's dialogue wouldn't work? Did you have input from anyone, or was it just your own sense?

A: I would just look at it and say, "This word Taylor doesn't know, and she wouldn't be able to form a thought this way." To tell you the truth, I didn't put it in the trash can; I put it in the drawer and thought, "Maybe someday someone will say that, but not Taylor, not today."

Q: This was when you were alone in the closet?

A: Right. Nobody saw that book except Joe and Jessie, my dog, who can't read. I didn't have any feedback that I can remember besides Joe's.

Q: Did he give you a lot of feedback?

A: Yes. Joe was a good first reader because he is very intolerant of bullshit. And he's a chemist, so he can keep himself awake at night reading something like the agronomical chemicals from the family asterae. But, when it comes to fiction, if it's obscure or slow getting started or full of itself or if it doesn't have a good story line, Joe will fall asleep. So I give him a chapter around 10:30 and come back in a half an hour, and, if he's awake, then I know I've got something.

Q: Friendships between women sustain a lot of your characters.

A: Friendships between women are sustaining and they're worthy of writing about; they're important. I like to write about relationships between people and the things that attach people, rather than the things that drive them apart. Of course, this is not what literature is supposed to be, because I learned in eleventh grade English that the three great themes are man against nature, man against man, and man against himself.

Q: We added "man against God" in my school in Lowell, Massachusetts.

A: This is just eleventh grade in Carlisle. So probably God comes in college [she laughs].

Actually, in the novel I'm working on now, I'm writing for the first time about characters who have an extreme conflict of interest, and there is no way to resolve it to the complete satisfaction of them both. And I'm finding it so hard that it gives me knots in my stomach. In all my other books the villain is offstage: it's the community against the bad mining company or it's women against poverty. Or something more abstract. This [new novel] is actually Taylor against someone who wants to take her child away from her. And both sides have a point. That's really hard for me to do. But it's still not man against man [she laughs].

Q: There's a lot in *The Bean Trees* about the situation of Central Americans, about racism, about sexism. Would you object to that being called a political book or to your being called a political writer?

A: Of course not. It's a catalogue of everything I believe in. I'm only going to write a book if it's addressing subjects I care about. Otherwise, why write a book? It's not worth my time, and it's not worth readers' time, and it's not worth burdening the world with another pile of pages. It surprises me constantly that almost everybody else in the United States of America who writes books hates to be called a political writer. As if that demeans them.

Q: That doesn't seem to be as true outside of the United States, does it?

A: Living outside of the United States, I realized that's a very American thing. In Europe and in South America, if they're good, if they're read, writers are political. Look who's been winning Nobel prizes for the last fifty years: Naguib Mahfouz and Nadine Gordimer and people who write about conflicts between people and the state. People who write about racism and sexism.

When *The Bean Trees* was released in Barcelona in Catalan, I went there to do interviews. Everyone was very excited about the political issues and the immigration issues and the poverty dealt with in the book. It was such a different experience from interviews in the United States because no one asked me to justify putting political issues in a novel. I realized then that in the United States art and politics got this divorce in the fifties and there's never been a reconciliation. Artists working in the United States remain, by and large, afraid of being labeled political, even though they're no longer afraid that they'll lose their jobs or lose their readership. They're afraid they'll lose their badge that says, "I'm an Artiste," with a capital A. And I'm bored with this provincial, silly little idea.

Q: Why did you go to the Canary Islands?

A: I really wanted to get out of the United States for a while. I thought it would be a good time for Camille [her daughter] to learn Spanish. She's four, and she's bilingual now. And I wanted to be near Africa because a future book is going to be set there. There's something buried in me that I really need to write about from that experience of living there when I was seven and eight.

Q: Let's move to *Homeland*. What's the difference between writing short stories and writing a novel?

A: Writing a novel is like a marriage. You've got to make it work. You get into this thing; you're invested. Halfway through you find you hate your main characters, so you go through therapy. You figure out how to make it work. Writing short stories is like dating. You try that character; you try this character; you try this point of view. You like it; you don't. It doesn't matter that much; you're only in it for a short while. You try to make it a nice date, but you don't have to go out with it again.

Q: I was struck in the stories in *Homeland* with how many different voices you use—a male middle-class narrator, a working-class woman narrator. Were you consciously experimenting?

A: I did that consciously because I had written *The Bean Trees* in a very unself-conscious way. And then, boom! I had to write another book with the awareness that my mother and my neighbors and other people were going to read it. Since I was scared to death, I decided to write a book of short stories—maybe to avoid the second-novel syndrome.

But whatever I wrote seemed to be coming out in the voice of Taylor Greer. She had such a strong voice, I suppose, because she talks a lot like me and like the people I grew up around. Friends tell me that when they read the book they heard me talking. Anyway, Taylor wanted to tell every story I wrote, so I quite deliberately put her in the closet, and I moved out.

Q: And you told the stories in these very different voices.

A: Yes. As an exercise in stretching my vocal range, I would deliberately set up a story told in the voice of someone with a very different vocabulary than Taylor Greer's. Like a male, middle-class biology teacher. And finally I got to pull those nice scenes out of the drawer and say, "Now, who could say this?" [she laughs]. Writing a story collection after the novel was a really good exercise. I tried out a lot of things, some that worked better than others. But, since I was just dating, it was okay.

Q: "Bereaved Apartments" has some strange characters. What inspired that story?

A: That story has an embarrassing history. It was Flannery O'Connor–influenced. A long time before I wrote *The Bean Trees,* when I was writing fiction as a hobby, I would send stories out to magazines and they always came back. We didn't have very much money, and I really wanted to sell something. A friend read Ellery Queen mystery magazines and said, "Barbara, you could do this." I looked at these stories and said, "I could write this, and they pay five hundred dollars. I'm going to write a mystery."

So I wrote about this guy that lived next door to a woman who believed people were stealing from her. So of course he did it and no one believed her. The perfect crime. I sent it to Ellery Queen's magazine, expecting my check for five hundred dollars to arrive any day. Instead, I got this letter that said, "We're sorry but your characters are too developed" [she laughs]. "Damn it," I said, "I can't even sell garbage."

Q: So you resurrected it for the collection?

A: Yes. I stuck it in that famous drawer, and when I was working on the short-story collection I got it out and started thinking about this metaphor of a divided house and a divided sense of morality. The woman who's been imprisoned but is honest, and the establishment guy who's actually a thief living in two parts of a house. I created the Sulie character, who's kind of like Taylor with a past, and I wrote a draft from Sulie's point of view. That was all I'd done up to that point—first person point of view or third person limited—but it wasn't working. There was all the stuff going on that Sulie didn't know about—Gilbert's thievery—and I was only trying to *suggest* something that the narrator didn't know, which doesn't work.

Q: How did you come up with a solution?

A: I always go to my bookshelves and cast around for answers when I get stuck. And I pulled out Virginia Woolf's *Mrs. Dalloway*. Here is this woman and here is this man across the street proceeding along parallel paths and you got to jump back and forth between their consciousnesses. And I said, "Bingo! That's what I need to do."

Q: In "Poem for a Dead Neighbor," you write about an old woman with a black wedding dress.

A: Yes, that's the neighbor.

Q: Were they the same person? Someone real?

A: After I've told you that I don't base characters on real people, I'm a liar. That's one of the relatively few times that a real person's peculiar character suggested a story idea. I had a neighbor whom I loved very dearly who was quite old. She felt so embarrassed about the fact that she couldn't keep her house up and the fact that she didn't have anybody in the world except me to help her that she began to believe that someone was coming in and messing up her house. That's where the idea came from.

Q: And the poem is a more direct treatment of her situation?

A: The poems are about real people and things that have really happened in my life. She was afraid that the boy, as she called him, was going to get her black velvet wedding dress. So she gave it to me.

Q: Some writers talk as if they would be contaminated if they read other writers while they are working.

A: To me contamination is not the issue. I feel like maybe I'm Lake Erie and a fresh stream coming in will up the level [she laughs].

Q: That seems tied in with what you said before about the myth of independence. This is the myth of the isolated writer.

A: Right. If I just went to a cave and wrote, I think in a week's time I'd really run out of anything interesting to say. Possibly because I didn't study writing in school, I depend really heavily on other writers—like Virginia Woolf who got me out of that jam with "Bereaved Apartments." For every story in that collection I could tell you the name of the author who pulled me out of some kind of a crisis because I was doing things I had never done before. There's an Ethan Canin story in there; there's a Bobbie Ann Mason story. Which is not to say that I modeled myself after these writers. They showed me a path out of the woods I'd gotten myself into. I looked at the elegant way that they had handled a sort of tricky writing situation and learned from it how to cut my own path.

Q: Who helped you with "Homeland," the lead story about the girl and her grandmother?

A: My absent great-grandmother. I wrote the first draft when I was nineteen and turned it in to one of the two writing classes I have taken in my life. It was called "The Last Remaining Buffalo East of the Mississippi." I was obsessed with that great-grandmother of mine: I rewrote that story every single year. I really wanted to include it in the collection, but there was still something really badly wrong with it.

Then I realized that the big problem was that it was too autobiographical. The hardest thing to do is write your own history because you're inclined to include all this stuff just because it really happened, not because it adds anything to the story. So I said, "All right, the junk that's in there just because it happened goes out. It needs to be more distant. It needs to be legendary in tone." So I went to the library and read nothing but Cherokee legends for about three or four days, from morning till night, and got a rhythm and a tone of voice in my mind. Then I went back and wrote the sentence, "My great-grandmother belonged to the Bird Clan." And I kept that high note all through the story, as far as I could.

Q: You must have been relieved to have finally gotten it right.

A: Yes. It was an albatross that had been around my neck for fifteen years [she laughs]. I buried her. But I also felt really happy because I feel "Homeland" expresses my reason for being as a writer. I hope that story tells about the burden and the joy and the responsibility of holding on to the voices that are getting lost. That's what I want to do as a writer, and that's what Gloria in that story had to do. That's what gave her a reason to live, and I think that's the reason I live.

Q: When your story collection came out, one reviewer said something like, "This writer is so good with women; it's too bad she doesn't create more men." There was some criticism of *Holding the Line* for not presenting the male point of view, too. How do you respond to comments like this?

A: I can tell you a funny story about that. The review in the *New York Times* about *Holding the Line* was written by Paige Stegner, Wallace

Stegner's son. His whole complaint about the book was that there weren't men in it. He said in the review, "Where were the men?" Somehow or other, this review got back to Clifton [Arizona, site of the copper mine], and [striker Anna] O'Leary called me up and said, "We got this review and we read it and we asked ourselves the same thing, 'Where were the damn men?'" [she laughs].

The fact is that during the strike the men literally weren't in town. Paige Stegner doesn't believe that, but it was true. You could drive through the streets and see only women. It was the opposite of Morocco where you don't see women anywhere. For economic reasons the men all had to leave to get jobs elsewhere. That's where the men were.

Q: Does it bother you to be misunderstood in that way?

A: A review like that doesn't bother me because I feel that my audience is going to recognize that old chestnut. I hope that people are beyond worrying that a book has to be about men to be important.

Q: I asked Gloria Naylor what she told critics of *The Women of Brewster Place* who asked why there weren't more men. She said, "I tell them to look at the title."

A: Good answer. When I talk to college classes, a lot of times some cocky guy will wave his hand and say, "This is kind of a chick book." That's a quote. And I say, "Yeah, it kind of is because all my whole life I've been reading white guy books and there's plenty of those in the world. And since I've never been a white guy, the most interesting stuff I have to write is going to be chick books."

Q: In reviewing *Animal Dreams,* Ursula Le Guin said it belongs to "a new fiction of relationships," along with the work of women of color. She puts you specifically in the same family as Leslie Marmon Silko and Louise Erdrich [*Washington Post,* 2 September 1990].

A: A family I'm very proud to belong to. Those are my favorite writers, the ones I feel a kinship with.

Q: Is Codi [in *Animal Dreams*] the most like you of the characters you've created?

A: She's the least like me. When I began to write the story I understood it was a triangle of Codi, Hallie, and Doc Homer, and it was going to be about the ways that memory creates a family and creates a culture. I knew it would have to be told from these three points of view. Hallie would have been easy because Hallie is me. If I didn't have a family, I would have been helping build a new society somewhere. Doc Homer I could manage because, for some reason, I can deeply relate to a person who is losing his mind. I say that glibly, but it's true. Also, my Grandfather Kingsolver died a year ago of symptoms exactly like Doc Homer's, so I knew what the world looked like to him.

Codi's motivations mystified me, and her personality scared me because she's so detached; she's so wounded and she's so cynical. Her cynicism is frightening because I feel it's always walking along beside me; and if I ever once turned and embraced it, I couldn't let go. So I didn't like Codi much, and I didn't want to get close to her. But I knew that if I couldn't understand her the story wouldn't work. And the only way to force myself to understand her would be to write the book mostly from her point of view.

Q: It sounds like you've had bouts of cynicism yourself.

A: Before we moved out of the U.S. [to the Canary Islands] I got really fed up with the Americans who supported the [Persian Gulf] war. I started thinking that they deserved the war; they could just vote for whomever they wanted because I was just going to get out of here.

Q: Are you less cynical now?

A: I feel a lot better now because I feel like there's another America to come back to. Hope is a renewable option. There's a lot to love here and a lot to do. I can write about other places, but only through the travel section.

Q: But to make Codi live, you had to participate in her cynicism.

A: And I had to think a whole lot about what would make a person that afraid of life. She and Hallie I see as opposites. I always start a novel with a question that I can't answer. And the question that began me on that novel is, How is it that two people could come from the same family and be so different? I thought that starting with a pair of sisters—one of whom was very engaged with the world and one of whom had turned her back on the world—would help me to arrive at some answer to that question. And for me it did. It's not a simple answer, but at least for that family, for that situation, I found an answer. In a novel you can only create a situation and tell the truth of that situation. Otherwise, it's a pamphlet.

Q: *Animal Dreams* is a painful book. Did you plan that Hallie would die from the beginning?

A: Yes, I always know what will happen in my books. I do a plot summary and an outline first. I think like a scientist.

I tried really hard to come up with other solutions, though. I wrote several different plot summaries, but I was just trying to avoid the necessary thing. She had to die because that's part of what the book was about.

Q: It seemed in keeping with the horrible atrocities happening in Nicaragua.

A: Right, and the book was dedicated to Ben Linder, and I knew all along that it would be. So I couldn't cop out on that.

Q: Would you talk about him?

A: He was the real Hallie. He was an engineering student from Oregon who worked in Nicaragua during the eighties, helping to build a hydro-electric dam. He was one of the internationalists, mostly young people from all over the world who were there working to make that society what it could be. And some contras shot him in the head. I didn't know then, but he was close friends with a lot of close friends of mine.

I wanted to dedicate the book to him, but I felt a little presumptuous doing that, since he wasn't a personal friend. So I wrote to his mother and asked how she felt about it, and we've been in correspondence ever since. Being a writer has brought a new richness of people into my life that I could never have had otherwise.

Q: Let's talk about your poetry book, *Another America/Otra America*. Have you always written poetry?

A: I've been writing poetry since I was eight, and one of the poems in that book I wrote when I was twenty. Most of them are much newer than that, and all of them have been brought up to date as far as my technical skill. So I've been writing poetry all along; I just never meant to publish any of it. Since I consider myself a storyteller, even my poems are little stories. Everything I do turns into a little story. I come home from the grocery store with a story. They tend to be little morality tales, little fables, that have points.

Q: So how is writing poetry different from writing stories?

A: The poems are deeply felt moments that don't necessarily have a beginning or an end. There are big, complicated ideas that lend them-selves to novels, and there are some ideas that lend themselves to poems and stories. I've always written these things spontaneously, and I col-lected the poems because they were personal moments I wanted to keep for myself. Some of them are very painful moments. I just put them in a notebook in another drawer.

Q: What's the meaning of your title: *Another America/Otra America?*

A: When I was in Barcelona I figured out the meaning of that title because all these interviewers said they found it strange to be reading a translation of the book from the United States that's about poor people who live next to this park that's all run-down. They said, "We see *Dallas* and we read Danielle Steel and we have a good idea of what America looks like." And I said, "I could see that America on TV, too, but if I look out my window I see another America, and that's the one that 90 percent of the people live in, and that's the one I want to write about."

We call ourselves Americans, but we forget that there's an America that's not in the United States, that's full of people who speak different languages and have different creation myths. The main one is the America that starts in Mexico and goes south. Initially, that was the America I had in mind.

Q: That's why all the poems are published in English and Spanish?

A: Yes. I feel that it's appropriate that a book that's about these other Americas besides the one on *Dallas* be accessible to the citizens of that other America. In Tucson about a third of the people speak Spanish at home, so that's the world that I'm accustomed to.

Q: How did you choose the translator?

A: Rebeca Cartes, who is a Chilean poet who has lived in Tucson maybe twelve or thirteen years, did the translations. I've known her quite a long time. In years past we did a lot of readings together at fund-raisers for groups like Sanctuary. She liked my poetry and asked if she could translate some of it, and I enjoy the increased accessibility. My poems always sound better to me in Spanish.

Q: There are poems on other topics besides Central America.

A: When these poems first got up their nerve to come out of the notebook, I looked through them and realized the main theme there was a sort of conversation between the United States and Central America. A lot of the poems were about the way the one world looks at the other. And so the "other America" I had in mind was Central America.

Then, after the book was up for publication I realized I wanted to make it a little broader than that. And so I included a lot of poems that were newer and that were about other things.

Q: You critique many things in this book: homophobia, racism, colonialism, sexism. This is the angriest I've seen you.

A: That's because it's poetry. These are my moments of truth. The poems are little steam vents on the pressure cooker. Most of the time the novels or the short stories are cooking along in this sort of gentle way and once in a while—Pstt!—you have to turn that thing, and the steam shoots out so the novel won't blow up.

Q: Are you at all anxious about publishing these poems?

A: I'm nervous about this book reaching the shelves, not because I'm embarrassed for people to know that I get angry or have strong emotions—I think there are strong emotions in my fiction—but because the poetry is much more personal, and it makes public some terrible things that have happened to me and some terrible things that I've seen happen to other people. It's very intimate.

The United States is a culture that regards its victims harshly. We have this big myth that anybody can make themselves rich or happy or even cured from cancer if only they believe it. This culture believes in the self-made person, this myth of individuality again.

And what helps people to live with the fact that there are very rich and very poor, without being overwhelmed and destroyed by their guilt if they are the rich, is kind of a corollary myth that if you're bad off you deserve it. You did something wrong to let that happen to you. You're poor because you're not a hard worker. If you're Anita Hill [who charged then-Supreme Court nominee Clarence Thomas with sexual harassment], the majority says, "Somehow or other, you caused that to happen to you." So naturally it's going to be a little hard to see a book published that itemizes specific ways in which you've been hurt.

Q: Two poems, "This House I Cannot Leave" and "Ten Forty-Four," describe a rape. That must have been terribly painful to write about.

A: The rape poems were written mostly a long time ago. Only the release is new. The hard part is anticipating the response of a culture that believes victims deserve their fate. I don't believe that I got raped because I asked for it, but I know that there are people who think that. It's not so easy to add on top of the humiliation and the pain of having been raped, the pain and humiliation of having to look people in the eye who think that you're less than they are because of that experience.

Q: Why have you decided to go public about it?

A: You've got to do it because if there are enough Anita Hills, if there are enough case histories, other people will start to believe. Keeping your pain in the closet helps to support the myth that there isn't any injustice, that there isn't any pain. And it doesn't serve those people whose pain still is in the closet and who need the support of community, of knowing that they're Lake Erie—they're part of a sea of people who have suffered similarly.

Q: Would you talk about the organization of the poems?

A: I tried to organize these poems that were written in these little vents of emotion over twenty years in a way that made some sense. Because the book is about another America that people don't like to acknowledge exists, I started with a section of poems that are about alienation, how far from each other we are. How far the janitor is from the rich women in the same elevator who are talking about his people as if he weren't even there ["What the Janitor Heard in the Elevator"]. Then the book moves into "The Visitors," about people who have come here ["For Sacco and Vanzetti"]. Then it moves into "The Lost," people who have been hurt very badly by this alienation. "The Believers" are people who have saved themselves from being lost by believing in spirituality or love or family or history or something that gave them a path out of the woods. And the last section is "The Patriots," about political activists who have reclaimed that word.

What I hoped was I could lead the reader through this visit with a lot of people but end with a suggestion that there is another America that's getting its act together. That we can be as empowered as I was in 1971, saying, "Stop the war"—and the war stopped.

Q: "What the Janitor Heard in the Elevator" could be overheard in an elevator in New York today.

A: I really shouldn't be able to sign my name to that poem because that's an exact transcription of a conversation I heard between two women. I went home and wrote it down [she laughs].

Q: What are you working on now?

A: It's a novel called *Pigs in Heaven.*

Q: Is that anything like pigs-in-a-blanket that I ate as a kid?

A: Actually, in the Canary Islands, I was walking by a shelf in a market and saw a sign that said, "Tocino de Cielo," bacon from heaven. I couldn't believe it, so I bought it [she laughs]. Actually, it's a sort of pudding, but I had to buy the box!

My *Pigs in Heaven* is a novel that's about Taylor and Turtle from *The Bean Trees,* four years later. The situation is that Turtle, who's Cherokee, who was adopted by Taylor, who's white, gets suddenly famous in a way that could only happen in America. I won't tell you what it is. It's just one of those fluky things that happen in my novels. And she comes to the attention of the Cherokee nation and the tribe wants her back because there's a law, the Indian Child Welfare Act, that says Native American children cannot be adopted out of their tribe without tribal permission.

Q: This law has been very important for Native Americans, hasn't it?

A: It's one of the most valuable pieces of legislation that's ever happened for Native Americans in the United States because, throughout this century, a very strong and insidious form of cultural genocide has been the adoption of Native American children out of the tribe. As many as a quarter or a third of kids up until the seventies, up until the enactment of the ICWA, have been adopted by white families. There have been some very famous cases in the last few years in the Southwest of kids who'd been raised by white families for years and whose tribes asked for custody.

It's an instantly interesting and emotional situation. What struck me was the case of a Yaqui baby, who had been with her adoptive Hispanic parents for a year, who went back to the tribe. All of the media, which, of course, was written by white people—was saying, "How could this possibly be the best thing for the child?" And the tribe kept saying, "How could that possibly be the best thing for the tribe?"

Q: Here's that cultural difference between individual and community again.

A: Exactly. They were thinking community, and we were thinking individual, and there's no point of intersection in this dialogue because it's two entirely different worldviews: one that values individual rights above all else and the other that values the connections between the members of an entire community above all else—above individual rights, certainly.

From reading the transcripts of court proceedings I learned that some very cagey Native American lawyers have argued individual rights. They've argued that when these adopted kids reach the age of puberty they start to have all sorts of emotional problems because they don't belong anywhere, and so they end up with no identity at all. That's something to think about, but I don't think it's the reason that the tribe wants the kids back. . . . [It's] because they belong to the tribe, and the tribe needs them. But they have to frame the argument in Western terms to get anywhere at all in a Western court in front of a Western jury.

Q: So you were inspired by these real cases?

A: Right. I started thinking that I'd set up a perfect situation in an earlier novel. Also, I realized with embarrassment that I had completely neglected a whole moral area when I wrote about this Native American kid being swept off the reservation and raised by a very loving white mother. It was something I hadn't thought about, and I felt I needed to make that right in another book. Otherwise I don't think I would want to write a sequel. I would just start from scratch.

Q: What stage is this book at now?

A: Page 245 [she laughs]. I'm about halfway through it. I told you I think like a scientist.

Q: What effect, if any, has motherhood had on your work?

A: I used to get almost annoyed when people asked me that question because I thought, Nobody asks John Updike about being a father.

Q: Why not?

A: They don't ask John Updike, and they do ask me, and they do ask Leslie Silko and Doris Lessing because it's assumed that what a man does is his job and someone else is going to take care of things. There's almost this sense that if a woman writes, it's a hobby. That's kind of in the back of people's minds.

Q: So do you answer the question when asked?

A: I've rethought my answer. I used to say, "Day care, like every other working mother," but it is a little different. I mean, if I were a bank teller or a biology teacher, it would be assumed that what I do for a living is a job and someone else takes care of my child while I'm doing it. The fact is what I do is a job and a career and it's feeding my family. But it's very flexible, and it can come and go. There are weeks that I do it sixty hours a week, and there are months when I can take off.

Motherhood is a huge investment for me. I think it's as important to me as writing. I get very grouchy if I stop writing for more than a week or so at a time, but I'm glad from time to time when my daughter really needs me. And I give her the time she needs. I'm married to someone who is just as much of a parent as I am, so that's lucky. No, it's not luck. It's planning. I take credit [she laughs]. I wouldn't have had a child by myself because I know I couldn't quit writing.

Q: What difference does it make that you've made money from your writing?

A: Because I got a big check for *The Bean Trees* right after I became a mother, I got this validation in a culture that only values work that you get paid for. I got this stamp on me that says, "This woman is a real writer; she gets paid for what she does. So it's okay for her to put her child in someone else's care while she writes six hours a day." If that hadn't happened I would still be working on *Homeland*, and maybe I would have finished the copper strike book by now [*Holding the Line*], but *Animal Dreams* would not exist. I would have been struggling both with myself and with those around me to believe that I'm a real writer even though I'm not getting paid very much.

Q: At a recent session on contemporary literature at the 92nd Street Y [in New York City], the writer Stanley Elkin said that if you were a good writer, you just got published. Mary Gordon and Toni Cade Bambara, who were on the panel, too, disagreed. How would you respond to the question of who gets published and how? You got published pretty fast.

A: Timing was everything. I was lucky enough to get everything in motion to get published before I had my daughter. If you're a good writer and if you're lucky enough to have the time to do your work and improve your craft and invest the time also to find an agent or to send things out again and again—yes, you'll get published by someone. But that's something only a man would say—it's incredibly presumptuous because it assumes you've got nothing else to do.

Q: That's how many of us in the audience felt.

A: In the United States we're lucky enough to have a huge spectrum of publishers, from trade houses to university presses to small literary magazines. So somewhere or other, good writing will find a home. But the odds are good that it won't pay you very much. If it's poetry, it won't pay you anything; if it's an academic book, it won't pay you very much. So that statement [by Elkin] presumes some kind of financial arrangement that many writers never have.

Q: Is the problem more acute for women in our culture?

A: In our culture what you're doing that doesn't get well paid has to be fit in around all the other stuff that you have to do to make a living, to take care of your family. So for many women, especially, writing ends up being the thing they can only do if they have insomnia and don't feel like scrubbing the tile. I encourage women to make their writing a priority in their lives if they possibly can, but so many women just can't—not while their children are young or whatever. I feel enormously privileged that I'm able to make a living at my writing. But I still have to stop—in the middle of a sentence, in the middle of a word—the instant my daughter walks in. And dinner has to be got, and I have to look at the picture she drew in school. I want to do that, but it's a hell of a way to write a novel. It's much easier to walk around in this kind of altered state, where you're thinking of your characters all the time and don't have to go in and out of that world. But I have to because I also want to be a mother to my child. I don't want her to grow up and write some *Mommy Dearest* thing about how I ignored her for the sake of my art [she laughs].

Q: It sounds like your daughter has given you a lot.

A: Before I had a child I never knew what it was like to love another person far more than I love myself. Without a moment of thought I would throw myself in front of a moving vehicle to save her life. For Joe, maybe. But he could probably get out of the way of the truck himself, right? It's a very different kind of love. And I feel that among many other things I'm a better writer for having had my child. I don't feel any resentment, and I feel lucky that I have the luxury of being the sort of parent that I want to be, that I can be on call for her.

Q: Do you think there's a difference between the way women and men are treated as writers?

A: I think that women have to insist that our writing be taken seriously. For men it's automatic. The assumption is that what men do is important; it's making money. I think that women have to insist on our writing getting the same kind of respect.

Q: You do a lot of book reviews. What do you get out of being a reviewer, and what do you think the role of the book critic is?

A: Well it's not money, that's for sure. If you go on an hourly basis, reviewing books is less remunerative than mowing lawns or babysitting. I do it for two reasons. One is I feel it's a chance to give something back to the profession. I feel, perhaps arrogantly, that novelists are the best people to critique novels because only a novelist really understands that it takes just as much blood and sweat to write a bad book as to write a good book. So you go into it with a basic appreciation for the endeavor, and you're not going to be glib, and you're not going to do some sort of a hatchet job on some poor soul who's sitting there waiting for some sort of a review to find out how the rest of his career is going to be. The second reason I do it is that it brings me books that I would not otherwise have read.

Q: Will we see movies made of any of your books?

A: Everything I've written has been optioned at one time or another. Right now there's a script of *Animal Dreams* that I actually like a lot.

Q: What restrictions would you have on a movie based on your work?

A: It's a frightening thing to release the film rights because you know it's got to be changed a lot because film and books are not alike. They're a hot dog stand and a roller coaster. They do different things. But I want the moral point of view to remain the same, and I want the information to be accurate, such as it is. For example, if a movie is made of *The Bean Trees* I want it to get the story straight on the Sanctuary movement. I don't want it to be some screwy romantic comedy. Actually, the book has been optioned three times now, and the furthest along it got was a script which was a romantic comedy. And Turtle was almost not in it, let alone Sanctuary.

Q: How were you able to stop it?

A: The screenwriter didn't follow through, and they needed an extension from me, and I wouldn't give it. So they gave the rights back.

Q: Pat Barker's *Union Street* was made into a movie that wasn't anything like the book.

A: I saw *Stanley and Iris,* and that guy was barely mentioned in the book. When you sign that three-hundred-page contract you understand it's like giving up your child. And you know what can happen.

Q: So why would you do it?

A: I ask myself why I do it—because I don't need the money now. I can make the decision for other reasons. I say no a lot, and I only now give up rights to a director or a producer who seems like he's on our side of the fence politically.

Q: That's not most of the big ones, is it?

A: Oh, it's none. It's not most of the small ones. It's almost nobody.

Q: So what are your reasons?

A: My reason for saying yes, if I do at all, is, if I have a commitment to accessibility then I'm being a hypocrite if I won't allow movies to be made from my books. The best best-seller in the history of the world was probably read by fewer people than go see *Stanley and Iris.*

Maxine Hong Kingston's books and conversation are filled with stories she has heard and those she's imagined. Yet her involvement with people doesn't end here: She's also a committed activist who has moved from anti-war protests of the Vietnam era and union organizing activities during her schoolteaching days in Hawaii to finding "a language of peace" to use in her next novel. Her creativity, her humanitarianism, her commitment to pacifism are reasons why a Honolulu Buddhist sect honored her as a Living Treasure of Hawaii for her first book, The Woman Warrior: Memoirs of a Girlhood Among Ghosts (Knopf, 1976).

Readers of The Woman Warrior know some facts about Kingston's life: Her parents, Chinese immigrants, settled in Stockton, California. The oldest of six children, she worked in her parents' laundry, then at odd jobs to put herself through the University of California at Berkeley, from which she graduated in 1962. As a child Kingston felt silenced by racism—unable first to speak the language of the dominant culture, then to fit in with her white classmates; finally, as an adult, she found voice for her anger in writing. From her earliest childhood she rebelled against both her own culture's sexist assumptions about female inferiority and her mother's attempts to control her life. She wanted to be like the legendary Fa Mu Lan, the Chinese female avenger whose story is woven into the text as it was woven into her young life.

Photo: Copyright © Franco Salmoiraghi

In The Woman Warrior *and its sequel,* China Men *(Knopf, 1980), Kingston seeks understanding more than vengeance. Just as in the first book she tries to understand her mother, in the second she traces the lives of her father and her male ancestors—as settlers, sugar plantation workers, transcontinental railroad builders, laundrymen—in order to see them more clearly. Again she merges myth and reality to tell their stories, neither sentimentalizing them (most were painfully sexist) nor minimizing their struggles, particularly against racism and discrimination. These are American heroes, she tells us, refusing to let them or herself be marginalized as "other."*

Kingston's first novel, Tripmaster Monkey *(Knopf, 1989), continues this exploration of what it means to be Chinese American in a rollicking, surrealistic examination of San Francisco's 1960s youth culture as seen through the eyes of Wittman Ah Sing, twenty-three-year-old Berkeley graduate, nonstop talker, and aspiring playwright. Like Walt Whitman, for whom he is named, Kingston's protagonist celebrates himself and America. But this America is filled with moral and cultural contradictions that tempt the young hero to violence before his final apocalyptic conversion to pacifism. The ending represents the female narrator's hope for the still-maturing hero, Kingston explains.*

Kingston said she intended to continue stretching genre boundaries in her next book: The fiction part will continue Wittman's growth; the non-fiction part will examine the mind of the author creating him. In addition, she's searching for a new way to tell dual stories: a language of peace, a literature of hope, that will make us a less violent people. Not long after we spoke, however, fire ravaged her Oakland, California, neighborhood, destroying her home and the only manuscript of this sequel, forcing her to rewrite it from scratch.

*Despite the phenomenal popularity of her work (*The Woman Warrior *is the most assigned book on college campuses by a living America writer), Kingston, like many writers of color, still encounters stereotyped responses, which she handles with amazing tact. When Bill Moyers interviewed her for his* World of Ideas *television series in 1990, he said, "So much of what you write about, your own childhood, your ancestors, sounds so exotic to mainstream Americans that it's another world, and I wonder what they take away from that world." Unruffled, Kingston answered, "I should hope that at some point they would not think 'exotic' anymore, that they will see that I am writing about Americans. . . . I would hope that they would take away what it means to be a human being."*

I met Maxine Hong Kingston in May 1991, the day after she received an honorary doctorate at Brandeis University's commencement exercises. Again she was being honored for her ability to speak to us all.

Q: Do you consider yourself a political writer?

A: I do now. When I was first publishing I didn't want to be called a political writer because I saw it as a limiting category. I thought it meant that my writing would be defined by outside events and standards, and I wanted to write a literature from personal emotions and peculiar circumstances. I didn't want aesthetic standards and socially relevant standards imposed on me from other people. So I didn't want to talk about politics or to look at my own work in terms of politics. I really resented Marxist readings that came at art in a narrow political way, saying, "If this piece of art doesn't fit our propaganda, then throw it out."

But I now think that I am a very political writer in that I want to affect politics and I want to have power through the means of art. I feel that I am playing for political stakes and I want to change the world through artistic pacifist means.

Q: What do you mean by "artistic pacifist means"?

A: I want to make the world a more peaceful place. I want to help prevent wars. I feel very much a failure at this Persian Gulf war because if I had been more effective ten years ago, twenty years ago, then this may not have happened in February [1991, four months earlier]. Many people will say, "Well, where was the peace movement in January?" But that's too late already. We had to have been working a decade ago. So now we have to create a climate to prevent a war ten years from now, twenty years from now, or seven generations from now.

Q: How does the artist change the world?

A: An artist changes the world by changing consciousness and changing the atmosphere by means of language. So I have to use and invent a beautiful, human, artistic language of peace. This has rarely been done. The shape of the novel and the short story is violent because we have violent confrontations—[then] a denouement where things explode. You especially see this in movies.

Q: Have there been books that have had that kind of impact?

A: Art is so indirect that it's hard to pin down exactly—now here's this book and it prevented this action—because if we prevented the action we don't know that we did it. Maybe no one book can create an atmosphere of peace because no writer can ever be that powerful; but if there were many books and many readers we could do it.

I've been reading William Saroyan's short story "Cowards" [1974, reprinted in *Madness in the Family*, ed. Leo Hamalian (New Directions, 1988)], a wonderful story about a man who hid under the bed during

World War I. It's just the right short story to read right now in the aftermath of the Persian Gulf war. . . . [The characters] are Armenian Americans . . . in Fresno, California, but they are Americans, and they are all going off to fight in Europe during World War I. And now we are fighting again, all in different configurations.

The story asks, "What is cowardice?" Is it a refusal to fight or is it just going in to fight? But that's just one little short story, and it didn't stop World War II, but maybe evolution is longer than that.

A Native American speaker I heard once said we should think about the effects of what we do in terms of seven generations. How wonderful if in our energy policies we would think ahead seven generations instead of, "What are the gas lines going to be like next week?" Art is like that, too—maybe there is an impact . . . [down] seven generations. Maybe there isn't, but you've got to keep doing it.

Q: There's a connection here with the Chinese books of peace.

A: Yes. The Chinese have this tradition that once upon a time there were these three books of peace that had all kinds of directions on how to have nonviolent communication. The myth is that these books were burned, and so we don't know what was in them—we don't know their effects. So I think of it as, that's what I have to do. I have to rewrite them, to try and figure out what was in them, to bring them back. You see how rare these things are.

Q: At the end of *Tripmaster Monkey,* Wittman launches into an angry diatribe against racism during his one-man show. Yet he becomes a pacifist. What are you saying about anger here?

A: Even though Wittman is ranting and raving and is verbally violent, he doesn't do anything about it. His explosions aren't even explosions— he implodes quite often. He cuts his own hair. He burns his own socks. But he never hurts other people. And I'm very aware that he never does racist name-calling. It's very hip right now, as it was in the sixties, to call people by various racial names, but he never does that, even though he has a hip kind of language.

I'm working with [the question], Is it possible to get all the anger and the hate out verbally? And, if so, does that turn a person more peaceful? It's the same question that Wittman asks at the beginning: "Does playing football make you more violent or less violent?" Does it mean that you get all your violence out, and football players then become the most peaceful of men because they realize that the violence is just a game and they are not out there to kill anybody, and then it's over with and everybody goes home? Or does it aggravate it, and then you become more and more violent? What does letting the anger out do?

Q: Which is it?

A: I'm not sure that I answer that, except that my narrator comes in and says that he [Wittman] becomes a pacifist. It's more like her hope and her blessing for him rather than really knowing that it would happen. That's why I'm taking the book into a sequel now in which he is going to become older. Right now he is idealistic because he hasn't been tested yet. He's been a little bit tested—he managed to put on one show—but to truly be a realized adult man he has to continue. There have to be more shows, he has to have more nonviolent acts. In my next book he is going to become middle-aged and older, so that I can show a whole life of lived, involved, pacifist ideals. He's just barely even decided that he's going to try to be a pacifist. He's still reacting; he hasn't created himself yet.

Q: I got the sense that you wanted to get everything into this book.

A: But it's still not enough. That's why I want to do the next one.

Q: In *Tripmaster Monkey* you make more demands of your reader than you do in the earlier books. Were you writing an unfinished book on purpose?

A: Yes, this is a fake book [a term from popular music describing a book of melodies with, perhaps, only a hint at what the accompaniment should be]. I'll throw out a few things, and you improvise and finish it in your mind and imagination and life, and then also I, myself, will finish it in a sequel.

Also, I think it is demanding because an educated audience—one who has read a lot—will get more out of it than somebody who is not a reader. It is a book for readers. And it is about a reader. And the people in the book read. And I read. When I was writing it, I thought, I'm going to enjoy myself in this book—and my greatest enjoyment in life is to read. In my conversation I make literary references all the time and in my head I make them even more—I can hear Joyce and Shakespeare and Rilke. So why can't I use this in my writing? It's such a delight. It makes me really sad when there are so many readers who think it is off-putting to do allusions like that.

Q: You mention these literary presences. Did you have any specific literary models in mind for the novel?

A: I did in a really subconscious way. *Tripmaster Monkey* was going in all different directions. Chaos. Then, at the end, I thought, It will all come together when I do a monologue. That will pull the whole book to a point into one person. I thought I had really invented this wonderful form. And then my husband said, "Oh, that's exactly what Joyce did in *Ulysses.*

That's just Molly Bloom doing her thing" [she laughs]. And so I didn't invent it, but I didn't consciously have Molly Bloom's soliloquy as a model. Subconsciously, having read Joyce, it was there.

Q: The whole novel reminded me of *Ulysses*. I felt that, like Joyce, you were writing a comedy that would include everything—in your case, about being Chinese American.

A: The *New York Times* critic [Le Anne Schreiber] also said that *Tripmaster Monkey* was like Joyce, but she made the comparison as a criticism [23 April 1989]. She was saying Wittman was like Stephen Dedalus, and it was as if Stephen Dedalus took the book away from Joyce. I was thinking, Isn't that good, to sound like Joyce? Isn't that a tour de force? She made it seem like an accusation.

Q: Is the writing of fiction different from that of semiautobiographical stories?

A: Those categories were done by the publisher. I never categorize my work. It all feels like one long flow, and the process is not that different, although the first two books are based on real people and then I imagine about real people. Then, in *Tripmaster Monkey*, those [characters] are not real people. I make them up. But then they come to me in my dreams. They walk up to me. I can see them. They say things to me.

Q: Did Wittman take over the book? Did he write it?

A: No, it's me writing the book because I could always see a distinction between him and the narrator. The narrator is more myself, although Wittman is myself, too, because sometimes the narrator's voice and his voice come together and sometimes they are very separate. Even by the end of the book, when he [Wittman] is going on and on [in his soliloquy], the community comes in and they give him a wedding reception, and she [the narrator] at the end pulls his ear. She is often doing that.

I think also that the relation between the narrator and Wittman is the relationship between us and God. Sometimes God or Goddess is very close to us, and then sometimes we are being an atheist and she dies. Then, when she dies, his [Wittman's] voice becomes very strong and it takes over and it's very different.

I'm teaching Dickens now in my English class [at Berkeley], and the narrator is always an even distance away from the other people. The nineteenth-century God is not that far away—he is not right next door either—but he keeps an even, middle distance away from people. But my narrator comes and goes. And sometimes God is dead, and then the characters run wild as their voices take over and they become solipsistic;

then other times she returns and there is great joy. It is also a play of yin and yang [and a play] of the feminine spirit, which is dead quite often in this century.

Q: From what you are saying in the novel, I had the feeling that Wittman had to be a man.

A: So many feminists are mad at me.

Q: Pat Barker said the same thing when she left writing about women to write about a male character in *Regeneration.*

A: *Ms.* gives me a bad review, and I meet women who say that I wrote the first one [*The Woman Warrior*] and have been going downhill ever since.

Q: In a television special on you and your work, the actor Victor Wong talked about the humor in your books. He said that in order to get everything in *Tripmaster Monkey* you probably have to be Chinese. Is that true?

A: Wasn't he great? Wasn't he just such an alive person?

Q: Yes, he really was.

A: Well, he did say that. No, you don't have to be Chinese American, but I think that you can probably can get more out of it if you are. I think that I have written it in a way that just the average reader would be able to get a lot out of it. But if a person knew a Cantonese language they would get some more out of it. If a person knew village dialect, shtetl language, they would get even more out of it. I was very gratified by what Victor said because he was born and raised within miles of me [in San Francisco], and so that means he got that out of it, being another village home-boy. I've gotten letters from people like a Filipino American who said, "You wrote about my father's store, which was on the corner of such and such." He wrote me all about his store and the other store across the street. Now he got something really special out of it that nobody else could get because he knew that store and I knew that store.

Then there are my brothers and sisters, and there are a whole bunch of brother-and-sister, private, in-jokes that they got. They all think that *Woman Warrior* is a hilariously funny book. My brother said that it's the Chinese American *Portnoy's Complaint.* I think that you have to be my brother or sister to get that out of it. So there are many layers.

Q: Talking about humor, I'm surprised that more reviewers haven't discussed the humor in *Tripmaster Monkey.* Do you laugh as you are writing?

A: Sometimes I laugh, and sometimes I cry. I have a lot of feelings. I think there are probably more people getting the humor now than when the books first came out. But people come to them, as they come to any book written by an ethnic American, with too much reverence and respect, trying to be politically correct and thinking it's wrong to laugh at a racial joke. So maybe that's why people don't get the humor. It's like being in the audience at ethnic movies. At Wayne Wang's movies I've sat with audiences that were mostly Chinese American, and everybody is laughing and falling in the aisles. They just think this is funny. And then I sit in another audience at an art house, and there are scholars and anthropologists and liberals, and there is such reverence that either nobody laughs or they are not sure what to do.

Q: So reviewers of your earlier works have missed the humor?

A: *Woman Warrior* had some weird reviews from people in places like *The Atlantic* or *Harper's,* one of those magazines with no sense of humor [she laughs]. They said, "She has a quirky sense of ethnic humor that is questionable," or something like that.

Q: So you read reviews?

A: Sometimes. I read them less and less now and care about them less and less. But I used to read all the reviews. I don't like to read them when they make me feel bad because the reviewers don't understand. I think there were lots of reviews of *Tripmaster Monkey* in which they did not understand, and it hurts me because I think communication is life. Communication is love. And I often see people as refusing to understand. There is a denial. Because I think that I am writing very strongly and it's not that I don't say it well enough. My part of the communication is done well. It's the other end of it.

Another reason I don't read reviews lately is that I discovered that the reviewers aren't reviewing the books that the readers get on the shelf. Publishers send out these bound galley proofs [to reviewers]. Well, on the bound galleys it says, "This is not the final thing. Have it checked before you quote," but I rewrite my bound galleys completely. I rewrite the whole thing.

Q: That must drive your editors crazy.

A: Oh yes. Knopf charged me a thousand dollars. They reset the galleys. In fact, they sent out a new set of galleys, which I think never caught up with the reviewers. They reviewed the bound galleys and wrote about the ending of *Tripmaster Monkey* as being tedious, but I rewrote the ending. I thought it was tedious in a previous draft, and I made it much more dramatic by the time the book came out, but they had read the previous one.

Q: Why do you wait until it's in galleys to make these final changes?

A: [She laughs.] I can't help it. That is my pace. This is why I try not to give them my books until I do think they're ready, because I think that the various drafts are like building a tower. When you get to the top you can see visions, and you can see further, and you can see higher. Sometimes it's not till I get to the galleys that I can really see up there. I don't mean to rewrite; it's just that, as I'm reading it, I see what I ought to do.

Q: So it's a matter of seeing it as a final version, set in type, justified right column?

A: And I think, There it is; now I know what to do. Then I rewrite it [she laughs].

Q: Would you rewrite your earlier books if you had the chance?

A: I am going to do it. I am going to rewrite them, but in a different way. Not go back and pull those other books and do them over again, but, in the next book, say all the things that I didn't say earlier and correct myself. But I would make it a new theme in the new book. I would put things that I left out before into a sequel. Like this next one won't just be a sequel of *Tripmaster Monkey*. It will be a continuation of everything, so everything you make grows with sequels.

I've been really appalled that there are a lot of students now who are writing dissertations on my work and it looks like they just read one book. They don't write about it in the context of everything, which they should do because I think *China Men* is a sequel to *Woman Warrior*. I see each book as building on the last one. It's almost like I do the rewrites and then the next book is another rewrite.

Q: *Woman Warrior* was so successful, particularly among women. Has the popularity of that book been at all a burden?

A: Oh no, no. They all want me to write a sequel, but I just have to go where the compass points and where my interests are. I think to be a good feminist means that first you realize who you are yourself as a woman and, when you become a strong woman, then you face the Other. Whatever that Other is, whether it's men, the rest of the world, people of other races—whatever to you, in your psyche, the Other is. And so, when you become a strong woman, you also face the yang, and so, of course, the next book has to be about men, that's the other half of the universe. So to me it's profoundly feminist to write about men, to be able to create men characters, and to understand what I previously could not understand.

Q: You've said in other interviews that you wish you had downplayed the warrior aspect of Fa Mu Lan in *Woman Warrior.*

A: Yes, but that's okay because in the last story of that book she is less of a battle-ax–type woman. She is more of an artist. There are some things about Fa Mu Lan that I left out. I forgot that she was a weaver. I don't know why I left it out; I guess I didn't understand, as women do now, that sewing quilts is an art. I wish I had remembered because it would have connected her with Penelope and with Spider Woman and weavers in the sense of the text. So I should have done that. And then there is another scene [in the original version] where she comes home and becomes a woman again—a feminine, beautiful woman—with makeup and with flowers and with silk clothes. So I think I could have included that. But then I was at a different stage of feminism at that time [she laughs].

Q: Would it have been as effective to downplay her being a warrior? I know a young Chinese American woman who was quite inspired by that.

A: And that is the correct way to remember the myth or legend because that is history and that is what happened. She was a knight in armor, and so to take that away would be to distort history. But it was also part of history that she turned back and had beautiful hairdos and makeup and all that. And I like that ending a lot because it shows that any of us can come back from war and not be like Rambo. Rambo never comes back from war. He just stays that way. Whereas she [Fa Mu Lan] comes back, and she becomes a soft human being again. She is not brutalized by war. So it's good for me to bring in that ending, too, which the ancient people had.

But see the whole thing is part of the continuing problem of how do we tell the story of peace and how do we imagine peace and how do we live it? We still think that peace is boring—we think that peace is nondramatic. And if there isn't going to be a war, then what are we going to do with ourselves? After I leave here [Brandeis], I am going to Omega Institute in Rhinebeck, New York, to do a Buddhist retreat led by Chic Nhat Hanh, who is a Vietnamese monk who led the Buddhist delegation to the Paris Peace Conference. One of the things he says is that we don't know how to feel peace. We don't understand the joy that is peace. We think that it's boring. And that is an aesthetic and a social perception. He is dealing with many of these same problems we are facing, and I just know he has some answers.

Q: My students all want to know where you got the courage to finally speak, how you broke the silence you talk about in *The Woman Warrior.*

A: I don't know. I guess I never thought about it as courage. I think of it as secrecy—well, maybe it is courage. You know James Joyce said [in *A Portrait of the Artist as a Young Man*] that he would forge the conscience of his race with "cunning, silence, and exile," and I have always thought that those were very weird things to say because how could you do it with silence? But maybe he means secrecy, because as far back as I could remember writing—I guess I was eight or nine years old—it was my secret thing to do. I'd hide my work and I would pretend I was doing something else, and I would write all the things that were forbidden to say. And then I just kept that up forever. I was very clear from a long time ago that I didn't have to share this with anybody—so that makes me very brave. I can always write it, throw it away, and I don't have to publish. But I do have to say it. Everything has to be expressed.

Then, when you write well—with an understanding of people and situations from their own point of view—the writing becomes beautiful. At that point I thought, Well, now I can publish it because everybody will see how beautiful this is. It works out very well that way, but it means continuing with the secrecy and the working out of things inside until they become a very beautiful thing out in the world.

Q: Were the first things you wrote family secrets?

A: The first things I wrote were very much like the things I write now. So I think that I've been working on them for forty years because I began writing them then, but I didn't have the vocabulary yet. I didn't have the skill. So I just kept doing it over and over and over again until I had the understanding and the wisdom and the beauty of it. I began as a poet—I always had the rhythm and rhyme of language—but it would get bigger and bigger and bigger. I think that's the direction of all the work. It always seems to get longer and longer [she laughs].

Q: You begin *Woman Warrior* by telling a secret; that's a great way to open a book. How did your family react to your letting that secret about your aunt out to the whole world?

A: Well, I think the way I told it is okay. You see, my parents have only read my work in Chinese translation, and the translations are pirated editions and the translator works with ready-made forms, soap opera forms that don't have the power and the anger of the English. And so when my parents read that, I think they just see it as a nice story. So they feel good about it. They never talk to me about, "Oh, we told you not to say this and you did." My mother says, "Oh, everything is so accurate;

you described China so accurately." I guess she just feels fine. Maybe when she says that things are accurate, it is like saying that it is the truth and the truth is always right.

I do have a cousin-in-law who is Caucasian who said, "I only read the first chapter because it's just terrible for you to say things like that." She just never gave me a chance by reading the next chapter where things begin to work themselves out.

Speaking of secrecy, did you notice that Alice Walker and Toni Morrison both began books with almost that same sentence: "'You must not tell anyone,' my mother said, 'what I am about to tell you.'" Alice Walker's novel [*The Color Purple* (Harcourt Brace Jovanovich, 1982)] begins: "You better not tell nobody but God," and then Toni Morrison [in *The Bluest Eye* (Holt, Rinehart, and Winston, 1970)] has the line, "Quiet as it's kept. . . . " You see everybody has that same line; it's the same struggle to break through taboos, to find your voice. It's that same "exile, secrecy, and cunning" that Joyce was talking about.

Q: My students found *Woman Warrior* a painful book, especially one woman who is the daughter of Irish immigrants. She said your parents could have been her parents.

A: That's fine to let pain come in. I get lots of letters from women and from people of different ethnicities. They come from all over—Finland, and a lot of Jewish people—so I know that I am telling a human story. Even though it is very specifically Chinese American, it is also everyone, and I know that the people are feeling their own pain. Some people resist feeling by trying to understand my work as a Chinese book: The Chinese people are like that. And they understand it intellectually that way, but I see that as a sign of a person who's denying their own identity and their own feelings.

Q: Reviewing *China Men*, Mary Gordon said, "Mrs. Kingston's success at depicting the world of men without women must be the envy of any woman writer who has tried to capture this foreign territory" [*New York Times*, 15 June 1980].

A: She's such a fine writer. I remember her writing that. When I was working on *China Men*, I remember reading a critic who was praising the great male writers, like Flaubert and Tolstoy and Dostoevsky and Henry James, who were able to write great women characters. I don't remember if they said women had done men in this way or not, but I remember thinking that to finish myself as a great artist I'd have to be able to create men characters. Along with that, I was thinking that I had to do more than the first person pronoun.

Q: Did the things you tell in *China Men* really happen? Did you hear the story about your grandfather yelling his secrets into a hole because he couldn't say them out loud, for example?

A: Yes, I hear about those people from my mother. I met most of those men, but not all of them. But they were still a real presence. I never met my grandmother either, but they were [all] so real that I know, through my mother's stories, that they existed in real life. So they exist in my imagination. In fiction, there are people who I think about and I hear their voices, and then they are embodied in people who walk up to me and say things that are lines, exactly as I need. So the line between imagination and reality is not a sharp one.

Q: I like the history of U.S. discrimination against Chinese that you put in the middle of *China Men*.

A: Yes, isn't that a weird thing to do? [She laughs.]

Q: It gets the reader angry—there in the middle of the book, when we have come to know these people, to see the horrors of U.S. immigration policy.

A: Oh good. Those are the effects that I wanted. Also, I put it in that way because I found that readers don't have the information. Okay, so where are you going to put the information? Do I do an appendix? No, they'll skip the appendix. Do I do an introduction? No, they'll skip the introduction. Do I do footnotes? No, because that's too scholarly. Can I trust the readers to be interested enough to go to the library and do their own research? No [she laughs]. So, I'll put it right in the middle. I have seen Bibles with the Old Testaments and the New Testaments where, if you open them right up in the middle, it's the psalms, and I thought of that. If you open that book right in the middle it's like psalms; it's like commandments. It's laws that are implacable. So I was reproducing things that are set in stone.

Q: The language shifts there, too.

A: Oh yes. I wanted to say, "There's poetic language and there's legal language." I was contrasting the language of feeling, where you could make friends with the characters and feel for them, with this formal, distanced language. Actually, I didn't even write that part. My editor, who was a correspondent in Asia during World War II, wrote it to make it sound really legal, journalistic, and not my language.

Q: One thing I admire about your work is that in each book you seem to be taking new risks, experimenting with different voices, not replaying the same thing.

A: That's right. I was talking to my husband about that last night. How we, all of us, just have to complete ourselves by doing the next thing, and I'm not doing *Woman Warrior* over again. It wouldn't occur to me to do it over and over again. Isn't it interesting that a lot of poets lately seem to be writing prose and prose poems, and then you see short-story writers who are writing novels, novelists who are writing nonfiction, nonfiction people who are writing fiction. It's because you just want to continue with the other forms. I have been reading Henry Miller's [*The Paintings of Henry Miller:*] *Paint as You Like and Die Happy* [ed. Noel Young (Capra, 1982)], and he had this whole other life as a painter. And Gauguin was a great writer and I just read *Noa, Noa* [1900], and Van Gogh wrote the most amazing autobiography [*Dear Theo: The Autobiography of Vincent Van Gogh*, ed. Irving Stone (1937)]. So there are genres within literature, but if life is long enough, then I'm going to paint some more.

Q: Did you ever think of writing plays? The pull of drama is all over your work.

A: No. I think about it, in that these books have been optioned for movies and for plays. Everybody keeps thinking why don't I do it, because the playwrights haven't been able to adapt or translate right, but I don't think about it mostly because the next book is coming.

Q: You mentioned that it will take Wittman Ah Sing into adulthood. What else?

A: It's going to have everything in it. Right now I'm going to go to the J.F.K. Library [in Boston] to read the manuscript of *The Garden of Eden* [Scribner's, 1986]. That was Hemingway's last book. The published version is not the whole thing; it's only 250 pages. There are two thousand pages of manuscript. Hemingway was trying to find a language that was about relationships and about community. In some senses he failed because now he is known for shooting all those animals, for bullfights and his suicide. But he was reaching for something else. He didn't burn the book; he just left it there. But he wasn't strong enough to see it through to publication. A lot of it has to do with sexual roles, and so I just want to see what he was aiming for. He's got a map of the shape of a novel, and I expect him to take me so far and then I'm going to have to go the rest of the way. This has something to do with this next book. I need some sort of a map, in the way that I had *Ulysses* for a map although I didn't know it. This time I'm more conscious and know that Hemingway has got something going there, and I thought I would take a look.

Q: So reading Hemingway is for you—not necessarily for use in the book per se?

A: It's for me, but it's also for use in the book. I may even write about it and write about the whole process. You see, this next book is going to be fiction and nonfiction. The fiction part will be to show Wittman Ah Sing growing up, and then the nonfiction part is the mind of the self that is creating it—that will be how my head works, which is to think about Hemingway. I mean, he is our father. He is everybody's "papa." He told us he was, so I guess he is [she laughs]. He left some kind of a map. Like I say in *China Men,* my grandfather left the railroad as a message. Well, Father Hemingway left *The Garden of Eden* manuscript, and I want to find out where I'm going next.

Q: What role do readers play in your writing process? You've mentioned your husband. Does he read what you write?

A: He reads the last draft, when I think that it's perfect and there's no more to do. After he gives me his criticism and feedback, I do another draft. He also reads the galleys. The other role he plays is being the person who lives with me; I constantly bounce things off of him, and sometimes I don't even know that they are related to my work. It's just life perceptions that you exchange, and I'm sure that's very creative.

Q: Is he your best editor?

A: Yes. I wonder if that happens all the time? I know a lot of people say that.

Q: Jamaica Kincaid said that, too.

A: I wonder why people feel that the spouse is the best one? Is it that they really, objectively, are the best one, or is it an illusion that they are?

Q: Maybe it's the trust you have.

A: Or maybe they understand you and they would anyway, even if you were not a writer. And so, if you accept that they understand you, then they must understand the writing. Which I think they do. My husband does.

Q: It sounds like you are pretty private about what you do until that last point.

A: Yes, because everything is so invisible, and I'm just bringing it into visibility, and anyone can tell me that there's something wrong with it. I can see that it's not complete and there's so much more. I'm getting less shy about that now, though, because things are coming out more finished now. The early drafts are more complete and almost perfect. So I've been reading pages in progress to audiences and telling them that it's a work-in-progress.

Q: Do you feel that you are a better writer than you were twenty years ago?

A: Oh yes, much better. *China Men* is a better written book than *Woman Warrior*. The language is more lucid. The sentences are smoother. The rhythms are more interesting. The way I can tell a story is more dramatic. And I had much more control of narrative form.

Q: In an article on your influence on other Asian American writers, you said that you've talked to people who say that they get "Maxine Hong Kingston rejection letters" that tell them to read *Woman Warrior* and *China Men* and get an idea of how they should write.

A: Well, I was just quoting what I had heard from them, and I'm not sure how these publishers said this to them. It could have been said in a really condescending and racist way that made these young writers feel pigeonholed and discouraged them, making them feel that what they had to say has been said and, "Go away!" But it could also have been said in the way of a teacher to a student or an older person to a younger person: "Know what your tradition is." In a way like older feminists could say to the young lawyer who thinks that she's done it all on her own: "Know your history; be grateful to the people who went before." Also, you don't have to reinvent the wheel [she laughs]. I hope that it was said in that way and that the young people could receive that and take it seriously and, yes, go back and read.

Q: You once said you were "not a good person" because you knew people would not like your stories and you told them anyway. Several writers I have interviewed have talked about feeling a sense of responsibility to their racial or ethnic group, but it sounds like that didn't bother you at first.

A: Another way of thinking was that for about the first thirty years of my writing I wrote in the first person singular, and then at a certain point I saw myself as very selfish and solipsistic and narcissistic. I thought that surely I've got to be able to put another person into a scene, that I should be able to use the other pronouns. I saw it as a great failing as a human being and as an artist not to have a larger world. It's not enough to have a rich interior world because then I'm missing everything else out there. So then I struggled very hard to take in the rest of the universe, and I think of that as being a good person: to consider all of the other people and everything else, not just one's self.

Q: One critic wrote that despite recent gains, "Asian American writers often are expected to play the roles of cultural ambassadors, to speak for their race." Also, because their history has been largely untold, some feel they must "shatter stereotypes and honor the historical record with a religious fervor" [Edward Iwata, "More Asian Americans Suddenly Are Winning Mainstream Literary Acclaim," *Los Angeles Times,* 11 September 1989]. Have you felt any of this pressure?

A: Yes. This is the same thing that I have heard so many black writers say—that they have to take the whole responsibility of race. Then, at the same time, there are people of our own community, other Chinese Americans, who will say, "Well, how dare you speak for us? Who voted for you? How can you make fun of us?" I had a short conversation with Philip Roth as we were walking up from [the Brandeis] commencement ceremonies. I thanked him for the writing that he had done after *Portnoy's Complaint* [Random House, 1969] in which he faced the reception of some Jewish people who accused him of making fun of them and of his mother and all that. I told him that he said it, and all I had to do is take out where it said "Jewish" [she laughs].

Q: So you get attacked on both sides: You get attacked if you try to break down stereotypes and if you don't.

A: Oh, yes. That's right. There are people out there who are just trying to say, "Stop it, don't even do that. Don't write." It's sometimes from a masculine-feminine point of view. So many minority men are angry at minority women for saying anything, especially among Chinese Americans. For some reason, most of our writers are women, and most of our critics are men. And the men are saying that we [the women] have feminized Chinese American history because our history is mostly masculine. There were mostly men who came here for one hundred years, and yet there are women who write. So these critics are saying, "How dare you write it?"

Q: I know that the writer Frank Chin has criticized you for this. Describing that dispute, San Francisco writer Edward Iwata wrote, "The struggle between Frank Chin and Maxine Hong Kingston is a literary battle for the soul of Asian Americans" ["Is It a Clash over Writing Philosophies, Myths, and Culture?" *Los Angeles Times,* 24 June 1990]." How do you respond to this?

A: For a while I just thought, Why doesn't Frank Chin just shut up and go home and write? The only way he's making a literary reputation is to attack me. He doesn't have anything else going for him. That's his career. And by doing that he is destroying himself as a writer because he is just wasting his words.

This idea of writing for the soul of Asian America—maybe there is something there. I no longer read Frank Chin, but I hear that the latest works are an attempt to find Chinese American manhood through a violent, warrior mythos, trying to find an identity with killers, with knights from the past who solved things by going to war. He says that our history is one of battle, of blood. I know that he has battle cries and one of his mottoes is, "War." He says it in Chinese.

I am going in the completely different direction. I am looking for a language of peace. I am trying to rewrite a book of peace. And so maybe that is fighting for the soul, not just of Chinese American people, but the human soul. I want the human soul to be one where people care for one another and where people cherish and nourish and value one another, and I am trying to think of ways of conflict resolution that have to do with talking or hugging or something, whereas his idea of conflict resolution is to kill each other.

Q: Where is this going to go? This is very true of the African American literary community too. Writer Ishmael Reed trashing Alice Walker for her portrayal of black men in *The Color Purple.*

A: It's just so horrible. It's the same thing. And Ishmael and Frank are friends. The guys are doing all this criticizing, and the women are just going about creating. In general, also, the women don't answer the critics. I go back and forth on that. Most of the time I don't answer this. Frank does terrible things. He tells me when he sees me at a conference he's going to beat me up. And I don't answer it because I keep thinking I'm transcending, I'm not being reactive. But then sometimes people see this as weakness and say, "See, these women don't have an answer." But we don't want to answer, because any little thing we do to them will destroy their manhood even worse because they are already so fragile.

Q: Is this inherent in men and women, or is it part of the acculturation they go through that leads to this sort of split?

A: I think it's partly that and another part is that it is aggravated among minority people because minority men have even a worse time becoming men than mainstream men, so the battle in the general culture continues back home. They say that wife beating and all cuts across cultures, but I have a feeling that it is probably worse among the minorities. When you face the frustration of not being realized as a human being, that human energy comes out in this mad way. I'm so upset that even literary people act this way. We should be more enlightened—after all, we have other means besides fists and guns. So why are we using these means for the men to beat up on the women?

Q: In terms of the conflict between men and women of color, I think the press plays right into this.

A: Oh yes, they love it. And there are plenty of black men and Asian men who love Alice Walker's work. And they love my work. And there isn't even a battle going on. It's Ishmael Reed all by himself. It's Frank all by himself. But the press plays it up as if it's all these Asian men against me. I think that for a while Frank got so much press because the press didn't know who else to call. So every time a new book comes out, they call Frank and then he speaks as if he's speaking for everyone and says, "Oh, we hate Amy Tan; we hate Maxine." But it's just him; he doesn't speak for anybody.

Q: This raises another point: Who should review books by Asian American writers? Should it be a member of that community or not?

A: That's another one of those double binds because we all want it both ways. Everybody thinks, Well, if we get an Asian then that person really knows what they are talking about. And then, if they give a negative review, it's not from ignorance. On the other hand, they think, It's really terrific to have a white person review it because then it's being recognized by the canon-makers. And so people fight about it all different ways. A newspaper someplace in the Midwest—I think it was in Chicago—assigned *China Men* to the only Asian American they had on their staff. He was a sportswriter. He wrote about oranges. He said there is a whole tradition of citrus fruits that I didn't understand.

I was at a gender and ethnicity conference at Georgetown University where there was a great uproar started by a Chinese American young woman who was upset because most of the papers that were delivered on my work were done by Caucasian women and only one was done by a Chinese American woman. I thought that was a pretty good proportion right there, but I think that she felt that I was being coopted. But I think that if all the papers had been delivered by Chinese American critics, she could have been equally upset that we were ghettoized and not recognized by establishment critics.

Q: What would you say to all these people who are writing about you? What do you want them to bring to a study of your work?

A: I want them to read well and accurately. I don't want them to speed read or skim, which is a condition at college, I guess. I want them to have their hearts and their minds and their eyes open as they are reading it and to read with their feelings. It's not just an intellectual book. They have to let the images come inside of themselves for the images to do their work. Something amazing happens with images and metaphor: We see these pictures, and they go inside of our imaginations, and our imaginations change. So I hope that people will allow themselves to change as they are reading the books. I hope that they will become different people by the time they finish. Maybe this is why they resist it: They don't want to become different people [she laughs].

Q: You're back teaching at Berkeley, where you were an undergraduate. Does it feel strange?

A: I love teaching and being back after having been a student there. Some of the professors that I had are still there, and it is just so amazing being a colleague of theirs. I love talking to the students.

Q: You mentioned teaching Dickens earlier. What course is that?

A: It's called Reading for Writers. I'm teaching *David Copperfield* because it's the story of a writer and how he becomes a man and becomes a writer, and I wanted a book that was long so we get that sense of nineteenth-century time.

Q: It's a great book to study for narrative voice.

A: Yes. The older man who is the narrator will sometimes get very close and look at David and say, "Oh, that poor baby." Then, at other times, he's inside of David. It's really wonderful.

Q: What other authors do you like to read?

A: There are some people that are really special favorites. Right now I'm reading William Saroyan, as I said. I find he is just a great writer. I think [Toni Morrison's] *Beloved* [Knopf, 1987] is a great book, a very human, mythic, epic book. I expect a sequel because that young woman ought to grow up.

Q: You, Toni Morrison, Leslie Marmon Silko, Francine du Plessix Gray, and four other American writers went on a trip to China back in 1984 as guests of the Chinese Writers' Association. Did you have the sense that you were seeing for the first time these people whom you had imagined?

A: I saw them for the first time, but also I felt I was seeing them again. And I know they were seeing me the same way because there was my picture and all the other family pictures at their houses, and then also throughout China people would say, "Welcome home," or, "It's nice that you've come back." They knew that it was my first trip there, but still they referred to it as a return. I think we all think that way.

Q: Harrison Salisbury, who was also on the trip, wrote that people were lined up to see you—that everyone claimed to be a relative [*New York Times,* 20 January 1985].

A: Oh, yes. All my relatives at the train station. God, it was so wonderful! That whole journey was a linguistic adventure, too, because we traveled from the north to the south, and the closer we got to my home village the more I could communicate. It was quite amazing. Harrison Salisbury is quite amazing. Here's this man in his eighties who could walk faster and do more than any of us, traveling with his typewriter that he had since World War II.

Q: You mention dialect differences. When you finally gave a speech you used a peasant dialect, didn't you?

A: Yes. Really, the only Chinese language that I have is the dialect that my parents speak. It is a real minority dialect in the southwest, and it is not even the main dialect of people who are here in the U.S. So here I was traveling further and further south and listening to the dialect changes and having translators coming along. At Chinese school we studied Cantonese dialect, but that isn't my parents' dialect, which is the peasant, village dialect.

So we came to these formal dinners where various ones of us had to give speeches, and they [members of the delegation] just kept poking me, "Okay, you speak, you speak, and do it in Chinese. You do it." And I thought, No, I just can't. I don't think I can give a formal speech in Chinese. I can't do it in Mandarin. I can't do it in Cantonese. Then it occurred to me, I'll just do it in village speech. And so I did, and I translated myself. I would say a sentence and then I'd translate it into English. And I realized that no one there understood me because the Chinese there wouldn't either. And it felt really good when I realized that I was being more politically correct than anybody because my class credentials were impeccable! I bet no Communist ever did this because they would do whatever the official national language was. Or, if they were really feeling peasant, they would do Cantonese, but they wouldn't do this peasant dialect [she laughs]. I just got such a kick out of it. I felt so at home [more laughter].

Q: I get a sense that you like to poke fun at the establishment in this trickmaster way.

A: First I feel really shy and awful and out of it and déclassé, and then I get into it [much laughter].

Q: Do you think that you will write about that trip?

A: That is really interesting to me because no, I haven't written about it. It takes a long time for me to take things in and see what they become. And I notice that Toni Morrison and Leslie Silko haven't written about it. But Charles Wright has had some poems published already about the trip, and Allen Ginsberg and Gary Snyder were composing as they were going along, so they have their China poems. I think everybody felt profound connections with roots, and so it is interesting to see the creative process of people. Some people are faster, some are slower, and maybe it will come out in their work in other ways. Maybe there was an image [from the trip] in *Beloved.* I don't know.

Q: Has there been a downside to your success?

A: The bad thing is that people recognize me and trap me. Just on this trip [to the Brandeis commencement] a young man trapped me. I was in first class, and he came through the curtain, and he started talking to me, and pretty soon he was right up in my face [she moves forward to demonstrate]. He just wanted to tell me everything about himself, and he wouldn't stop talking. I couldn't figure out how to get rid of him [she laughs]. He introduced himself as a conservative, and then he had to tell me his whole conservative philosophy of life [she groans].

But then, in some ways, he's a character in my work. I've imagined him, and he appears. He was like Wittman, except that he's a right-wing Wittman. In another way, when he did that to me it's like he's saying, "Here I am! You write about me and take responsibility for me." How are you, as a good liberal, going to answer that?

Q: I think I would say, "Go away!"

A: But he can't go away; he's another being on the planet.

Q: So what are the good things about your success?

A: There are lots of good things. Wonderful things. My father says that I'm living the life that he wanted to live. My sense of community has gotten so wide. I now know that I can go anywhere in the world and I will run into a friend or I will make a friend. I actually have the power to make a family, a community, that's all over the world.

I'm having so much fun with the pronouns "we" and "our." When I say "my people" and "our people," I mean everybody [she laughs]. And I watch other people think that I mean Chinese people or Chinese American people or Asian American people or women. But, more and more, I'm spreading the meaning to mean every human being on earth, living and dead, because there are reincarnations, too—ancestors and root people. So I am feeling more and more like a Spider Woman. So there are all those good things, but also the responsibilities of all that kind of power.

Like many children who came of age in the late 1960s in immigrant working-class families, Valerie Miner grew up believing in the importance of hard work. As an undergraduate majoring in English at the University of California, Berkeley, she thought about becoming a fiction writer, but instead got a master's degree in journalism, a more practical field. Writing fiction "wasn't the sort of thing my people did," Miner remembers. It didn't seem like real work. Besides, that was 1970 and the war in Southeast Asia was tearing the United States apart. Miner left for Toronto in protest.

For the next seven years, she lived abroad—first in Canada, then in England—writing and traveling widely. She discovered feminism, became a peace activist, got divorced, wrote free-lance articles on subjects ranging from the Miss Canada Pageant to Tanzanian president Julius Nyerere, coauthored a feminist essay collection, Her Own Woman *(Macmillan of Canada, 1975), and collaborated on two collections of short stories,* Tales I Tell My Mother *(Journeyman Press, 1978) and* More Tales I Tell My Mother *(Journeyman Press, 1987). By the time she returned to the United States in 1977, Miner had an international perspective and impressive credentials as a writer.*

While teaching at the University of California, Berkeley, she began writing longer fiction. Her novels, like her essays, invite readers to think about pressing societal and personal issues, such as sexism, violence, poverty,

racism, homophobia, and war; but Miner doesn't give her readers easy answers. Instead, she invites them to think about these issues as they
manifest themselves in daily life. Her social criticism emerges from her
clear-eyed vision of the interrelationship between the personal and the
political.

First published in the United Kingdom, Miner's fiction reflects her varied
experiences. Set in London and California, Blood Sisters (St. Martin's,
1982), her first novel, focuses on the struggle by a family of Irish and Irish
American women to understand one another's ideals. It explores the rival
claims of feminism and nationalism, pacifism and violence, without coming down on one side or the other. Murder in the English Department (St.
Martin's, 1983) examines guilt and innocence in the story of a feminist
professor who defends a graduate student whom she suspects of having
murdered a sexist colleague. Movement (Crossing Press, 1982) examines
ten years of changes in the life of Susan, like Miner herself, a leftist activist, working journalist, and feminist. As the novel ends, readers don't
know what choices the protagonist will make.

Miner calls her next novel, Winter's Edge (Crossing Press, 1985), a turning point because it was the first time she wrote primarily about the lives
of working-class people—specifically, the friendship between two elderly
women in San Francisco's Tenderloin district. Her next and most ambitious novel, All Good Women (Methuen [London] and Crossing Press,
1987), continues this theme of women's friendships, tracing the lives of
four young working-class women on the home front during World War II.

Trespassing and Other Stories (Crossing Press, 1989) continues Miner's
exploration of what it means to cross boundaries—of class, culture, age,
and sex—in tales set in Europe, America, and Asia. Finally, A Walking
Fire (SUNY Press, 1994), a retelling of the Lear story from Cordelia's
point of view, brings together themes from earlier works: the importance
of family, the significance of class, the responsibility of the individual for
collective actions. Again, Miner makes connections: The family acts as a
metaphor for American foreign policy in Southeast Asia.

Miner has edited and written essays on many subjects. With Helen E.
Longino she coedited Competition: A Feminist Taboo? (The Feminist
Press, 1987), a collection of essays on the topic by women from diverse
backgrounds. In the lead essay of Rumors from the Cauldron (University
of Michigan Press, 1992), a collection of her essays, reviews, and report-
age, Miner explains that she cannot insulate her art from her politics. She
explains that she writes out of all her identities—feminist, lesbian, reluc-
tant American, woman with working-class roots—as part of "an
imaginative collectivity."

During our two conversations in June 1990 and January 1992, which
I've combined here, Miner talked about this "imaginative collectivity of
readers and writers" and how it has shaped her work. She talked, too,
about international feminism, the politics of publishing, and writers as

workers. Like her mother, who worked in restaurants until she was seventy-seven, Miner identifies as a worker. Having authored or coauthored twelve books, she's earned the title.

Q: Would you start by talking about your background?

A: My ethnic background is Irish Catholic and Scots Presbyterian. I identify much more with the Irish Catholic because I went to Catholic schools as a child. My mother was born in Edinburgh. When she was five, her mother died of an abortion on the kitchen table during World War I; her father died of tuberculosis when she was twelve. She grew up in what they now call a blended family—there were fifteen kids, some from each parent's previous marriage and some that they had together. She had to quit school when she was twelve to go out to work in a coffee shop. Then, at twenty, she came to the United States and waitressed in New York City and various other places. When she was seventy-seven, she was laid off her job in a coffee shop in the Tenderloin in San Francisco.

Q: Was your mother the model for Margaret in *Winter's Edge*?

A: She's not really Margaret, but that neighborhood is her neighborhood, and the book is informed by her experiences. I had her read it for local authenticity and because I wanted to dedicate it to her. I was pleased that she liked it.

Q: Did she make any changes?

A: There was only one thing she wanted me to take out, and it touched me, although it seems superficial. I had written that at the café where Chrissie worked, the policemen got 50 percent off their dinner because the owner wanted them to keep an eye on the place. My mother insisted I take this out because she said it would make the policemen mad and they might not come back. At first it floored me, and then I realized that I was writing about her world. And this isn't central to the book. I can tell the story now because the café where my mother worked is closed.

Q: So you took it out?

A: Yes. I knew that book would be read in her community; and indeed it was. People talked about it, and that was all very satisfying to her. It wouldn't have been so satisfying if I'd put that in.

Q: Many of the writers I've interviewed have said that storytelling was important for them as they grew up. Was your mother a storyteller?

A: I never used to think so. When I went to China with a group of writers in 1983, Paule Marshall and Alice Walker would talk a lot about their family being storytellers. I thought at the time, Oh, well, my family weren't storytellers, but then I realized that my mother was. She told stories as jokes, and it was an ironic, self-deprecating type of storytelling. She, like many Scots, had a great love of language which she passed on to me. And, taking off from that question a bit, I realized that the silences came from her, too, and the need to escape.

Q: What were your mother's silences?

A: Well, her family history was obscured. I was always hearing about a new aunt and a new uncle that I had never heard of before. Maybe six years ago, she was sitting having a drink with me, and she said, "Sometimes I think about Peggy and I wonder what happened to her." I say, "Who's Peggy, Mom?" "Peggy was my sister. She was between me and Colin [the youngest of the children]. Somebody wanted to adopt me, but I didn't want to leave my father—by that time my mother had died—so they let Peggy be adopted. Then we never heard from her again, and no one knows where she is." All of this comes from her saying, "Sometimes I think about Peggy" [she laughs].

One night two years later, she was telling me about visiting Jack in a juvenile home. "Who's Jack, Mom?" He was another brother. So when I was growing up, there were these relatives who would emerge, one by one.

Q: Were those the main silences?

A: What I learned after I finished college was that her parents weren't married when she was born. In Edinburgh in 1910, you cannot imagine the shame connected with illegitimacy, Presbyterians being what they are. She didn't tell that story, and there were a lot of secrets like that. My father's mother, who lived with us until I was eleven or twelve, had been institutionalized when my father was a child. My father also drank too much, so there were all the problems associated with that.

Q: What was your father like?

A: Because he was in the merchant marine for forty-four years, my father was away a lot when I was a child. I was born in New York City and lived in New Jersey until he decided to take a port job in Seattle. I had four years in Seattle, then we moved down to California, where I lived in a town called Hayward. I went to Berkeley, the first one in my family to go through college—my mother wanted me to go to secretarial school. Then, in 1970, I left the country because of the war in Southeast Asia and was away for seven years. I had no intention of coming back. More women went to Canada than men at that time, but not too many people know that.

Q: When did you begin writing?

A: I started writing for the grade school newspaper, *The Hilltop Herald.* Looking back after years of talking to friends and years of therapy, I think that I always wanted to write fiction. But I started out professionally as a journalist because it felt to me that fiction writing wasn't the sort of thing my people did. I never had the nerve to take a creative writing course in college.

Q: You felt a pressure to do something practical with your degree?

A: Yes. In a certain sense, literature seemed audacious. Also, the literature that we read in the late sixties—I graduated from university in 1969—was really British literature by middle-class or upper-class white men. My people, working-class people, were not represented in the material I was reading. I did a double major in English and journalism, then a master's degree in journalism. I think that I did the journalism part because it was the sixties and the world was exploding. I thought journalism was more useful than studying English literature.

Q: You published your first book in Canada. Would you describe that process?

A: That was a coauthored book called *Her Own Woman,* which was published in 1975, International Woman's Year. When I arrived in Toronto in 1970, I was beginning to become conscious of feminism. I had done a piece in graduate school about discrimination against women in academe, which I later published in the *AFT* [American Federation of Teachers] *Journal.* Anyway, I started working as a free-lance journalist in Canada in 1970. In '72 or '73, some other women writers and I became interested in starting a writers' union. When we interviewed other writers we knew about wages, working conditions, and the realities of their lives, we found out that everybody had legitimate complaints, but that women writers were treated worse than men.

In the beginning, none of the five of us in this writing group would have identified ourselves as feminist, in the sense that none of us would have said we had been discriminated against. But, boy, after a few sessions talking to each other and talking to some of the men about how their work was treated and where it was placed, we had a more realistic sense of what was going on. In response, we decided to edit a book ourselves, with no external editor.

We did this series of essays about contemporary Canadian women from diverse backgrounds and social classes who we thought were, in the language of those days, "strong role models." I chose an Olympic runner named Abigail Hoffman and [novelist] Margaret Atwood. Both of the pieces, but particularly the Atwood piece, were entrances for me into writing fiction. They were exercises in character development and lessons about the professional world. I then went on to interview Maryon Kantaroff, a wonderful Canadian feminist sculptor, and the writer Margaret Laurence, whose work I admire a lot. I used that process of being a journalist and asking people questions as a way of opening doors for my own courage and finding out where I could stick my toe in as a writer.

Macmillan brought the collection out in Canada, then, in 1985, it was brought out in mass paperback and is still in print, which is quite amazing. Formac Publishing [in Canada] publishes it.

After living in Canada for four years, I went to England, where I worked on my second book, another collective effort, which was called *Tales I Tell My Mother.* Then I started to write my own books.

The genesis of those first two books is key to the way I write and the way I think about writing.

Q: How so?

A: Those collaborative processes were very important to me. As a writer, I still strongly identify as a worker, partially as a consequence of working with those other people and partially as a result of my class background. I see my work emerging from some kind of imaginative collectivity, not from solitary genesis. That approach has been nurtured by my working in writers' groups, which I still do, sharing my fiction. I very happily claim those two books as my first books. A lot of American critics tend to dismiss coauthored books, particularly books that have five authors [she laughs]. But they were really crucial to me. And I think they are also great books.

Q: In "An Imaginative Collectivity of Writers and Readers," the lead essay in *Rumors from the Cauldron,* you talk about your work as integrally connected with your life as a feminist, a lesbian, a person with working-class roots. Would you expand on that idea?

A: My work is influenced by questions that hit me when I am walking down the street or in a meeting or in a classroom or some other way in connection with my communities. The themes in my work have emerged from that imaginative collectivity, from my activism. Also, my style has emerged from a consciousness of a larger world. I try to make my work accessible. Another way in which I see my work as being part of an imaginative collectivity is that I am interested in a kind of Brechtian raising of contradictions and asking of questions. A lot of the books end with questions.

Q: For example?

A: At the end of *Murder in the English Department* you don't know whether Nan will go back to her job or what she will do about her sexuality. In *Movement* you don't know what Susan will decide about motherhood, politics, or even geography. In *Blood Sisters* you have two very different points of view presented in Liz and Beth. So I see myself trying to raise the questions that I hear my communities asking.

Q: Like Maxine Hong Kingston and Pat Barker, you wouldn't mind being called a political writer?

A: No, but I think this American reflex judgment that if you write political fiction you are writing didactic fiction is funny because I see my fiction as the opposite. I see myself as somebody who is learning as I write, motivated, mostly, by questions. For me the process of writing a novel is to be thinking about the questions.

Q: Your talking about wanting to be accessible reminds me of what many of the writers have said about wanting to reach a wider audience than an educated elite.

A: Although I am a literary writer, I don't want to be obfuscatory. Some critics assume that if you write accessibly you are writing simplistically.

Q: Would you be comfortable being put in a kind of nineteenth-century fictional tradition? You seem to be interested in social issues in the way most of them were. I think of George Eliot, for example.

A: I'd not only be comfortable; I'd be honored. I don't know, in some ways, why we left those traditions behind. There were some things that needed to be left—a lot of social convention, of prejudice, of verbiage— but there was much that was really enriching—contexts in which to address social and political questions, for example.

Q: How would you describe your relationship with your readers?

A: One of the reasons I moved from journalism into fiction is that I wanted a deeper, more intimate relationship with the reader. For example, last night at a reading, I met a woman whom I felt I knew, even though I had never met her before. When we talked afterward, it turns out that she'd read all my books and talked about what they had meant to her. But I also felt as if I knew her. So there is a way in which people do open to you if you're open to them. I think this is particularly true if you are offering open-ended questions and your characters are open.

Intimacy involves a kind of trust that is built on an egalitarian, rather than an authoritarian, relationship. And that has to do with friendship. My ideal relationship with the reader is a reflection of the female friendships in my books.

Q: Would you say that women's friendship is the main theme of your fiction?

A: The short answer is: probably. The longer answer is that I go into a book because I'm excited by a set of questions, as I said before, so I'm not setting out to prove a point. I feel very strongly that didactic fiction is not successful fiction. So I don't think I enter a project saying, "This is the theme," except insofar as, for instance, with *A Walking Fire*, I knew I wanted to try to hear Cordelia's voice. I didn't know what Cordelia's voice was going to say.

Another theme is the difference between friendships and family relationships: what these relationships do to us, what we get out of them, the way they help us grow. Possibly because I've been such a mobile person, friendships have been very important to me. I never would have survived moving from place to place without really strong friendships—and, primarily in my life, these have been with women.

Q: The essays in *Rumors* cover twenty years. Are you a different writer from that woman who interviewed Margaret Atwood?

A: There are a lot of similarities. I like that young woman, that me of twenty years ago. But time has both taken its toll and given its gifts. I guess that now I'm more conscious of psychological subtlety, both in my everyday life and in my writing. I'm more conscious of nuance. I'm a lot less naive than I used to be, more confident. I think those things come out in my writing. It has a certain authority now, albeit a gentle authority. I can't believe that Margaret Atwood trusted me as much as she did when I was twenty-seven [she laughs]. But she was a lot younger then, too. I'm not sure that she would do it today.

Q: How has your fictional voice changed?

A: It's a tough question because I think that there are things about which I don't feel the same kind of urgency, topics with which I'm not so well acquainted. One of the things that has emerged over the years is an unapologetic interest in the lives of working-class people, something that I did not have when I started to write fiction.

Q: How did you stop being apologetic?

A: I think there are similarities between coming out as someone who grew up in a working-class family and coming out as a lesbian. The more often you do it the more comfortable you are and the more communication you have with people who are like you and with people who are grateful that you've come out—people who come out to you and inspire you and teach you. So writing about Margaret and Chrissie in *Winter's Edge* was a real turning point for me, even though my earlier fiction deals in different degrees with working-class families. *Winter's Edge* focuses more directly on working-class life. Those two women are still alive and with me.

Writing *Winter's Edge* allowed me to understand how much I owe my mother, how much I admire her and love her. I felt as if my feet were on the ground for the first time as a writer. My mother had a big part in that.

Q: Was the decision to be out as a lesbian—to write about the sexual marginality of lesbians—difficult for you?

A: I really came out, I think, as a lesbian after a friend of mine died of melanoma. She was a young activist named Lynn Campbell, and I was very moved by her life. She was active in the farm workers' movement and a number of other social or political groups. And she was a lesbian. I thought she was so brave. I remember thinking, This is really stupid to be living with the shades pulled down, when she gave so much to people by being her full self. So, for me, being out as a lesbian has to do with honesty and the vitality I get from honesty. It isn't a moral act or a question of conscience so much as it's a way of engaging more fully in the world by being who I am.

In some sense, coming out as a lesbian writer is a process of discovery, a journey, just as coming out as a writer from a working-class family or coming out as an American writer [she laughs]. And it's something that continually surprises me with new dimensions.

Q: Do you think that there are specific ways in which your perspective as a lesbian writer colors your fiction?

A: I think the definition of lesbian novel is much more subtle than, Is the protagonist a lesbian or is the author a lesbian? The definition is related to the perspectives presented, the angles from which the author views things and the types of questions the author raises. For me, one of the lesbian aspects of my fiction is that, although I'm not always writing about lesbian characters, I'm primarily interested in women's experiences.

Q: You hint in your essays that you get pressure from both sides. The lesbian community gets angry if you don't create lesbian characters, and the heterosexual community wants more straight characters.

A: It saddens me that people don't know the reaches of their own imaginations. It's very strange when people ask a writer to write about certain kinds of characters. Many people are hungry—certainly I am—to see more lesbians portrayed as human beings in serious literature, since there are so few. But there are a lot of bridges to be crossed by empathizing with people of different identities.

What I've experienced more from within the lesbian literary discourse is that sometimes there's a self-censorship that lesbian writers feel, myself included, because we don't want to portray lesbians in a negative light. We don't want people to think that because we show a battering couple, all lesbians batter each other, and so forth. But I think that kind of timidity is really self-defeating, because if you write the whole story and you write it well enough, people will see beyond their prejudices.

Q: This is so similar to what writers like Gloria Naylor and Alice Walker went through with African American men who said, "Don't create any negative African American men because then the white world is going to say that's how we all are."

A: I think that one of the things we're talking about with the question of people identifying across class or across sexuality or across national boundaries is the employment of imagination. It's one of my frustrations that we don't make demands on readers to use their imaginations and that, as teachers, we don't really teach imaginative skills, just analytical ones. As a writer, I don't want someone to tell me I have to write only about white working-class people, only about Scots and Irish people, only about lesbians. One of the reasons I became a writer was to try to develop some kind of empathy for my fellow human beings. If I'm always writing about the same kinds of people, I'm not going to get very far. I've got a long way to go, so I don't want any censors.

Q: Vivian Gornick told me that she can't write an essay about a subject unless she has an empathic connection to it. Did you feel that way when you were a journalist?

A: I very much agree with Vivian. I knew that I had to be a free-lance writer, that I didn't have the patience or stamina to deal with daily assignments to which I had no relation. One of the penances for free-lance work, at least in my experience, is poverty. I never made more than five thousand dollars a year until I was thirty years old; I didn't own a car until I was thirty; I've never owned a house. I'm not complaining because, in many ways, I had a kind of mobility and freedom as a free-lance writer that I never would have had if I worked full-time on assignment.

Q: Who influenced your style of journalism?

A: Talk about embarrassing: early on, I was influenced by Norman Mailer! Also, I was interested in Tom Wolfe, although I always found him a little bit frenetic. At one point I was very influenced by Joan Didion, although later I came to feel that she was asking questions that didn't interest me so much. And I was also influenced by James Baldwin because, although he wasn't a reporter per se, he wrote wonderful essays raising really important social questions in this accessible, literary, elegant style.

Q: Let's talk about your fiction. In *All Good Women* I was particularly struck by Moira, the one of the four central characters who has the most conventional life, in that she marries and has children. I felt that somehow hers was the least happy ending. Is that a fair assessment?

A: I don't think it's a happy *ending* for any of the characters. I see it as a book about continuing. One of the reasons I called her Moira is because people refer to her as "Moy" or "Moi"—me—and I see her as a mirror for the other characters' behaviors and choices. She's quixotic; she's explosive; she dares to say things; she's exploitative—of Teddy, for instance. But I also think that there is a lot of potential there, in her, in all of them.

Q: *All Good Women* must have been heavily researched. Did you make any discoveries about the period when you were researching the 1940s?

A: I didn't know before I began the project that it was a time of great "liberation" for gay people. Because people were so mobile, they often wound up being able to experiment or express themselves sexually in ways they weren't able to express themselves at home.

Q: Any other discoveries?

A: Although I knew about the internment of Japanese Americans, I didn't know about the experiences of daily life in the camps, which was very moving to learn about. I also had to do a lot of research about the German and Austrian refugee kids who were sent to England in '38 and '39 and about women's lives in the war industries. It was an important book for me in many ways because it provided me with a sense of context and a sense of history I didn't get from my conventional American education. Although I went to school in California, we never heard about the internment camps, for example. I gained a lot of courage from those individual women's lives.

Q: Where did the impetus for *Blood Sisters* come? You mentioned in the introduction to the book that you were living in London at a time when there was widespread violence.

A: Given my family background, "the troubles," as they're called in Ireland, have always been of deep interest. The book is, in part, about the struggle of Irish people to maintain their national identity. I'm very much an Irish Republican, in the sense that I believe that the troops should be out of the north and that the north should be part of Eire. I was also interested in what seemed to me the two major choices feminists were making in the mid-seventies—between separatism and male-identified politics.

Q: Your characters embody this political struggle.

A: I wanted to look at somebody who was involved in a group that had both men and women in it, like the Provisional wing of the IRA [Irish Republican Army], and I also wanted to look at someone who was exploring the possibilities of separatist feminism or cultural feminism. Those are the cousins, Beth and Liz. I was also very interested in mother-daughter relationships, in whether expatriation was a self-indulgence, and in intergenerational questions about families.

I also wanted to rewrite *Hamlet*. I remember riding my bike home to north London after a virtuoso performance at the National Theatre and thinking how much of *Hamlet* was missing from that very male performance. I decided to rewrite it from a woman's point of view. I tried to have Hamlet split in two—into Beth and Liz, the daughters of the twins who were literally split in two. If you go back and read the book, you see all these *Hamlet* references—to Aunt Claudia and Saint Gertrude's Church and Denmark Hill—that no one saw [she laughs].

Q: Are you going to write another mystery like *Murder in the English Department?*

A: I started out wanting to write a book about a woman's relationship with her working-class family, raising questions about interclass travel and what happens to us when we move from a working-class primary family into a middle-class life. It's also a book that examines loyalty among women and asks some philosophical questions about the nature of innocence and guilt.

I was also interested in the whole question of sexual harassment. It seems to me that an extension of sexual harassment is rape, and that's what wound up happening in the book, an attempted rape. One response to an attempted rape is self-defense, in that case, murder.

So, I didn't actually intend to write a murder mystery when I wrote *Murder in the English Department.* That's just what happened when these people got together. Every book is, in some sense, a mystery.

Q: At one point in the novel, Nan, your protagonist, says, "The English department is embarrassed by my conscience." Was that autobiographical?

A: No. One of the things that's so startling to me about that book was that it's much more autobiographical in the sense of premonition than in the sense of memory recorded. I actually set the book in the English department because I was teaching in an interdisciplinary program, not an English department. One of the ironies is that after the book was written, but before the book was out, I was hired to teach a couple of creative writing classes [at Berkeley]. There were many people in that department in those days—it [*Murder in the English Department*] came out in '83—who insisted and still today insist that it's autobiographical and that they know who Angus Murchie and Marjorie are and that I'm Nan. After the book was published I was never again hired by the English department to teach creative writing.

Q: I think the novel shows the extent to which Angus is universal. We all know him.

A: Many women have congratulated me for having a murder in the English department.

Q: Let's talk about *Trespassing,* your collection of stories that was nominated for a Lambda [literary prize in lesbian fiction]. In these stories you explore relationships between many different kinds of people. Was that a conscious attempt to create really diverse characters?

A: Again, it happened. I didn't set out to write a book about trespassing, but when I pulled the stories together, I found that they were all about trespassing in one way or another. Although the stories are not directly autobiographical, obviously all fiction emerges from some seed of experience. And I think that the notion of trespassing is so visible in the stories because I feel as if I've been trespassing my whole life in one way or another: Literally trespassing, as someone who has lived abroad a lot and traveled widely; but trespassing morally, in the sense that I've made some unconventional choices in my life and, although I certainly am not a practicing Catholic anymore, I still have echoes of a Catholic conscience that tell me that I'm trespassing. I'm also trespassing in the sense of being from the working class and moving into a middle-class environment; and trespassing in the sense of transgressing literary conventions because that book plays with a lot of different forms.

Q: Would you talk about your most recent novel, *A Walking Fire?*

A: It's a rewrite of *King Lear* from Cordelia's point of view, fiddling with the gender in the sense that Goneril and Regan are men, Cordelia's brothers rather than sisters; fiddling with the social class in the sense that King Lear is a working-class merchant seaman; fiddling with the history in the sense that it's set between the 1940s and 1980s. The backdrop of the war is American involvement in Southeast Asia and then, in the more contemporary parts, American intervention in Central America. So I'm trying to look at family as a metaphor of American foreign policy and vice versa. It's also a psychological drama about a family and what happens to them over a forty-year period.

Q: You chose *Hamlet* for *Blood Sisters;* what made you choose *Lear* this time?

A: I've always been very moved by *Lear,* but most of the interpretations of Shakespeare's *Lear,* which is the version most Americans are familiar with, are male-oriented. I was interested in Cordelia's lost voice and very interested in silencing and types of censorship: overt censorship, covert censorship, self-censorship. I'm also very interested in questions of loyalty, which runs as a strong theme throughout my work.

Lear was not an invention of Shakespeare's; he stole it from someone else, who stole it from someone else. It's a strong archetypal story. I was interested in unleashing some of the voices. Initially I thought of Cordelia's, but I found, in the process of rewriting it, that I had to listen to other voices, too. I had to do something with the lost mother. I had to look closely at how Goneril and Regan—or, in my book, George and Ron—got to be the way they are. That made me look at the childhoods of Cordelia, Goneril, and Regan much more closely and gave me a deeper sense of family.

Q: Did the voice of the Lear figure emerge as you expected, or was that different, too?

A: One of the really devilish things about being a novelist is that you wind up having compassion for all sorts of really unlikely people. I wound up liking Lear a lot more than I had.

Q: It sounds like you are criticizing the working-class family in this book.

A: The book questions the notions of heroism and family. The brothers, who fought in Vietnam, are invested in the notion that they were heroes, while the sister, Cora, fled the country after burning down a draft center. I'm looking at the often-forgotten working-class protestor as well as at the complicity that some working-class men had with the military during that war. This is something that I feel people are not really talking about, and I may get in a lot of hot water about it.

I was very frightened to write about it—not because people will disagree with my point of view, but that they will misinterpret my point of view. I am *not* saying that working-class men started that war. But a number of them were complicit in fighting it. The rhetoric of Vietnam, particularly in the last five years, has made all of the soldiers heroes. Not just survivors, but heroes. And I don't think that's true, and that's one of the things that has led us into further aggression in the Middle East and in Central America. So there is some urgency in confronting this.

But I do feel that issue of self-censorship. Why don't I write about a middle-class family where middle-class men go off to war?

Q: Perhaps because, for the most part, they didn't. They left the country.

A: That's right. Many didn't fight that war. Many got deferments through various friends of their fathers who were doctors; many who went were the officers, who didn't have such a high casualty rate. But the other reason that I don't write about a middle-class family is that I don't know those people so well. They are not my family and I don't care about them as much.

To say that working-class men during that war were heroes and to exonerate them is the worst kind of castration. It's taking all their power and all their culpability away from them. In the book I am trying to look at working-class protest against the war and support of the war. One of the things that really bothers me is that often working-class lives are presented as having no choices.

Q: What's your next project?

A: I started a new novel set in the High Sierras of California. There's not much I can say about it right now because it's at a very tender stage, but I think of it as a book that's exploring the edge of the western imagination. It's set in eastern California, and I think of the Sierras as a kind of backbone to the San Joaquin and San Fernando valleys and the barrier between part of California and the rest of the country. And that's what I'm interested in right now, with the book. I'm interested in place and the question of the borders of imagination.

Q: Is this going to be as big as *All Good Women*?

A: I hope not [she laughs].

Q: We don't have to wait five years for this?

A: I hope not.

Q: Let's talk about publishing. In *Rumors,* you wrote that you submitted *All Good Women* to thirty-six mainstream publishers before you went to an independent company [Crossing Press]. Why is that? Your books have gotten wonderful responses from readers.

A: The book came out first in England, from Methuen, the first house that saw it. I thought I would try returning to the mainstream press here (I had published two previous books with St. Martin's in New York and then the most recent one with Crossing). But I found the mainstream houses resistant.

Authors don't talk enough about their "failures" or the "failures" of the market or publishers to respond to them. If you ask a number of feminist writers you'll find many rejection stories. But since "success breeds success" in this country, the idea is to keep up a good face and to appear as if you're being well published and people are seeking your work. One reason I mentioned it in *Rumors* is that it's liberatory for all of us to talk about context and how the marketplace creates values, shapes values, manufactures reputations, and so forth.

Q: This has come up in almost every interview. Joanna Russ, Gloria Naylor, and Paula Gunn Allen were vehement about this.

A: Great; I'm glad. So, number one, I think there are many women to whom this has happened. I know women who have published fine work, who, in their middle years, can't get their work published. I'm lucky because my books do come out. And they stay in print. With the economy the way it is, mid-list authors are getting squeezed and squeezed; I don't feel isolated in this struggle.

Q: What criticisms have you gotten from mainstream publishers?

A: That my work is too literary, too intellectual, too political. I've received these criticisms, which I think are compliments, since *Blood Sisters,* which was the first book I submitted in this country.

One reason I experience resistance from mainstream publishers is that I'm writing about working-class people. Another is that I write a lot about sexual identity, sexual marginality. Also, I'm interested in racial issues and relationships among people of various races and ethnic backgrounds. And I care a lot about accessible prose. People often fail to see the subtlety in a sentence that has been honed, worked, and reworked, unless it's written by Ernest Hemingway and has a penis in it.

Most of my books come out in England first. You see, I tend to write a lot about Americans—and the British are more likely to be appreciative of that critical eye than Americans are. Also, the British are more interested in novels of ideas and novels that raise social questions. We don't have as much of an articulated tradition of that in this country, although there are many good social-political novels.

Q: In *Rumors* you say, "Writers have a lot to learn from coal miners and steel workers, whose unionism erases any false notion of privilege about the right to be paid or to be treated decently for work done." What kind of dialogue would you like to see happening among writers?

A: One reason I feel more comfortable in Britain or Canada is that in these countries there are strong labor movements and professional people identifying with the labor movements. In this country we don't have that, even with heavily unionized teachers.

I would like to see a serious writers' union in this country. I have been involved in the National Writers' Union since it was founded in the early eighties, and I think it's a very important organization; but it needs to branch out and get more support from poets, playwrights, and fiction writers. It's done fine work getting good contracts for journalists, but it needs to do more work in the book industry.

We also should develop an international consciousness of our work as writers—that's crucial to our own individual welfare and to the kind of imaginative collectivity that I mentioned. If my books sell it will help your books sell. And the better treated I am as a worker, the better treated you will be as a worker [in any country] if publishers start developing standards of professional treatment.

Q: Is the publishing industry exploitive?

A: Yes. For instance, when we sell our foreign rights we seem to think that we should have no say in how our work is treated in other countries. A few years ago, when I was a writer-in-residence in Australia for six months, it took about five months for my books to get from England to Australia, even though the publisher knew six months before I left that I was going there. And it was only through my badgering and screaming over the telephone that Methuen, which is a major house, with big distribution through Heinemann, got a few books over there.

If we had stronger relations with Australian writers—where we could help them get better deals with American publishers, and they could help us get better deals with Australian publishers—we'd all be better off. We tend to forget that it is a labor-management issue, that publishers are our employers, that we are workers. We like to believe in this rarefied notion of the artist, an idea that does us in. In the long term, one of the benefits of this labor consciousness on the part of writers might be a more realistic consciousness of working people altogether. We don't write very well about work in this country.

Q: We don't write much about work at all.

A: Right. We tend to write a lot, perhaps too much, about—capital R— Relationships. But what about all those relationships we have from 8:00 to 5:00, or whatever our shift is? It seems to me it's a very fertile area.

Q: You've written about international feminism. Would you talk about that?

A: Because of the gift of my mother's experience and perspective and family, because of the gift of living abroad all those early years, I'm very influenced by international writing, particularly by Canadian and British writing. Since both Canada and Britain are more open to international writing generally, I became conscious of African writing and Asian writing and Latin American writing. So, in a certain sense, my experiences between the ages of twenty-three and twenty-nine living in England and Canada and the traveling I did in other parts of the world then and in later years were a kind of graduate school for me as a writer.

Recently, for a complicated reason, I've had to read a lot of contemporary American novels, and I am bored to tears [she laughs]. Some contemporary American writers I admire tremendously. I very much like the work of Paule Marshall, Bette Pesetsky, Randall Kenan, Marge Piercy— but to have a steady diet of American writers is like eating Rice Krispies for 365 days; it is boring.

I find international literature appealing because, as a writer, I'm curious about place and find it provocative to see what people do with place. I'm very interested in rhythms in language, in seeing and hearing on the page how people write English differently. And, of course, it's fascinating to see how translators translate into English differently.

Q: How is the sense of place different in international literature?

A: Much of European writing, African writing, Latin American writing, Asian writing seems to focus more on the individual in a context—in the context of a history, in the context of a community, in the context of social issues and questions. Of course this is a generalization. There are exceptions. But I feel less alone and less foreign when I'm reading literature by people who are not my people. That's strange.

So I find myself wanting to read a lot of international fiction and using a lot of international fiction in my classes, for which my students are grateful because they don't get it elsewhere. I also find myself, as a reviewer, really preferring to review international books. Right now, for example, I'm writing a foreword to a collection of international feminist fiction that Julia Penelope and Sarah Valentine are editing for the Crossing Press. I feel an almost impresario-like commitment to letting American readers know that there's more material out there.

Q: What writers have influenced you? I've seen your work compared to Doris Lessing's. Is that a fair comparison?

A: When I was splitting up with my husband years ago, I found behind the couch either the first or the second book in her Children of Violence series. My husband had bought it to give me for the Christmas past, but he had lost it. This was the first time I read Doris Lessing. After the epiphany of finding her in this way, she became a big influence. I share her interest in Africa, and generally admire her a lot, even though I don't agree with everything she says. I was also quite influenced by those conversations with Atwood, and I love all of Margaret Laurence's books, particularly because she writes about people who are obscure, who lead hidden lives.

Since I was a young writer, I have been captivated by Toni Morrison, by Tillie Olsen, by Grace Paley—particularly Grace Paley. Again, the attention to the commonplace, the language she was using, and the politics of the books. I'm still very drawn to British women writers, especially Iris Murdoch and her impossible esoteric characters and the philosophical questions that they ask. The wonderful satire of Fay Weldon, and the work of my friend Zoë Fairbairns. I'm interested in what Muriel Spark does because she's a very weird combination: She's Scottish and she's Catholic. There are not too many of us around [she laughs]. I'm a great fan of Brian Moore and Randall Kenan. I am provoked by Ralph Ellison's *Invisible Man* [1952]. Somewhere along the way I developed a real appreciation for Shakespeare's language and his ability to nick the right plots. When I was researching *All Good Women* I came to really appreciate the way Mitsuye Yamada distills images in her poetry, and I read *Obasan* [Lester and Orpen Dennys (Toronto), 1981], a wonderful and moving novel by Joy Kogawa.

Q: Have any other foreign writers influenced you?

A: I'm interested in the South African writer Bessie Head's work. She has a fascinating novel called *Maru* [McCall, 1971] about friendships among women. When I think about the writers who have influenced me, I also find it hard to separate the writers from their work and from what I know about their lives. There are people like Buchi Emecheta, a Nigerian writer who lives in London and who has raised five children, managing to write exquisite fiction and do all the sorts of things a writer has to do to survive. I often look to the strategies that writers have employed to survive with integrity. When I was in Australia I met yet another wave of writers I was unacquainted with because of the provincialism of American publishing. And I particularly loved the writing of Thea Astley and David Malouf, both from Queensland.

Q: You are so prolific, Valerie: six novels, a nonfiction collection, a short-story collection, four coauthored books. How do you manage to do all of this and teach full-time, too?

A: I've developed a schedule where I go to school in the afternoon on most afternoons, so that I'm available to my students. That way I don't feel guilty when I say to them, "You can't call me at home." So they know that they can see me during my office hours. Then I can write in the mornings.

I think that this work ethic is related to class a bit, too. If you grow up in a family where people are always working, you believe that work is normal, and so I'm always a little baffled when people say to me that I'm so prolific. That's what writers do. That's their job. They write [she laughs].

Q: Do you enjoy teaching?

A: Teaching was kind of an accident for me. I fell into it because I wrote an article about the Upward Bound program, part of the poverty program in the sixties, on the UC [University of California at Berkeley] campus where I was an undergraduate. I started to teach in Upward Bound, first as an assistant teacher, then I ran a journalism workshop. I became a counselor in that program and then worked as a teaching assistant in an inner-city community college [Laney] in Oakland.

One of the reasons that I enjoy teaching is that I never had any enormous ambitions as a teacher. I found that I liked it, that somehow I knew how to do it, and that I seemed to be useful. And over the years I found that teaching is the most helpful way I found to support my writing. It is tough if you're writing serious literary fiction in this country to make a living from your work, so you have to have an additional job.

Over the years I've taught primarily university students. Eleven of my teaching years were at UC-Berkeley, a very privileged environment where the Xerox machine usually works and you have postal privileges and a very light teaching load. That makes an enormous difference.

I'd like to have more time for my writing. I would like to get a Guggenheim or an NEA grant or some kind of external support so I could take a year off [from] teaching. I've never had a paid sabbatical, only unpaid ones. But I feel basically lucky that I have the job.

Right now, I'm teaching in an M.F.A. program at Arizona State University [at Tempe] and I enjoy those students tremendously. For the most part they're returning students who have had a lot of experience in the world. They're interesting as people, and they're very good writers. I find them provocative and inspiring. [After the interview, in September 1992, Miner began teaching at the University of Minnesota in Minneapolis.]

Q: You've mentioned that other people have nurtured your work. Do you get input all along in the process or do you wait for a certain point to show it to others?

A: I tend not to let anyone see the first draft. After that draft, I tend to share it, on a regular basis, with members of my writing group. (I've been in a series of them since the early 1970s.) Depending on how the group works, I'll either read a chapter aloud or give them a chapter to read.

Also, after each draft of the book, barring the first draft, I give it to two or three people outside of the writing group, sometimes asking them to look at specific things. For instance, as I mentioned earlier, when I wrote *Winter's Edge* I had my mother and three other people read one of the drafts for details about the Tenderloin. And these people also gave me linguistic comments and so forth.

I tend to do a lot of drafts of a book, and I think something that is very important in my writing process is that I erase the disk after each book, which horrifies my students. But I believe in the old-fashioned notion of a draft, so I use the computer as I would a typewriter. I'll type the book, print it out and give it to friends—say, the second draft. I tend to give them six weeks to two months to read it. Maybe five weeks into that period I, myself, will read the whole draft again, making my own editing comments, because I want to read it with my own fresh eye before I read it with their eyes. Then I'll take their comments, look at them, decide what I agree with and what doesn't work for me. I make further changes on the hard copy, then I rewrite the whole by retyping it into the computer again. I print the hard disk and go through that process again and again and again.

Q: That retyping must be very time-consuming. Why do you do it?

A: With *All Good Women,* the retyping was quite a production because it was eight hundred pages in manuscript. My friends really thought I was nuts. But I find this erasing of the disk and the rewriting is helpful because I actually do rewrite, not just retype what's on the hard copy. Things go on in my head as I'm retyping it. I have to let all the words go through my bloodstream. If I'm just editing on the disk I don't do that. Also, I now type very fast. I got a D– in high school typing from Miss Jenks, and she would be so proud of me now [she laughs].

Q: You said that you never read reviews of your work anymore. Is that true?

A: Yes. I get reviews during all of those drafts when I have all of those people read the manuscript. And that's when it's most helpful to me. I like that Virginia Woolf essay, "Reviewing," in which she talks about the ideal relationship between a writer and a critic being that of consultation. I used to read reviews of my work, but I haven't learned nearly so much from them as from critical comments during the process of the book.

Q: To what extent is your fiction autobiographical?

A: I think that people have different relationships with autobiography in their fiction. As I said earlier, my work strikes me as more autobiographical in the sense of premonition than in the sense of memory recorded. I tend to get ideas for my books from the world around me rather than from my own life.

I'm more interested in my characters' lives. I do understand that they are figments of my imagination and, therefore, in some sense, autobiographical. But I really don't want to sit down and expose my life for the world. It's not interesting enough. I felt much more vulnerable publishing *Rumors from the Cauldron* than I have ever felt in publishing any other of my novels because that is a very autobiographical book. That exposes the voice I had twenty, eighteen, fifteen years ago. It reveals the attitudes, questions, and biases I had, and I describe myself in some of those pieces. Six months before that book came out I wanted to pull it back; I was so embarrassed by the notion of all that self-revelation. In a certain sense, *Rumors* is a literary intellectual autobiography. But I don't think of my novels as autobiography.

Q: Maxine Hong Kingston said that she thinks that literature can change the world. When I asked Pat Barker what she thought of that, she disagreed, saying it doesn't change anything. What do you think?

A: Oh, I think it does, absolutely. That's why I'm a nineteenth-century writer [she laughs].

When I met Gloria Naylor in December 1991, she was busy with several projects—adapting her recently completed novel, Bailey's Cafe (Harcourt Brace Jovanovich, 1992), for the stage; producing a film version of her earlier novel Mama Day (Ticknor and Fields, 1988); and raising her teen-age nephew, Roger, who lives with her. However, sitting in the living room of her apartment in Manhattan's Washington Heights, her back to the Hudson River view, she seemed amazingly unharried. This daughter of former sharecroppers, who traveled the United States as a missionary, worked her way through college, and wrote four novels in just over ten years, knows all about juggling conflicting demands, I soon realized. And she knows that a writer must write, no matter what the distractions.

Naylor learned about ignoring distractions when her first novel—The Women of Brewster Place (Viking, 1982), written while she was a student at Brooklyn College—earned her international attention and the American Book Award for first fiction in 1983. Seven interconnected stories of strong women whose support for one another enables them to survive de-spite crushing poverty and personal tragedy, the novel established Naylor as a powerful new voice in fiction. Readers found the book's celebration of women's friendships convincing, and its depiction of violence and homophobia, including the rape of a character who is lesbian, chillingly believable. In her acceptance speech at the award ceremony, Naylor noted that the novel was only the beginning of a career that, she hoped, would be "*as long and consistently excellent*" *as that of Alice Walker, who received the fiction award for* The Color Purple *(Harcourt Brace Jovanovich, 1982) that same year. She was determined to avoid the fate of so many novelists who never live up to the promise of that celebrated first book.*

She needn't have worried. Linden Hills *(Ticknor and Fields, 1985), Naylor's second, very different novel, confirmed her reputation. Using Dante's* Inferno *as a model for her hero Willy's journey into a black middle-class community, Naylor exposes the hollowness of the American dream of success. She again explores the connections between women in a second plot: Willa, the abused wife of the novel's demonic antagonist, finds her own identity in the pictures, domestic objects, and diaries of her husband's female ancestors.*

Love, tragedy, self-sacrifice, and the enduring strength of women remain as themes in Naylor's most recent novels: Mama Day *and* Bailey's Cafe. *In the former, George and Cocoa, doomed lovers, learn the meaning and power of love from Cocoa's great-aunt, Mama Day, medicine woman and healer. In* Bailey's Cafe, *inspired by the improvisational quality of jazz, Naylor explores the painful lives of several women who end up living at Eve's Place, a brothel, and frequenting Bailey's, a kind of last-chance café located "between the edge of the world and infinite possibility."*

Since her days as a student at Brooklyn College, Naylor envisioned these four novels as forming the foundation on which she would build her career. The groundwork completed, she shows no signs of letting up, with plans for a play, a movie, and another novel. During our time together Naylor explained that she has made a conscious decision to make writing her first priority, that she considers herself a "filter" for stories that haunt her, that she hopes to have something to say to readers of the twenty-first century. With her determination, she certainly will.

Q: You describe yourself as a New Yorker, Gloria, but I know that you have deep Southern roots.

A: I was raised in New York, but I was conceived in Robinsonville, Mississippi. My parents were from sharecropper families, and they were young—nineteen and twenty-one—when they married. They left the South when my mom was eight months pregnant because she did not want to raise her children in Mississippi. They grew up in the Depression South and came North a month before I was born in January of 1950. So I am, technically, a native New Yorker. But even though people change their locations, they don't change who they are overnight. I'm the first of the three girls who came of that marriage, and we were raised in a very

Southern home, with our foods and our language and a certain code of behavior. The way we were disciplined came from the South.

Q: So you got hit if you misbehaved?

A: They weren't always hitting us—we were not abused—but you knew you were the child and they were the adults. Southern children grow up to be quite respectful of their parents and other people, older people. My parents are now very well off, but in the 1940s they were poor, and living in the deep South was like being in another country.

Q: Did they move North to give their children more opportunity?

A: Exactly. My mother couldn't use the public library in segregated Mississippi, and there were no schools for blacks in Tunica County beyond the ninth grade. So there was no access to books and no decent education if you were poor people. And she wanted those things for her children. She wanted music lessons—basically, what had been promised to every American, promises that were not forthcoming if you were a poor black in the South. My parents knew they would be poor people, working-class people, for most of their lives, and they weren't naive about what it meant to move North. It did not mean, in their minds, an end to discrimination. They encountered that full blast here. But it did mean that, at least as far as tax-supported facilities were concerned, their children would have equal access like any other taxpayer's child.

Q: When you won the National Book Award for *The Women of Brewster Place,* your first novel, you said that you accepted the award for your mother.

A: That's right.

Q: What is she like?

A: She's very much a part of my life—I just talked with her this morning. She was a very quiet woman and a little bit shy when I was growing up. My mother didn't have a lot of friends. She devoted herself to her family. My maternal grandmother, who died in 1977, and my mother's sisters and brothers ended up here [in New York] ultimately, so my mother was always very close to them. She was always very sensitive to our needs. People say to me that perhaps we were too sheltered as children—from my father's end for other reasons, because we were girls—but she was a woman of the fifties.

I think I kept writing as a child because I had my mother as a model. She always encouraged us to dream. Whatever you wanted to do, she would just be behind you. And she never made me feel odd. I was an odd child; I was extremely introverted, very quiet. And she would allow that because she was also an introvert; we were kindred spirits. She'd let me read a poem or a story to her sometimes, and she would encourage me to write. I think I kept going through her.

Q: So many women I've spoken with have credited their mothers with keeping their creative spark alive.

A: Yeah, these women who let you be a little different, as long as you weren't doing anything that was harmful to other people or to yourself.

My father worried much more than my mother did, as I said, I guess because he didn't get the sons that he thought he wanted. With three girls, he just wanted us to go out and be girls—be feminine and that sort of thing. My being so quiet and my scribbling away all the time and staying in my room so much bothered him, I think, more than her. My dad is not shy at all. Put him in a room of people and he works the room, but not my mother.

Q: Women's support for one another is a central theme in all your books—from the community of women in *Brewster Place* to Willa discovering the Nedeed women in *Linden Hills* to the sisters, Miranda and Abigail, in *Mama Day*. You must see a real power in women's love and support for one another.

A: I do, beyond a doubt. Historically, women have only had each other. It is only very recently that they have been given any exposure outside the home or even the ability to work outside the home and to live and make a living. Maybe because my mother had six sisters and two brothers, I saw this support of women for one another all my life. And my grandmother was like the matriarch there. I saw what women would do for each other. In my own life, when there's a problem of any nature, I turn to a woman. Your female friends are the ones you have the longest history with, for the most part, because they understand; they understand. The bonding of females will always come up in my work.

Q: Is there any of your mother in all these women you've created?

A: I'm sure there must be. I'm positive that if I ever had the inclination or the time to take them apart I would find things that would surprise me. Maybe she's there in a mother that worried excessively—Kiswana Brown's mother [in *Brewster Place*], for example. The kind of mother who would come visit you and check out your apartment.

Q: Does she ever give you suggestions for your books?

A: No, never. She definitely reads them, though.

Q: In doing research for this interview, I discovered that you spent a number of years as a Jehovah's Witness. Would you talk about that?

A: I did become a Jehovah's Witness after high school, basically out of disillusionment. Martin Luther King had been assassinated in my senior year, and I lived through the Vietnam War for all of my high school years. I had the mind-set of a lot of people in that generation that there was nothing good that this system could offer me. So joining a fundamentalist group allowed me to preach about the coming of a theocratic government that would just tear everything up from the roots and build anew. I devoted seven years of my life to believing and preaching about the coming of that theocracy, the coming of a decent living for human beings. I saw no need to invest time and effort in a system that I believed was going to be destroyed and that I felt should be destroyed.

Q: Why did you eventually stop preaching?

A: Seeing that the theocracy had not arrived and that things were not really getting any better. I was twenty-five years old with a high school education and no marketable skills because I had been on a college track in high school. If I had been on a vocational track, I could have gone on to be a secretary or a printmaker or something. But liberal arts! What in the heck do you do with that at twenty-five? Not too much. So that's when I decided that I would try to make a difference inside of the system, as opposed to hoping that the whole thing would just somehow go away.

Q: That's when you went to Brooklyn College?

A: I went to Medgar Evers [College in Brooklyn] first for about a year and a half because initially I thought I would be a nursing student. That was a quick, two-year program. It was practical, and it pays well. But I found that I wasn't interested in medicine and in learning about digestion and all that stuff; I was spending more time with my English classes. That really had been my first love: books. And liberal arts. So that's when I transferred to Brooklyn College as an English major.

Q: When did you start writing?

A: I've written all my life. I started writing poems when I was seven, then I moved into *Twilight Zone*-type short stories. There were other popular shows at that time called *The Outer Limits* and *One Step Beyond*. I liked that kind of thing. When I was twelve, my mother gave me a diary, and I would write in that and then ultimately in notebooks and journals. What I do today is just a continuation of what I did then—putting feelings on paper, sorting out things.

Q: What got you to the point where you decided you'd try to publish your writing?

A: Well, I had been publishing in our high school literary magazine, the Andrew Jackson High School *Star,* and at Brooklyn College I would enter poetry contests and place maybe second or third. I really decided to venture out because of a creative writing course I took at Brooklyn College with [poet] Joan Larkin. Joan is a wonderful woman. She told us, "Well, grow up and join the real world. Send your things out and start learning what it's like to be rejected." And she also said, "Remember that when you write these query letters you always pretend that more is going on. Really build it up. Be assertive."

Q: So you would pretend this story was part of a larger piece?

A: Exactly. Don't say, "Please publish me." So I sent out a story to *Essence* magazine, and I told them in the query letter that this was a part of a larger collection. And the people wrote me back and said, "Well, this is wonderful; let's see the other stories" [she laughs]. I didn't have any other stories. I was doing a classroom assignment. So I hurried up and wrote another one.

In the back of my mind I did have a collection that I wanted to do, but I just hadn't done it. So after I wrote them this second story, that's when the editor said she'd like to have lunch with me and find out who I was. That was kind of heady and thrilling for an undergraduate—to sit with a real magazine editor. I've had many, many lunches since then, but the first is always thrilling. So those stories that became *Brewster Place* were written at Brooklyn College over the course of my last two years there.

Q: Which was your first story?

A: The one that dealt with Lucielia Louise Turner, the woman who had aborted one child and lost her baby girl when the infant stuck the fork into the electric outlet. Then Ciel's rocked back to health by Mattie. That story was written in a creative writing course. It began with the ending, the woman healing the other one by rocking her. I wrote that as a catharsis for myself, to get myself over a moment of pain. I projected my imagination out by thinking, Now, who could be feeling this kind of pain? It's not my story, not my specifics, but I tried to imagine what could hurt this badly. I had written this scene earlier and put it away. Later, for the class, I took it out and re-created a beginning leading up to what I call "the rocking scene." So that's what they published.

Q: A lot of the women I've interviewed have talked about the fact that, when they started writing, no one had told their stories—I'm thinking particularly of Maxine Hong Kingston and Paula Gunn Allen. These women are a decade older than you, but was the situation different when you started writing?

A: Well, your standard high school English curriculum, even in the mid-to-late sixties, was basically classes in nineteenth-century male classics. That's what I cut my literary teeth on. If you go through these bookshelves, those books are still here. I learned about language and how to discriminate in my reading through the English classics. I was not taught any book by or about black Americans.

Q: So they weren't teaching black writers even in the sixties?

A: Not as a group, no. When I was in a senior dramatics course in high school, we did *A Raisin in the Sun* [1959]. I had very progressive Jewish teachers at Andrew Jackson. But somehow it never connected with me that Lorraine Hansberry was a black writer because, in our integrated school, whoever auditioned the best, that's the part that they took in the play. These teachers never said there was a whole body of work, this whole literary tradition of black writing in this country, no. It just wasn't taught. I did not find out about black writers until I hit Joan Larkin's class at Brooklyn College. Ultimately I took courses in the Africana studies department and discovered there was this whole discipline there. That's why, when I went to Yale for my master's degree, I majored in Afro-American studies—because I wanted to learn more.

Brewster Place really got written as a result of my discovering these writers. I realized all that I had been missing and the pain that I had gone through all those years in those journals and with the poetry and the stories, thinking that somehow I was freakish for doing this because, after all, black women didn't write books. How could I presume to do so? So it was liberating to find out not only that they had been writing, but also that they had been writing as well as they had. It was incredible when I discovered the kind of gorgeous language you get in writers like Toni Morrison and Alice Walker and Paule Marshall. That was when Ntozake Shange was extremely popular, too. It was quite something.

Q: When it was published in 1982, *Brewster Place* created a literary sensation. How did you deal with that?

A: Well, writing *Brewster Place* did for me what those journals did when I was a painfully shy, very troubled teenager. It got my life in order. Because I was now older, I had a messier life, okay? *Brewster Place* was one of the first things in my life that I ever finished. One of the very first things.

I was living in an eighty-eight-dollar-a-month apartment in Flatbush [in Brooklyn], taking the bus straight down Flatbush Avenue to the school on Flatbush and Nostrand. I will never forget the feeling when I had finished it. It was saying so many things that no one had ever said about me. It pulled me out of a year of horrendous depression, a time when I had had so many failures on many, many levels. Not with school or any of that, but in my personal life. It kept me sane. It was an affirmation of what I could do, my God-given gift. Nothing can surpass that, you see.

The writing did something for me that kept me going because I can be suicidal. That's why, in my work, I'm always looking at ways that people do these odd forms of suicide. My art saved me once again from that. So, you see, then there was nothing that the world could do to top it.

Q: So the writing itself was more important than the success.

A: Exactly. It was the fact that I did it as well as I possibly could. And since that point I have always striven for this internal sense of excellence. With this last novel, *Bailey's Cafe,* I have done the quartet that I had dreamed about [*The Women of Brewster Place, Linden Hills, Mama Day, Bailey's Cafe*]. As I look back, I wasn't keeping stock of time or anything, but this is 1991, and I finished *Brewster Place* in 1981, and now I have finished the quartet. This was to lay the basis or the foundation—I saw it like this little square foundation—for a career I was going to build. So I now believe that I will have the kind of career I want.

People have approved and sometimes disapproved of things I've done, and it hasn't mattered. Not in any great sense. We're human beings, so when you applaud me I am pleased; when you don't like me, I'm a little bit troubled. But it's never, ever central to what keeps me going. What does is that moment when I completed that manuscript and it was done well.

Q: How do you know when it's done well?

A: It just feels right. Nine times out of ten, I know that I hit whatever mark it was I was aiming for. I said what I wanted to say in the way I wanted to say it. I didn't get sloppy and lazy and tired. As I went on in my career, I knew that often readers and editors would accept things that you knew you could do better. So sometimes, one time out of ten, you don't keep pushing for what you know could be "perfect" with that moment or that sentence. You say, "The heck with it" [she laughs]. But when I had hit the mark, when I believe that those characters are living for me and that the stories I have been entrusted with have been told to the best of my ability, then I think it's well done.

Q: You say "stories I've been entrusted with," which sounds like what writers like Leslie Marmon Silko, Paula Gunn Allen, and Maxine Hong Kingston say about their responsibility as writers. Do you see yourself almost as an intermediary?

A: I do. I've often said I'm like a filter for these stories.

Q: So you feel like you're telling a story that's been given to you in some way?

A: The process starts with images that I am haunted by and I will not know why. People will say, "How do you know that's to be a story or a book?" I say, "Because it won't go away." You just feel a dis-ease until somehow you go into the whole, complicated, painful process of writing and find out what the image means. And often, when I've gotten into a work, I have been sorry to find out that that's what the image meant. But the die is cast.

Q: Would you give me an example of one of those images?

A: I noticed after *Linden Hills*—I think of *Linden Hills* because I had stayed so long down in the basement with this dead child—that the children die in my books. I didn't even give it a second thought in the first book because it was in [only] one story, but with *Linden Hills* I began to wonder. Willa and her dead baby were half my life for three or four years or so.

One image that kept haunting me from even before I finished *Linden Hills:* a woman carrying a dead male baby through the woods to this old woman. I didn't know why she was carrying the dead baby, but I knew her name because the old lady said, "Go home, Bernice. Go home and bury your child." So years later I'm into *Mama Day* and the story is unfolding, and I realize what that image meant: Bernice, who went through all that trauma trying so hard to have this child, is going to lose him. And I said, "Oh, my God, he's going to die!"

Of course, I'm not a robot. I could have not had him die. But it never occurred to me because I was entrusted with that. I don't know why all of this happened. I don't worry about it. But I like to think that I did it justice. Believe me, I didn't have much heart for it. When that baby died, I said, "Well, I really feel sorry for you, Bernice, but this was one of the early, early images."

Q: Do these images come in dreams?

A: Not sleeping dreams. They're just waking, psychic revelations that will happen.

Q: *The Women of Brewster Place* aroused strong feelings. Like Alice Walker and Ntozake Shange, who created equally powerful women characters, you've been criticized, particularly by black male critics, for what they call your "negative portraits" of black men.

A: From the very beginning.

Q: How do you respond to this?

A: I tell them to look at the title. If that is not self-evident enough, I will say to them, "I was not writing about men. This is a book about women."

But I've always thought that was not what they were really asking. I always thought what was under that was not, "Why haven't you written about men here?" but, "How dare you write about women? How dare you highlight or celebrate this which we have despised to the point that we weren't even taught that they existed or that they did such wonderful things for this country and the arts? How dare you be so militant about this happening?" But I never apologize, never ever. I will say, "I was not telling your story; I was telling your mother's story. Now please tell me what is wrong with that?" And then they'll say, "Well, but the men are all so negative." And then I have to explain to them the nature of creating art.

It goes back to Aristotle, who said there were three themes in all of drama: man against man, man against fate, man against God. Therefore, there has to be some obstacle that your protagonists climb over. You have to introduce conflict. Now, because of the kind of women they were— who weren't going out to General Motors or to Congress; they were staying on that street, on Brewster Place, in their homes—nine times out of ten my conflict bearers were the men in their lives.

Q: But the women have other conflicts going on, too.

A: Exactly. People tend to forget there are two stories in that collection where my conflict-bearers—the heavies, if you will—were not men. With Kiswana Brown the conflict came with her mother and that whole clash of social classes. With my two lesbians the conflict bearer was the stronger lover and the whole theme of power and struggle in relationships. But that criticism is all about the kind of society we live in. The underlying presumption has always been, until lately, that anything male should be central, and if males are not central, then it's jarring. And if something jars us we tend to think, Well, what is wrong with it? as opposed to, What is wrong with the way we have been programmed to think? I tended to explain all this in the beginning, but now I don't even bother. I'm getting old and cranky, and this country needs to grow up.

Q: Pat Barker said that she didn't feel that she had to create a sympathetic rapist just to appease critics, that sexism is a fact of life. Aren't you just saying that there's sexism among black males?

A: There's sexism in this country. Probably everywhere on the planet, but it's been concretized and institutionalized in the Western Hemisphere.

And how on earth can someone escape that because of the color of their skin? How can women escape it? I also got that question [about the "negative portrait" of men] from women. I think it's important that that be said. I've done a lot of rethinking about the socialization of females when, half of the time, a woman will stand up and say to me, "Where are the men in this book?"

Q: So women themselves are socialized to value men's stories over their own?

A: Sometimes, yes.

Q: Your books show that women are subjected to violence every day.

A: Violence is everywhere. We're all going to die, and some people inflict violence on themselves, by suicide and that sort of thing. A woman is raped in this country every six minutes. I don't think my books are any more violent than the reality of living, one, as a human being in this country, and, secondly, as a woman in this country. You know, every six pages I don't have a rape. What I do find in my work, and that comes back to how I cut my literary teeth on the English classics, is that I enjoy dramatic situations: the clash with nature and unfolding of human passion.

Q: I know that you've been in contact with Pat Barker, whose novel *Union Street* was made into a movie. What did you think of the made-for-television movie of *The Women of Brewster Place* that Oprah Winfrey put together a few years ago?

A: I saw it when it first came on television. I wasn't involved with that translation. I was not displeased with it, though. I felt that they kept the spirit of the book.

I did not see the movie made from *Union Street* [*Stanley and Iris*], but I read about it. At first I was so excited because Pat's a friend of mine, but I guess they just took two of the characters and went off and did something else. I'm now into producing because we are turning *Mama Day* into a feature film.

Q: How will this project differ from the adaptation of *The Women of Brewster Place*?

A: I've started my own production company. It's funny because, from a producer's standpoint—and I'm now wearing that hat—you prefer not to have the writer involved, because some writers don't understand that film is a different art form. From the writer's point of view, if you care at all about the initial thrust of your work or its message, then it's best that you leave it as a book.

Q: Other writers have talked about the risks involved in making movies out of their books.

A: You can protect yourself if you have a contract where you have a final script approval, but you don't usually get that. If you don't much care, if you trust your producers, you hope they carry the spirit of your work to this new art form.

Q: Were you pleased with the casting of *Brewster Place?*

A: What they [the producers] did do, which I thought was extremely sensitive, is that they tried to match the skin colors of the characters. Kiswana is light. With Lorraine and Theresa: Lorraine is fair; Theresa is dark. Skin color matters in the book, and they kept this in mind with the casting [of Robin Givens, Lonette McKee, and Paula Kelly].

Q: You talked earlier about the influence of the classics. Where did the idea for modeling *Linden Hills* on Dante's *Inferno* come from?

A: When I was a sophomore or junior at Brooklyn College I took a survey course called Great Works of Western Literature. When we began to go through the first part of *The Divine Comedy, The Inferno,* I said, "Yeah, that's how this neighborhood could be structured." I have some early doodles from class when I had sort of concentric blocks, but that didn't work. I ultimately devised the idea that there be circular drives that would go down the side of this hill; so I guess the structure came from there.

Q: And you stayed with Dante throughout the book, didn't you?

A: That was conscious. I was with Dante until Second Crescent Drive. Winston and David, my two homosexual men, were Paolo and Francesca. Everything up to that point was transliteration with Dante: the green on First Circle Drive, Mrs. Tilson, and all that. I left Dante there because I had my own schema. Then I picked him up again at Sixth Crescent Drive when they enter into the lower regions of Hell for the Tower of Dis and are stopped by the demons. And then Beatrice sent the archangel Michael, I think, to cast out the demons. I went to Dante for that. I picked him up again at the very end with his image of Satan being a three-headed creature frozen in this lake and crying; that's what Willa and Nedeed and the baby are, coming out of that house, one body fused together with three heads. But that was perhaps my most formulated work. Some critics would say too formulated [she laughs].

Q: In this novel you made a conscious shift to the middle class.

A: Right. That's why Kiswana Brown is at Brewster Place: She's from Linden Hills. I knew that the next one would deal with the black middle class.

Q: You level quite a scathing indictment of the black middle class in the novel. Other than in Toni Morrison's *Song of Solomon* [Knopf, 1977], has there been another critical portrait?

A: I don't think so. During the Harlem Renaissance, in works by Zora Neale Hurston and Langston Hughes and Arna Bontemps and Claude McKay, the political thrust had been to emphasize the color and the vitality of the "black folk." But before that, black writers had basically dealt with the middle class—writers like Nella Larsen and Jessie Fauset—but in a very different way.

Q: Larsen and Fauset weren't commenting on the dangers of becoming middle class.

A: No, their books were taking black people and really just putting a black face on white middle-class jargon. Basically that's what it was about: the bourgeois [she laughs]. In *Linden Hills* I'm looking at the whole phenomenon of hyphenated Americans and their ascension of the [so-called] ladder of success.

Q: You certainly suggest that such a rise has too great a cost.

A: It was about the stripping away of your soul when you move toward some sort of assimilation. That happens to any hyphenated American when you lose that which makes you uniquely you. We've finally, thank God, stopped that nonsense in this country where the ideal concept was a melting pot. Now we're saying, "No, it's a patchwork quilt, not a melting pot." Because—guess what?—nobody was melting. It wasn't happening. The novel was a sort of cautionary tale about that, about attempting to do the impossible—especially for the black American, because we're also a racist society. When you take on the accoutrements of success, you go to all the right schools, you wear the right clothes, you have all the right vocabulary, and you go as high as you possibly can, you still get that ceiling. You come up close to the fact that you are always going to be the Other; you will always be black.

Q: You split the perspective in the book between Willa and Willy, so there's a double vision and dual center of interest.

A: For male and female.

Q: In terms of the story, there's more stress on Willy, the poet, though.

A: You think so? You don't think they got equal time?

Q: I think Willa is powerful when she's there, but there's just more space given to Willy; and I wondered if that was an attempt to try something different from *Brewster Place.* Why the decision to focus on a twenty-year-old man?

A: I wasn't at all thinking of *Brewster Place.* I basically followed *The Inferno,* in that Dante sets out with Virgil on this trip.

Q: The character of Willa, Luther Nedeed's abused wife, down in the basement with her dead child is haunting. What's happening to her down there?

A: She's going from being a woman who was so faceless that she did not even have a name—no one in the upstairs and throughout her neighborhood knew who she was—to someone who reclaims herself.

Q: She's always described as "Luther's wife."

A: Exactly. But down in the basement of his house she is moving through history, reclaiming the other Nedeed women. That opening section of the book is sort of a chronicle of the Nedeed men and how they made history by procreating themselves. The wives were not important; they were shadows. Then, boom, you get to the last generation, and this woman produces this fair child, this white child. All those women had been light skinned. Willa produces something that, in Luther's mind, is illegitimate because it is evidence of the fact that there had been women in this historical dynasty.

Q: Even though the Nedeed men tried to efface them.

A: Exactly. When Willa is thrown into the basement with the evidence of the bastardization of their [the Nedeed women's] history, what she uncovers is the history of the women. She uncovers the way that women left their mark. No, they did not build huge real-estate empires and deal with political figures, like the men had done. But they left photographs; they left scribblings in their Bibles; they left recipe books. That's what she is doing. I'm taking her through the ways in which women have made history; and, through doing that, she ultimately claims for herself an identity. It was not the identity that I would have wanted her to claim; but now we get into the autonomy of your characters and when they start to live. What that woman finally came to, after that whole travail, was that she was a good wife and a good mother and that she could go upstairs and claim that identity. That is not what I thought Willa would do, but Willa was Willa.

Q: I wanted her to come out of that basement with an ax and kill Luther.

A: Yes, exactly. Me, Gloria Naylor, I would have said, "Go up there and kick his butt!" But no, it did not happen. You can't impose your will. Like we started talking about before—the writer is a kind of filter.

Q: It makes sense, though: She's reclaiming the house, too.

A: Yeah. I knew the Nedeed dynasty would be destroyed, but I was confused about how on earth that was going to happen if Willa wanted to go back up and be a housewife again. But then it all worked out. Personally, I think it worked out more powerfully than it would have if she had gone up there to try to push past him and get out the door and knock over the [Christmas] tree. There's something so eerie about the fact that this woman is cleaning up. And her husband misunderstands. He thinks she's going to run out and tell the world [that she's been abused], and she's just getting some dust in a corner.

Q: Laurel Dumont, the character who kills herself when she has all these material things, is a tragic character. What is the significance of her death?

A: Laurel was very hard for me; it was very depressing. I don't know when I knew she had to die, but I knew she was going to be in that swimming pool. It was sad for me to know that with all that she had accomplished and how hard she worked she had indeed lost her sense of self.

Q: I kept hoping she would get back in contact with life, especially when her grandmother stayed with her.

A: It's too late by then. She was an empty shell. And because I think I identified more with Laurel than I did with Willa it was kind of hard for that to happen to her, for her not to be able to just pull it all together. But that can happen when you live so much in what you do [that] you forget about where home is.

Q: The idea of home brings us to *Mama Day*, where going home is a central theme. You said you're making a movie out of that?

A: Yeah. We have a second draft of the script, which I did, and now we're raising the money to do it. I would like to see a black love story in the mainstream film media.

Q: Other than Spike Lee?

A: Yeah. Spike did a good job, but we need another vision. I think more black women filmmakers need to be out there getting exposure. No one has said the things that *Mama Day* will say on screen yet about black community, about connections between family, between the black male and the black female. They haven't. And also about a part of this country few people know about: the Sea Islands. It's going to be a beautiful film for as much as I can control. That's one thing about making this transition: Film is a collaborative medium. So even though I know how hard I strive for excellence and how hard I work at something, you have to pray that you get the kind of people around you with the same mind-set that ultimately will be reflected in the product.

Q: Do you have a director you like?

A: A few people I would like, sure. Jenny Wilkes—she's a British director and also a friend of mine who has been really helpful to date; Rhonda Haynes, who did *Children of a Lesser God* and *The Doctor,* with William Hurt; Joan Micklin Silver, who directed *Crossing Delancey.*

Q: You feel like you want a woman to do it?

A: For this book, sure. You need someone to handle this powerful older female and that relationship between the young man and the young woman sensitively. This is going to be a film that's going to pluck at the heartstrings of women, the same way the novel did, for various reasons and for women of all different ages.

Q: Where did you get the inspiration for *Mama Day?*

A: Maybe by listening to my parents talk about the South. Like I said, they're from a little rural hamlet where there were women who would work as lay healers. For the book I went back to interview one, a friend of my grandmother's who's still alive and who lives in Robinsonville.

Q: Was that Eva McKinney, the woman you interviewed for *People* magazine [11 March 1985]? She sounds extraordinary.

A: Oh, you read that. Yeah, I didn't see her when I was growing up, but she had come to New York once or twice to visit. I went back and actually put her on tape. Those are precious, precious tapes about the different herbs and things that she would use and about her life. Those women also dabbled in magic and the supernatural. So I grew up listening to my parents who would have these friendly give-and-takes about whether or not those things actually happened or not. I think the structure of *Mama Day* got born with letting you choose what side you're going to come down on. The story's told from three perspectives. You have to choose which to accept.

Q: What about the role of magic in that book? Are we supposed to believe the extraordinary events—like Ruby's spell—or not?

A: Well, you get a hint with the opening of the novel. I moved from the most universally accepted forms of magic into those things that we're more resistant to accepting. You're first made aware, in the first twelve or thirteen pages, that the act of reading, itself, is an act of magic. That's when the narrator turns to you and says, "Ain't nobody really talking to you." And yet, by that point you've laughed with these people; you've been moved by certain parts of their stories. And they say, "We're not real." And then the reader should go, "Oh, of course: the magic of the imagination!"

I move from that into having a man like George and a woman like Cocoa, who are totally incongruent, meet and fall in love. We all have in our circles two individuals who we don't know what in the hell they're doing with each other. We do accept that; we accept the magic of love. And then, from there, I take you to the last frontier. That's where there are indeed women who can work with nature and create things which have not been documented by institutions of science, but which still do happen. So the book's an exploration of magic.

Q: Cocoa and George *are* an unlikely pair. Why is she so afraid of George's love?

A: Because that's just the late-twentieth-century female dilemma. Living in an urban area like New York, women don't trust. There are so many bad experiences with men that if the right one came along, forget it, there's no way you could see it. She's a *Cosmo* girl.

Q: I found George one of your most interesting and sympathetic characters to date.

A: I really like George; I think he's a wonderful character. I cried for a whole year, knowing that George was going to die. I think that was a very believable love story [between George and Cocoa]. I'm very proud of that.

Q: He's really transformed when he goes into that chicken coop to save Cocoa's life.

A: His heart gives out on him. He was meant to find nothing there, to just bring back his hand to Mama Day. That was it. And she would have just held his hand, which would have been a physical holding as well as a metaphysical holding of hands with him and with all the other parts of Cocoa's history, the other men whose hands had worked and who had broken hearts. But George could not see that because he was a practical individual. There was nothing there for him. But he still saves Cocoa through the powers of his own will.

Q: That idea harkens back to the scene with Mattie and the rocking in *The Women of Brewster Place.*

A: The laying on of hands and the healing, yeah, a little bit, except there were two different dynamics going on. In that earlier scene, it had to be a woman doing the healing and the rocking. That was important to connect them up with other women throughout history who had their children torn away because of the machinations of the patriarchy—that's the reference to the concentration camps and the sacrifices [mentioned in that chapter]. A man could not have done that. In *Mama Day* George's laying on of hands was possible.

Q: What is wrong with Cocoa? Is she really under a curse?

A: She's had a spell cast on her, and she's being eaten alive by those worms.

Q: So that was black magic?

A: Some people will say this; some people will agree with George, who never accepted that and who has a third of the book. He just sees her getting sick and dying; he does not accept that she has worms or that Ruby cast a spell. He has just determined that he will not let her die. I have seen people healed by the power of the human will, through love. So it didn't matter to George. Me, because I'm a believer in these things, I think she was being eaten up by worms [she laughs]. It doesn't really matter—just like my parents and their different perspectives. It's not the point whether Miss Eva dabbled in other things or not; it's whether or not you believe.

Q: Did Shakespeare's *The Tempest* influence *Mama Day?*

A: Consciously, no, although people have commented on that.

Q: The name Miranda, the idea of the island . . .

A: Exactly. Shakespeare has appeared in each of my works. For *Mama Day,* he was consciously there because of *King Lear* and with the star-crossed lovers idea from *Romeo and Juliet.* I read *The Tempest* ages ago, so even though I wasn't consciously doing that, who knows?

Q: Your novels have a certain theatricality.

A: I knew before I began *Bailey's Cafe* that ultimately it would be presented for the stage. It was the first time that material came to me three-dimensionally. But the first step was to get it down, literally. And that's what I did in August [1991]. Now I'll have a reading at the Roger Furman Theater [in Manhattan] in March [1992]. It will be open to the public and to backers. So the theater is something I'm going to go into. I find I like the headiness of it all because your gratification is more immediate with a play or a film than with a novel.

Q: Would you talk a bit about *Bailey's Cafe*?

A: *Bailey's Cafe* is going to come out in the late summer of 1992. It deals with female sexuality, and I've structured it around a set of jazz, in that you have the maestro come in—that's Bailey—and then you have a section called "The Vamp." This, as you know, in music is the introduction of all of the notes and all of the things that will be used. That happens; then there's a section called "The Jam," which has these different songs, if you will. There are no quotation marks in the book— this is all supposed to be in music. You'll have the different songs that will occur, all involving most of the women and also a man, Miss Maple, who happens to come to this café.

Q: Where is this café located?

A: On the margin between the edge of the world and infinite possibility. It is there as a situation that embodies a turning point in each of these characters' lives. The next step they take is that step into the café, where they will either redeem themselves enough to go back out into the world or they will exit the café into oblivion.

On that street is a brownstone owned by a woman named Eve. Women come to that café looking for a place to stay, and Bailey directs them to Eve's. It's about their stories and the story of this man, Miss Maple, who meets Eve there at the café and becomes her housekeeper.

If you take the stories apart, you are going to look at some aspect of human sexuality. I didn't go in doing that, but that's what came out: the ways in which women are victimized and men are victimized by our definitions of what it means to be a woman or a man. And, since there are these series of voices, it works out that, while it's not going to be easy to adapt to the stage, it's very adaptable for stage. It's my job to figure out how to do it.

Q: The themes of female sexuality and definitions of female and male have been in your work from the beginning.

A: Very much so, yes.

Q: In *The Women of Brewster Place,* you talk about C.C., the man who rapes Lorraine, as someone defined by his sexual prowess. And the lesbian couple, Lorraine and Theresa, are threatening to the young men because they are outside their control.

A: They're outside, exactly. Outside of C.C.'s definition of what they should be.

Q: Will the play have music?

A: Yes. I'm excited about it. I'm also going to write a play about the whole Anita Hill–Clarence Thomas case. I didn't know what I was going to do with all of that at first because I had to digest what it meant. After I got over the horror of discovering that we are leaderless in this country, I said, "Okay, it won't explode tomorrow, but, God knows, this society won't last if this is how we're being led."

Q: Will your play parallel the televised hearings?

A: What happened will be one issue in the play. There will be one woman on a stage and three male voices that you don't see. You don't see these men, these inquisitors, these judges. There will be voices and this one woman.

Q: How do you see your responsibility to your community, and does it have anything to do with your writing?

A: I believe that as I, Gloria Naylor, the real Gloria Naylor, the real person, live, I definitely do have responsibility to my family and my community. Personally. I do not feel that I have that responsibility in my work. I know that these stories do filter through who I am and what I think and believe. They ultimately reflect my sensibilities.

But I don't agree with this thing black middle-class people have about positive images. They say, "Well, you should try to portray positive images. This system is only too willing to show blacks negatively, and these negative images have destroyed many of our children. When we [these middle-class speakers] were growing up, it was just that we were invisible. But now, when we become visible, it is usually as someone doing something destructive." The idea these people have is that your writing should reflect the other side, what's good.

Q: You disagree.

A: Absolutely. I don't see that, I don't believe that. I think that my books are something separate and apart from how I live my life and try to help my community. What I write really are other people's stories and they come forth, I would hope, as complex as people are. Some of the characters are not great role models; some of them might be. But, ultimately, I think that human nature is dark; I really do. Whoever the human beings are. But that's just me. Other writers—take Eudora Welty, for example—have very different visions of human nature. That is my vision, and that vision comes through with all of my characters. But, no, I do not feel that my art should serve some political end. I can do that with my checkbook; I can do that with what I do with my private life. This is another world for me, and I don't want to tamper with it.

Q: What would constitute tampering?

A: I don't want to censor what my characters do. A case in point: I'm a feminist. And when I worked with Willy and Lester [in *Linden Hills*], they were twenty-year-old males who would sometimes say things and hold attitudes that would make me cringe. But that was them. I allowed them to live, to do what they had to do. Now, my plays might be a different story [she laughs].

Q: From your first book, you critique bourgeois, establishment values. Etta wants respectability and marriage to the preacher; he wants a good time, exposing the myth of romantic love. In *Linden Hills* you show us the evil, dark side of so-called "success." It's as if you are saying, "Respectability, middle-class life, house in the suburbs, good job, fancy car: it means nothing. It means not having a face." In *Mama Day* Cocoa and George must leave their rational, city selves back home. Is any of that turning of things on their heads going on for you when you write?

A: That's really interesting. Not consciously. I have always been a little odd. I think I started out saying that, being a little different. I remember how I believed in Santa Claus only one Christmas, just about one. I remember pretending for many Christmases. That was the case. I used to enjoy catching adults in lies because it gave me a sense of power and control as a child. I liked seeing behind the evident facade of things, or to pretend I believed in Santa Claus when I didn't—that kind of deal. You see me turning things on their head. I think you're probably right. It's not what I set out to do, but there's probably a reason for that.

Q: I was reading about Charles Johnson, who won the National Book Award for *Middle Passage* [Macmillan, 1990]. He said that he doesn't have any politics, and the author of the article quoted you as saying that "every writer has an ideology."

A: Every single writer from Homer. Every piece of art has an ideology. There's an ideology in my books. The problem has been that, depending upon whose ideology it was, it was considered a universal truth versus something that was a particular truth. The great writers, the ones who last, are those who take the specific and somehow manage—a little bit through their talent but a lot through this intangible mixture of life being sparked into it—to make the specific spring into the universal. We all start from who we are and what we know—Henry James, et al.

My quibble is with people who construct literary canons and who construct book reviews and how we determine what is real writing and what is fringe writing. Those are all political decisions. I don't back away from saying that I'm a political being. I think, as a black American, I'm more political than others. My existence in this country was an act of politics. My continuing existence is such. And that's why I think it's more difficult.

Q: How different is the world for African American writers today than it was twenty or thirty years ago? Is it easier for them to publish now?

A: No, I really don't think so. The double standard still applies today. It's up to the whims of the publishing houses. The old myths are still there, that black consumers don't buy books. Publishers will often publish and tout that which makes them the most comfortable—e.g., why all this attention given to Shelby Steele's *The Content of Our Character* [St. Martin's, 1990] versus this book I'm reading now, *The Alchemy of Race and Rights* [Harvard University Press, 1990] by Patricia Williams? Because, right now, we're in a terribly conservative climate in this country.

We have not solved the problem of living together in America so, therefore, some kind of bomb that will come from a Shelby Steele takes the emphasis away from the fact that it's the society that's guilty. Not that his is a simplistic work; it's not that. But because he shifts the emphasis onto the people who are suffering, he makes the white system feel a little bit more comfortable. They can say, "I'm tired of being guilty; I'm tired of being uncomfortable. And these problems haven't been solved because it's *them*!" I think that controlling the means of production is the only way that a whole myriad of voices will be heard equally.

Q: What do you think about mainstream publishers, in terms of encouraging hyphenated Americans or anyone out of the white middle-class mainstream? Several of the writers I've interviewed have criticized the marketing of books.

A: Marketing is the word, if you're talking about commercial publishers. If you're talking about the health of American literature, I don't think that's a problem because of the university presses and the smaller presses which are saving our literature for the twenty-first century. But commercial publishing, no. It is by accident that art will be perpetuated with commercial publishing. That's not their function [she laughs]. Their function is to make money. At one time publishing may have been about art, but that's no longer true.

Q: Literary criticism is certainly changing—it's exciting to see so much diversity in the field.

A: You are getting critics from diverse backgrounds looking at the literature that has really composed America: Asian critics, Native American critics, Latino critics, and, of course, a plethora of black critics. That is heartening. I think what should be done is a reexamination of the canon, but that's just academic politics. We know how the canon came about, but these critics are re-creating it. For the literature of hyphenated Americans to be discussed seriously is a big move from before, when it was just ignored.

Q: But your stories were published by Viking.

A: That's why I tell you I was extremely fortunate. It just happened.

Q: If, as you say, the publishers want books that will make their readers comfortable, yours certainly don't. You don't make anyone comfortable.

A: Donna, I would be writing this way if a publisher sold two copies or two hundred thousand copies, because I'm not writing for the publisher; I'm not writing for the reader. Bottom line: I'm not. It has just worked out that the publisher sells more than two copies. But if they didn't I would still be doing this stuff. When I wrote it initially, I wrote it for me, to resolve things within me. It has just been luck that people cared.

Q: Do you read all these articles and books and doctoral dissertations that deal with your works?

A: No, of course not. I think criticism is an art form in itself. They are creating, in that space between the text and themselves, an understanding of the text. Criticism works with its own rules, its own languages. You couldn't go through Yale and not be a structuralist; and I keep up because some of that stuff is just so wonderful. It's marvelous what writers like Northrop Frye and Jonathan Culler do with language. But it has not a damn thing to do with the book. I don't believe it does. I will just read Derrida for Derrida's brilliance.

At Yale I realized that I was suspicious of playing the part of the critic because there was a part of me that was afraid of tampering with the creative process. At that time I thought it was like Hawthorne's "The Birthmark," where the scientist destroys everything, trying to find out the secret of his wife's beauty. I had already written a book before graduate school, so I knew that the creative process is mysterious.

Q: So you don't read criticism because, basically, you don't think it unlocks any mysteries?

A: Not really, no. But there's another reason I haven't read this stuff that's been written about my work: For years and years I was afraid of getting caught up in the one-book phenomenon, the whole idea of seeing yourself as a kind of celebrity, where you don't do your work. I didn't want that to happen. Now maybe I could read that, now that I'm more secure.

I only read an analysis of my books if I like the young person; otherwise, I give them [the critics] the space and respect to do their own thing.

Q: Do you get upset by reviews?

A: I read them when they come out, but I don't get upset. Some people do, but I don't. I would get upset if someone said that I couldn't write. For each book I have gotten bad reviews. I have only gotten one dishonest review and that was a political review of *Mama Day*. The reviews are there for the purpose of selling the book. My goals for my career go well beyond that. I want my art to be meaty enough or to say something important enough that there are doctoral dissertations on it, that it can be taken apart. I want to have something relevant to say in the twenty-first century.

Q: Is it hard to stay focused when there is so much hype in the publishing industry? Book tours, promotional interviews, that sort of thing.

A: Exactly. But you have to understand that this kind of celebrity is cyclical. I know this: that real artists create, no matter what. And since I am so dis-eased when I am not working, I make conscious choices throughout my life to put my work first. Some people might call them sacrifices. So be it. Right now I'm very fortunate because I don't have to do as much physical labor as I had to to support myself earlier. It's better-paid subsidiary work; I call it my secular work.

Q: What kind of job is it?

A: I'm on the executive board of the Book of the Month Club. You read manuscripts and meet once a month. But for years I taught—the whole idea being that this work was a way to support the writing.

Q: Did you like teaching?

A: I enjoyed it tremendously. The only hope I have is for young people. If you can get to them, not with an ideology, but just with the idea that they need to examine assumptions, there's hope. I would try to teach my young people to question everything. When I taught creative writing, I could never teach as a sort of guru because I know that's not how the process is. The only thing that separates me from them is that maybe I wrote a sentence that day and they didn't.

Q: So it doesn't get easier?

A: I thought it would get easier. I thought it would reach a point where you would pay your dues and it wouldn't be so demanding. But, no. You are into new territory each time [she laughs].

Q: You just raised an important point about writing that is rarely discussed: the need for money. Valerie Miner talked about how poorly paid writers are. Did you have to begin teaching right after graduate school to support yourself?

A: I received a fellowship to George Washington University—the Jenny McKean Moore Fellowship—after I got my master's degree. When I realized I was not going to stay on at graduate school and get my doctorate, that meant I would no longer be supported by scholarships. I knew I would have to hustle. So I said, "Okay, I will get a teaching job." I moved to Washington to teach at GW. They gave you time to write, so I finished *Linden Hills* there.

Q: So you had a light teaching load?

A: I taught an undergraduate literature course of my own design twice a week and, one night a week, I taught a creative writing workshop for the community. So I had basically three days. I gave those three to the university, and I finished my novel. That was the idea—they made the teaching schedule light because they brought writers in to give them a chance to write. After that, it was another teaching gig, and I got a fellowship one year at NEA [National Endowment for the Arts]. They gave me like twenty thousand dollars and a whole year that I could work. And that's how I hustled for seven years. And after about the seventh year, it reached a point where I could make a living from just being me.

Q: So now you live on your writing, supplemented by these other jobs?

A: Yeah, but my needs are simple. Bottom line: I need a warm and quiet place to work. I have been more fortunate than some; I really have.

Q: What's your writing process like? Do you let people read your material as you are writing?

A: No. I have done public readings if I am not sure. I enjoy hearing the response to the stuff and seeing if I achieved what I wanted—like if people think it's funny.

Q: So you basically show the book only when it's done?

A: Usually. My editor, Cork Smith, is my friend. I've had only one editor since I started publishing, although we've changed [publishing] houses. I'll read something to him. With this last book, I read a section to another longtime friend. But I don't read for them to tell me if it's good. I've lived alone for so many years that I'm used to being independent in that regard.

Q: Do your books pretty much appear as you wrote them?

A: Exactly. All of my books.

Q: Your editor doesn't change much?

A: Not except editing for clarity. For example, in *Bailey's Cafe,* my editor suggested that I cut some of the opening chapter because he thought it was too long. Another longtime friend said the same thing, so I will, indeed, cut it. But I won't put up with ideological changes—no kind of nonsense like that. It's always on me, anyway. As my editor says, "Your name's on this, not mine. Not Mr. Viking or Mr. Harcourt or whatever—your name. So you have to be pleased with what's here."

Q: Do you revise a lot?

A: When I'm working on it; not after it's finished. I think what I did on *Bailey's Cafe* is the most I've ever done with a book after I called it finished. The way you see my books is basically the way they came out, except for copy editing.

Q: I see a computer in your work area. Is that how you compose?

A: The last two books; the first two were written longhand, and then I would type them. Now everything—letters, too—gets done on the computer.

Q: Do you ever have to do background research for your books?

A: Sometimes. When I found out that George was a football fan, I had to do catch-up with the character and learn about football. In the case of Laurel Dumont, I had this image of her listening to classical music with her grandmother. The grandmother says, "That's nice, but he ain't made peace with his pain, child." I was at Yale then, and there was this guy in my program who used to play the classical flute. I went to Gordon and told him my problem; I wasn't going to go through the whole canon of classical music. He said, "I think you should try to listen to Mahler because he will make you want to cut your throat on a rainy day" [she laughs]. He was right. It turns out that's what Laurel was listening to.

Also, from time to time, I have to go to a certain place. For *Mama Day* I went to the Sea Islands, a chain of islands running from the coast of North Carolina down to the tip of Florida. And for that book I also read loads of books on magic.

Q: What do you like to read when you have a chance?

A: Well, look around me. There are a whole slew of *Nation* magazines over there. I'm reading Jamaica Kincaid's new book now [*Lucy*]. I love

Anne Rice dearly; now I'm into her erotica, but *Interview with the Vampire* [Knopf, 1976] hooked me on her. She did what Stephen King did for me. She made me believe that if I went down to New Orleans I would run into one of these jokers. It was all so plausible. Jo Humphreys and Robb Dew are friends; I read my friends. Louise Erdrich and Michael Dorris. I've already read all of the black women writers—I studied them in graduate school. Now it's nice because it's hard to keep up—you get galleys and books from new people all the time. I thought that John Irving's *Cider House Rules* [Morrow, 1985] was a really well done, sensitive book, although I couldn't get into him much before. That's who I read, but I don't have much time for it. I'll be reading more plays now. One year—maybe my fiftieth year—I'll take off and go back and reread all of the classics. I would like to do that, return to where I began.

Q: You've gone from being on your own to having responsibility for a teenager. What is it like having your nephew live with you?

A: Well, it's been different, incredibly different. Roger, my youngest sister's son, came when he was fifteen. I have learned things about myself since he moved in. I didn't think I could write with another human being sharing a space with me because I'd never had to, but I wrote *Bailey's Cafe* while he was here. Also, having to literally rear him, I could be sitting here typing and turn and give a lecture, and then go back to work. I found that was possible. Sometimes I'd be so into it [the writing] that I'd forget he was here, and then, aha! It would be a shock. It has shown me that you do what you have to do. It's taught me a lot about the human spirit and how it can expand and how it can love.

Q: Has his presence affected your writing habits?

A: I used to write in the early morning, but because I was mothering and working on the production company, I wrote *Bailey's Cafe* at night, from about 10:00 to 2:00. After Roger would come in from school and we'd have our time together, he and I would settle in to do our work.

Q: Are you a different writer now than you were when you started?

A: Oh, sure. I'm more confident than when I first started. I do think I'm more conscious of language. *Brewster Place* was just a gush of raw emotion. I haven't looked at the book in ages, but just thinking back, I know that I would just decapitate a writing student of mine if he did some of the things I did in that book [she laughs]—that's too hokey; that would never work.

Q: It's a good thing you aren't your own student.

A: It's a good thing I'm not. The book just drove itself in its own passion and innocence. But there is that point in your work where you don't control it and you don't want to because that determines whether or not life gets breathed into something. That's the magic.

I interviewed novelist and short-story writer Éilís Ní Dhuibhne (pro-nounced Ay-lish Ne Guivena) in her book-lined living room in Shankill, a seaside community ten miles south of Dublin. Her two sons asleep, her University College professor husband, Bo Almquist, working in his study upstairs, she relaxed with a glass of wine one chilly January evening in 1991.

Trained as a folklorist, Ní Dhuibhne has written two short-story collec-tions and a novel that feature strong, sometimes eccentric, contemporary women who stand up for their beliefs despite the consequences. In Blood and Water *(Attic Press [Dublin], 1988), her first collection, the stories differ from one another in tone and voice, from a straightforward, first person account of a midwife's moral dilemma when a poor infant she delivered is found dead, to a dark comedy about an ex-folklorist who makes a living killing pesky dogs and selling the meat. Her characters en-act revenge against society's constraints in the stories collected in* Eating Women Is Not Recommended *(Attic Press, 1992). A housekeeper goes mad when she no longer has time to crochet; girls rebel against cooking and sewing; a woman becomes a self-styled "menstruating tiger" after being embarrassed in a supermarket for having stained trousers.*

If her stories focus on the individual and choice, tying the present to the Irish past, Ní Dhuibhne's futuristic novel, The Bray House *(Attic Press, 1990), probes the violence and abuse of power by nations and individuals*

Photo: Copyright © Tommy Clancy

which lead to the destruction of the earth and of Ireland's population. The book follows the adventures of a Swedish archaeologist and her crew as they embark on a voyage of discovery to an Ireland laid waste by nuclear disaster.

At thirty-six, Ní Dhuibhne has already received considerable critical acclaim: inclusion in Heinemann's Best Short Stories of 1986 *and in several recent collections of work by contemporary Irish writers; a 1987 bursary (fellowship) in literature from the Irish Arts Council; and, in 1990, short listing (finalist standing) for both the Irish Book Awards medal and the Irish Children's Book Award for* The Uncommon Cormorant *(Poolbeg [Dublin]). A second children's book,* Hugo and the Sunshine Girl *(Poolbeg), appeared in 1991.*

In person, Ní Dhuibhne seems shy. She speaks softly and looks younger than she is, but she had no trouble subduing the neighbor's Irish setter who bounded in with me when I arrived, nor was she reticent about stating her opinions on topics ranging from the Persian Gulf war (which had broken out the day before our interview) to the situation for women writing in Ireland. As with many of her heroines, her placid demeanor conceals the fire within.

Q: Why did you decide to stay with the Irish form of your name?

A: I was brought up speaking Irish and going to Irish schools, so I just called myself by the Irish form because I was used to it. It can cause a lot of problems with the Irish themselves—mainly because they can't pronounce it [she laughs]. And they probably think those of us who have Irish names write in Irish. But, at this stage, I'm going to hold on to it since names are almost the last thing we have of the language.

Q: You write about poor country people and middle-class city people. What was your background?

A: My father is a carpenter and my mother is a housewife. I was born in Dublin in Ranelagh [an area south of the city center], and I've always lived in Dublin. I've got a brother and a sister, both younger than me, and we've all stayed here. It's our generation, really. If we had been older or if we had been younger we would have left.

I went to Irish-speaking primary and secondary schools, even though we spoke English at home. There were only a few schools like this when I was growing up, but now they have become quite common. After that, I went to University College, Dublin, where I did a B.A. in English, and while I was doing that I got interested in folklore. Then I went on to do postgraduate work and became a folklorist. I studied in Denmark for a year, doing research for my Ph.D. Since then, I've been working on and off in the folklore department. I've done some adult-education courses at People's College, Dublin, and I have a part-time job at the National Library.

Q: You talk about staying in the city, but there's a real love of the countryside evident in several of the stories in *Blood and Water.* Did you always feel at home in the city?

A: As a child you always take for granted your immediate surroundings, so I felt as if I belonged. On the other hand, my parents were very rural sort of people, even though my father had left Donegal when he was about twenty and lived in Glasgow in Scotland, like a lot of Donegal people. He had also lived in Manchester and Birmingham in England, but he seemed to blot out all of that and talk about the Donegal background a lot more. That was much more real to him. My mother was from Wexford.

It's strange what happens to these immigrant people. My father retained his Donegal accent—he's a native Irish speaker. He speaks a dialect that doesn't even exist anymore. All of that is much more real to him than his city life. So, yes, we did somehow have a very strong sense of our rural origins, and they loved the countryside and nature, like a lot of country people. We always went out on the weekends to the countryside around Dublin, and we spent all of our holidays in Donegal.

Where we lived in Ranelagh, about two miles from O'Connell Street [the main street in Dublin], was very dingy and we didn't see very much greenery. I guess I inherited from them a kind of romanticizing of the countryside.

Q: How do you think your working-class background affected you?

A: My background was a definite strength in that it laid a foundation for me. My mother was determined that her family would rise in the world. She was there pushing her children to go up and up. I was pushed into these schools where a lot of the other kids came from backgrounds that were more middle class. Those differences seemed quite big to me at the time. I used to be a little embarrassed by my working-class background. It used to irritate me when my parents spoke—they dropped their *g*s.

I think I was a nasty little girl, really. I was a little snob. I never noticed [my parents' speech and background] affecting my siblings, but they were younger and that helps. Once I got into college I began to feel at home. Now I don't feel different from my parents.

Q: How have your parents reacted to your success? Do they read your books?

A: My father reads them. My mother starts them. I think they read the short stories. He likes *The Bray House;* my mother didn't really like it. She didn't get past the first chapter. Parents take things pretty much for granted. In Ireland it isn't at all surprising that children write books. I don't think they consider it that strange.

Q: Were you the first in your family to go to college?

A: Oh, yes. I was the first in my family to go to secondary school. I belong to a wave of Irish children who would have been doing that. They were all working-class children going to college in the early 1970s because, when I was starting secondary school, they introduced the free education, which meant that you didn't have to pay fees anymore, so more people could go than before. Then they introduced certain college grants. In reality, the statistics are that very few working class went— they can't afford to do it anyway—but the opportunity was there.

I suppose that what inevitably happens to people like me is that I would have changed the way I spoke. I might have acquired a sort of posh accent different from what they had at home. I might have lost something of the language that was there at home. It's interesting to imagine what would have happened if you hadn't gone to college. I really can't conceive of myself remaining—working in a shop or something.

Q: Were your parents storytellers?

A: They didn't tell traditional tales or anything, but my mother has a real gift for narrative. She turns her whole life into a story, and she's one of these women who never stops talking. She describes every step of her day in the most complete detail. So I think she has a gift for turning life into stories, which I didn't appreciate at all when I was growing up.

Q: Were there family stories that got handed down?

A: It's surprising how little of that there was. I'm beginning to ask questions about that now. Sometimes it comes out; sometimes my father tells stories about his childhood, which was very strange. When my father was growing up, he lived in a house where they did all their own spinning of wool from sheep they raised themselves. They made the clothes they wore, and they fished. It was a very self-contained, old-fashioned and traditional household. He would tell stories about how he was cured of a malignant wound on his leg by a stone from the Holy Well. He's very sturdy and strong, as I am, physically. Once his grandfather was supposed to have carried a plow from Scotland to Donegal on his back, and that's the first plow that came to the parish.

I think a lot of Irish literature has been about the rural Ireland, about these people. John McGahern, one of our most important novelists, writes about them in *Amongst Women* [Viking, 1991], for instance. I am interested in that sort of writing as a transition, but I'm not interested in writing that myself. I think there's a danger in succumbing to this romantic fallacy because it takes you away from the way life in Ireland is right now, which is very poor.

A writer I like a lot now is Alice Munro from Canada. I think she is very good on rustic Canada—she reminds me of Irish writers.

Q: How did you first get published?

A: I started getting published in a page which used to be in the *Irish Press* called "New Irish Writing." You probably haven't heard of it, but any Irish writer probably started getting published there. It was in the paper every Saturday for about twenty years probably. It was edited by a man named David Marcus, who's a writer himself now.

I just sent off a story I wrote when I was in college. I was about nineteen, and it was really the first story I wrote. He published it, so that's when I started. And I used to send my stories to him for the next eight years; and if he published them I felt that was fine, and if he didn't publish them I threw them immediately into the wastepaper basket, which I now realize was not the right thing to do. It took me that long to realize that editors of pages in newspapers are individuals and that they would have their own taste.

Q: Do you think that's a good thing for a writer—to write for a particular kind of publication like that?

A: The taste of someone like David Marcus, who edited that page, the main outlet for Irish short stories, had a really strong effect, I think, on the way people wrote. And he didn't like a certain kind of fiction. I was happy because he gave me a lot of encouragement, but there were people who were not so happy. Perhaps he encouraged a certain kind of writing. On the whole he was very positive and encouraging toward women, one of the very first in Ireland to be that.

Now, he didn't publish "Fulfillment" [the dog-killer story in *Blood and Water*]. He did say some good things about it, but he said, "It's too bizarre for me." At that time there really wasn't anyplace else to get published here, so I sent it to England and got it published in the journal *PANURGE*. They made quite a fuss about it, and they included it in this anthology of *Best Short Stories*. So I began to see that there were other ways of getting published. My eyes were opened a little bit.

Q: Do you have an editor you work with now?

A: Ailbhe [Smyth] at Attic Press is the one I work with. I don't have a regular place for my stories now. David Marcus has retired—to write—and "New Irish Writing" has stopped. Caroline Walsh in the *Irish Times* runs a good summer fiction series, which I contribute to. There are very few outlets for fiction now.

Q: Let's talk about your writing. In *Blood and Water* I was struck by how different the stories are, one from another.

A: I am aware of that. The reason, I think, is that the stories were written over a long period. I had been writing in a sort of desultory way for at least ten or twelve years before that collection came out, and it was a collection of stories that were published during those years. So some of them were written when I was really very young. Some probably shouldn't have been included, like "The Duck-Billed Platypus." That was written when I was around twenty-one. "Blood and Water" was one of the late ones, one I wrote just before the book came out—that and "Kingston Ridge," "Fulfillment," and "Midwife to the Fairies."

Q: Do you do research for your stories?

A: I had to do a bit of research for *The Bray House* and for a historical novel I've done, but I haven't done research, per se, for the short stories.

Q: I see your affection for the country in "Blood and Water," your story about a girl who spends her summer holidays with her aunt in Donegal. She says, "I have an aunt who is not the full shilling." Did you visit an aunt like that?

A: Yes, that story is kind of autobiographical. I had an aunt who's a bit like that one, and I have this connection with Donegal. When I was very young there was a real contrast between the life there in the country and the life back in Dublin. It was almost medieval. Now that has gradually evened out. I'm quite interested in that gradual urbanization of Ireland.

Q: I really liked "Fulfillment," your story about the dog-killer.

A: People either love that one or hate it. It's quite black, you know.

Q: I like the way you don't let the reader know that the dog-killer is a woman right away. Was that deliberate?

A: That was quite deliberate. I wanted there to be a shock. Well, it's about work, really. It is a bit about the dogs. I wrote it when we moved out here to the suburbs. You met Rua from next door already [the large Irish setter who greeted me when I got out of my car; the name means "red" in Irish]. Well, he's a typical example of the canine population of this area, and when you are new here—for the first month or so—all the dogs are after you. I'm a wee bit afraid of dogs so it does make life vaguely unpleasant if they are constantly nipping at you.

The story's also about being frustrated about not getting a job. I felt at the time that a woman working was the same as a man working, that the reaction to the actual work would be the same. I'm not sure that I feel the same now.

Q: In "Midwife to the Fairies" [in *Blood and Water*] and "The Wife of Bath" [in *Eating Women Is Not Recommended*] you use material from earlier authors, like Chaucer and Jane Austen. Would you talk about your use of sources?

A: "Midwife to the Fairies" comes straight out of my folklore background, my academic background. I'm very interested in interpreting these legends in a new way. "The Wife of Bath" I wrote because I've always read a lot, and literature is part of my bread and butter. It's my life. Reading is very important to me, yet I feel that, as a writer, you write as if nobody ever reads. You feel somehow as if you ought to write about characters who don't seem to open a book, or for whom literature means absolutely nothing. That struck me as interesting. I admire what Antonia [A. S.] Byatt has done very much, for example. I think she gives reading the right place in life, really. Her novel *Possession* [Chatto and Windus (London) and Random House (New York), 1990] is really about the experience of textual criticism and about literature.

So "The Wife of Bath" is about a literary character coming alive and influencing a person in a real situation and in a Jane Austen locale. I am very fond of Jane Austen.

Q: "The Postman's Strike" presents a strong woman who leaves her man at the end. What were you saying about women and power?

A: It's my experience observing sexual politics at work. In some writers, someone like Margaret Drabble, for example, you always have this woman being abandoned; but when I looked at my friends, it was quite often the reverse. And my own mother has been an extremely dominant woman, the dominant partner in the marriage. My father is a quiet, submissive man, and that isn't unusual in an Irish working-class family. You have the idea of the Irish matriarch running everything and the husband kowtowing.

But when you analyze economics, you find the woman doesn't have any say. As families get more bourgeois, you find the woman is fading out of the picture, but where there isn't much to control in terms of money, the woman is ruling the roost.

Q: Your novel *The Bray House* is about a strong woman—a Swedish archaeologist named Robin Lagerlof—who goes to Ireland after a nuclear disaster has destroyed the country. I was amazed that you wrote this before the nuclear plant meltdown at Chernobyl.

A: Yes, I wrote it before Chernobyl when there was, for some reason, a lot of publicity in the media about the effects of a nuclear disaster. Everyone was thinking of nature and what that would mean. Then I revised it in the aftermath of Chernobyl and made it more ecological as I was writing.

Q: Some critics have called the book science fiction. Have you read much of that genre?

A: No, I haven't read any science fiction. I don't really like science fiction, I'm sorry to say. I know it falls into that category, but I don't think of it as science fiction, really. Maybe many people who write what they call science fiction say that, but I just felt I was using that sort of futuristic device as a framework to look at contemporary Ireland, an imaginative way to look at Ireland the way it is today. I feel strongly about the threat to ecology and the survival of the world. I don't see myself writing other futuristic or science fiction sorts of novels. I'm a different kind of writer. I think a lot of writers have thrown up one novel of this kind. They've thought about the future and wanted to write about it. Doris Lessing has done it, of course, and Margaret Atwood.

Q: Actually, I liked the fact that it was an adventure story with an archaeological angle.

A: I was thinking about *Robinson Crusoe,* that kind of adventure novel, and the lust for power that people get. It's about how dangerous that is. I was thinking of Maggie Thatcher, but you can also think of Saddam Hussein or anyone who has this awful lust for power.

Q: Your Robin lusts for power to the point where she becomes inhuman. She's ready to abandon her comrades to return to Sweden, for example.

A: Yes, she's supposed to be someone who is completely ruthless and crazy. She is completely mad at the end by the time she commits suicide.

Q: Was it a challenge for you to create such a ruthless and crazy character?

A: Yes, it was quite hard to create this character. I have done this before—in "Fulfillment"—but that character's more of a caricature, in some ways. I do have a certain amount of sympathy for Robin—her background and everything and why she turned out that way. Some people who have interviewed me have said, "Is Robin yourself?" and I've said that in some ways every character you create is going to include some elements of yourself. Some people have had some admiration for her because she is a person who gets things done.

Q: Compared to the three others on board the ship, I admire her, too.

A: I suppose they are all kind of wishy-washy. They aren't very attractive. Karen [Robin's principal assistant] is more attractive to me. I know she has a lot of qualities that would put you off initially, but at least she has a heart and a conscience about humanity.

Q: What about the irony that no one cares when Robin gets back to Sweden with word that she has excavated an intact house in the seaside resort of Bray?

A: Well, that's just life. If you have an enormously big ego you eventually have to get your comeuppance.

Q: *The Bray House* is a very powerful indictment of society. Do you consider yourself a political writer?

A: Not very political, but I have certain strong views on some aspects of political life. Now I'm a sort of mealy-mouthed, pink liberal. I mean, I have been in the Labour party, and I have socialist ideals, and I'm worried about environmental issues, though I'm not a member of the Green party. I simply wouldn't have time to be politically active; my life is so busy. I have a pretty strong social conscience, and I feel guilty about a lot of things. I don't know whether that is a legacy from my Catholic upbringing, but I really wish I were doing a lot of things. I want to be in Romania cleaning up orphanages, and it worries me that twenty million people are going to starve in Africa. And sometimes I feel that I would want to do something about it through writing. So I'm just politicized to that extent.

Q: Since you are so socially conscious, do you ever feel a tension between being a writer and being more active in the world?

A: I have mixed feelings on that. I have mixed feelings about the Gulf, for example. I know that it's about oil, and I am against war and all that, but Saddam Hussein seems to be such a crazy tyrant that someone has to do something.

Q: To return to your work, what prompted "The Garden of Eden" [in *Eating Women*], about a mother's reaction to the death of her son?

A: It wasn't sparked by anything real. I just think that if you have children you are always afraid of what might happen to them. The house next door does have a nice garden, and mine is pretty messy [she laughs]. I don't know how they feel about the story, though.

Q: Would you talk about this new collection?

A: It's called *Eating Women Is Not Recommended.* The title story deals with menstruation taboos in contemporary Irish society. Many of the stories are concerned with "shapeshifting"—the tendency of people to change bodies, personalities, moods. I am very prone to mood swings myself, partially due to PMS. I'm interested in the phenomenon and in the question of what constitutes reality—the real individual or the real situation. I'm not talking about clinical schizophrenia, but something much more commonplace and normal.

The short stories use very feminine imagery very deliberately: metaphors drawn from needlework, embroidery, and other "female" crafts or arts. I think this is a low-key, very female collection of stories; I hope they are subtly crafted. That is my intention. I am happier about them than I have been about any of my other books. I like them.

I've also got another novel under the bed. It's historical and I'm revising it. I haven't talked to Ailbhe [Smyth of Attic Press] about it yet.

Q: Is it set in Ireland?

A: Yes, of course. It would have to be [she smiles]. It's about Roger Casement's cousin [Sir Roger David Casement, 1864–1916, an Irish revolutionary], Gertrude Bannister. [Roger] Casement was a diplomat in the English foreign service. He exposed the exploitation of wild-rubber gatherers in the Belgian Congo and investigated the treatment of Indian laborers in the Putumayo region in South America. In the end he dropped out of the foreign service, became a nationalist, and went to Germany to get aid for an Irish uprising. So he became a traitor to the British. In 1915, after he landed on the beach in Kerry from a German submarine, he was arrested and hanged for treason. He was a homosexual, as well. His "black diaries" were produced when the trial was going on, and it was probably because of that that he was convicted.

My feeling about his cousin, Gertrude Bannister, is that she was in love with him, and she didn't know he was homosexual. She did everything to help him when he was in prison. She was running to the Home Office and making appeals. She was always working for him.

I got involved in this story when I was helping someone who was interested in making a movie about Casement. They wanted to know if there was a woman in his life, and she was the only one. I don't know if there's enough in her for a novel, although the topic is very interesting to me. What you can find out about her is very limited—as a character she would have to be fictionalized.

Q: What is your process of writing? I read somewhere that you like to write at night.

A: When I was working full-time during the day, I used to write at night; but I much prefer to work in the morning. I do that now. The children are in school in the mornings and now I have this job-sharing and I have time to write in the morning. I write out in longhand—I prefer that, especially for the stories. Then I use a primeval Amstrad [computer].

Q: Do you revise extensively?

A: I revise a lot—especially the short stories. I find that they gel after I've written the first draft: I get ideas about images that tie things together. I might write a story and come back to it after three or four months or a longer period of time and change something. On the other hand, I write rather quickly. I've come to accept it. For a long time I was ashamed of myself for writing fast because I talked to people and I thought I wasn't taking enough pains or something. But I do write the first draft very quickly, and then I come back and work on it.

Q: You speak in a lot of voices for someone so young.

A: [She laughs.] I'm thirty-six now. I recently met a young man aged thirty who has published thirty-five books. He writes a book about every two weeks. A lot of them are retellings of old Irish myths. But it just makes you think.

Q: You mentioned liking Alice Munro. What other contemporary writers do you read?

A: I like a lot of writers. I like Margaret Atwood a lot. I like Antonia Byatt. I like American and Canadian writers: Ann Beattie and Toni Morrison.

Q: What is the situation for women writing in Ireland today? I get the sense that there is this sudden eruption of talent.

A: There are more women writers than there ever were before, that's for sure, and there is the concept of the woman writer, which a lot of them reject but which is still there. And it's a useful thing, even if they don't want to be known as women writers.

Q: Do you mind being called a woman writer?

A: It's fine being described as a woman writer, as far as I'm concerned. But I didn't become a writer because I was a feminist. I wanted to write when I was seven years old. Writing was the great escape from my drab life. My consciousness was low until I was well into my twenties. I was a conventional girl.

Q: What do you think of the writing Irish women are doing today?

A: It seems to me that there are a lot of women writers, but still none of the major Irish writers are women. So far, no woman seems to have really broken through. I suppose we're not always waiting for another Joyce or something, but I sometimes feel that women writers put themselves under some sort of pressure to be a lot more conventional than men are and to write in kind of a popular way.

Maybe Irish women are always conditioned to please people and to be nice and to do the nice thing, and that even in their writing they want to be what most people would find easy and pleasant.

Q: Do you want this when you write?

A: No—well, perhaps a bit. Perhaps you come under this kind of pressure, especially after you've written a book or two. You begin to feel it would be nice to write a best seller. It may be exerted in ways that you aren't even aware of. It may be exerted by editors and by whether they will accept your material. I mean, when you consider that the main outlet for Irish stories was the newspaper page and that the newspaper is sold to thousands of people, well, there will be a certain pressure on the editor of the literary page to make the thing fairly accessible to a large readership because they would be hoping to sell more copies. That could be a kind of pressure, but the more experimental stuff would be weeded out.

Q: Are there publishers that encourage women to be more experimental?

A: Attic would be the most experimental now, and that's because it's small. It's the sort of publishing house that is going to be more unconventional and daring because they're not commercial. But the London houses which publish Irish women often do kind of middle-of-the-road, straightforward, realist, domestic sort of fiction. I'm not sure if that's in any way a bad thing, but I just have the feeling that Irish women aren't making any breakthroughs in the way they write, and that they're a little bit afraid of experimenting with the language, for instance.

I was in Norway a month or so ago on a kind of cultural exchange, and I got the impression talking to the women there that they were trying to create their own women's language, and this sort of thing just isn't happening in Ireland. Not yet, anyway.

Q: Do you think this experimentation should happen?

A: I don't know, but I think it would be interesting to try it, rather than to keep turning out social novels that are good bedtime reading. This is, in a way, a bit unfair—I read a lot of this myself. I mean, I like reading

Margaret Drabble and so on, but it's not going to change English literature or move it forward or anything. I think a little more experimentalism would be good.

I know that is elitist, though. If you start getting experimental, if you start writing in a way that is breaking conventions and developing new kinds of language, you're probably going to be addressing a very small elitist group, probably academics, whereas the way the women in Ireland write, they are accessible to women, who read a lot of fiction. I do think that women read fiction more than men do. I'm talking about fiction. Poetry's different. It's the nature of poetry to be not so worried about accessibility.

Q: So the shadow of James Joyce still looms over Irish fiction.

A: It can be a bit of a hindrance. I think you are always measuring people against Joyce and wondering if a successor will come along. Some really good naturalistic novelist like Kate O'Brien, for example, you're always asking, "Well, why did she still write like a nineteenth-century novelist, after Joyce?" I'm sure she was very well aware of Joyce, but she probably just didn't want to write like that. But you wonder why certain writers—men, too—why they would just reject modernism. They seem to go ahead writing in a kind of nineteenth-century way.

Q: How have male reviewers in Ireland treated women writers? I know that you have gotten generally favorable reviews.

A: I think lately the male reviewers have been extremely fair. You occasionally open to a male reviewer who says, "I am afraid to say anything bad about this woman writer because I am a man," and then they go on and do it anyway. And they do criticize women for writing about issues like love, marriage, and sex—really classically stupid male views that you probably just couldn't get in the United States because they are so clichéd and silly. But many of the men seem to review women's work fairly. Whether they read it or not when they aren't reviewing it, I don't know.

Q: One reviewer said he was relieved that you weren't a strident feminist. Do these reviewers resent women writers?

A: Sometimes you get the impression that they are expressing a kind of tiredness with women writers and that they resent that there are so many—a sort of backlash or resentment that if you are a woman that's all you have to be; you don't have to know how to write. So maybe there's a feeling of that here.

For example, we have all of these prizes here that have become really big. In 1989 there were a few novels by women and none were shortlisted for one of the literary prizes here and in England. Traditionally, women have not been given the same status as men. After all, it's still the early days for women writers in Ireland. Molly Keane and Mary Beckett made a new debut in their fifties after retiring temporarily to raise their children. Nowadays, we don't stop because we have children. I think these earlier writers may have been under such pressure. There was this climate where women didn't write. Mary Lavin was the exception.

Q: Do you think there is a difference between women writers from the North and South of Ireland?

A: Yes, because of the political atmosphere and what they are writing about. Sometimes I feel women in the North are stronger because they are more used to work. In cities like Derry women had jobs in shirt factories, while men were at home, unemployed. That might have given the women a sense of strength and solidarity. My feeling about the North of Ireland is that there are a lot of women's groups there; there's a lot of support. But here [in the Republic] I don't feel that.

Q: I sense that you have gotten a lot of support from the past—from those stories you unearthed as a folklorist. How do you think your interest in folklore has influenced your writing beyond the obvious way of providing you with stories?

A: I'm very interested in narrative—folk stories and legends. I'm interested in the way people tell stories and the sort of meanings that stories have. I think that as a folklorist I tend to shy away from using it as a basis for stories. I mean, I'm a bit of a purist—I'm not going to do up an existing story and make something else out of it. It's too good as it is.

I would see *The Bray House* as a kind of fantasy; but even though it's a fantasy, it's about something real. I think a lot of fairy tales are like that— they're about unbelievable characters, but they have a deeper truth. Things seem to be fantastical and unreal, but, in fact, they are about very ordinary, real problems and people. The big fairy tales are all about children growing up and maturing sexually and coming to terms with adulthood. And it's disguised as magic realism. I think folktales are magic realism.

Q: Would you describe your work as a folklorist?

A: The work that I have done is very interesting. The collecting is quite exciting. I've worked in Irish-speaking regions in Donegal and Kerry— the old shanachies [Gaelic tellers of legendary romances] and storytellers. There is a great romantic excitement about collecting these ancient stories from these storytellers in the Irish countryside in their little cabins.

I really sensed this when I interviewed Joe McCafferty, a man who was about eighty, who lived alone in a prefabricated hut when his house became uninhabitable. He lived out in the wilds in the middle of a bog. For some reason I was up there in the wilds of Donegal in January, and it was snowing, and I really felt like the Brothers Grimm. I had a sense of being in touch with something great from the past, a great culture and heritage.

Q: Have these stories been published?

A: There have been some collections of rural stories published already, and I've had some of mine published in some folklore journals. I collected from Joe about half a dozen stories; but, in the context of the archives of the Department of Irish Culture, it's just a drop in the ocean. There's so much there.

Q: Aside from those already published, are these rural stories being preserved? It would be a shame if they weren't passed down.

A: The stories that I collected have been transcribed and are in the Department of Irish Folklore. They are not lost, but the people are not interested in them. People who are interested in Irish culture can get to them, but, unless they are popularized or made into stories for children, nobody is interested in them, really. I don't think they would have a big readership.

I have also collected a lot in the city, in Dublin. I've investigated the modern legends which you come across—modern stories that people tell in cities.

Q: What are the city stories like?

A: A lot of studies have been done on them in the States. They are what we call legends. An example of a typical urban legend would be: a family takes the grandmother on holiday, and on the way the grandmother dies. In order to avoid the cost of sending her body home, they prop her up in the back of the car and start out on the journey home. On the way home they stop to have a meal in a café and they leave her in the car. While they are inside, the car is stolen. And that's the last they ever hear of her.

Q: I'm amazed. I remember that story from my childhood in Massachusetts.

A: These stories are everywhere. One that I've heard recently is about a woman who goes on holiday to New York. She's come down to dinner in her hotel when she discovers that she's forgotten her handbag. She goes back to her room and gets the bag, and when she gets in the elevator to go down there's a black man there. When she gets in he says, "Hit the floor." She dives onto the floor, and he says, "No, I just meant press the button for the floor." So she does, and she goes down to dinner. A few days later, when she's checking out of the hotel, the receptionist says that Eddie Murphy has paid her bill.

Q: Why are they called city stories?

A: They have an urban setting, but they are told everywhere. They have microwave ovens and cars in them, modern trappings. In some ways they are modern, but of course they're often using very old plots. What I have found out as a folklorist is that all good plots are as old as the hills, and that as a writer it is very hard to beat them.

When I arrived at Joan Riley's house in West Norwood, in southeast London, on a sunny July afternoon in 1991, she greeted me warmly. "I've been away, so I'm afraid the house is a bit of a mess," she said, although it looked comfortably lived-in to me. "I do hope you like fish because I've made you a Caribbean lunch." For the next few hours, over baked mackerel ("I wasn't sure if you would be ready for parrot fish"), callaloo, mastic bread, and guava jelly, I discovered how and why she writes such powerful fiction about the difficult, often painful lives of ordinary people. And I came to like and respect her.

Family and community—the Caribbean community in Britain or her native Jamaican community—have inspired Joan Riley's fiction from the publication of her first novel, The Unbelonging (The Women's Press [London], 1985). About an eleven-year-old's psychic dislocation at having to leave her native Kingston, Jamaica, for Britain to rejoin a father she has never really known, the book was based partly on the life of a woman Riley met when she was working as a residential counselor and partly on her own experiences.

Born in 1959 in Saint Mary, Jamaica, the youngest of eight children in a family of laborers, Riley came to Britain for college, receiving a B.A. and M.A. from the Universities of Sussex and London, respectively. She was shocked by Britain—the hardness of the life, the coldness of climate and people, the racism—but she was older than her fictional Hyacinth

Williams, and she wasn't sexually threatened by her father or crippled by romantic dreams of a Jamaica that never existed, as Hyacinth is. However believable this harrowing account of the lives of the poor and the consequences of a racist and neglectful child care system, it's fiction, not autobiography.

In Waiting in the Twilight (The Women's Press, 1987), Riley again explores the combined effects of racism, sexism, and poverty in the lives of the forgotten: in this case, a middle-aged Jamaican cleaning woman, living in Britain, crippled by a stroke, and dreaming that her husband will return to her. Romance (The Women's Press, 1988) traces the different choices made by two sisters—one a defiantly fat woman who escapes from her boring life by reading romance novels and having affairs with old white men, the other a wife and mother about to rebel against her oppressed state.

Her most controversial novel, A Kindness to the Children (The Women's Press, 1992), exposes the epidemic corruption Riley finds in contemporary Jamaica, extending from church pastors to government officials. Sparked by several factors, particularly the abuse of women and children leading to madness, the novel has so angered Jamaican clergymen that Riley has been read out in church as a sinner for writing it.

Such criticism doesn't bother the outspoken Riley, who claims to be used to it. In the course of the interview, she talked candidly about her own work and many subjects, from differences between African American and Afro-Caribbean women writers to the responsibility she feels as one of the handful of black women writing and publishing in England today. This desire to make connections between people is evident in Riley's latest project, Leave to Stay, an anthology of fiction and poetry exploring how the landscape acts upon and is acted upon by the writer as migrant. Coedited with New Zealand poet Briar Wood and due to appear in 1995, the collection brings together writers from around the world who share the experience of leaving one home for another.

Toward the end of the interview Riley's children came home from school. I have five-year-old son Bayhano's voice on tape: "I've been to school," he says into the recorder several times, in a slow, serious voice. Then I hear his ten-year-old sister Lethna in the background, annoyed because the "dinner lady" told her not to intervene when her brother was in trouble. "It is my business," she tells her mother, "he's my brother." The self-confidence of her daughter and both children's affection for one another isn't surprising, given their writer-activist mother's example.

Before I left, Riley gave me a hug: "That's how we do it in Jamaica," she said. And smiled.

Q: Your first three novels are powerful indictments of racism, Joan. Yet you've gotten some negative responses from the British for them.

A: I think [that's] because I'm writing about their backyard. It's okay for people from elsewhere to write even similar things, but it's not right to write about British systems in the same way.

Q: The British seem to like black American writers.

A: Oh, they love American writers. I think that is a kind of twofold thing. It's a kind of Americanization of the world. If it comes out of America, then it's radical. And I mean that ["radical"] in the sort of sixteen- to eighteen-year-old's sense of "good" [she laughs]. Secondly, it's because they always like to think that they are different here. I don't just mean the host population; I'm talking about the black population as well. They like to think that somehow they are superior and the sort of things that would hold true in America wouldn't hold true here. Then there's also the Caribbean thing: that most of us came out of Caribbean nationalism and this belief that you must always be positive. They don't like you to write that the Caribbean is riddled with racism, for example, which it absolutely is. Colorism actually forms social policy, even though they would never admit it. That's in my new book [*A Kindness to the Children*]. Negativism is seen as reactionary and a betrayal of the revolution, whatever that is.

Q: So among the black community in Britain, there has been criticism as well?

A: Yes, but what's interesting is that I get lots and lots of letters from black women in particular that are very, very supportive. They have been through those sorts of things and nobody ever wrote about them. There are these set vogue figures that you are supposed to write about, and I don't. When *The Unbelonging* was finished and my cousin sent it to black publishers, they said, "Nobody's going to want to read that. Why don't you write about the youth?" That was the vogue figure at the time. They also said, "The black woman isn't very strong, is she? We want a strong black woman. This woman is a waste of time."

Q: So they wanted you to write stereotypes?

A: That's right. At the time it was rather horrendous because the gay movement thought that . . . [my protagonist] should become gay, and the fact that she didn't showed that I was in some way homophobic. The radical feminist movement thought that I was divisive because I actually said that white women were also racist. And the radical black women said that the character was a betrayal because I was not talking about the strong black woman, but making too much of this type of woman, who we all know exists. I didn't write anything for six months because I was so traumatized by the experience [she laughs]. I thought you wrote a book and went home.

Q: How have your books been received in the Caribbean?

A: Ambivalently. It [my work] is taught because they can't avoid it. But if there was anything happening in Jamaica, I would never be invited— absolutely never. Under any circumstances. They are very bitter about other criticisms which, until this last book [*A Kindness to the Children*], have never been that full-fledged. This is the first book that has ever been absolutely Jamaican, and they've only heard bits and pieces. In the rest of the Caribbean they can stomach what I write to some extent, but they still think it's very much a betrayal.

Q: What you are exposing is different from what most other Caribbean writers are writing about.

A: I think I'm an odd kind of Caribbean writer in the sense that I don't come out of the rich, middle-class elite who are the traditional writers. It's almost like cloning themselves, you know. So what they write is very much their image of the world. There's never been a voice that's been a poor voice, and I've never, ever seen myself reflected in Jamaican fiction. To some extent in Olanda Paterson, but very little. All of them, including Olive Senior, can't get into the psyche [of poor people] because they don't know it and it's an alien place, something they are afraid of. And so what happens is that they create a distorted image of people like me and my family.

Critics can't throw out that I don't know the Caribbean, because I do. And they can't say that I've got an ax to grind or I'm in one faction or the other, because I haven't got the educational background for the petty jealousies. Finally, I've got the most jealously regarded [quality] of all: "street cred." So I'm a very odd person for them to deal with.

Q: By "street cred" you mean credibility?

A: Yes, I have credibility. I know the masses, but I can speak their [the establishment's] language. And it's a very hard thing for them to come to terms with.

Q: How did you earn that "street cred," Joan? I know you were the youngest of eight children. What's your background and how did you become a writer?

A: I don't suppose you want to hear about my poem when I was six years old? [She laughs.]

Q: Sure I do. Most of the women I've spoken with had something at seven or eight at least.

A: When I was quite young I started writing, but I never thought anything would come of it. Writing was something other people did. I loved books. I think this is what started it. I didn't have a particularly nice childhood. It was a very bewildering childhood, with the extremes of religion and politics. Like most Caribbean childhoods, it was an extremely violent affair. Books were an escape. You could go to anywhere. When I discovered Greek mythology I was about ten. Talk about a world! But I wasn't satisfied; I had to create all these other adventures. So I used to scribble away like crazy.

Q: What other books were you reading when you were young?

A: Odd things, like Shakespeare. I loved the language in Shakespeare. It took me a while to kind of work out what it was saying, but I loved it. Then I found Dickens and Norse mythology and Molière [she laughs]. Can you imagine that in translation? You've got to remember that the books we got were the discards of Europe and America. I also came across Zora Neale Hurston. *Their Eyes Were Watching God* [1937] still remains one of my favorite books.

Q: So these were books you were getting out of the library?

A: Yes. I used to sneak to the library and get them out and return them before the library closed. You had to sneak them into the house because it wasn't allowed. Or you would have to read them on Saturday when you were sick because you were supposed to go to church.

Q: At school, was your education pretty traditional?

A: It's peculiar how classical even the poorest education is in the Caribbean. For a lot of people, that was all the education they got. I was reading people like Robert Frost and Thomas Hardy. I loved Frost's poetry. I still do. But then you weren't supposed to like it because he was a white imperialist. But when I was in school in the seventies we got Caribbean literature and African literature and black American literature. I came across [Nigerian writer] Chinua Achebe and people like that.

We have a word—I don't know if you have anything like it in America—we say that something "clide" you. It gets so strong that you get sick of it. That's how I used to feel about black American literature, especially that of the men, because it was very defeatist. It's a certain something very much like fundamentalist Christianity. It never actually looked at internal blame, which is as important as external blame, because if you can't take responsibility you're not human and you're not adult and you're not able then to ask for a share in things.

I remember reading Ralph Ellison's *The Invisible Man* [1952]. Everybody was raving about it and I hated it. I like a lot of [James] Baldwin's stuff. I think he's definitely different, but a lot of the American stuff—I'm being blanket, I know, because the American writers were absolutely adored—but a lot of it I really don't like to this day. I feel that same sense of oppressiveness when I read them. It's not black being oppressed by white, because I can tell you about that as much as anybody. It's the sense of making a culture out of oppression. Black Americans are very anti-Afro-Caribbeans, and it's quite ironic because here Afro-Caribbeans use the same language against the Asians as Afro-Americans use against Afro-Caribbeans. They are not looking at why things are as they are. It's the white man, the white man, the white man. I get so sick of hearing "the white man."

Q: So did you continue writing into adolescence?

A: When you turn twelve or thirteen, you start thinking about the family and buttering your bread, or buttering the family's bread, really. I don't know if you know much about poor Caribbeans, but one thing they had was that only one child could have brains. That person was going to save the family; that's what it boils down to. And in my family, it wasn't me; it was my big brother. But he died after they had educated him—all their money went down the drain.

Q: Is that child usually the son?

A: Oh yes. The first-born boy. But the second-born boy, my brother, wasn't particularly scholarly anyway, but then he didn't have to be. Those were my two brothers. The next person who seemed to have an aptitude was me. There were all sorts of other things as well: being born last and my mother dying and all—it was all my fault, anyway. So I had to put away frivolity and foolishness like ideas about art and ideas about books, and I had to do real things that were going to be concrete. So I stopped writing. I wrote enough to get through English language and literature, but nothing else because it was out of my reach. I was going to be a librarian because then I could read books all day. Then I realized that you couldn't.

Q: When did you begin writing again?

A: I really started when I was here [in England] at university. There was a whole load of upheavals going on—Jamaica was just bleeding to death. I had lost so much family—they'd just been shot. And the other thing that happened was that, when you're a student and you've not got a work permit, the one work you could do is work in children's homes as a residential social worker. I was shocked by the situation there. Lots of black children that had been so neglected and are still so neglected. They really hated themselves. Their general self-image was so poor—they couldn't comb their hair; they wanted to be white. Just listening to them, talking to them, made me very angry—it wasn't just anger about white society and what it was doing, it was anger about these black people marching up and down like idiots with their banners for South Africa, for the Panthers, for everybody except for what was right under their noses. And when you raise it up [as an issue], it just wasn't high profile enough.

Q: So your working with these children and getting angry pushed you to write?

A: I started to write because I was getting so angry that I thought that I was going to explode, because the images on the television I was seeing about Jamaica were deliberately misleading images. It was at the time that Jamaica was going through a very bad patch, you know. It was fermenting; there was lots of destabilization. I saw it from the other side . . . from the mean streets of Kingston. On television they would only spin the shacks and they would say, "This is Jamaica." And of course the way it was being portrayed didn't happen.

I also got very angry with the peace movement because I was saying that I felt that, even being here, all of us here do violence to other people. We can't talk about nonviolence and just limit it to nuclear weapons. We've got to talk about what caused the whole philosophy which created the kind of mentality that could do that. And if you get rid of nuclear weapons something else will take its place. People were not listening to that, so I started writing poetry.

Q: This was the seventies?

A: Yes. I've been told my poetry is anti-male and anti-white. I think that's very unfair because it raises issues like, Have I not got a right to protest against your exploiting me because you are being exploited, too? I mean, isn't that how we get into hierarchy? And isn't that how we get into trouble? Well, people don't like those questions.

Q: How did you get to *The Unbelonging*?

A: I kept doing this [residential social] work in the holidays. It's good money for a student, and money was very tight. In one children's home I remember there was a young black girl who was the housefather's slave-girl. She just was so happy that he was paying attention to her—even though it was quite inappropriate attention—that she went along with this and really internalized this by kneeling to give him things. I just got more and more angry.

Then I started to meet people who'd left care and were really bewildered. They didn't really belong anywhere because they couldn't fit in. They had no coping strategies for living in a white society and they were terrified of black society. I met one person who had come to England at eleven, which most of them did. And because the parents who were here had new, British families, these arrivals were never seen as children of the family. Because there was this breakdown in relationship, a lot of black girls were inappropriately treated. And she was. The story [*The Unbelonging*] is loosely her story.

Q: So you wrote this book. How did you get published?

A: There was a series of coincidences. I wasn't writing it to be published. I was just venting my anger. And somebody who knew Ros [de Lanerolle] at The Women's Press [in London] told her that I was writing this thing that people were reading bits of and suggested she might read it. She said, "Yes," so I went to see her when it was about a third finished. When she said, "I will publish it," I thought, Good heavens! Obviously she doesn't know what she's talking about; I had better keep my mouth shut! And that is really how it happened. There were one or two other people that my cousin sent it to who wanted to publish it, but I went with The Women's Press because I wanted the book to be focused properly on the issue of the human being, not seen as a political novel or as a sociological text. And I thought to put me amongst women's books might force that issue. As it turns out, it's now a sociological text in many social work courses.

Q: How do you feel about that?

A: Mad as anything. I don't want them to study it. I want them to go out and do something about the issues, not think that this is the definitive voice, because it's not. There was no empirical data collected. What can you do? At least it has caused some change in social work practices which you can't complain about.

Q: Has the book had an impact?

A: Not much fundamental has changed, really, [but] I think that the book has added fuel to the thing about having more black people in residential situations; it's exposed the racism there, and it's contributed to the move for better training.

Q: When *Unbelonging* came out, did everyone ask you if this was your story?

A: Yes. My father was very angry. He said, "How could you do this? People think it's me. I never lived in England" [she laughs].

Q: In a way it's a tribute to the sense of reality in the book, but it's also a bit of an insult to any writer to wonder how she could imagine something if it didn't happen to her.

A: I just think you have to read what's there, and if it creates a certain reality, then the person succeeded. I get really cross when people say that to me. I remember at Sheffield I was speaking once, and, afterwards, I was left hanging about on this [train] platform. So I rung up and I said, "Who's going to come to collect me?" And they said, "But you weren't there." They were looking for a fifty-eight-year-old Guyanese woman, the character in [my second novel] *Waiting in the Twilight*. You see, that happens all the time.

Q: Do you think they do that more with writers of color than they do with white middle-class writers?

A: Yes, I think they do and I think the reason they do that is because of the whole thing about sociological context. There's a sense that somehow black writing has to be something other than literature. I remember the most insulting thing that was ever said about *Unbelonging* was, "Structurally it's quite good, surprisingly so." Also, the people here in England never quite worked out whether they should call me an English writer or a Caribbean writer. To my horror and shock, I was the first black Caribbean woman writer to write about the British situation in this country. And so immediately you become a kind of minor celebrity.

Q: They have to find a place to put you instead of just reading your books.

A: Yes. They don't realize that poor people are poor people, no matter where they grew up. If I wrote about a child who grew up in England, that meant I must have grown up in England. Those who would be my friends quite often say to me, "You've got to explain." But I can't understand why I should give them this huge polemic for them to be able to get something out of the books.

Q: You open *The Unbelonging* with that dream Hyacinth has of the secret place in Jamaica that she left at eleven. What do you see as the role of the past in that book?

A: In *Unbelonging* the past is a handicap, just as it is for so many people here. It's something that stops them from going forward because they've never actually come to terms with exile. It is as much exile if you emigrate as if you came because you had to, particularly for young people who came in their preteens. They had no choice. They are as much exiled as a political refugee. Memory is a funny thing. It keeps you sane because there is another, better dreamland that you can escape to. It commonly has that function here. But what happens when memory comes up against reality? That's what has caused so much pain for people here. When they were able somehow to find the money—half of them actually went to the moneylenders to get it—and went back to paradise, paradise was an illusion. What happens with memory is that it's very faulty. It edits out pain.

Q: You certainly show that in *Unbelonging* with Hyacinth's idealizing of Jamaica.

A: The image of the Caribbean in this country horrified me because they had this image of this place where everybody was well off and they lived in harmony and there was lots of food to eat and everybody went to school and did really well. It was so incredible, and I'm thinking, my goodness, there's a gunfight every night in Kingston. Can't they understand that it never existed? That's a child's-eye view.

It struck me that memory is actually quite negative in lots of ways because it stops you from creating new, sustaining memories as a kind of other to survive with. In the heir to *Unbelonging*, my new book [*A Kindness to the Children*], the heirs to these eleven- and twelve- and thirteen-year-olds are the late-thirty-year-old women who are going mad in this country. It's almost like an epidemic, as though if you don't resolve all that luggage you carry around with you, it somehow is going to come back and haunt you. This is what's happening.

Q: When Hyacinth goes back to Jamaica it is so traumatic. I like the scene with her in the cab—she's this middle-class success who is even more of an outsider back home.

A: But the reason she's an outsider here [in England] is because she never ever made a life here. She lived there in the past, but time continued.

Q: You talk about one horrible reality of life among the poor in Jamaica: incest. Is it really epidemic there?

A: Yes. I met a cousin of mine who had been here and [I] asked how her youngest sister had died. She said some kind of venereal disease or complications, and I said, "Well, how did she get that?" And her father had systematically raped all nine daughters. And I said, "Well, I never knew about it," and she said, "Of course you did. You just never wanted to know." After she said that, I suddenly saw how epidemic it was.

Q: How did the character Perlene manage to survive?

A: Perlene grew up in Jamaica. Poor Jamaicans—the ones who manage to get out and get an education—are very resilient simply because to survive childhood is so hard. Coming to England is like a picnic compared to that. I remember the first three months or so that I was here, any time a bike backfired my instinct was to hit the deck. Literally. At once. Surviving that and coming out the other end does make you take everything in your stride; so, instead of being bitter and anguished about everything, you make relationships. Perlene can make relationships. It doesn't matter where she goes.

Q: She seems more like you [than Hyacinth].

A: I think of her as being based on all these Caribbean people I grew up with.

Q: Do you share Perlene's political activist views?

A: No, but it was a very typical view of the time. I'm very squeamish about violence because violence always kills people I know. It's never the people who are sitting there being armchair Marxists who die. Because I know the individuals, I can't see the mass. But, at the same time, I feel Perlene is an interesting character because that's the backbone of Caribbean society now. I remember a Jamaican academic, a Marxist, saying to me, "If a million Jamaicans die so a million can live in a socialist state, it would be worth it." For him, that is fine. It's so easy to get rid of lives when it's not one that is going to cause you pain.

I had hell at university. When I said I didn't like [former prime minister Norman] Manley, they lynched me! [She laughs.] I was thinking, Everyone knows how much of a convenience Jamaica is to this man. That means he must be like [prime minister] Edward Seaga [who had close ties with the United States]. I've always been very unhappy about leaders. I see my brother with his cap in his hand, with his head bowed just like my uncles—probably like my grandfathers and my great-grandfathers—and he's saying, "Mr. Manley, liberate us, man." Then I think, But, you're not liberated. And that's because we look always to somebody else. I never write about the leader. It's always the antihero because the antihero is the salt of the earth. And if this earth is to have any chance, it is the antihero we are going to have to look to.

Q: Adella, the protagonist of *Waiting in the Twilight,* is certainly a salt-of-the-earth character.

A: She's well hated because when that book came out everybody said to me, "How could you write about a cleaner?"

Q: Why did they object to that?

A: Because they said it was reinforcing the idea that black persons are nothing, no-accounts.

Q: A lot of people are cleaners, though.

A: Exactly. And what I say is that you've got to look beyond the mop because there's a human being there; and until you can accept the fact that people are people and stop seeing people through the eyes of occupation segregation then you are always going to be prepared to step on people. If you really want to talk about people suffering you can't get a more common denominator than a cleaner. And it's not only black people. Cleaner is a job you start with whenever you migrate. It's really interesting because in the Caribbean a cleaner is my class. We are the people who spend fourteen hours leaving our children unattended to go and iron somebody else's skirt. It's a question of class.

Q: What sparked *Waiting in the Twilight*?

A: I wrote it because one day my aunt, who is the mother of the cousin I lived with, was rushed to King's College Hospital. Poor people are terrified of King's College Hospital in the south London area because lots of them go in there and they don't come out. There's really a chronic shortage of staff, discourtesy, a shortage of beds, the wrong operations— like somebody who went in to have an ingrown toenail cut out of the left foot and had the right toe cut off.

Q: This really happened?

A: Oh yes, it happens all the time. So my aunt had a stroke. It happens a lot—black women who don't speak good English really suffer. If you can get a child who can speak for you, then things aren't so bad. A lot of them did have strokes—can you imagine a stroke in your thirties? She dies waiting for a bed in King's College Hospital. And so many people die waiting for a bed. It's so ironic because for so many of these women, their whole life is waiting. It's all they ever do: waiting to do the cooking, shift cleaning, waiting to retire, waiting for the husband to come home, always in the twilight because they have to save electricity. But also in the twilight because they can't really live. What kind of life is it?

Q: Is her feeling that her husband is going to come back anything like Hyacinth's belief that this Jamaica she will return to is going to be wonderful?

A: No . . . well, yes and no. It's also to do with the way that she's been socialized. When you are a poor Jamaican there's nothing worse than to lose your man. You're good for nothing. You have no home training. You're worthless—all of the things you can think of.

Q: So a woman puts up with anything—even being beaten—just to keep this man?

A: Yes. Concubinage is very strong in Jamaica. You talk about outside children—it's almost an institution.

Q: And wives have to accept that?

A: What choice do they have? They would get a good battering. So she lost her man. What kind of woman is that? Obviously it is her fault.

Q: What about the fact that Stanton wants his own son so badly? Is that part of the culture?

A: That is such a strong thing. Girls don't count. My father had two boys and six girls. My uncle would see him and he would say, "So how is—the boys by name—and the rest is all right, too?" My mother died trying to serve my father's craving for sons. She should never have had more children. She had seven, and that was supposed to be it. She was obviously not doing well. It happens among the youngsters now. They are breeding warriors and leaving the woman to cope—fifteen- and sixteen-year-old kids and they are being stuck with two kids. It's disgusting, but it is a thing about having someone to carry on your name.

Q: Those John Wayne movies that Sybil watches on television tie in with this hero worship you mentioned before.

A: [She laughs.] John Wayne and cowboys and Indians. When I was young we used to go to the Rialto—that's the cinema in Jamaica; they've torn it down now—and they had to put a concrete screen up in the end because the gunmen used to come in and shoot Indians in the eyes [more laughter]. These fantasies. They say that we are a practical and stoic people, and to some extent we are, but this need for the hero figure is very big. That's why they put a personality cult around leaders.

Q: Dialect is central in your books. It gives texture to your characters' lives.

A: I think that's what it boils down to. When you meet somebody, the second thing you know about them is their voice. That shapes that person so much in your mind because everybody is oral. British people say we're not oral. Every time I do workshops I say, "Listen to everything. When your eyes are on the paper, listen to the sound of the words because if you want to shape a person, what comes out of a person's mouth and the way it comes out is so integral a part of them that if you take that away from them it becomes a different person." And I think that for me it is very important for that reason.

The second reason that it is important is because the Jamaican language is what we call a running joke in this country. And I get really mad.

If you want somebody to laugh, you use dialect. If you're being serious, you wouldn't use dialect. But for a lot of people it's the only language of expression they have. It is their whole life, their whole identity. And this is because middle-class Jamaicans use dialect in a funny way. The poet Louise Bennet did it—so everybody else did it. And so what happens is that it makes a person even less of somebody to respect or to have any regard for. And I made a conscious decision that if I used dialect to write somebody, that person must have some form of realism and they mustn't come over as some wise-cracking, laughing jackass.

Q: And the language is very rich.

A: It is. It is the language of my childhood, but the only language of my early childhood. When I went to school I couldn't speak English. You weren't allowed to speak dialect of any sort, you know. For me it is the language that comes out when I get stressed. I don't mean this pantomime cursing that they do. We're really not like that at all, but what happens is that you can't think of the English expression quite often and that's why your speech changes. It's certainly the only language my aunts understand. People laugh, they cry, they feel pain in that language. Why only the laughter? I actually get a lot of stick for misusing dialect because there's no humor in it.

Q: There's humor in the books, though. The grandparents in *Romance* are wonderful.

A: I think so, but they say that's not humor. The grandparents actually are based on my grandparents. In the Caribbean that's the old people. I'll give you an analogy. When I was growing up and even now, a woman smoking was a loose woman. But when you reach seventy or thereabouts, you actually earn the right to smoke a pipe. You earn the right to be whatever you want to be. Age confers rights and respectability on everything that you do.

Q: In *Romance* you mention the Brixton riots and a group called the BUF. What's that?

A: Black United Front. I was going to write its proper name, which is Black Unity and Freedom Party, but then I thought I better not because it might be a bit upsetting.

Q: That's a British group?

A: It's affiliated to all sorts of weird and wonderful things in America. But it's the same things: a little elitist group of people who set the agenda. I thought that you had to see a meeting because it's so typical [she laughs].

Q: There's this young man in jail, and everyone's talking all this rhetoric.

A: Yes. First of all you have got to go through procedure. Most of these people come out of a white socialization. Most of them have been brought over here by lower-middle-class parents and were told they're better than other black people. So they organize with white people because they think they're nearly as good, but then they find out there's a little bit of racism there. Then they go back to the black community where they can be big fishes in small ponds.

Q: And, according to your character Verona, they don't really know what's going on.

A: Yes, because she lives out there and they don't. I wrote that because I was living in Brixton at the time of the riots in 1981. The Brixton Liberation Front—there's always one—was set up. They met in Tooting, miles away from Brixton, and they wouldn't be seen dead in Brixton after dark, in case they were attacked. And that's really typical, you see. Average radical black men are very much like that, and I just wanted a little flavor of what it was. Notice that John, when he got disillusioned, went and bought the *Sun*, the most racist newspaper in Britain. It's a bit like he went from being a Marxist to a racist: Both of them are dogmas.

Q: Your latest novel [which I read in manuscript], *A Kindness to the Children,* is the first one set totally in Jamaica. In it you indict those in power for their abuse of children and women. What led you to write this?

A: I had to do some work with a woman who is mentally ill, and I started to try to get her to piece her life story together. And it sounded really so typical that I started to worry about it—to worry about this woman going mad and why she went mad. It seemed she had been kind of tottering on the edge, and, when she went to Jamaica, it pushed her right over into madness. Then, very quickly after, [Jamaican writer] Olive Senior wrote a couple of stories about madness where she made a joke of it, and I read them and was really horrified. Finally, I heard that my aunt was going mad. She's got a form of Alzheimer's disease, but the family are so frightened of the idea of spirit possession that they won't have it treated. They're fundamentalists, and they don't want people to know. Manley had a child who is mentally disabled, and I don't know if a fifth of the country knows that that child exists.

So it was just me thinking about madness in the Caribbean and fretting about it. My father worked at Belleview [a mental institution in Jamaica] and it was like Bedlam in the nineteenth century. They do lobotomies as a production line measure. But I started to write something totally different. It was kind of going on a parallel track, but I really wasn't getting anywhere with this [other] book.

Q: So you incorporated this madness plot?

A: It was like three strands of the book were coming together at the same time, because I am writing about this woman who is thirty-seven and is going back to the Caribbean—she's never been to the Caribbean, but she was born here. And this madness just kept bothering me.

Then, when I was in Jamaica, I met this madwoman who was being raped by these young boys trying out their sexuality. I don't think she was even mentally ill—I think what happened was that she was mentally disabled and she was classified as mad. This happens more often to women than men, because a madwoman is then actually common property, you see—no rights at all. And everyone I would interview would say, "But Joan, you were away for a long time. You don't understand this is the way society works." And thinking about Olive's stories and the laughter she evokes about this woman who is mad and talking to herself—suddenly you've got this character who comes into this book.

Q: That's [Jean], the character who goes mad?

A: Yes. She leaves Jamaica and comes to England at eighteen. She has her education here, but she carries this old luggage of childhood rape and brutalization, which she has totally forgotten. Her brother had died, and she had internalized blame for it. The pastor had actually encouraged her guilt and taken advantage of her.

Q: How is this going to go over in Jamaica?

A: It's already causing me all sorts of trouble.

Q: In what way?

A: Well, Jamaicans don't like to admit to all of the things that are wrong with their society. Children are unprotected. They are fair game, basically. Violence against women and children is endemic and accepted. Academics write about it as if it is a subversive act. Women are simply expendable, and when they write about it, it is always a woman's fault somehow. A woman is mad because she is drinking or something. There's never any rational reason why somebody reaches this point.

And the thing about Jamaica is that the twin pillars of society are the fundamentalist church and the state. Fundamentalist Christianity, which is really based on American fundamental Christianity, is chipping away the few things that women had in terms of comfort and support and leaving them bare. With fundamental Christianity, you never have to take responsibility. It's always somebody else's fault. And both political parties are strong in fundamentalism.

Q: So you are in trouble for writing negatively about the church?

A: If I had written a book which was about somebody who sinned because she was weak, that would have been fine. And even if pastor had sinned and you had explained why pastor had sinned, that is fine. If I had written a book about the church but hadn't looked at the political context and how bad corruption is and how everybody actually colludes with the situation, that would have been fine. Then at least the academics and the politicians would have been on my side. But because I have written a book which actually goes to the heart of how poor people are kept in control—which is by the church actually doing the job for the government—people are resentful.

Q: So some Jamaicans have read the book in manuscript?

A: Yes. To try and make the book as fair as possible, I did send copies down. Some of the people who have been asked to read the book are actually Christians, but everybody is, at least nominally, Christian. And what they felt, basically, is that I have no right to undermine the church by attacking the practices. Now, I mention the practices in passing, but I never actually talk about the rituals of the church or the beliefs of the church. But they read me out in church.

Q: How, exactly?

A: They call out your name and your sins and you are read out because you are a sinner.

Q: And this happened because of the way you wrote about pastor?

A: Yes. Pastor is a very interesting figure. You're very unsafe in church; they even have a folk song about pastor. When he offers to give you extra lessons, that's his shorthand for molesting you. And because in fundamentalism you never have to take responsibility, what happens is that you're tempting pastor and you forced him.

Every day you see it in the papers: Pastor gets caught with one child or another. But they'll say, "This child, however, is a very provocative child," or, "This child is known not to have been a virgin."

Q: So it's always your fault.

A: It's always your fault. When I was in Jamaica my niece said to me, "Oh, Auntie, pastor want to give me extra lesson and I don't like the way pastor touch up my foot." And I thought, oh, my God, and I got very,

very angry because if you get pregnant, which eventually you do, then it's your fault and you get read out of church. If you get pregnant in Jamaica you are finished. You are fair game. Going to Jamaica is like going back into the nineteenth century.

Q: Why doesn't anyone stop it?

A: Because everybody, including the government, colludes with it. A Jamaican academic woman in Germany at a conference I was at was talking about "slackess," you know the real rudeness and horror that reggae music is becoming—really disgusting, really antiwoman—we say "slack." She stood up on the stage, and she said the only thing worse than being a sex object is not being a sex object. Well, she's okay; she's safe. Who isn't safe are my nieces, my little cousins. Those are the people who are not safe. My favorite aunt was raped when I was very young, and she had a child, and she was kicked out of home. She's going mad now because what happened was that during the troubles they tied her up and shot her son through the mouth and left her with his body. It was about two days before they found her. So this is the Jamaica you never hear about.

You hear about middle-class Jamaica, but we never had a voice. There is nobody to say, "This is what's happening," because you can't do that to a middle-class woman. But one of my cousins has just been killed because a policeman raped her and he had to kill her. In Jamaica the poor are expendable. Many a time my brother and I would be walking along the street and you would hear, "Hey, boy!" and a policeman has got a gun on him. Fortunately, I have now got an educated accent, but yes, that's Jamaica.

Q: Are you afraid when you go back there?

A: Yes, Jamaica frightens me. You don't know how much it frightens me. I'm afraid of the violence. My daughter's [Lethna's] father was shot [dead] in Jamaica, so it's just one of those things. That's our lives. There isn't a poor person in Jamaica who hasn't had two or three deaths in the family. And if you talk to middle-class Jamaicans, they are horrified: "Surely it was just American propaganda."

Q: Was he shot by the police?

A: No, he was shot by the JLP, Jamaica Labour Party. He was one of the people who believed that they should work it out and not kill one another—he belonged to neither side. Who is killing? The poor people in the ghetto are killing each other for the politicians' sake. Both of them were looking to kill him, anyway, so one of them did, which makes the point that it really didn't matter.

Q: So writing this book was very important to you.

A: I've always wanted to write about Jamaica and I've never had the guts. It's taken me years. And, in fact, it took me two years to write that book and a year of total paralysis when I decided to write it. I was going to write another book—one that was funny and full of sun—but I'm writing this book because I had to write it.

I wanted to write about how the church has done more to destroy people in the Caribbean than any other institution. I grew up with the church. I also grew up with fundamentalist Christianity and that part of growing up is probably the most horrendous, painful time of my life. I still have nightmares about it. The nightmare I used to have was the devil had dug a hole but I couldn't fit in it, so he used to take this silk cotton tree, which is kind of a symbol of ghosts and things, and hammer my head to try and get me in. And the church really does have that grip.

Q: I understand that you have also written some science fiction. Would you talk about that?

A: I have actually written a science fiction novel which will go out after *A Kindness to the Children*. It's called *The Diaspora on the Twin Suns*. It was just a what-if? thing. I wanted to make a statement about how mad and stupid the world is. It's a really crazy novel. The whole concept came about because of the possibility of South Africa actually becoming a multiracial society. And also there was this thing about America trying to find the neutron bomb, the ultimate capitalist bomb [that would destroy people, not buildings]. The book asks, What if it went wrong, as things tend to do, and they actually destroyed the land and saved the people? So it's half a joke.

Q: Is this going to come out?

A: It will be coming out, but I'm not sure which publisher I'll be going with.

Q: What is it you like about science fiction?

A: I think you can say everything you want to say in science fiction and get away with it. I always wanted to know what would happen if roles were reversed. Black people are always saying very smugly, "You know, we've never gone out to commit genocide." But if we had had the development pattern where you knew you had to survive the next winter, we would have been no different. Human beings are human beings.

Q: I want to ask you about something you've said elsewhere: "A writer is just an ordinary person who happens to write."

A: Yes, I think so. Because most of the people who have had leisure to write were middle-class people, there grew up this myth about the writer being somebody who was somehow peculiar, different, exalted, and the whole mystique of the printed word came about. I think that cuts off people from the right to tell their story. Everybody has a right to own their own life. That's what it boils down to. And you can't if you're told that you're handicapped by not having "talent." I think it's not so much talent as hard work. I have seen people who have come to workshops with me for a year or two and they actually produce something which is fine, which they can learn to edit for themselves. They might not all start off being able to, in one go, write something publishable, but persistence pays off. I just think that writing is probably about 5 percent talent and 95 percent hard work. And I think most people have got 5 percent talent.

Q: You wrote this about African American women writers: "Although this is a valid part of the black experience and an essential part of the growing body of women's writing, the idea of Americans writing based on American traditions and values as the definitive influence on black women's writing is disturbing and unacceptable in its implications. It raises questions of cultural imperialism and ethnocentric values" ["Black Literature's New Dimension," *Concord Press of Nigeria*, July 1985].

A: I remember writing that. I am very concerned about the fact that there is a certain amount of imperialism which is going on because America isn't so open to other experiences, and other people, in a sense, take on board the American experience as something that is [at] one remove. I have heard American writers say things like, "Oh, we've been there, honey." And because they do put themselves forward as the definitive black writing, that then means that I have to dismiss the whole of my history, which is not at all like the American black history. There are similarities, but it's not the same.

Among Caribbean writers, I find that someone like Zee [Edgell], who is writing from Leeds, is writing something which is much more similar. We have much more commonality, and yet I wouldn't say that what I say from Jamaica is definitive for the Caribbean any more than what Zee says from [her native] Belize or what somebody like Merle [Collins] says from Grenada. I think that difference should be celebrated and we should talk about a body of literature, but the Americans don't. They actually do believe that they set the trend and we follow. When they talk about a particular experience of racism, it is an American experience of racism. A British black person's experience of racism is very different. When Britain has tried to tackle things by looking at the American experience, it has just gone disastrously wrong. They haven't understood that the values, the belief system, all those things are very different for Caribbean people.

Q: Which black American writers do you like?

A: Paule Marshall is absolutely gorgeous; she is well respected here. Toni Morrison is brilliant; she is one of the best writers around. With Alice Walker, although I think she is a very nice person and a good writer, I have lots of quarrels with things that she writes. I accept that it comes out of an American-centric, if you like, view of life, but it is very neocolonialist. We can see what she said and say that it is good, and I really feel I've got a sense of what it is; but then, on the other hand, we are seeing that she is calling us savages.

Q: You mean in *The Color Purple* [Harcourt Brace Jovanovich, 1982]?

A: Yes. Now this isn't going to be taken up in America because of the guilt. But it's Alice; it's not just her characters. I feel about some black American writers that they don't understand us. And because they don't understand who we are, we are savage, exotic, and different. So, yes, we take exception to that.

Q: You said that Jamaica Kincaid has a hard time.

A: Jamaica really has hell because Jamaica writes about the Caribbean in a kind of no-holds-barred way. She is attacked because she writes about some of the Caribbean's own prejudices, which you are not supposed to do, and because she speaks out about issues that anger her. She's a lot braver than I am because quite often I will sit there and I will shake with anger and I won't say anything, because I know that they are going to come down like a ton of bricks—but she does. She'll say, "You people, you think that you can talk for the Caribbean, but I am living in America, and I probably know as much about it as you do, and I'm less scared." And they can't stand that.

Q: Did you read Kincaid's *A Small Place* about colonial and post-colonial corruption in Antigua?

A: I thought that was great and quite true. She's actually saying what we all see, but the middle classes will not accept. I go to Jamaica and the people they stop to search [at the airport] are either black or working class, and when they throw these people's clothes out it's like some obscene insult. You are going into your own country and you have to have a landing card. The nationals' line is always the longest line. I put this into my new book. It really is a hangover from British colonialism.

Q: Like some African American writers, you've gotten criticism for negative portraits of black men.

A: [She laughs.] If you look in *The Unbelonging* there are very few negative black men. But everyone jumps on the one [the father who rapes his daughter]. I feel that it is unjust that people don't actually read the work with an open mind. Black men have been defining black women in the most awful, negative, horrendous ways. It's like the point where white men defined white women in this horrendous way, and this portrayal would be taken as gospel.

I think that when women write they write about the human condition—it's how I think of how I write—and the human condition I know most about is the condition of women. Men are there, of course they are there, and so you write about them, but they are always peripheral to what I am writing about.

Q: So *Unbelonging* did engender most of the criticism?

A: Yes. And it's interesting because it's been criticism of the two boy-friends. Nobody actually, openly, to my face, criticized that father. When I've asked them, "Don't you think the father is a little bit over the top?" they say, "Well, you know, it's quite obvious that the father is sick." And every time I've said, "Well, do you think it's an unjust portrayal of the boyfriends?" they've said, "No, it's not an unjust portrayal, but you've got no right to make it sound like that." And it's always been that it hits too close to home.

I'm saying, "Everybody has feet of clay. We're all products of our society, whatever that is. And men have been socialized to be men, and to be men there is a certain amount of callousness, there's a certain lack of sensitivity which is actually seen as desirable." But they don't like that. They say, "This is what gives white people ammunition against us." The irony is that lots of criticism I've had from white people is that the book isn't really about black people. It's really dishonest.

Q: It sounds like you can't win.

A: You can't. I really do feel like a pig in the middle most of the time, because I feel like I'm getting it in the neck from every possible side.

Q: Do you see your work, as you step back, as part of any kind of tradition?

A: No, I don't. People have said that I write in a realist tradition, whatever that is. I don't, actually. I just write what grabs me, I suppose. And probably that is why there is so much difference in the things I write. They are always trying to think of what school I might belong to, who have been my influences, and all of that; but I think I have read so widely anyway that certain things probably have had some kind of influence on me. I think that probably the thing that has had the most influence on me was [L. S.] Lowry's painting—he was a working-class English painter who is dead now. It was really fantastic for me to see working-class scenes in museums! If anything ever influenced me, it was that. I never wanted anyone to say that I wrote like anyone else.

Q: So you don't see yourself as writing like other Caribbean women writers?

A: I think my work has got a lot less in common with theirs than most Caribbean writers you are likely to come across, simply because it is not saying the kind of things they say. Many of them take on this working-class mantle, and everybody believes it because they don't know what the working class really is. A lot of stereotypes about poor people get tangled up in what they write: It is taken as a given that poor people are promiscuous and shiftless. And when they write something totally unbelievable there's nobody that's refuting it. When you actually find something that is coming out of that particular experience, you see the difference. People talk about "walking barefoot over the field" and "getting the stones hurting their heels." And I'm thinking, Well, how could the stones hurt your heels? By that time, you can't feel a thing. So it's little things.

Q: It's looking from the outside.

A: It is. But then to get credibility, you have to say it's coming from the inside.

Q: Do you read or interact with other people as you are writing?

A: Whilst I am actually physically writing, I never read anything at all. A lot of the writing is actually me thinking and going around and talking to people. It is very interactive; like when I was writing *Waiting in the Twilight,* when I finished it, I realized it didn't read properly because inside of an older person's head doesn't run like that. I could see it because I've lived with older people, but I couldn't think what was wrong. So I went out and talked to lots and lots of older people and absolutely listened to them for the first time with a view to hearing how their minds worked—the way it skips and the way it flows and convolutes. I think I have an ear to the ground more than I have an eye to literature.

Q: You talk about interacting with the people, Joan. How do class differences work in your fiction and your life?

A: I used to really want to be middle class. If you go to Jamaica you have to go to the university and look at this huge wall there. For years the metaphor for my life was this wall that divided the university and the affluent, heavily subsidized housing from the shacks and the open sewers of the gutters where I used to go to town. For me good was middle class. It was having a starched petticoat underneath my skirt and a new dress and new shoes and white socks. Fortunately, I grew out of it, but that I grew out of it probably had as much to do with getting a scholarship and stuff like that and also loving the old people. And, for a lot of people here, they'll get ashamed of their parents 'cause their shade's too dark. And their parents themselves are just as much to blame, because they say, "Oh, you're too dark." And that's the racism which nobody is tackling because it's all nicely hidden. White people don't realize racism is not a white problem; it's a problem of the world.

Because Caribbean people who speak English all have the same accent, you can't tell class differences by how people speak. This is a real difference between the Caribbean and Britain, where speech is a class marker.

Q: You write a lot about women supporting women, and you have these wonderful friendships between women. Can I conclude from that that you see that as a positive force?

A: Yes, I do. In fact, the new book talks about the evolution of friendship between women—of course this isn't even the right word, because you've got this woman who is one step above the working poor. This isn't easy to explain. It's very jealously guarded in the Caribbean. I think that women sustain women, and I think that middle-class women often lose that because they become separated and put into like a hole, you know, with their washing machine and their house.

There's two things poor people know: Children are their wealth, and the person whom you're going to have to rely on is another woman. And you're talking survival. Working-class women really do know how to make friends.

Q: Would you talk a bit about your children and the effect of being a mother on your work?

A: I have two children: My daughter Lethna is ten, and my son Bayhano is five. I often feel strangled. I write early in the morning and very late at night. I'm not a day person. The children are very well behaved. I always think of them as well-brought-up writer's children. Bayhano's never known anything but me writing. So I don't see the children being so much as I'm raising them—sounds like chickens, doesn't it?—as that they're people, individuals, who come along and we're making relationships. Part of that relationship is each other's space. They have absolute time which belongs to them, and they have to respect each other's time, but I also have writing time. I find allotted time for them, and I put writing around them.

Q: Do they travel with you when you go on book tours and such?

A: My daughter used to go away with me a lot, but my son doesn't like traveling. He hates flying. Generally we have a carer who lives here with us and looks after them. When I am here they have me.

Q: Tell me about your job.

A: I free-lance now; I don't actually work for anybody. Since I'm a writer, it means I've given up a [so-called] "lucrative growth industry with lots of prospects." But I do crisis counseling. I'm a trained social worker, not that I ever use it. For many years I worked with people having drug addictions. I still do intervention work with them and with people who have been tortured because of drugs. And I often get called to work with people who are mentally ill, because I think having that kind of background along with the writing helps you to restructure their lack of perception.

Q: And you do writing workshops, too?

A: I do writing workshops, and I also teach literature for University of London in the external department. I always think of myself as a bit of a fraud in writing terms because I haven't got a literature background and I tend to prefer interactive approaches.

Q: In your own writing, do you do a lot of revisions?

A: Yes, I guess I do. I write until, say, about chapter five, and that chapter will probably be something like fifteen or sixteen chapters after I go back, because the book expands in all sorts of directions. In terms of revising the whole book, not really, no. I revise so much as I go along that I don't have to. I write a chapter today, and tomorrow I revise it before I write the next chapter, so that by the time I finish I do have a whole book. It takes forever from the first writing down to having a digestible book, I must be honest. It's an ongoing process. I can't write a whole book and then rewrite it. I can't wait that long [she laughs]. No discipline.

Q: Do you use a computer?

A: Yes, I used to use a typewriter but the carriage fell off and now I have a creaky old Amstrad.

Q: Some of the women I've spoken to have talked about this pressure to create certain kinds of characters and their resistance to it. Have you felt any of this?

A: There is such a thing as being too positive. What you create is a new stereotype which is just as destructive. I was really horrified at how cardboard we had gotten in literature. There were two sides to it: Black people were these people who only suffered racism. I mean, black people don't sit at home and say, "Oh, last night, the racism that man did to me . . . " [she laughs]. It's important that a white audience can pick up that book and say, "I can identify with that." I hate it when people say, "Oh, well, I couldn't identify because I just couldn't understand the context."

Q: And the other side?

A: That we are these strong black women: I always think of a donkey; this black woman who drops the baby at 2:00 and at 2:15 on the dot she's back out there working. It depersonalizes the individual. What I keep saying is that we are people. People are people, with the same pains, the same hurts, the same uncertainties, regardless of race.

When I met science fiction writer and essayist Joanna Russ at her home in Seattle in October 1991, she was confined to bed with chronic back pain and chronic fatigue syndrome. Despite exhaustion and discomfort, she spoke with me for nearly three hours, about topics ranging from her life and works to the politics of publishing and the attraction of science fiction for feminist writers. A prolific writer and elegant talker, Russ sounds like many of her narrators: irreverent, smart, and passionate.

With eight novels, three short-story collections, and two critical books, as well as dozens of articles, Russ has established herself as one of the most innovative and controversial writers working today. She's best known for her award-winning science fiction, but within the feminist and academic communities she's equally famous as a social commentator and literary critic with strong opinions on everything from capitalism to pornography (two subjects she sees as interrelated). How to Suppress Women's Writing (University of Texas Press, 1983), in which she traces the ways women's voices have been silenced throughout history, remains a feminist classic. In essays collected in the irreverent Magic Mommas, Trembling Sisters, Puritans and Perverts (Crossing Press, 1985), she exposes the limitations of feminism (due to the lack of class analysis), criticizes the antipornography movement (for lacking data and detracting from more serious issues), and unearths the sexual fantasy elements in stories written by female Trekkies [fans of the 1960s television series Star Trek].

But science fiction has remained Russ's first love ever since she discovered Jules Verne and H. G. Wells in the stacks of the New York Public Library at age eleven. A precocious only child, the daughter of New York City schoolteachers, she began writing her own stories at about the same time, vowing to become a writer someday. After college, a graduate degree from Yale Drama School (her second love is the theater), college teaching, and the publication of a few stories, at thirty-one Russ published her first and most accessible novel, Picnic on Paradise *(Ace, 1968), later incorporated into* The Adventures of Alyx *(G.K. Hall, 1976).*

*Alyx, Russ's tough, emotional, self-sufficient, sexual heroine, challenges gender norms in a novel that critiques contemporary imperialism and sexism. This was followed by more Alyx stories; a feminist fantasy combining Sleeping Beauty and vampire legends (*Kittatinny: A Tale of Magic *[Daughters Publishing, 1978]); and an experimental novel, the difficult* And Chaos Died *(Ace, 1970), dedicated to Nabokov and featuring Russ's only male protagonist, a gay Indian man who finally reaches a telepathic, communal utopia. In* We Who Are About To *(Dell, 1977) and* The Two of Them *(Putnam, 1978), Russ continued her social critique in more traditional narratives: the first, an exposé of the imperialist underpinnings of the Robinson Crusoe story; the second, an adventure pairing a feisty heroine and a young woman escapee from the harem on a quasi-Islamic planet—a thinly veiled 1950s United States.*

But The Female Man *(Bantam, 1975), combining verbal experimentation with biting social satire, remains Russ's most successful novel. It features four protagonists, the same woman in different social contexts and life stages: a 1970s feminist named Joanna; a librarian from a sexist, pre-World War II past; an alien from Whileaway, an all-female future society, and an assassin from a future earth where women and men are at war. At times funny and horrifying, the novel examines the tragic consequences of sexism and the nature of political violence.*

Russ spoke more personally in On Strike Against God *(Out and Out Books, 1980), an honest, funny, sexy, at times poignant story of the coming out of a lesbian college professor who is a thinly disguised stand-in for the author. Again the style dazzles: chatty, filled with asides and direct addresses to the reader. Again the political savvy and intelligence shine.*

Russ's stories, collected in three volumes, vary from fantasies and reworkings of traditional SF plots to parodies and satires. Reading The Zanzibar Cat *(Arkham House, 1983),* Extra(Ordinary) People *(St. Martin's, 1984) and* The Hidden Side of the Moon *(St. Martin's, 1987), it's hard to believe that one person imagined such different worlds.*

"I just wish I had the energy to do all the things I want to do," Russ said to me just before I left. I wish she did, too.

Q: You've had a long and varied writing career, Joanna. Was there any person or event in your background that led to your becoming a writer?

A: If anybody was pivotal it was my mother, who wanted very much to be a poet and a short-story writer and didn't. She swears that she started reading poetry to me when I was eighteen months old. We would play games about guessing poems from first lines. As soon as I could talk I would ask for "Gaily bedight," which was a poem by Edgar Allan Poe that begins: "Gaily bedight,/ A gallant knight" ["Eldorado"]. I remember thinking it was thrilling, especially the verse about "Over the Mountains/ Of the Moon," which I took quite literally. And my mother's voice would change. She was a wonderful storyteller.

Her father was a Polish Jew, an immigrant, who wanted very much to write for the Yiddish theater. I found out years later that he was told that he could become a very fine playwright, but he would have to do it full-time, and, of course, he couldn't. He had a family to support. So I feel as if there are two generations behind me, pushing.

Q: Does your mother enjoy your books?

A: Yes. She sometimes complains that she doesn't understand them, but that's only in the last few years.

Q: In *The Female Man*, Joanna's teenage ambition was to "stand up fearless and honest like Joan of Arc." Was that yours?

A: Yes. I knew that I was going to be a writer by the time I was twelve. I had it all decided. And I remember telling myself that I would tell the truth no matter what. I didn't even quite know at the time what I meant by that, but I meant it. It was very important to me.

Q: How did you start writing science fiction?

A: I wrote it because I was crazy about it and I still am. I still love it. I discovered it in my adolescence, like most fans, and for a long time I throught it just sort of grew in the library. When I found out there were [science fiction] magazines, it was wonderful. I think I was reading some of [SF writer Robert] Heinlein by the time I was twelve. I still read some of the really early stuff that's very crude and conceptually very daring, and it's still wonderful.

Q: I read "Little Tales from Nature," a story that you wrote when you were fifteen. It had violence and revenge visiting this proper family at Carlsbad Caverns National Park. It seemed like a kind of macabre Jane Austen.

A: It is. By the way, Jane Austen's juvenilia is like that. It's funny and it can be surreal in much the same way.

Q: What influenced that story?

A: I don't know. I remember as a teenager reading a lot of S. J. Perelman and reciting it to anybody who would listen. I was reading horror stories at the same time I was reading science fiction. I loved them. They both scared the wits out of me, especially at night. But I couldn't keep away from them. I still write horror stories from time to time.

Q: The voice of the narrator in that story is pretty nasty. Is that a voice you like to use?

A: It's a voice that has come back in one book I can think of: *We Who Are About To.* But that was a different use. I've been cultivating for, my God, thirty years, a first person voice which will sound absolutely personal, absolutely spontaneous. But it's not spontaneous. I sweat blood to make it sound that way.

Q: Many of the women I've interviewed talk about being outsiders. Do you feel that you're one?

A: I know just what they mean. I've been reading [Gloria Anzaldúa's] *Making Face, Making Soul* recently, and that raises many of the issues in [Anzaldúa and Cherríe Moraga's] *This Bridge Called My Back.* I'm an outsider in every way but one. I'm a woman, first of all. I'm a lesbian. For the last fifteen years, I'm a disabled lesbian. I'm sort of an outsider in being an Ashkenazi [a Jew of Eastern European origin]. I am starting to think that is much more important than I did. I was also something of an outsider via class, which I didn't realize until I moved to the West Coast. The one way in which I am an insider or can have pretensions to the dominant culture is that I am white, but I know what they mean. It keeps you honest. First I was pushed this far by being female; then I was pushed this far by coming out as a lesbian; and then I was pushed even further by my disabilities, of which I have several. I am trying to write a book now which relates all of these things to each other.

Q: What do you mean that you were an outsider via class?

A: There are funny parallels with Zora Neale Hurston, who grew up in an all-black community. I grew up in an essentially all-Jewish community in New York. I thought everybody was Jewish. It was only after I went away to college and found out my best friend was Italian that I realized in a dim sort of way that they weren't. That really surprised me. But most of the places I worked in, certainly the places I taught in, had a very large, New York Ashkenazi presence. When I moved to the Pacific Northwest fifteen years ago, it was pure culture shock.

Q: This was when you came to the University of Washington?

A: Yes. I didn't get over it for ten years. As I'm coming to the end of this book I've been working on, which started out with feminism and its theoretical links with socialism, I'm now saying what the links are with racism. And I'm seeing that it all fits together. It's the people who are on the "wrong" side of the equation in all these splits who are making theory and doing coalition work and are absolutely crucial for our future.

Q: What is the status of this book now?

A: [She laughs.] Well, it's hit about four hundred pages, and I've got CFS [chronic fatigue syndrome] and I seem to be able to write in it once a month, and I don't know when the bloody thing's going to be finished. But I'm going to try.

Q: CFS must make it pretty difficult for you to work.

A: It's a lollapalooza because it leaves very little energy, constant exhaustion, all sorts of other symptoms. I've had chronic back pain for fifteen years. I've had episodes of depression which have been diagnosed as physiological. And, let's see, oh, problems with my feet, which really didn't matter until I got problems with my back.

I think people with disabilities have an awful lot to teach everyone else about human mortality, human limitations, and interdependence. And that, of course, plays right in with a lot of feminist analysis.

Q: It also ties in with the theme of anger, which I see in all your books.

A: Oh, heavens, yes. Anger turns up in *The Female Man* with, literally, claws and fangs. She is what pulls the whole book together in the end—that actual, open experience of sheer rage. In the first few years after I become a feminist, which was '69, '70, '71, I remember wondering if I was going to live through the anger because it was so awful.

Q: But I find your work at that period was pretty restrained. There's humor in those books, too.

A: Well, it was more than anger. Anger isn't the only thing that happens. There's also an enormous access of energy that comes from finally turning the oppression the other way and saying, "There's nothing wrong with us. There's something wrong with all of you."

Q: So you are saying that anger energized you?

A: Oh, yes, absolutely.

Q: Does it get you to write?

A: Yes. Once the anger comes out, what you have is gay liberation. When Larry Kramer or any of the other gay liberationists start writing openly about their eroticism, there's a tremendous gain in clarity. The crucial experience of my life is that difference between inner conflict and outer conflict. Outer conflict clarifies and energizes; it can be very difficult to keep doing, however. I am very, very privileged to live in a time when women's liberation and gay liberation and class and black liberations have all happened. I think they are going to have to converge.

Q: I read an early play you wrote called "Window Dressing" [in *The New Women's Theatre: Ten Contemporary Plays by Women,* ed. Honor Moore (Vintage, 1977)], in which a man falls in love with a department store mannequin. It reminded me of an episode I saw as a kid on the *Twilight Zone* television series.

A: Yes, I saw it. I loved that program and I loved *The Outer Limits.* I think I had that episode in mind when I wrote this. What really started that story was going down Fifth Avenue at night in a snowstorm and looking at the elaborate shop windows in mid-Manhattan, all brilliantly lit. The image was just so eerie and striking that I thought, What would it be like if they had real consciousness?

Q: You do some plot switching here, because when the mannequin is rescued from the window she is miserable. She says to the man who takes her home, "You're not going to take me dancing." She's disappointed.

A: Well, my idea was that she absorbs his reality at that point. She becomes real. She takes her reality from her clothes, from what's outside her. As soon as her clothes tear, she doesn't know who she is. He then puts his bathrobe around her, and so she takes her reality from that, and then she looks and says, "Why do you do this? Why do you do that?" And he gets terrified and pushes her out the window. Somebody once called it a reverse Cinderella story. I was very sympathetic with him [the man who takes home the mannequin] in the story.

What fascinates me as well as what fascinates an awful lot of horror story and supernatural fantasy writers is that for human beings it's so easy to confuse a representation of something with the real thing. Theater works with illusion in that way. I worked for one summer on costumes for Shakespeare in the Park [in New York City] when Joe Papp was producing it, and at the rehearsals I would look at this picture that was perfect and then move around to the side of the stage and I could see the back and the front. It's amazing because the illusion is so good. Fantasy often says, "Illusion is real; walk into the mirror and you find a world on the other side."

Q: Why did you stop writing plays?

A: Most of them were terrible. I went to Yale Drama School for three years to get a master's in playwrighting. The theater had always fascinated me, and it still does. And I love the art of acting, although I cannot act very well. I was in plays at Yale and for about six years afterward in off-off-Broadway and amateur but quite good theater in Brooklyn Heights, where I lived for a while. But playwrighting is a much more bare art than any of the others. I can hit it sometimes. I think that play you mentioned isn't fully there. I made a story out of it later ["Window Dressing," reprinted in *The Hidden Side of the Moon*], but as a play it's not fully expressed. Too much of what I write about is internal.

Q: That's true. I often feel that your narrators are the most interesting things in your books—their quirks and oddities.

A: And when the narration is third person there are still oddities in it. There are times when it suddenly falls to pieces. At the end of *The Two of Them* the whole book falls into fragments. I think I am doing what a lot of my contemporaries outside of science fiction are doing. Does that make us postmodernists? There's something that started in the forties with people like Nabokov, and it's no longer possible to make the same kinds of distinctions between what's real and what isn't or what's objective and what's subjective. Science fiction doesn't make the same distinctions as realism between what's possible and what's not possible. I think they go together beautifully.

Q: You also have a terrific narrative sense.

A: When I was in drama school, I spent three years learning dramatic structure, until I could stand on my head and do it. So I can do acrobatics with plot because I know the traditional, conventional, stereotyped way of putting a story together so well. I can pretend to do it and do something else. I got some very good teaching on this from John Gassman at Yale.

Q: Has it worked the other way? Did anyone ever think of making your books into plays or movies?

A: There was an independent investor who wanted to make a movie out of *Female Man*. He took an option on it, but the script they submitted to me was, I thought, so ghastly, so incoherent in a Hollywood way that I said, "No." What happens when you give something to Hollywood is that they say, "Well, we can't do that, so we'll change it." And you end up with an incoherent story, and I didn't want that to happen.

Q: Another early work of yours that turns a traditional plot—Sleeping Beauty—on its head is the children's book, *Kittatinny*.

A: I don't think it should be published as a children's book . . . [but] as one of those fantasies for children of all ages.

Q: I like the way you make the princess a vampire in the book, but one aware of her suffering. She says, "They made me scared of everything in the world and now I'm the scariest thing in it. Don't ever let anybody lock you up."

A: That came from an area that still makes me feel kind of crawly: There was a story by Terry Carr in which Sleeping Beauty is a vampire. I thought the saddest thing was the little girl herself and the stasis she is in. Unchanging. It's just horrendous.

Q: Here you lead us down the garden path then you shock us, a technique you use a lot in your fiction. Will you explain what you're after?

A: Sleeping Beauty is part of a thoroughly patriarchal tradition. It's not the witch who did it; it's the king who did it. And the sheltering of the little princess and the spoiling her is going to make her into something grotesque and awful.

You remember, just before that, Kittatinny finds the story of Russalka, a story of violence and sexism which is not for kids. When Kittatinny hates that story, Baby Brother says, "You've been listening to too many stories with wedding dresses in them." She says, "No more stories like that. I want the stories I heard when I was a girl." And this [Sleeping Beauty] is quintessentially the story she heard when she was a girl: a patriarchal story.

If you take things and turn them on their heads you often get the truth. If you push things logically further and further until they explode into their opposites, then you've got something artistic and truthful.

Q: I found your experimental novel *And Chaos Died* difficult to read.

A: Yes, it is. I remember reading somewhere that we do not have just five senses, but more like twenty, and most of them are internal. The sensory apparatus that tells us where parts of our body are, whether we are standing or lying down, whether we are cold on the surface or internally, are we hungry, etc. And I thought, Why not try to use those senses and tell a story directly like that? I've always been a very kinesthetic writer.

Q: Why did you make the protagonist of that novel a gay Indian man who looks Aryan?

A: I haven't got the slightest idea. I had a friend in mind. I think if I wrote it now I would be rather more in control of my material than to do that. He's not really presented as a gay man. I think he was a stand-in for you-know-who—me—or parts of things of my own that I projected onto him.

There's a whole tradition in literature of a woman's man, a woman author's man: characters like Heathcliff [in *Wuthering Heights*]. He's the kind of man the author would be if she had been a man. My character is in that tradition of projecting oneself into the other sex.

I feel rather apologetic about that book because I didn't know beans about gay men at the time. What I was trying for was what finally came out in *The Female Man,* and it was a romance between women. And it was a roundabout way of doing it. Adrienne Rich has also written about "the man who was on our side." There's some of that in it, too.

Q: *The Female Man* is your best-known book. Where did it come from?

A: Right out of my guts. What happened was that I went to this symposium on women that was held at Cornell University about four months after I had first come there to teach. It was the very end of December of '68 into the beginning of January '69. It was the first time feminism had hit Ithaca.

Q: It sounds like it struck with the force of a blizzard.

A: It did. Marriages broke up; people screamed at each other who had been friends for years. It absolutely astonished me. The skies flew open. Shortly after, I wrote a short story called "When It Changed" [reprinted in *The Zanzibar Cat*]. Then everybody started saying, "You should write a novel." And I said, "Nonsense. Go away! I don't want to write a novel. It's too much work." And about six months after that I just sort of felt like I might mosey down to a gay liberation meeting. I didn't know why. I didn't know why I had gone to the women's symposium, either. I had a vague idea that I ought to.

Q: Did you know you were lesbian then?

A: No, I didn't consider myself so. I had kind of come out at the age of eleven and a half and gone in a few years later.

Q: You sort of peeked out.

A: Yes. I said, "It's hopeless. It's dangerous. I'll never be able to do it." I tried to find information, I tried to find people who would know about it, and I couldn't. It was totally taboo. I read [Radclyffe Hall's] *The Well of Loneliness* [1928] and thought, I'm not masculine, you know. I mean, I'm tall, but I hunch over, and I'm not physically strong, and I'm not athletic, and I don't ride, and I don't fence, and I don't have lots of money, so this isn't for me.

Anyway, I went on down there and I realized that a lot of people there had been in my classes and were the students I had especially liked. What does that mean? [She laughs.] And there were two students of mine who stood up and said, "We've been lovers for several years," and I went out of there on cloud nine, thinking, it's really possible. It can be done. And that's when, suddenly, "When It Changed" started growing all the apparatus for the novel. I started writing the novel and it was finished in 1971. It didn't get published until 1975.

Q: Why the delay in publication?

A: It was rejected by hardcover publishers all over Manhattan. I had some very amusing letters. One woman editor wrote and said, "Well, you know, I don't like this sort of self-pitying whine." Another one said, "We published one already." I think it was *Les Guérillères* [by Monique Wittig; English translation, Viking, 1971]. I had read *Les Guérillères* by then.

Q: Were there other influences on *Female Man*?

A: A movie called *August at the Hotel Ozone,* which was a science fiction film about a future in which most of the men have died off. And it was a group of women surviving somehow in this world. It was Polish, I think. It was well done and it wasn't Hollywood-stupid.

Q: So this book comes out in 1975. What happens?

A: Well, first of all, it got reviewed all over the damn place. I sent a copy to the head of each NOW [National Organization for Women] chapter in each state, including Hawaii. The publisher [Bantam] didn't want to, and I threatened to blackmail them. I showed them the letter and I said, "I'll send it myself, and I'll pay for the books, and I'll pay for the postage, and look at the letter I'll send with it," which said, "My publisher would not do this. Look at the cover they put on my book, etc., etc." They said, "We'll do it! We'll do it!"

Q: Why didn't they want to publicize the book?

A: I think that the simplest explanation is that they were a paperback house that's not really set up for individual publicity on books. But I think that it was highly likely that they thought it was going to be a failure. I think they just didn't want to throw money away.

The two books of that whole series which really did make money, I have heard, were *The Female Man* and Sam Delany's *The Einstein Intersection* [Ace, 1967], two of the most difficult, artsy, radical, daring books in the whole series.

Q: The book must have brought you a lot of attention.

A: I got letters and letters and letters for the next five years. I still have them inside. It's a file this thick [three to four inches]. I got all sorts of requests to speak and lecture, most of which I had to turn down because I just didn't have the time. And it got all these reviews. There was one review in which the writer said it was insane and bitter and crazy and awful; but there was an enormous number of favorable reviews, many of them from fan magazines, and many, many of them by women, who said, in effect, "This is wonderful and funny and exciting and angry, but it's not really a novel." You see, I'm kind of in between three places: I don't write as a feminist only; I don't write as a science fiction writer only; and I don't write as a sort of—what?—artsy postmodernist only. I do all three, which means that somebody is always saying, "What's that?" It's a problem for publishers and for some readers.

Q: Where are they going to put you?

A: Yes. That's capitalism. If you're going to sell it, you have to put it in a slot so everybody can recognize what it is. On the other hand, I have to say that science fiction has also been a wonderfully congenial place for me to become an artist. I've gotten, in the main, a lot of appreciation in the field. And there is a closeness between readers and writers that's marvelous; fans are very active in science fiction and they let you know what they think and feel. You don't find that in a lot of other places.

Q: Was *Female Man* a turning point for you?

A: Yes, I think so. It was a great freeing of a whole lot of energy and relief. I could address my own life and the situation I was in straightforwardly. I once wrote an article on Willa Cather and I think it's beyond question, although the feminist journal I sent it to did not believe me, that Willa Cather was a lesbian. And when she wrote about her experiences she gave them to her male characters. Once you don't have to do that anymore, there may be a decrease in the kind of murky strains and echoes that critics love to explicate, but there is a terrific gain in honesty and breadth.

Q: Is that why you wrote *On Strike Against God*?

A: Yes. It was my coming-out novel. It's got some of the limitations of its situation. It was: If I came out, this is what it would be like. And the narrator, as well as me, is rather ignorant in some ways. I remember somebody coming into my office here years ago and saying, "You're homophobic!" And I said, biting my lip, "Why?" And she said, "I was reading *The Female Man*, and you don't describe the love between the

women in the same detail as you do the love between Jeannine and Cal."
And I thought, but did not say, That's because I didn't know! I knew one;
I didn't know the other then. And there is some of that in *On Strike
Against God*.

Q: What was the reaction to that book?

A: It came out with a small feminist press [Out and Out], which means
that basically it was not reviewed much. It was reviewed in the feminist
medium and it did well. It's a nice book. It's a good book. *The Female
Man*, because it was published as science fiction, hit many more people.
One of the things about paperback publishers is that they can distribute.
Small publishers have much more trouble.

Q: Why did you decide to go public about being lesbian?

A: It wasn't a decision; that was just the next book. My books are a lot
less politically conscious than people think. I will write them first because
it is sprouting and I have to do it. Afterward I can look at them and say,
"Now, that's what I was doing." In *Kittatinny*, I know that it looks like it
was planned, but it wasn't.

Q: Where did you get the inspiration for "Souls," the fantasy story of
the Abbess Radegunde who resists the Vikings?

A: The visiting alien in "Souls" is a character who has been in SF for
years. It's often put in historical context: Leonardo da Vinci was really an
alien, etc., etc. Or there was a group of these people who came to earth
from time to time to give our culture a little nudge, and I thought, What
would it really be like?

I think I do what Delany and [Tom] Disch also do: to say, "Here's
something from pulp science fiction. Let's do it seriously and complexly."
I often read something and I say, "That's a goddamn lie. I'm going to tell
the truth."

Q: Like *Kittatinny* and the Sleeping Beauty story?

A: Exactly. My stories are often haunted by the commonplace story that
isn't there. The situation in "Souls" has occurred many times in SF
stories. All the ones in that book [*Extra(Ordinary) People*] are traditional, conventional SF themes. The hidden society of homo superior, telepathy, the visiting alien. In *Female Man* the whole idea of alternate realities
is commonplace. I got it from Keith Laumer and A. E. van Vogt. They
didn't use it for the same thing.

Q: How are you and these writers you mention different from other SF
writers?

A: As I see it, there are three stages of science fiction. The first is inventing things: telepathy—geez, wow, gosh!; robots—wow! The second stage is what [Isaac] Asimov does with his robot stories, where you construct a plausible society for this to happen in. And the third stage is when you use it for some other purpose. I think that Delany and Disch and [Ursula] Le Guin and Gene Wolfe and I are third-stage writers.

Q: What do you say to critics who find religious themes in your books—in "Souls," for example?

A: I am not religious. I am a socialist atheist just as my mother and her parents were. I come out of that radical Jewish socialist tradition that started in roughly 1900. These secular Jews took the messianic, utopian promise of religious Judaism and transferred it to this world. I'm very much part of that tradition, and I didn't even realize it until recently. I've been reading books about the Pale in Russia [where the czars allowed Jews to live] and the ghetto life there; I recognize a lot of things that I didn't even know came from there which deal with me.

Q: But there's no belief in a higher power?

A: I do not believe for a moment that there is anything like a being of that sort. No matter how attenuated you make the theology, I still don't believe it. I am, as I said, a materialist. I am a religious mystic in the sense that George Bernard Shaw was, and he was very important for me when I was a teenager and has been since. To call it religious is to mistake it. They are using terms like "spirituality" now, which I think is just as fuzzy. I have the temperament, and I certainly did in my teens, of a religious mystic, which doesn't mean that I believe in religion. They are not the same thing, and the world that I paint in my work has nothing like that in it.

Q: What exactly do you mean by the term "religious mystic"?

A: If you put baroque music and mathematics and something about the incredible beauty and excitement of the physical world together, you can get that. Lucretius said that in *De Rerum Natura* [On the Nature of Things]. I don't really know the poem, but I know the little bit that I've seen quoted which is, you know, when I look at the starry heavens and I look at the order and the magnificence and the complexity, I feel more than mortal.

You find that all over science fiction and it's not religion. You are talking about an experience that certain temperaments have, but it doesn't necessarily have anything to do with religion. There is a fan term for it: "sense of wonder," "sense of awe." It's all over the stuff from

[H. G.] Wells on. Wells's depiction of the time machine or the death of the sun is awesome, but it doesn't mean that you believe in God. The ending of *The Two of Them* is full of that feeling, and it's not religious. It's about revolution.

Q: I'm struck with how different your stories are. Something like "My Boat" [from *The Zanzibar Cat*], for example, is such a different voice from that of other stories. Where do you get your ideas?

A: All over the place. People who write science fiction or fantasy are always spinning these off.

Q: So you could overhear a conversation . . .

A: Anything, anything. It is a constant, semiautomatic, speculative mechanism that keeps going. As I said, I'm between genres and modes and so I like them all. And I can pick things up from all of them. "My Boat" is a work I can defend up to a point. It was an affectionate tribute to a writer whose work I like very much: H. P. Lovecraft. Very few women have I ever met who like his work. The names, the places are tributes to him. The little Italian boy in the story has Lovecraft's book, and the narrator knows about those books. He's a real cult favorite. . . . The other source was seeing Cicely Tyson in *The Autobiography of Miss Jean Pittman* [a movie made for television] and thinking, My God, this women is one of the greatest actresses who ever existed. It ["My Boat"] was sort of a homage to her. They're an unlikely couple, I know, but when you put unlikely things together you can get some very nice results sometimes.

I wrote an article once about Lovecraft's writing a fiction "of extreme states"—I used Adrienne Rich's idea of "a poetry of extreme states." That kind of writing can do something that more [so-called] adult realistic writing simply cannot do. It can render what it feels like to be there in that situation, to have that kind of psychology operating inside you. These are concerns that literature in the academic canon does not treat and cannot treat from the inside. In fact, I suspect what they call paraliterary genres are precisely those that are connected with what has been censored, tabooed, made impossible.

Q: You've written other tributes to writers, haven't you?

A: Yes. "The Extraordinary Voyages of Amélie Bertrand" [in *The Zanzibar Cat*] is a homage to [Jules] Verne, and "Sword Blades and Poppy Seeds" [in *The Hidden Side of the Moon*] is a tribute to Amy Lowell. I've done a lot of what you might call metaliterature; that is, literature that's saying, "Isn't Amy Lowell wonderful? This is sort of like what she did."

Q: Lowell's underrated now, isn't she?

A: She was a wonderful narrative poet, but narrative verse is totally out of fashion now. I think it was one of her reactions to being a woman and a lesbian. An outsider has to write outsider verse. She's one of those people who wrote so prolifically that a lot of it is not good, but some of it is absolutely superb. She has a collection that attracted me called *Down East*, which is poems in New England dialect, and she has written stories of the supernatural in verse that I absolutely love. So, I simply took one of the plots that she does in verse and put it in prose—the one about women writers.

Q: Sounds like you saw her as a kindred spirit.

A: As a woman writer in that white European tradition I felt a lot of sympathy. I think [Sandra] Gilbert and [Susan] Gubar say [in *The Mad-woman in the Attic* (Yale University Press, 1979)] that, at least in the white European and Anglo-American tradition right now, the effort of men is to get out from under their predecessors; the effort for women is to find them.

Certainly when I was growing up, I, personally, would have given a great deal to know that there were more of them and that they were good. I found the Brontës by myself; my parents had some of the books, and it took me a long time to find the others. Women like [critic] Susan Koppelman helped. What she has done is so wonderful because she says, "It's not just the white Anglo-American tradition; it's not just the white European tradition; it's also Mexican American and African American, etc." She's one of the few who has really done the primary research. We became acquainted when I sent her a manuscript for a collection she was doing [*Images of Women in Fiction: Feminist Perspectives* (Bowling Green University Popular Press, 1972)].

Q: You talk about influences. Was "Little Dirty Girl" influenced by Truman Capote's story "Miriam"?

A: It may have been. I read the story and liked it years before. But no, "The Little Dirty Girl" comes out of something else that was personal to me: that is, what they now call the child within, the inner child, the squashed child who comes out later. I spent two years reading ghost stories. I didn't know why; it was like a vitamin deficiency. I just gobbled them up and then wrote that story. It was also the first time I ever wrote a story about Seattle.

Q: That was a very popular story.

A: Some stories that I write are much more accessible than others. Like "Souls" and "My Boat," it was not metafiction. When they are like that they get a much broader response from people who read. That story hit a nerve.

"Souls," for example, got all sorts of awards [such as the 1983 Hugo Award] because it struck a chord, particularly among science fiction fans because they tend to be highly educated, bookish, a little odd—people who, some time in their childhood, have experienced quite a lot of isolation. Therefore, this fantasy of "Am I really an alien?" speaks to them.

Q: Could you rework some of the things you have done that have been so popular? Could you write a variation on "Souls" or "Little Dirty Girl," for example?

A: No, I couldn't. It has to be different from what I've written before, in some respect, and it has to have some personal resonance with me or I bore myself to death.

I once tried to rework something. I wrote notes for a lesbian gothic. I found a gay male gothic book [called *Gaywyck*] in a bookstore near the University [of Washington]. It was the first gay gothic that I had ever seen and the cover was your pure standard gothic cover: the mansion in the back with the one lit window and this blue-green color scheme and out in the front a tall, dark, brusque handsome hero and next to him a pretty, docile, romantic, sweet-looking blond, but it was a hero and not a heroine. I don't mean this as an insult, but the cover was extremely funny and delightful. It was like taking a cliché and changing one term, and the whole thing makes you go, "What? What's wrong with this picture? Shadows are pointing the wrong way."

Q: So you decided to change the genders?

A: I had a vision of a book cover like that which would be two women and in curly gold letters it would say, "Lady Sappho." It would have to be early Regency because then you could work in Wollstonecraft's book [*A Vindication of the Rights of Woman*, 1792]. The dark one would be an aristocrat, and you would have her as the assertive one; then you could have the blond, sweet heroine and how they got together. I was writing just a plot outline and it got better and better and I put in all these wonderful things. She would be called Lady Sappho because she was a poet, you see, but the modern meaning would be a lesbian.

Then I tried to write the thing and I couldn't write it in the ordinary way. So what I did was write it in the form of a letter, which is what all the other stories are in that volume [*Extra(Ordinary) People*; the story is "Everyday Depressions"]. . . . By the way, if anyone wants to take the plot from that novel and write it, I wish they would. As far as I'm concerned, that would be wonderful because then I could read it and enjoy it.

Q: So each work you write has to be different?

A: Real artists, it seems to me, are those who don't repeat themselves. From very early in my writing—sometime in my early twenties—I made two technical rules: One is, "Go around." Remember what the Boyg says to [Ibsen's] *Peer Gynt?* There's a scene in which the Boyg says, "Go around," and Gynt says, "I won't. I want to go straight." And the Boyg says, "No, you won't. Go around." Most of what's worth saying in fiction cannot be said straight. You have to go around; you have to use all of your technical resources. The other thing I consciously said to myself was, "Never say anything twice, except for emphasis." It makes the story somewhat harder to read, but I think it's a marvelous technical precept. It makes them [the stories] tight and supple and gymnastic.

Q: "The Clichés from Outer Space" [in *The Hidden Side of the Moon*] pokes fun at some of the books written by women SF writers. Are they this bad?

A: A lot of them, yes. What happened was that Vonda McIntyre, a SF writer friend of mine here in Seattle, was editing an open anthology called *Beyond Equality.* Open means that you advertise in the SF newspaper *Logus* and places like that, and everybody on earth sends you stories. And most of the stories she got were ghastly. She got one, she says, about telepathic cabbages [she laughs]. The story ["Clichés"] included a preface about Vonda's anthology in which I called her Ermintrude. And things that I had read went into the story.

Q: There's a lot of bad stuff out there, it sounds like.

A: Ooo-hoo! You're telling me! They were frightful. But I seem to do that with parodies a lot. There's "Dragons and Dimwits" [her parody of Stephen Donaldson's fantasy series that appeared in the *Magazine of Fantasy and Science Fiction* (December 1979)] and so forth. It becomes irresistible.

Q: You've said elsewhere that you can afford to be a noncommercial writer because you have another source of income: teaching. Do you enjoy it?

A: Yes, I like it. What I don't like is not essential to teaching. It's the conditions. Everything is wrong with it that everyone says is wrong with it, but doing it can be very, very satisfying and very exciting.

Q: Except for your realistic novel, *On Strike Against God,* and your literary criticism and theory, almost all of your work has been science fiction and, to a lesser degree, fantasy. What have you found there?

A: Science fiction is so freeing and it can be so daring and so wild and so imaginative that I really don't want to abandon that. It's also such an intellectual form: it is literature of ideas. That's why you find [George] Orwell writing *1984* [1949] and [Aldous] Huxley's *Brave New World* [1932] and the work of H. G. Wells.

Q: Do you feel as though literary critics know how to read science fiction?

A: No, no. Absolutely not. They don't have the tools at all. I think there are some individual exceptions, but I think they are fairly recent and they come out of SF. Delany is a critic, just as I am a critic. But most critics don't accord SF any status as a field; they are not familiar with its history; they have no idea of its ruling paradigms; they have no idea of the traditional resources we're drawing on. And basically what they don't do, as we do and as our readers do, is know that everything that happens in science fiction is literally true, logically prior to anything being coded or symbolic or anything like that. This is what absolutely has to work. They [critics] can make the most ludicrous mistakes.

Q: Is it that they are trying to find a label for SF within what they already know?

A: They are trying to use the resources that were developed to deal with different kinds of writing. This is like a critic whose critical tools were developed to handle modernist works like [T. S. Eliot's] "The Waste Land" [1922] going back to the eleventh century and trying to find the same things. They just aren't there. The assumptions are different; the techniques are different; the whole aim of this is different.

Q: To some extent, this is the dilemma that has faced writers of color when their works are forced into limited genres and modes as a way for white critics to understand them.

A: Yes. I remember when [writer] Marilyn Hacker and I were in the audience at Ntozake Shange's *For Colored Girls Who Have Considered Suicide / When the Rainbow Is Enuf* [1976]. At the end of the performance, when the chorus speaks of "I found God in myself and I worship her," I looked around covertly, as I was sobbing. Almost all the women in the audience were either crying or laughing in that crying-laughing kind of way—and the men were all sitting like this [she crosses her arms]. They clearly didn't like it. And Marilyn said later that the white male reviewers liked it because they thought it wasn't about them. So it's the same thing.

Q: Many people say that science fiction and fantasy are the genres for women—that here they are doing things that they can't do in other places.

A: I think that's true. I think that science fiction has always been a natural, easy, fruitful place to do social criticism of any kind. If you pick up H. G. Wells, you'll see things like *The War of the Worlds,* in which he says that Europeans have gone and exterminated the Tasmanians. Suppose we turn it around? *The Time Machine* has Marxist and socialist speculation. And *When the Sleeper Wakes* is pure Marxism. Lots of writers have done social criticism, including those who are politically conservative.

Q: What about lesbian SF?

A: You've had a lot of fantasy and futuristic kinds of writing in lesbian writers. You have had a lot of radical lesbian writing about future utopias as a political stance. Sally Gerhart has done that. I encouraged Sally to publish; other people did, too. I feel a little like the mother of Godzilla sometimes because I did it early. All of a sudden, those of us writing in those early days are seeing our grandchildren everywhere [she laughs]. And I'm not always sure I like them. It [lesbian SF] has turned into a little subgenre of its own. It's just plain freer. I remember somebody saying, "I'm tired of unhappy housewife books." Either you write what is essentially autobiographical or you have to do something else. You cannot imitate a genre which was intended to exclude you.

Q: So you have to remake the genre in a way that you can fit in?

A: Yes. [Maxine Hong] Kingston is obviously writing between genres. Her books are fragmented, very like *The Female Man.* I think we all reach for the same solutions when we are in the same place.

Q: Four other writers I have interviewed have done science fiction or fantasy kinds of books: Paula Gunn Allen, Gloria Anzaldúa, Éilís Ní Dhuibhne, and Joan Riley.

A: I would really love to see those. And I hope they understand that they have got to be as correct, as truthful as possible about the science, as well as everything else. I mean, every once in a while a Doris Lessing will write science fiction and drive the rest of us absolutely bananas because she pays absolutely no attention at all to plausibility. When I heard about her SF, I thought, Oh, Christ Jesus, not that, because a lot of people venture into the field who are utterly unaware of what they are doing and trip over their own feet. I think that what I would find is that parts of it are very good and parts of it would make me want to shake her.

Q: Did you like the old Doris Lessing?

A: I couldn't read that, either.

Q: When you say that these writers need to pay attention to the science, what do you mean?

A: As Delany says, "You have to avoid offending against what is known to be known." You cannot write a serious science fiction novel or story and put helicopters on the surface of the moon. It's ridiculous.

Q: So you have to know about the moon if you are writing about it?

A: You have to know at least what kind of science is popularly known among people who watch channel 9, say [Seattle's public television station], or who have read a good deal about it. I have my little reference shelf with a lot of Asimov and other stuff.

Q: So when you write your books, do you do some research as you write about these worlds you create?

A: No, I don't. It's stuff I knew. I was a Westinghouse Talent Search Winner, in 1953 I think it was.

Q: So you know science?

A: It's not up-to-date. If you were to ask me, for example, to do something with computers, I couldn't. I don't know the language. But I do know enough to know what I must not say. I tried to make a little comedy with that in that plan for a gothic romance, "Everyday Depressions." At one point I ask, "Is there an East Wessex? (West Sussex?)." And I would say, "Must do research, must do research." I hate research, and I don't do it.

I do what Delany does, which is to ask my friends who happen to be in the field. And there are ways of explaining the explanations of science that do not exist because this is fictional. The point is in making that sound right. You must avoid glaring errors.

Q: Are you working on any fiction now?

A: I do have a novel that I was working on five years ago that I had to stop because my back was giving me a lot of trouble. In the middle seventies, as a result of *Star Trek*, the old television show, a lot of women became science fiction fans. I want to write a book that is sort of influenced by that.

Q: I read that article [in *Magic Mammas*] where you talk about these women Trekkies writing stories about the Spock–Captain Kirk relationship as a kind of model for a heterosexual relationship.

A: That's what sex is like when women write about it. I might amend it now to say that these are almost all white women who seem to be, by and large, pretty well educated. They have the air of being in the professional middle class, and if you read the stories, everybody is in the professional middle class. Signally, nobody does housework, and nobody does any kind of working-class job, and so on. It's tailor-made for them. But since I am more or less in the same position, I am rather fond of it. And some of them are damn good writers.

Q: How does *Star Trek: The Next Generation* compare with the original *Star Trek*?

A: In some ways it is better. The production is better. I am told that their computer technology is quite state-of-the-art. And Patrick Stewart pulls the whole thing together because he is such a fine actor. In a way, it's less daring because you have to put the old *Star Trek* in the context of its time, which was *Wagon Train,* for heaven's sake! There were at least token gestures toward being sexually egalitarian, international, antiracist, etc.

Now it is reflecting more the state of what life is for a lot of the people who watch it, or what they want it to be. I don't find it as feminist, by contrast with its surroundings, as it was.

Q: In 1983 you published *How to Suppress Women's Writing,* a landmark study of the silencing of women writers. How are women writers being silenced today?

A: It's still happening today, only one method has shifted: We now have inclusion by partial incorporation. SF is filled with men who are writing adventure stories with female protagonists, but that doesn't mean that there is anything else in the story that has changed.

Q: So the person going out on an adventure and making war is now a woman?

A: Yes. This can make a difference, but it doesn't make much of a difference to do only that. I think a lot of that partial incorporation would not have been operative when I wrote the book. I wrote it when I was in bed for several months with my back and I had nothing else to do. I had to make do, basically, with what I had in the house. I couldn't get to the library. Oh God, that thing was work! I wrote the first draft in only a few months.

Q: Would you change anything in that book today?

A: I would add something probably a lot more explicit about class differences. It's there in a couple of places. Also, I would do a hell of a lot more with racism, which I didn't even think of then until the end. I seem to do that: I'll push a line of thought as far as I can go, and I find things eventually.

Q: What would you say about class now? Do you think there is a difference for people from working-class backgrounds, for example?

A: Absolutely. I say this especially after having a couple of writer friends—Marge Piercy is one—who come from the working class. It's a different ball game. I came from being sort of in between. My mother's parents were very poor. She had made that jump up that a lot of their daughters had done, becoming a grade school teacher. My aunt was a social worker, but we lived in what was essentially a working-class neighborhood. And my mother's family was working class. Both my parents were members of the New York City teachers' union, which was very militant at that time, and I lived next to the Bronx projects. One of my little friends once said, "Don't bother her. She's a good little liberal." I was used to that kind of thinking.

So, yes, I think that writers from the working class also have to go around, as I explained before. Or they write in a bare sort of way that makes middle-class critics say, "Oh this isn't dense enough or ambiguous enough." But when the presence of money in your life was a daily worry, you don't think in the same way.

Q: Several writers from working-class backgrounds talk about consciously wanting to make their work accessible, but I don't sense that in your work. Is it there?

A: I'm beginning to feel that as a real pressure in nonfiction, although I certainly didn't start out that way. In fiction I don't do it because I was educated very expensively at Cornell University, besides my education at home by my mother and father. My father was a science buff. And if we were different from our neighbors it was because we were cultured people. That's a very Ashkenazi sort of thing. And I never assumed that you should not be as cultured as possible. I tried very consciously, as [critic] Susan Koppelman does, not to use jargon in *How to Suppress Women's Writing.*

Q: What would you add with respect to race?

A: I think now I would add more on women of color. For example, Zora Neale Hurston was another one who was slandered sexually in a ghastly fashion. I think some things cut across color as they cut across class. But I wrote it as I could do it at the time.

Let me add something else about silencing: Most academics have no idea of the economics and the politics of publishing.

Q: That theme has come up in almost every interview, too.

A: What books are chosen to be published. What books stay in print. What books are widely distributed. *The Color Purple* [Harcourt Brace Jovanovich, 1982] was not accessible for a long time. That [Pulitzer] prize going to any white author would have meant that it was all over the goddamn country. But you couldn't find it.

And then you have the business of choosing one Chinese woman and saying, "She's it, and we don't want to hear of the others." And choosing me often as, "You are the science fiction writer; we don't want to hear about the others. We don't want to hear about your tradition. We don't want to know where you come from." People who should know better have said to me, "You are so original in your stories. Look at these wonderful things that you have invented, like parallel universes." I keep saying, "That is not original with me. Nobody on earth has ever been original in that way."

Art is collective. Always, it has a tradition behind it. Always. And they will let some of us in but they will not let our traditions in with us or our aesthetic in with us. Again, I just come back to these goddamn critics who have no sense of reality.

Q: Are things getting worse?

A: Much worse. For the past twenty-five years or so, the big fish have been eating the smaller fish, and the bigger fish have been eating the big fish, and what you've got now is essentially monopoly capitalism, corporate capitalism. You've got a very few huge conglomerates controlling the media. I think there's something like five of them worldwide. And my field, for example, was an idiosyncratic, quirky little field that you couldn't really make a living at. You had to do it for love. You had to read it for love. And that was true in the thirties and forties, even the fifties and the sixties. And now most of the science fiction I see in the bookstores are just war stories, just Rambo in space. And the fans, whose taste is a lot broader than mine, will say, "I can't find anything to read in this stuff. It's crap. It's not speculative anymore; its physics is ridiculous." Yes, it's getting worse. Absolutely.

Q: You've written about the current debate among feminists about pornography. What's your position?

A: I kept trying to get to what I perceive as the bottom of the split and I always find another layer. I'm going to put something on this in the book [that she is currently writing]. Society can constrain your behavior in two ways: to make you do things you don't want to do . . . [and] to keep you from doing things you do want to do. The difference between the antipornographers and the group who call themselves pro-sex—that is, the ones who fight about it—has everything to do with differences in experience.

I think women with Andrea Dworkin's experience were forced to do things that they did not want to do, and that often had something to do with male sexuality and with pornography. If you've been battered as a lover or as a wife, if your husband has used pornography to belittle you or humiliate you . . . you are going to be utterly appalled by pornography.

On the other hand, if you have grown up aware of sexual impulses that you have been forced to suppress, if you've been told that you are wicked and that sex is wicked, if you have been beaten up because you dress [in men's clothing] like [writer Pat] Califia does on the street—and if one of the things that helped you realize that your sexual impulses were legitimate was pornography, as it was for Califia—then you are going to have a very different point of view [see Califia's "Among Us, Against Us: The New Puritans," *The Advocate*, 17 April 1981]. I think it is ghastly that the fight is going on. I would like very much to be able to bridge that.

Q: You wouldn't want to outlaw pornography then?

A: I don't think it's possible. What I would like to do, although I'm not at all sure how, would be to stop pornography from being a way to make money. I don't see anything, per se, harmful in books and movies and pictures which are supposed to get people all aroused, just as I don't see anything harmful in fiction which is supposed to involve you in the joys and sorrows of imaginary characters. But much of the fiction of this kind is what I would call sexist, violent, vicious, racist, etc. And much of what is done for sexual arousal is the same.

Califia's position is: look, we're not recommending real cruelty; these are rituals that we go through because it arouses us and makes us feel good. I think not to investigate why you like it is bad. I would say to Califia, I would say to Dworkin: "Your experience of it is not the only experience of it."

Q: Would you make any changes in your life?

A: There is a poem by Brecht which says, in effect, we did the best we could. And I did the best I could with what I had. I would not change any of that. The wonderful and terrible thing about politics in the very broadest sense is that you never know enough, you always find out more and more, and, of course, as you find it out, it changes, too. I think the poem goes: "We tried to make the world safe for kindness,/But we ourselves could not be kind," and I think there's a lot of that in my work. I think of some of the nonfiction of Mary Anne Evans [George Eliot] and think, Oh, God, are we going to look like that in one hundred years? Yes, absolutely, but it's still worth doing.

Leslie Marmon Silko lives on the edge of the Saguaro National Monument northwest of Tucson, Arizona, down a dirt road best suited for a four-wheel-drive vehicle. Her older son, Robert, twenty-five, had just moved back home with Silko and her companion, Gus Nitsche, when I did this interview in January 1992; her younger son, Casimir, twenty-two, was on his own. Silko is a private person—the entrance to her driveway has a skull and crossbones and a "Do Not Enter" sign—but she's also funny and self-deprecating. The winner of a MacArthur Foundation "genius" grant, Silko seems singularly unimpressed with awards and celebrity, except insofar as they enable her to devote herself to writing, a task she has, sometimes joyfully, sometimes painfully, taken on since she was in fifth grade.

Born in Albuquerque of mixed ancestry—Laguna Pueblo, Mexican, and white—Silko was one of three sisters raised at the Laguna Pueblo Reservation in a setting she describes as "sheltered." From early childhood, she was influenced by family stories and tales of the Laguna and Keres people told by her Grandmother Lillie and Aunt Susie; she retold some of them in Storyteller, *a collection of stories, poems, and photographs (Little, Brown, 1981). From her father, a tribal officer, Silko learned about injustice: When she was seven or eight, he sued the state of New Mexico for sixty million dollars in land rights.*

At the University of New Mexico at Albuquerque Silko intended to become a lawyer, but fate intervened when she took a creative writing course and discovered a natural gift for writing. In that class she drew upon her Laguna background for "Bravura," "Tony's Story," and "The Man to Send Rainclouds," the last earning her a National Endowment for the Arts Discovery Grant for short fiction. After three semesters in the American Indian Law Program at the University of New Mexico, Silko decided to leave law for writing. And the moral indignation against injustice took a new path.

In 1974 Silko published a book of poems, Laguna Woman (Greenfield Review Press, 1974), and several of her most famous stories were collected in Kenneth Rosen's The Man to Send Rain Clouds: Contemporary Stories by American Indians (Viking, 1974). Her work from this period falls very much under the influence of the storytellers she has known and the poets she read in college. The language is beautiful and haunting in poems celebrating the Southwest landscape and the individual's connection to the land. The stories are based on episodes Silko witnessed or heard about, like the title story about a traditional burial given an old man and the parish priest's subsequent anger. The most famous is probably the first-person narrative "Yellow Woman," about a contemporary woman's connection with the legendary Yellow Woman, through her adventure with a mysterious stranger, and her eventual return home. Controlled, objective, these stories and others, along with poems and photographs, appear in Storyteller.

Silko's widely acclaimed first novel, Ceremony (Viking, 1977), celebrates storytelling and the role of language that traditionally has been part of Pueblo curing ceremonies. But the book is also about the harsh realities of life on the reservation—the despair that leads to the suicide, the alcoholism, and the violence prevalent in so many Native American communities today. The protagonist Tayo, a Laguna World War II veteran and former POW, returns to the reservation broken by the war and estranged from himself and his people until he's saved by a Navajo medicine man's healing ceremony.

Tayo's growing recognition that "his sickness was only part of something larger, and his cure would be found only in something great and inclusive of everything" could describe Silko's own process in her ambitious second novel, Almanac of the Dead (Simon and Schuster, 1991). In what she describes as "a 763-page indictment of the United States," Silko spins dozens of interconnected tales to rewrite five hundred years of American history and envision a future where the tribal people of the Americas retake the land from governments that are corrupt at every level.

The characters aren't likable in any conventional way. The stories are what matter—a cocaine-addicted white woman's search for her kidnapped baby; a Native American psychic's attempt to transcribe the notebooks that comprise her people's history; a drug-runner's brutal elimination of his competition; twin Mexican brothers who follow the instructions of sacred macaws and lead their people north.

That Silko manages to pull off this tour de force is amazing; that she does it with humor is incredible. But humor has been part of her vision all along. In With the Delicacy and Strength of Lace *(Graywolf Press, 1985), a collection of letters between Silko and the poet James A. Wright, she tells the ailing Wright a funny story about a man she knew back home whose claim to fame was an incredible ability to cheat death despite a series of catastrophes and illnesses. In "Storyteller," one of her most famous stories, an Eskimo woman held on suspicion of murder laughs when she sees that her jailer will be forced by the white attorney to stay and translate for him. Humor functions in her real life, too—Silko wrote both* Ceremony *and* Almanac *in spaces rented from lawyers.*

Before I met her I had wondered which Silko I would find—the rhapsodic nature poet, the vivid letter writer, the weaver of stories of Native American life and legend, the realistic chronicler of contemporary life on the reservation, or the fierce rewriter of American history. She had just returned from an exhausting book tour to promote Almanac of the Dead, *and, as we sat in the backyard of her house under a cloudless sky, the cactus-strewn desert sweeping away to the mountains behind us and her pet macaws calling from the living room, I found myself falling under the spell of the woman as I had the writer. And hearing traces of all the voices.*

Q: You once told an interviewer that the Marmons, your father's family, were controversial. What did you mean?

A: In the 1870s, Presbyterian missionaries came out this way. One was a man named Gorman, who, I think, later went up into Navajo country. Anyway, around 1878, '79, my great-grandfather's brother and cousin from Ohio heard about this place through Gorman. The Civil War was over—they had been in the Union army—but there must have been a kind of restlessness in the family.

So these two men, who were government surveyors, came to the [New] Mexico Territory first, then my great-grandfather settled there and married a Laguna Pueblo woman. He taught school up at Acoma Pueblo. There are stories about him: I know that his saddle sores from riding were so bad that he walked most of the way from Albuquerque because it hurt so much to be on the horse. I know he married my great-grandmother's sister first. They had two children, and she died; then my great-grandfather married my great-grandmother, and they had six more kids—something like that.

During Geronimo's last tear around the Southwest, he [her great-grandfather] was part of the territorial volunteer militia with the Laguna scouts, who were supposed to track Geronimo. Of course, they were careful not to find him. That wasn't something you wanted to do. Both he and his brother must have been eccentric for white men of their time and backgrounds. What possessed them to leave? They never went back, even to visit. They were called squaw men by other white men.

Q: Do you know anything about what he was like?

A: He was the kind of man who could just blend in. He was very generous, very quiet. His behavior was sort of in line with a lot of the most important Pueblo values. He also spoke the Laguna Pueblo language well enough that when [ethnologist and linguist] Franz Boas and [his protégée] Elsie Clews Parsons came through, he contributed a couple of little children's stories for texts in Keresan [the family of languages spoken by Pueblo tribes] that they were collecting. There's a picture of him in the back of *Storyteller* with his sons. He must have been really sweet and special, this white man.

My great-grandmother's family was very strong politically [because they raised cattle and sheep when most other Lagunas were still farmers]. I knew her quite well, but, by then, she was in her eighties. She took care of me a lot when I was growing up; she didn't die until I was fourteen. It wasn't typical in the pueblos at that time for families to allow their daughters to marry white men. And so, the being different started a long, long time ago. My life has not ever been typical.

Q: I know that for a time you went to Indian school. What was that like?

A: It was a completely hideous, traumatic experience. The Laguna Day School was a stone's throw from my house. The irony was that my great-grandfather had helped facilitate the federal government building it there. It was when I started there, at five years old, that I first learned about these invisible borderlines that authoritarian figures use. When you crossed the line and stepped onto the school grounds, you weren't to use the Laguna language anymore. If you were caught using it, you got in a whole bunch of trouble.

Q: So your experience was pretty bad?

A: It was just full of anxiety. And I could sense the horror of what was being done to the other kids, especially the kids who didn't speak English. At the same time, I had had all of this reinforcement about education from my great-grandmother and from old Aunt Susie, who were Carlisle Indian School graduates. Of course, the reason the Pueblo people have survived as long as they have and as intact is because they were real thoughtful about how to outlast people who come along and hassle you and push you around. There was the sense that if you learned enough about the whole wide world, especially the western European way, you might be able to survive. They've outlasted a lot of people—the Spaniards, the Mexicans.

Q: So the extended family expected you to succeed?

A: They were book people. We had books because the old folks had this strategy for survival. Also, the Pueblo people always wanted to include knowledge from other people. It's an all-inclusive culture, unlike western Europeans who wanted to exclude anything that wasn't western European. So I excelled in school. But I never got over the horror of it or feeling how badly the other children felt. They used to run us through in September like cattle and dip us all. Put lice medicine on us all. They'd give us every kind of shot in the world. Ooh! I remember typhoid shots!

Q: It sounds as if the whole purpose of the schools run by the federal Bureau of Indian Affairs [BIA] was to cut you loose from your own community and to turn you into "Americans," as opposed to what you were.

A: Oh, absolutely. That's really what they tried to do to my great-grandmother and that generation. Actually, what you see by the time I was going to school was a softening, because it was a day school where we could go home. The worst were the times when my dad was growing up and earlier, where they took you away from the reservation. But no, that was still absolutely what it was all about.

Q: Were the teachers white?

A: No, the Bureau of Indian Affairs is a wonderful racist reflection of America: The teachers were African American and they were Native American because these were the positions in the boonies. No one wanted to be there. The school principal was a full-blooded Laguna Pueblo man who had gone through the BIA system. You learned pretty quickly that sometimes white people will be nicer to you than your own. Of course, that's also good to learn, too—to see how the fact that people get twisted cuts across lines of skin color and culture. It has to do with who buys that authoritarianism.

Q: Did you learn much there?

A: The teachers just took attendance so they'd get paid, and then they let school out . . . tell us we could play baseball or softball. I was acutely aware of how the teachers made fun of Pueblo beliefs about animals and plants. It was really shoved in the faces of Native American people how backward they were and how white man's science was just so great and so wonderful.

Q: When did you leave Indian school?

A: My father hated Indian boarding school and he said we would never have to do that. So, after fourth grade, if you weren't going to board, you had to either ride sixty miles a day round-trip to Grants, New Mexico, that scum-hole, or you could go twenty miles more [each way] and go to Albuquerque every day. So we carpooled with a couple of other kids' families who could just barely afford it, and we made the one-hundred-mile round-trip [to Albuquerque] every day from the time I was in the fifth grade.

Q: What kind of school was that?

A: It was Manzano Day School, a real liberal little school. They had little scholarships, and they wanted to get some diversity. Needless to say, we were the diversity. It was good because it was real liberal arts, and I had come out of the Indian school totally deficient in mathematics and science. They hadn't taught us the times tables, and here I was in the fifth grade. But I could read because that goes back to being around people who loved language and would tell stories all the time.

Q: Were the teachers better at Manzano?

A: The teachers were good. Their curriculum was really, really heavy in the humanities and I could handle that. I didn't get the feeling that the teachers cared that much about science and math—it was the same way at my Catholic girls' school [to which she transferred in the eighth grade]; the nuns were that way. So I'm really an illiterate in math and science. I was. I've been reading on my own.

In that fifth grade year I had this big awakening about writing. I was in this classroom with Mrs. Cooper. She was a war bride from England. One day she gave us our spelling words and she told us to write a story and use each word at least once. It was such a silly, little, easy assignment, but that was the first time a teacher ever did that. And something incredible happened. I can almost remember the piece of paper. In making that story out of those words, it just clicked. It's the high that you get from writing when it just all comes together. Then I turned it in, and I got lots of praise because I just had a knack for it. And that was it, that was the turning point for me.

From then on I was always writing something in the back of the classroom. When I was a kid my dad took us hunting, and I have really good eyesight. I can look off and it's almost like my eyes can make things look bigger. So I'd sit in the back of the classroom and hurry up and do the assignments and then I would trip off. Bye, I'm gone! You can be other people in other places in time.

The other thing I learned real quick was whether there was any way that what I was good at could possibly be twisted into what was needed academically. I actually did get through the University of New Mexico [she laughs].

Q: How did you manage that?

A: I outsmarted the system. In the general honors program in the College of Arts and Sciences, a science seminar would serve the same as a mathematics or a real hard-science class. I never would have graduated Phi Beta Kappa or anything if I had to take hard science.

But in those science seminars I got to read Freud and Jung. In the history of science class I fought with the professor all semester saying, "Western European science is just one way to order experience." And I read Michael Polanyi and all these Frenchmen with these wild notions about anthropology, because my first husband was in graduate school then. So I was always eavesdropping on their seminars and looking at his books.

Q: What about the fact that your background is filled with strong women?

A: I was really fortunate because I was surrounded by generations of women. I never thought that women weren't as strong as men, as able as men or as valid as men. I was pretty old before I really started running into mainstream culture's attitudes about women. And because I never internalized the oppressor's attitude, I never behaved in a passive, helpless way. Instead of being crushed by sexism, I was sort of amused or enraged, but never cowed.

Q: As a child you weren't treated differently because you were a girl?

A: I can remember men in Albuquerque saying to my dad, who had three daughters, "Gee, you must have wished you had a son," or, "Too bad you have daughters." No one in Laguna would say that because it would be completely stupid. But my dad would always say, "Well, my girls can do anything your boys can do and my girls can do it better."

Of course we could. We could shoot. My dad would come along when they were target practicing and he'd talk about how I could shoot. And then these grown men would go ahead and want to shoot against me. But a child has a pure heart, hasn't been doing lots of caffeine and alcohol and cigarettes. And I had good eyes. I had a .22 rifle when I was seven years old. So at fourteen I could almost always outshoot grown men. My dad was a rebel in his own way and he must have understood that it was flying in the face of something. He enjoyed it when I won, you could tell.

The other thing he taught me was, "You don't ever have to let a man hit you. This gun will make you equal to any man no matter how strong he is." He was real strong about that. So it wasn't just as a little girl seeing the women plaster the walls and own the house and all of that. It was this being treated as someone who could do anything.

Q: How does this show up in your writing?

A: I choose different themes. I didn't even think twice about having a male protagonist in *Ceremony* until I finished the whole book and then went, "Oh, God, the feminists! Women are supposed to write about women!" And they ignored it; they didn't like it. And then this other voice said, "Oh Leslie, you don't ever do anything like anybody else anyway." Now, of course, the feminists are very supportive of me and my work.

Q: How are Laguna attitudes toward gender and sexuality different from white, mainstream ideas?

A: Laguna people just didn't go around thinking, You're a man, you're a woman. When I was growing up there was a transvestite, a man who dressed like a woman, and nobody—nobody—jeered him, nobody beat him up. To this moment he's the coordinator for the community health outreach. He's a nurse, and he works with women mostly. Nobody doesn't want to have him because culturally that was always accepted. I say I am a feminist, but I'm a feminist like you join a party because it reflects your beliefs. Where I came from you don't need to have that concept because women own all the property and everything.

Q: Because it's a matriarchy?

A: Yeah. Before Christianity had a lot of impact, the creator is female and all things are created with the female. Thought Woman and her sisters create everything that is. Women own the land, the house. Who's the father of the child is not very important, since the children belong to the mother and the mother's family. So the attitude toward sex and premarital pregnancy is completely different.

Q: Is the figure you most identify with Kochininako, Yellow Woman, who appears in so many of your stories?

A: Probably. When you're in the kiva [underground chamber used for ceremonies], that's the ritual name that every young Pueblo woman is called. So I think I somehow internalized that.

Q: So when did you first run into sexism?

A: When I started college, when I was seventeen, they could try all of these things. But the bottom line was that even with dating and men on the outside, I always had my trusty deer rifle and a pistol. I still have the rifle. My grandmother and all the family people had little purse guns. I sit up here [in the desert] and think about women and being scared at night. I think now of the terror that women who can't protect themselves must feel and the toll that must take on their bodies.

Q: In 1969 your story "The Man to Send Rainclouds" gets published. How did that happen?

A: I had always kept writing on my own. I wrote poetry. My eighth grade teacher, an old nun, has written to me since I got the MacArthur award, and she said she remembers that I was always writing. She said I did it for extra credit, but I thought they were assigned. My freshman year at the university, I found out that I could write those English 102 papers like that [she snaps her fingers]. So that's cool. I thought, I think I'll stick with what I can do. I didn't want to teach. I had always wanted to go to law school.

Q: Why?

A: Back in 1955 or '56, when my father was a tribal officer, the tribe sued the state of New Mexico for six million acres that they stole from us . . . [based on] a land grant from the king of Spain. So, it took twenty years, but the people got the land back. When you grow up and look around you every day and say, "Oh, there is stolen property. It was ours and it was stolen," you're not nearly as quick to swallow the kinds of rationales that everybody else accepts. That's one of the tragedies of the United States—a sort of collective amnesia about the past, sort of like the Germans during the Jewish Holocaust.

Q: So how did you end up becoming a writer instead of a lawyer?

A: In the first semester of my sophomore year I got pregnant. My folks found out that Dick wanted to marry me, so we got married. It was the best possible thing for me because his family was real supportive. And so I just kept going to school. In my senior year of high school my parents had split up, and so many things just came undone. And so I had not been writing for my own pleasure like I had ever since I was in fifth grade.

That semester that I was pregnant with Robert, Dick said, "You ought to take a creative writing class this semester. It would be an easy A." I wasn't even thinking about writing; I was thinking about how to get into law school. So my conscious self was saying, "Nah," but my unconscious said, "Yeah, okay, I'll do it."

So I took that class and . . . I could just do it. I could write short stories. Something just happened. It's not something you can consciously control.

In the very first fiction class I wrote "Bravura." And I wrote "Tony's Story"—that was in *Redbook,* but it also was the first thing published—and then "The Man to Send Rainclouds." And then Professor George Arms, who's just a totally wonderful professor who made you love Henry James, asked to use that short story, which had been published in the campus publication, in a college textbook. That was in 1969. And then in '71 I was in law school but I got an NEA [National Endowment for the Arts] Discovery Grant for writers.

Q: Did you apply for that?

A: No. I've gotten more things where you can't apply. Gus Blaisdell, a writer who has the Living Batch Bookstore in Albuquerque, was asked by somebody who was on the NEA screening panel to kind of scout for things, and Gus asked me to give him some short stories. So I gave him everything I had written in beginning fiction and intermediate fiction. I just had the stuff I did in class. And those were the stories that were published.

Q: So what happened to law school?

A: I went halfway through and was actually in danger of becoming an attorney. I thought they would weed me out, but that whole system is so lame that a total anti-Christ could get through. But I, early on, decided that I would tell my clients to use self-help. I would say, "The law here is fucked, go throw a rock through his window." And I thought, "No, I better quit." So I got out of there because really I felt sorry for the people who would have me as their attorney. It crushed everybody at home. But I had already figured out that we weren't going to get our land back with a lawsuit.

There were five women and ninety-five men in my class, and they [the men] harassed us continuously. The men were so threatened because the women were so much better students than they were because you had to be. The other thing was that a little voice said, "Leslie, do you want to have to work with these assholes the rest of your life?" So I got out of there.

Q: Do you think that ease which you had in telling stories came from the storytelling of your Aunt Susie and others?

A: I don't have an ease in telling. You mean the ease I have in writing? Absolutely. It must come from being immersed in a community where every interaction reinforces a narrative vision of oneself and one's belonging. Narrative is the only way they keep track of all the rituals, all the hunting places, all the history, all of the chemistry. How you do this, how you make that, how you bend this. Nothing written down. All in the human memory and kept collectively. So that you'll go clear to the next village to ask some old woman how was it exactly that they used to do this. They used human brains for books.

Because the information is stored in narrative, it's ordered completely differently than western European ordering of, like, technical botany or biology, by taking things apart. It puts things together and reinforces stories. So that one deer hunting story can contain valuable information in a number of different areas that you'd have to cross-catalogue.

Q: How is writing different from telling the story?

A: I've been trying to figure that out all along. The book *Storyteller,* in a sense, is one time that I've considered it, and I still don't have any answer. The answer would have to be, in part, that you read through the material. The anecdotal pieces about the family are stories you listen to. And, of course, the Aunt Susie stories really are remembered from how I heard her tell them. There are those repetitions, which, in literary terms, are not good and are not done. You don't need that because the reader can scan the page. But the storyteller repeats; there's repetition in the book. And it's a little bit different.

I used to tell students, "Oh, it's so easy. If you can stand here and tell me or talk to me you can write." But then I realized that it isn't necessarily so, any more than an Olympic swimmer saying to me, "Just get into the water and you can swim."

Q: I guess one difference is that when you're writing you can rewrite. You don't have to perform on the spot, on the moment. It's much more a considered way of expression.

A: That's it. And because it's more considered it does take on different structures. At the same time, there's something pretty wonderful about oral narrative and the way it was practiced at Laguna Pueblo because it's always contemporaneous—past, present, and future always in one moment. Because the storyteller footnotes herself and makes fun of herself and recollects. But when you go into the room alone to write, you're swimming in the sea of all that language and a huge and collective sense of the past. It's real spooky. Well, I guess it isn't any more spooky than evoking the ancestors. You're alone in a room with the language and the spirits of the ancestors. That language has been used and given and used by the people—Freud was just beginning to try to explore that. But you're working with a whole other territory and it's pretty dangerous to work alone. Storytelling in the group is safer. The writer alone is in a really dangerous position.

Q: What's the danger?

A: Somewhere along the line you realize that all of everyday life is made of narrative. That you need narrative to live your life. That you can't get up out of the chair and walk back to the front of the house without narrative, really. And, finally, when you once understand something about narrative, and you work and you live in narrative that isn't in the community, you won't need people anymore. And you won't be social. Hawthorne dealt with this in "The Minister's Black Veil." I think that's what that short story is trying to talk about—this idea that you could just live there or stay there in that world of narrative or imagination.

Q: So is it that when you start being the generator of the narrative you become godlike? You create your own community?

A: It's more like Zora Neale Hurston's "Tell My Horse that You're Ridden"—that I'm ridden by the narrative. I believe that stories are alive. They're not just archetypes in a way those dudes went around the world and said there's all these archetypes—but they were on that track.

I believe that there's a kind of living spirit in stories that can't be seen—it's there when the story is all together, but if you break the words apart and say, "Where is the spirit? Is it in this word or this word or this word?" it's like pulling a human apart and saying, "Does this make you alive, does this make you alive?"

And the danger for a writer is that you can get saddled up and ridden. You can just end up not having a life as a human being that eats. When I was writing *Almanac* it was like I was totally serving the novel and the stories, without time to eat and rest. And you need to stop, because after four or five hours, usually the writing just isn't good quality. And you can keep writing if you want to, but it's a waste of time. Also, it isn't good for you. It makes you feel bad. So I felt less like a god and more like a tool of the spirits.

Q: So you felt out of control, in a way?

A: At some point when you're writing a novel, the characters really are more interesting and exciting than living people. That's one of the reasons people read novels. It's almost like you become seduced by your own making, except that I know damn well that even though I imagine so much, especially in *Almanac*, that it's not something completely separate from all of the past and all past stories and things I've heard. With

Almanac I felt like once the stories got started I didn't really control them very much anymore. I had to do what the writing wanted it to do. So when *Almanac* got bigger and when it took longer, there truly was nothing I could do about it.

Q: You didn't envision having a book that big?

A: Absolutely not. A poet friend of mine said, "For your second novel you should do something short and simple." So I thought, right. You don't want to live in the shadow of your first novel. Two or three years, and so I thought cops and robbers, cocaine smuggling novel set in Tucson. Simple. And that's what it started out as. I even experimented with a shorter sentence because, as I said to my friend, the poet Mei-Mei Berssenbrugge, "I'm going to get it on the wire racks at the checkout counter in Safeway."

Q: It is a new voice. You've left the reservation in this book.

A: Absolutely. And all my characters are cut loose too. I've always been real aware of language. I hate repeating myself; I don't want to just stick with the same anything. My Italian translator said the sentences are shorter in *Almanac*. She liked the longer ones.

Q: So what happened?

A: I started talking to this guy downtown and heard about the Salvadorans with suitcases full of cash. I heard about the CIA and the landings and started saving clippings. I still have the clipping describing what happened: They spotted on radar a plane crossing the border. They chased it to south of Casa Grande [Arizona] in the air, radioing in people. When it landed in the field at Casa Grande, when the authorities got there, there were like fourteen suitcases full of cocaine and twelve men. They wrote down the names of the men and let them go. While they were standing there, the pilot took off and landed right over here at Marana Air Park [she points over the mountain to the east]. In the [official] report it said, "The pilot eluded authorities and disappeared into the night, as it were." As it were!

Q: So the authorities were in on cocaine smuggling?

A: Senator John Kerry of Massachusetts has been trying to prove that Oliver North and his people were resupplying the [Nicaraguan] contras with cocaine that came into Miami and Tucson. A lot of the contra airplanes would fly out of here over my house—these unmarked transport planes. My neighbor did welding on some doors out there in Marana right before the Oliver North thing broke. He said they had all kinds of security. Go over there today and try to get around.

Q: So this was the inspiration for the drug smuggling plot in *Almanac*?

A: When I started I ran into the story about the connection between the CIA and the dope right away. At the same time I was already playing with Dillinger and Geronimo, and it just hit me. Boom! Look at this. This is the Indian Wars, the Vietnam War, the whole history of the country. This corruption.

Do you know what happened? The CIA and Oliver North brought in so much dope that they drove the price down. It was really funny. Allen Ginsberg was chanting, "Don't smoke government dope" in August when he was in Seattle. We found out over here that they brought eighty thousand pounds across the border, that the police brought it in, sold it, and kept the money. *Almanac* really goes easy on how corrupt the police in the state of Arizona are.

There's something about Tucson, about Arizona, that's so corrupt. The land is very beautiful. There's nothing wrong with the earth. New Mexico is crooked, but Arizona is totally corrupt.

Q: You have your drugs, you have your cops and robbers and your smugglers. Then the book makes this enormous political jump into the native peoples and their desire for the land. Where did that jump come from?

A: From the fact that the CIA runs drugs to finance weapons to keep the native people from taking back the land down there. You begin to see the incredible anxiety in this town and all of the things that are done with the border patrol—the regulations, the rules, the laws, the concerns in Tucson. The underlying fear is that the native people are going to take it back. They want it back. They're already coming. And in the border cities, like Los Angeles, it's in the air.

So there's incredible repression right now. A lot of police crime. It's not just that they're after money, but the police are completely out of control—in Los Angeles, Tucson, Phoenix, San Antonio.

Q: So why did you put all of this in an almanac?

A: I was thinking about trying to do something completely different with the novel as a genre. The Mayan almanacs had really strong images that are often repeated. And since a lot of the remnants covered war, destruction, politics, war, destruction, politics, I thought that my almanac is going to be crammed full of narratives. That's what you can do with any kind of almanac, whether it's a Mayan almanac or a farmer's almanac. Old almanacs had all kinds of information and details and stories, stuff you just wonder, Why would this be here—except that it's a part of the time. But I didn't write the novel the way it's put together.

Q: How was it written?

A: It was written the way you would make a film. A lot of it was written as narratives. I didn't expect them all to so interconnect. I suppose I expected it to be more mysterious and fragmented. More destroyed. Maybe more like the old Mayan almanacs were. But it did something that I didn't plan and I would have been afraid to hope for: It did all finally fit together. That's all *Ceremony* is: You just build, and your pieces are narratives.

There are four or five different books in there. Someone said I could have split them out, but I said, "No, we're not making tidy little books." But also I was resisting writing a book that's so radical. At some point I had to say, "Oh my God, here go all of the aesthetics of the novel, all the rules." Luckily the genre has very few rules, comparatively. But I was horrified.

Q: Besides form, the content is so radical.

A: Yeah, I asked myself, "Do I really have to write about all this incredible twisted sexual torture? Do I have to write about America's fascination with blood and violent death?" But I knew I had to because nobody really wants to talk about it. I had to connect that with Christianity and the Holy Eucharist and the Church and the Inquisition. And I knew people weren't going to like it, but I had to do it.

Q: You say you had to tell this story. Why? To lay out what happened to the native peoples? Or to grab ahold of the white middle-class readers who were going to buy the book and shake them by the shoulders and say, "Hey idiots, wake up"?

A: This is my 763-page indictment for five hundred years of theft, murder, pillage, and rape. So is *Almanac* long? Sure, but federal indictments are long. The one returned against Charles Keating, who took one billion dollars just in one savings and loan in Arizona, is long. And mine is a little more interesting reading than a straight-on legal indictment.

Q: You have a chronicle in the middle of *Almanac* where you talk about that legal history.

A: I've never lost track of Indian law decisions. Also, in the back of my mind, I was thinking that Native Americans will think it's funny that this appears in 1992 as . . . [Anglo-Americans are] making all their Columbus bullshit. Since I started this ten years ago, obviously it wasn't conscious that I will write this to tell the truth five hundred years later. Also, do you realize that both *Ceremony* and *Almanac* were written in offices sublet from lawyers? That is weird.

Q: So you finish this book. You bring it to Simon and Schuster and what do they say?

A: I need to finish the book. I'm running out of money. The MacArthur is long over. And I tell my agent [to] sell it and that will force me to finish. See, I was still resisting what this book wanted to be. It was just totally like Freud said. Then I read Freud, volume one through eighteen. When I got through volume eighteen it was like some magical thing had happened and I finished the book.

Simon and Schuster, though, bought only the first 660 pages of manuscript. They had no idea. They thought they were buying a cops-and-robbers, doper story set in Tucson. In 1987 I had about 1,100 pages in manuscript. It later came out to 1,793 pages. So from '87 to '89, I wrote the last part, where it all started to come together. I always knew that when I finally accepted that somehow it has fallen to me to do this kind of book, I would be okay.

Q: So how did the book assume the shape it has now?

A: When I handed in the manuscript to Michael Korda at Simon and Schuster, he understood the spirit of what I was trying to do. He did work with the Hungarian freedom fighters in the fifties. But it didn't have the chapter names, and it wasn't broken into the geographical sections. So it was still happening when I handed it to him.

And he said it was this daunting monolith of prose. "We've got to do something to help the reader," he said. And I said, "I'll help the reader all I can." And he said, "Well, could we break it into chapters?" And then I got really excited because it reminded me again about how almanacs have all these little short sections. I've collected all kinds of almanacs over time.

When we started editing there was an instant where we could have edited it to be more of a best-seller and actually pulled whole books out of it. But I knew that the damn thing was an almanac. We did cut about 350 pages. I did most of the cuts, although Michael did make suggestions. It took us both a while to figure out what the book wanted to be.

Q: When you saw that it was going to be an almanac, what difference did that make?

A: Then I started to think about the notion of time reckoned not with numerals and numbers, but what if you just talk about time as narratives, day by day. What happened that day is the identity of the day. More in the direction of what the Mayans thought. Once we did that, the editing went differently, and it became a whole different book.

Q: Your sense of time in the book is very non-Western.

A: The way time is computed in western European cultures is completely political. Colonialists always want time and history not to go back very far [she laughs]. My great-grandmother lived to be 99. My Aunt Susie just died at 113, and I grew up listening to her tell me about times long ago. There's an immediacy there when you have living voices. It's not just something that's in your ancient history books. Here [among Native American people], five hundred years is nothing.

This is something that the Anglo-Americans, the invaders, the colonials, never want to face—in China or India or Africa—especially when there are native people who have an incredible spiritual connection to the very earth. Time is totally political—especially when they are on that mother ground and especially when it's such a short period of time, where somebody living today could have talked to somebody who had talked to somebody who actually was at the scene of some of these events. Then you completely miscalculate how well things are going.

[An airplane flies over the desert.] See that plane that just took off? That's one of their planes. Before they caught Ollie [North] they were just going down eight and nine at a time.

Q: Let's talk about the book's structure. What was your thought in having opposing pairs of twins, triplet relations, triangle relationships?

A: That just happened. That wasn't conscious. See, I wasn't aware of that triplet idea. No one's mentioned that. I was sort of amazed when I saw the twins. I started out with the twins when it was just the two old women. And then I realized in the end that it goes back to the Mayan twins and the Pueblo twins, and then I found out that "West Africa" [a section in the novel] has the twins.

Q: You have two homosexual triangles, Calabazas and the two sisters, Menardo and the two women.

A: Yes, there was this triangle thing, too. And then Alegría was still seeing Bartolomeo while she was with Menardo. You couldn't even say that Alegría does triangles because, remember, she'd [also] been sleeping with Sonny Blue.

Q: You create some pretty awful characters.

A: Even though there are parts of them I didn't like, I have to say I liked all my characters quite a bit. I had planned on killing a bunch more than I did, but the characters knew in a way that I didn't know. It was almost as if some other part of me was trying to save them. A lot of the characters developed—they became more than what I thought they were or could be—and they saved their own lives.

Q: Alegría's one of the strongest characters in the novel.

A: I originally planned to have her dead. I just thought I'd probably get rid of her on that long desert crossing [coming illegally to the United States from Mexico]. But by the time she got there I really kind of liked something about her. She's so ruthless. But I guess what I loved about her was that, by God, she was determined to survive.

Q: I don't know how you liked that sadist Beaufry though. He's pretty vile.

A: He is—he's just the worst. What do I like about him? The darkness I guess. You get fascinated with him. What can you do when you're writing about five hundred years and it just happens to be five hundred years of slaughter, slaughter, slaughter? What do you do when that's your task, and all these other people before you have cleaned it up, and you're the one that has to come and say, "No, the priests didn't come for God, glory, and then gold. The Church came here for money"? But with Beaufry, I just get fascinated with the language and the description. He's really awful, and he does all these awful things. He's a repository for just a lot of Arizona karma [she laughs].

Q: He's an embodiment of evil.

A: He kind of is. And the only hope for the reader is to get something going either with his relationship with some of the others or maybe just with the language or where he can take you. He's like a guide. This guy's set up to take you to all these places that you just never imagined. So, working with that kind of character, you're less sympathetic with him as a possible living thing and more sympathetic with what he can let you see or do. As a novelist, I'm always saying, "I want to do this. What can let me do this?"

Q: Is Sterling what in the old days we used to call a moral center or a connection for the reader?

A: Yeah. I did that because I felt sorry for the reader. But then I felt sorry for myself, too, and I was thinking the reader can't cry or whine because I suffer as much or more. The reader can at least throw the book down and run away and never have to think about it again. But I have undertaken to do this and I have to go over these five hundred years. I did like Sterling. He's kind of all of us. Sterling was always trying to fix things up for people. He knew that it was a dangerous and bad world. My friend [novelist] Larry McMurtry said that Sterling was his favorite character, and couldn't there be more of Sterling? And probably there could have been. But maybe there will be more Sterling in some other place, I don't know. He is a messenger, finally, too.

Q: At a recent session on American literature at the 92nd Street Y in New York City, Toni Cade Bambara held up *Almanac* and said it was an important book and that Simon and Schuster wasn't pushing it. And that is what's wrong with American publishing.

A: Wow. That's really nice. I'm really glad to hear that, and I'm so gratified that Toni said that. Some part of me always feels like, "Oh gosh, I don't really deserve it." And I *don't* deserve it, but I have to say that those stories have a separate life of their own, and so I can say, "Well, the book deserves it, but certainly not me."

In the beginning the bookstores were full. I guess if something doesn't sell like Kitty Kelley's biography of Nancy Reagan or something, they start pulling them back out. But they got twenty-six thousand copies out, which, for a book that's as long and as mean as mine, I think is pretty good. It took *Ceremony* fifteen years to get to where it is now, but when people came to the book signings for *Almanac* they came because of *Ceremony.*

Simon and Schuster didn't spend as much money on me as Norman Mailer's publishers spent on him or anything like that, but I think there hasn't been too much of a plot against it. Except I know that the *New York Times* was really horrified about it. They would probably just as soon not [have] had to deal with it. Of course, the review that the reviewer did was great [Elizabeth Tallent, "Storytelling with a Vengeance," 22 December 1991].

For the kind of book it is, I'm real pleased with the reaction. It's also because of academia. Now there's just this huge cadre of people waiting [she laughs]. They waited a long time, so I gave them a big book.

Q: What do you think about these academics?

A: People write to me all the time. I think it's just fine. I know that people have to write dissertations on something. And that's sort of the way I look at it, and I don't pay too much attention.

Q: You mention putting Sterling in for the reader and being concerned about the reader. Are you worried that some people might be badly bothered by *Almanac?*

A: At signings, people would come and buy three or four copies of *Ceremony* when they bought *Almanac.* And they said things like, "I give these out to my friends." I was so embarrassed [she laughs]. Then I've also felt real protective of people, thinking, Oh no, these dear little people that love *Ceremony,* what's going to happen to them when they get sucked into the maelstrom of *Almanac?* In Seattle a man told me he thought *Almanac* was affecting his sanity, and finally I just said, "I hope it won't harm you, or if you think it is, then stop."

Q: The reviews seemed all over the lot. It was like some people got it and some people didn't get it. And some people loved it and some people hated it.

A: Oh absolutely, it's extremes.

Q: It's not unlike Kingston's *Tripmaster Monkey* in terms of the responses.

A: Right. I was just rereading *Tripmaster Monkey* and thinking that in an odd sort of way Maxine is doing the same sort of thing, except in a different area and a different way. Which is great. Same instincts, same direction. And it made me feel good about what I was doing. Another book that made me feel good was John Edgar Wideman's *Philadelphia Fire* [Holt, 1990], because it's a very political book and it's also working with recent history. You feel like you're on the right track.

Q: I enjoyed the letters between you and the poet James Wright, collected in *Delicacy and Strength of Lace*. How did that get published?

A: Sometime after Jim died, I got a letter from [his widow] Annie Wright saying that she thought the correspondence was beautiful. Jim had kept copies of his letters, but I don't keep copies of my letters. Anyway, she said that she wanted to publish it. And I wrote back and said, "Great, go ahead." And when she sent the manuscript out, I couldn't read it. I just started to cry.

Larry McMurtry was here, and I asked him to please just look through the letters to make sure that there isn't something that my [second] ex-husband John Silko, who is a lawyer, will take exception to and sue me. So Larry read it through and said it was very beautiful. I sent the manuscript back and said to Annie, "Go ahead. I'm told it's very beautiful." I couldn't read it. And to this day I have not read that book. How could she put those letters together? But Annie is strong. And readers who didn't know me from a pile of sand that loved the work of James Wright read that and—boom!—I get all these people who are appreciative of my work. So it's been a wonderful thing.

Q: What was the connection you two had?

A: Language. It happens in narrative. It's this place. I could feel it when I was writing back to Jim. I just knew. And he read it, and he knew. There was the opening, the first letter, there was that simpatico. And even that he chose to write when he did was uncanny. We knew that we could know one another, not consciously, but through the work. He had read *Ceremony,* and I was familiar with his work. Believe it or not, the connection was made through the writing and then the letter writing was just a conscious crystallization.

Q: Both of you used stories in those letters. When you got word of his illness, you wrote the story about the person who refused to die.

A: The man who wouldn't die [she laughs]. And then his whole life was that. That's all I could think of that he ever accomplished. Of course that's good. It goes to show you that that can be valuable, too.

Q: And he used the story of his own situation with his son when you were having your own custody fight. You both recognized this value of stories. And this made me want to read Wright's poetry.

A: Oh good, that makes me feel better. I was thinking that all of these Wright fans were coming this way, so Silko fans can go the other way.

Q: What did you respond to in Wright's poetry?

A: Wright is 100 percent of this continent: his language, what he does. Just like Larry McMurtry's narrative and the way his characters are related to time and the land and the West. And it comes out in the language, and in *Lonesome Dove* [Simon and Schuster, 1985], the way the cowboys talked to one another. That's not English, that's American. My favorite kind of writers are the ones that recognize where they are and where the English language has come.

Q: Were you surprised at the success of *Ceremony* and the way it took off?

A: Yeah, really. I had the book contract on the basis of short stories. Went to Alaska, wrote the book, meant to write a collection of short stories. But my editor, Richard Seaver, wanted me to try a novel, and I was really naive not realizing that they want novels because books of short stories don't sell very well. Maybe Seaver thought that expanding the form would be good for me. I'm sort of a structure nut, and sometimes I think the failings of my short stories are that they are too tightly structured—even though I don't do it consciously. They end up clicking too much together like poems or something. Or maybe he didn't see any of that, and he just wanted a novel to sell.

Anyway, I said, "Oh no, I couldn't possibly write a novel. I didn't take that class at the University of New Mexico." And then this other voice said, "Yeah, stupid, but you have read a bunch of them." So I went to Alaska and I had a couple of stillborn novels, about page 60. And then I decided I'd write a funny short story, which turned into *Ceremony.*

Q: So then you sent it to Seaver?

A: I had written it to please myself because I didn't think anything would come of it. So, when I finished it, I sent it to Seaver, who had moved from Grove to Viking by then, and a copy to my friend Mei-Mei [Berssenbrugge]. And Mei-Mei called and said, "I read it. It's just great; it's wonderful. And what I really like is the way you didn't break it into chapters."

And I went, "Oh God, I knew there was something I forgot." So I didn't say anything. This other voice said, "When you hang up the phone all you have to do is sit down and break the manuscript up into chapters. It's not a big deal, don't freak out." So I hung up and I rushed back to the manuscript and I tried to break it into chapters to send off to the publisher because I still hadn't heard from them and I thought that was really bad.

And as soon as I sat down and tried to break it into chapters I thought, This book does not want to be in chapters; therefore, this book isn't meant to be, it's not supposed to be. Of course, it's very important that it be the way that it is.

Q: So the positive reaction must have been surprising.

A: I was surprised, yes. I got a bigger review of *Ceremony* than I did for *Almanac:* the whole page in the Sunday *New York Times.* Of course they have cut down on how long their reviews are, too. But I didn't expect that reaction, because I meant to be a lawyer. I hadn't gone to graduate school at Iowa or Columbia. I hadn't thought about being a writer.

Q: You were also raising two small children then.

A: Yeah, but I never fooled myself that I would be remembered for how good a mother I was. I knew they'd turn out and be whatever they're going to be.

Q: I asked Paula Gunn Allen if she thought there were any differences between the writing of Native American women and African American women. Do you have any sense of that?

A: No, I really don't think so. You can go and impose differences, but I think that really strong writing springs from such depth of the psyche that there aren't such differences. You might be able to say that all writing from those considered Other by the powers of life and death has some similarities. But that includes gay people, immigrants, people who have maybe been insane. Maybe when you come back from having been insane, you're Other.

But to say, "This is how Native American writing is different from African American," I don't think so. Maybe you can only say that this person always felt he or she was part of a group—women or Jews or blacks—that was about to be exterminated, that there are threads of what it's like to be called Other. I really think that's the main difference, whether you're an insider or an outsider. And there I think you can definitely see similarities. Because with what I was working with and I think what Maxine [Hong Kingston] was working with, there really are way more similarities and wonderful synchronicities and meanings. And they're not just superficial; they're real deep.

I think this is this sort of outside mentality of wanting to pick things apart. It's very political, too.

Q: Are there certain writers who have influenced you?

A: Not particularly. I told you about lights going on in the fifth grade. That was the most important thing that ever happened to me. I think I felt the influence not so much as a writer but as a reader and an appreciator of literature. Shakespeare. There was a moment reading *Macbeth* that something happened with my sense of, oh, this is what it means. Talk about his language. I love *Paradise Lost.* It's so cataclysmic. When I was in junior high I read Steinbeck and Faulkner, and I liked them because they seemed to be closer to a kind of a more rural world. And of course Flannery O'Connor. I just like all different kinds of writing. I probably get the least out of contemporary writing and writers, but I still check out what they're doing.

Q: What's missing in contemporary writers?

A: They're disconnected. The sense of not being a part of anything. The anomie. It's the great malaise of the twentieth century. The autonomous, lonely little character—what Harold Brodkey wrote about. But language is so connected to other times and people. Words are so alive with other connections. It's almost as if some of the postmodern fiction, some of the experimental fiction, is trying to start a fire by dumping ice water on the wood. Something's a bit off because the medium, language, is connected historically. And yet the feeling of that poor individual, that disconnection. The only time you *are* connected is when you're writing and using language.

Q: So for you that connection is crucial—the connection with the external world and the connection with the whole history.

A: Absolutely. Otherwise you fall into this abyss where everything that's Other is completely irrelevant. It's almost a kind of death.

Q: A moment ago you said you wanted to write a funny book when you started *Ceremony.* I picked up a lot of humor there and a darker kind of humor in *Almanac.* Can you talk a little bit about the role of humor?

A: One of the dumbest stereotypes about Native American people is this stern, straight-faced Indian. Actually, Native American people are laughing and joking all the time. Maybe they should be more stern, if you could reflect upon the future. But humor always has had this really special place. And I sensed that it was a bigger role at Laguna.

When I got in the outside world and the university and started studying what the critics and scholars said about Shakespeare and humor and comedy and started reading philosophy and theory, I started to think about the role of the clowns in Pueblo ceremonies and how humor is sacred. Laughing is sacred. The world would become sterile and cold and die if there wasn't the clowning and the joking and the laughter. And that in order to have a perfect balance or harmony you have to have humor. *Almanac* is supposed to be really a big joke as an indictment, but if there's not enough humor, if I didn't manage to get enough humor in *Almanac,* Native American people would still think its appearance at this time [the year of the Columbus quincentennial] is funny.

As I wrote *Almanac,* all I could think of was Hamlin Hale, this professor [at the University of New Mexico] who offered the American humor course. They'd study all different types of humor and black humor—meaning as in dark, not in African. I was intrigued. He talked about [J. P.] Donleavy, the English writer who wrote *The Ginger Man* [1955] and the black writers who write with black humor, like Terry Southern.

Q: I love the shooting of the English poet in *Almanac.*

A: I think there's a lot in there for everybody to laugh at. Like I told people: If you're turned off by corporate technocracies and the Bushian types, you'll like this book all right. You'll see the humor of it. But if you've cast your fate with them, well, I feel sorry for you.

Q: How was this book tour you were on for *Almanac?*

A: Simon and Schuster had me on this circuit that you go on if you have a record album or sell shoes or whatever. It's the second tier. Bookstore signings were the first tier. So you go to these radio stations and they play the tape of your interview at 6:00 in the morning during the public access time.

No one had read the whole book, which was particularly funny here in Tucson because they didn't know how really mean and strange it was. This radio guy here in town had a feeling that this book wasn't friendly to Tucson. But it was sort of poignant because he was a reformed alcoholic and he went on about how that character Seese really reminded him of what he had gone through. That's when I started to get scared about the power of language. I started to worry about readers. This guy finally said, "There weren't any heroes in this book. Only time was a hero."

Q: All right, he got it.

A: He got it, the poor man. I said, "That's right. Time is the hero."

Q: So what are you going to do now? You must be exhausted after *Almanac*.

A: World Famous Autorama Auto Salvage and Towing. It's a little business that [her companion] Gus and I are going into. We're starting from scratch an auto recycling and auto salvage business, which we feel is righteous and fun. We love old cars. You saw our old cars [in the driveway]. When you crash your car and because of the economy you're not going to buy any more cars but it's crashed up pretty bad, you'll call us and we'll say we have the fender for you.

But we're also doing it because I really can't in conscience affiliate with a university, at least not like these state universities in the Southwest. Actually, I don't believe in college, university curriculums, and educations anymore at all. I believe they're a great consumer ripoff. I even feel hesitant about going onto campuses and speaking, but what I try to do is to talk about that. I did that when I was teaching, too. I'd tell my students that they were getting ripped. So we hope that the auto recycling will just cover expenses because the writing doesn't. Maybe in fifteen years *Almanac* will finally do what *Ceremony* did. *Ceremony* is selling more now than it ever did.

Q: Is this like a junkyard?

A: Yes. A junkyard. Recycling, auto salvage. That's the term of the art, and that's what they call the license. We're trying to get an auto salvage, auto recycler's license. If we pass that, we have to be investigated. It's a big deal.

I've also been doing some painting, but I'm not a good painter.

Q: What have you done?

A: I did a mural downtown on a wall on Stone Avenue [in Tucson]. It's still up, and it says mean things in Spanish, and it has skulls so the graffiti guys don't touch it like they destroy all these other people's murals in the city. I think the reason they don't graffiti-ize it is because it says, "The people are cold; the people are hungry; the rich have stolen the land; the rich have stolen freedom; the people demand justice. Otherwise revolution." I put it in Spanish because Stone Avenue is the main route downtown and most of the powers that be and the police go right past it.

And the police park in a vacant lot right by the mural. I knew if I put it in Spanish everyone that I wanted really to know would know. One time someone even wrote me a little note on it in Spanish. People sometimes leave notes on it. Like "thank you."

Inside of where the mural is is where I wrote most of *Almanac*. I had a little window, but it's boarded up now.

Q: You're moving into auto salvage and painting. Are you just giving yourself a breather from writing?

A: Yeah, just giving myself a breather. I'm already having ideas. I'll have my writing office down at the junkyard. Ever since I was a little girl I thought junkyards were neat. And the rules are different. It's things that people say they don't want; but it's a lie, they do want these things.

Q: So maybe your next novel will be about a junkyard.

A: I don't know, but new things bring new material. I needed to rest after *Almanac*. I really couldn't have done that book if everything hadn't been just perfect—everyone so nice to me; no worries; the MacArthur fellowship and all of that.

Almanac spawned another novel about a woman who is a serial killer. She just kills policemen and politicians. She's different from Andrea Dworkin's killer woman who kills bums and stuff. It was way more radical than *Almanac,* and it was so American. Such a love affair with guns and handguns. And so scary and threatening to police and the white-male-in-authority kind of thing. The character uses Mexican tarot cards and, as I was writing it, they would work for me. It was so cool.

I put that novel down because I didn't think it was fair for me to serve the narrative again so soon on something so hard. I also had the feeling that it was *Almanac* trying to keep hold on me because it really didn't want to end. Simon and Schuster made the *Almanac* end. I, the one who was in the day-to-day world, made it end. But the *Almanac* didn't want to end.

Q: We had the apocalypse in *Almanac* and now a woman who's a serial killer. What happened to the nice, charming Leslie Silko who used to write poems?

A: [She laughs.] Well, what happened is just classic. Mr. Jean-Jacques Rousseau would be so happy. I was so sheltered, even though there was always this incredible thing that these wildflowers and these trees and those clouds are over mountains that were ours, that the Forest Service took them away from us in 1903. I was really young. I was twenty-three or twenty-four when I wrote those poems. I haven't written poems for about ten years—you could look up when I last wrote a poem. I think it was just development. Reading, learning, time, life. Or it was just bound to happen?

Q: Poetry just doesn't appeal to you anymore?

A: Well, I have no control. I sit down and I write. And I might start out with one intention and then something happens. And the poetry is the greatest mystery of all in my writing. I have no idea how I do it exactly. It's not that I'm in a trance or something. I just mess around, and it just happens. Also, *Almanac* has dominated me for so long. I would like to and I'm going to try to get back to these other things. I tried to do some nature writing: I have some essays on rain, on rocks. I started reading Buddhism again, but then I get sidetracked.

Right around then, I was thinking, You gotta cool out. You gotta think peaceful thoughts. No more guns, no more death. Buddhism, Buddhism. Then what happens? When I turn on my TV a few months ago, I find out they killed nine Buddhists in Phoenix. Blew their heads off. It's like a message from all that's evil in Arizona.

It was good that I had been reading because I knew where those guys went to who got their heads blown off. It was okay. Buddhism helped me get through.

Q: Why do you stay in Arizona?

A: Turn tail and run and go to some little Shangri-la? Ha! I am a part of this. You don't just run off and leave your land and your people and the animals and the trees. You stay here.

Laguna has its problems—the reservation has unemployment, and they have suicides. But they have this wonderful culture and cohesion and history, and they have themselves. No matter how bad things are at Laguna, they're way better than here. But the truth is that somebody has to come over here and say, "Look, this is criminal. These policemen, these judges, these legislators in Arizona are criminals. The people shouldn't listen to them." I feel that way on a national level, too. When you find something like this, you have to tell about it. You just can't ignore it.

Q: What is it like living here at the edge of the desert?

A: The desert protects me. For years I lived up here alone after Robert went off to school and before Gus and Larry [McMurtry] were around. People would say, "Well, aren't you scared?" And I just said, "No." The people who do bad things are scared of the desert.

I'm at the end of the road; there's nothing here. That's Saguaro National Monument [just beyond her house]. These saguaro are very old.

They're special and vulnerable. And when saguaros die, their bodies are warm. There are some things that happen out here that make you think twice about whether these cactuses are just dumb inanimate things. Up in Phoenix a guy got drunk and went out on a shooting spree a couple of years ago and blasted away at them. A saguaro fell on him and killed him.

Another reason I'm not afraid is that nobody's going to come out here alone. They know about my target shooting and hunting. You'd be surprised how well things can go when you live up in a scary place and people know you have guns [she laughs].

Donna Perry is a professor of English at William Paterson College in Wayne, New Jersey, where she also teaches in the women's studies program and codirects the writing-across-the-curriculum program. She has conducted workshops on transforming the curriculum to include race, class, and gender concerns and has published essays in several journals and in *Teaching Writing: Pedagogy, Gender, and Equity* (State University of New York Press, 1987), *Gender/Body/Knowledge: Feminist Reconstructions of Being and Knowing* (Rutgers University Press, 1989), and *Caribbean Women Writers: Essays from the First International Conference* (University of Massachusetts Press, 1990). For 1989–90 she received a New Jersey Governor's Fellowship in the Humanities to study the work of several of the writers interviewed here.

Like most of these women, Perry comes from a working-class family. She was born in Lowell, Massachusetts, and received a B.A. from Merrimack College, an M.A. from Duquesne University, and a Ph.D. from Marquette University. She lives in Riverdale, New York. This is her first book.